THE TWENTIETH CENTURY:
AN AMERICAN HISTORY

THE TWENTIETH CENTURY: AN AMERICAN HISTORY

ARTHUR S. LINK
Princeton University

WILLIAM A. LINK
University of North Carolina at Greensboro

Harlan Davidson, Inc.
Arlington Heights, Illinois 60004

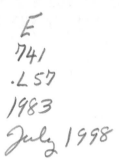
Cover illustration: "Macomb's Dam Bridge," oil on canvas by Edward Hopper, The Brooklyn Museum, bequest of Miss Mary T. Cockcroft, detail.

Library of Congress Cataloging in Publication Data
Link, Arthur Stanley.
   The twentieth century.
     Bibliography: p.
     Includes index.
     1. United States—History—20th century. I. Link, William A. II. Title.
E741.L57 1983   973.9   82-22080
ISBN 0-88295-815-1
ISBN 0-88295-816-X (pbk.)

PRINTED IN THE UNITED STATES OF AMERICA

83 84 85 86 87IN10 9 8 7 6 5 4 3 2 1

PREFACE

It is a truism to say that we live in a world of kaleidoscopic and unpredictable changes. So fast is the velocity of that change that we sometimes tend to become disoriented, lose our bearings, and wonder where we are going. It is no wonder that we should feel perplexed as we look upon the world around us.

A study of our history during the past eighty-odd years will not assuage all our perplexities and doubts about the future, but such a study does say to us in a loud and clear voice that change has been the one constant feature of American life since the 1890s. A Rip Van Winkle who went to sleep in 1900 would not recognize the landscape and environment should he awake somewhere in the United States in the 1980s. Much less would he recognize the society and its mores, its government, and the mighty nation that plays so important a role in the world at large.

The theme of this book is the transformation of the United States from a largely rural society, composed of disparate and isolated communities and sections, into a nation united by bonds of a common economy and culture—some 230,000,000 people who, wherever they live in this vast continental empire, share the same basic political, social, and cultural values in spite of important yet fundamentally superficial ethnic, cultural, and religious differences.

It is a forbidding task to try to tell this story—not only the *what* of it, but, more important, the *why* of it. We have tried to describe how the American people, in their politics and diplomacy, have met the challenges of momentous and unsettling change in the twentieth century. And we have tried to include all the people in our narrative: blacks, women, young people, ethnic groups, Chicanos, etc., who, after all, constitute the great majority of Americans. Their struggle for freedom and opportunity has been one of the chief causes of change in the American society during the past century. That change has been unsettling at times, but it has been, and still is, the movement of a people to realize the ideals and objectives so eloquently proclaimed in 1776.

We live in a world of change, but we are no different from our grandparents in this respect. They adjusted to change and rebuilt their institutions to make them constructive and socially beneficent. The present generation of young people is just as resourceful and even better equipped to do the same.

In writing this book, we have accumulated a burden of debt which we can never repay. We owe our greatest debt to the hundreds of historians whose books have been a light to our hands. Our book is a tribute to the progress of historical scholarship in the United States during the past thirty-odd years. We thank our editors, Maureen Trobec, Margaret D. Link, and Susannah H. Jones, for improving the style of this book, and Harlan Davidson for his suggestion that we collaborate on this book and for his unfailing friendship and encouragement. It goes without saying that we are responsible for any errors that remain.

Arthur S. Link

William A. Link

Princeton, N.J.
Greensboro, N.C.
November 15, 1982

CONTENTS

CHAPTER 1
THE AMERICAN PEOPLE
IN 1900

1. THE BIRTH OF MODERN AMERICA

Building the Industrial Infrastructure

Americans today inhabit a social, political, and economic world which was largely born between 1865 and 1920. In 1900, most Americans—rural and urban, black and white, male and female—lived in a radically transformed environment which their parents and grandparents would have regarded as quite alien. Taken together, the emergence of modern America constituted one of the most important transitions in the history of the United States.

One of the most obvious ways in which Americans in 1900 were unlike their ancestors 100 years earlier was their ability to move and ship goods with more speed and at considerably less expense across large distances. The transportation revolution was an essential ingredient of the industrial revolution, for it made possible greater and more efficient trade, created new markets, and, for many areas of the United States, ended centuries of isolated self-sufficiency.

Although the expansion of transportation facilities began in modest proportions during the early nineteenth century, by 1900 it had wrought a fundamental transformation of the American economy. Much of this expansion took place in water transport in two distinct ways. Americans constructed canals which linked major markets and created new centers of trade. The Erie Canal, for example, was begun in 1817 and completed in 1825. It connected the Hudson

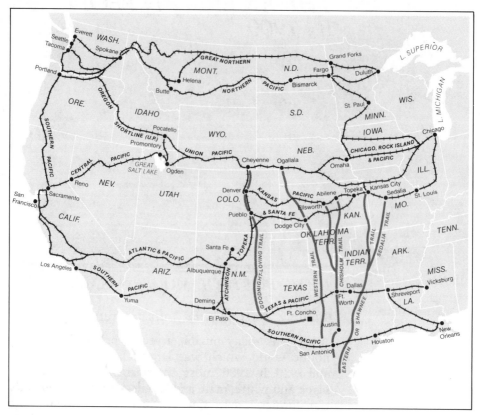

Railroads and Cattle Trails, 1850-1900

River at Troy, New York, with Lake Erie at Buffalo and linked the farmers of western New York and the northern Middle West to New York City. Canal building continued throughout the nineteenth century and reached its peak about 1880. At the same time, innovations in steam engines and the widespread use of steamboats permitted upstream traffic on such great water highways as the Mississippi River.

But the revolution in transportation occurred most profoundly in the growth of railroads. Beginning in the 1830s and 1840s, and accelerating between 1850 and 1900, railroads became the dominant force in the American economy. They extended far beyond the geographical limits of water transport, and innovations in railroad machinery had made rail transport the most efficient form by 1900. Railroads particularly expanded during three tremendous "waves"—during 1868–1873, 1879–1883, and 1886–1893; by the latter date the total mileage of track was more than quadruple the mileage existing in 1861. Railroads were able also to penetrate to the outreaches and hinterlands of the United States; by the end of the nineteenth century, they had created the basic components of a truly unified national economy.

Railroads also had a "multiplier" effect on the American economy. The biggest single industry in the nation, railroads generated large amounts of income, not only for their owners but also for the vast army of railway managers and workers. Railroads also provided an enormous amount of employment and income in industries as diverse as construction and iron and steel.

The Manufacturing Revolution

Another profound economic change in the United States was a tremendous expansion of manufacturing. In 1850, most American manufacturing was small-scale, artisanal, and powered either by humans or animals or water power. Fifty years later, the face of industrial America was completely changed. A substantial portion of industry was large-scale, steam-powered, and organized in a sharply separated division of labor. All of these changes—most of which took place in the urban industrial areas of the Northeast and Middle West—resulted in an undreamed of geometric growth in the productive base of the American economy and in a steady expansion in income for all Americans.

In 1859, the value of manufactured goods in the United States was about $820 million; forty years later, it had increased to over $5 billion. Gross national product (in 1929 dollars) during the period 1869–1873 stood, annually, at $6.7 billion, while in 1897–1901 it was, annually, $37.1 billion. Even more important, during the last half of the nineteenth century, the American economy achieved a "modern" rate of economic growth on the average of between 1.5 and 2.0 per cent per year, as compared to an average of about 1 per cent per year during the period 1800–1860.

Much of this increase in productivity was the result of the formation and use of enormous amounts of capital during the late nineteenth century. Although only 14 to 16 per cent of the national product was devoted to capital formation before the Civil War, by the 1880s that figure had risen to 28 per cent. American industry, partly because of an overall labor shortage, turned to mechanization and capital-intensive innovation. In "older" industries, such as textiles and shoemaking, new looms and steam-powered machinery combined with a strict factory discipline to maximize production.

The most startling advances in American manufacturing before 1900, however, occurred in the production of iron and steel. In 1871, American firms produced less than one sixth of the total British output. Yet, thirty years later, American output, led by mills in the Middle West, was double that of Great Britain. In steel production, American manufacturers had also achieved supremacy, and they even exported over 1,000,000 tons in 1901.

The growth of the iron and steel industry in the United States was the result of innovation and large infusions of capital. At the same time, the industry became more concentrated; great factories, which integrated all phases of production, emerged in which labor was extremely specialized and the work routine highly organized. By the turn of the century, moreover, fewer firms—Youngstown Sheet and Tube, Jones & Laughlin, and, most notably, United States Steel (founded in 1901)—were organized with a professionalized force of executives and middle-level managers.

"The Visible Hand": The Emergence of the Modern Corporation

Today, the corporate mode of organization dominates American industry. Yet, as late as 1900, most firms were probably owner-operated and run by a single capitalist or his family. Nonetheless, the beginnings of the emergence of the modern corporation—and its ultimate dominance in the American economy—were evident by the turn of the century.

Late nineteenth-century corporations had similar characteristics. By definition, they were "incorporated"; that is, they lowered the risk of investment —and attracted capital—by placing financial responsibility in a chartered corporation. Incorporation not only led to an infusion of capital but also to the introduction of a highly organized managerial corps committed to long-range planning, cost cutting, and maximization of profits. Because of streamlined organization, mechanization, and economies of scale, corporations also tended to facilitate the integration of all stages of the process of production.

A few examples of late nineteenth-century corporations stand out. In meat packing, Edwin and Gustavus Swift of Chicago formed a partnership in 1878 and, through the use of refrigerated railroad cars, built a national system of distribution and marketing. By the end of the 1880s, the Swift brothers had incorporated and possessed a fully integrated corporate structure. Other firms, such as John D. Rockefeller's Standard Oil Company and James B. Duke's American Tobacco Company, exploited the advantages of incorporation to achieve industry-wide dominance.

Since its colonial beginnings, the United States had been rural and agricultural. By 1900, however, although many Americans still subscribed to Thomas Jefferson's dream of a land of yeoman farmers, the Sage of Monticello's conception no longer corresponded with the socioeconomic reality. Indeed, a striking alteration in the American way of life occurred in agriculture at the end of the nineteenth century. Even in 1900, the majority of Americans earned their livelihood as farmers and lived in communities which contained fewer than 2,500 people. But these same Americans were beginning to feel the full force of a process which—when it had run its full course by 1970—would result in an almost total transformation of their environment and way of life.

The transportation revolution catalyzed much of the change in American agriculture. Water transport and railroads began the end of rural isolation and made farmers part of the regional and national market economies. Farmers in heretofore isolated areas thus increasingly produced almost exclusively for the market. Moreover, as the nineteenth century came to a close, the various regions came to specialize in the production of agricultural staples. In the South, farmers raised cotton for the domestic and international markets, as well as tobacco, sugar, rice, and hemp. The Middle West, meanwhile, specialized in the production of grains—particularly corn and wheat. Around the urban areas of the East, farmers could not compete in the production of staples. Those farmers who remained on the land turned instead to vegetable, poultry, and dairy farming and exploited their proximity to large urban centers. Particularly in New England, the rural areas experienced a substantial depopulation.

The commercialization of American agriculture also involved a higher capital investment in machinery. The growth of the farm-implement industry—spearheaded by Cyrus H. McCormick's International Harvester Company in Chicago—made agriculture more productive, particularly in the cultivation of wheat. At the same time, the opening up of new lands after 1870—particularly rich lands in the eastern areas of the Plains states, Texas, and California—caused a substantial increase in the level of agricultural production.

For many persons, the transformation of agriculture was a traumatic experience. Because of increases in production (throughout the world as well as in the United States), prices declined steadily for both manufactured goods and agricultural products. Over the short space of thirty years, farmers watched a precipitate decline in prices: wheat, which sold for $1.21 a bushel in 1879, brought only sixty-one cents in 1894; cotton declined from twenty cents a pound to about five cents in 1893.

The Political Crisis of the 1890s

The reorganization of American life also caused profound changes in the political system and the practice of politics. Americans faced a political crisis of major proportions, particularly during the last decade of the nineteenth century, and to many persons the very safety of the Republic seemed imperiled.

The political crisis erupted in both the countryside and in the cities. Agrarians, mainly in the South and parts of the Middle West, organized themselves as an interest group. During the 1870s, farmers in these regions organized the Grange, or the Patrons of Husbandry, in part as a social club where agriculturalists could enrich their otherwise dreary lives. But soon the Grange had acquired a reputation as an interest group, and, on the state level, it pressed for a variety of laws, most notably laws to regulate railroads. The Grange was, however, small by comparison with the Farmers' Alliance, which, during the late 1880s, claimed close to 2,000,000 white and black members. The Alliance attracted new members when it began to establish cooperatives for the purchase of manufactured goods and the sale of agricultural products.

By the beginning of the 1890s, however, agrarians had begun to turn to politics as an answer to their problems. During a series of meetings across the South, leaders of the Alliance concluded that farmers could obtain redress only through the formation of an independent third party—the People's or Populist party—which they formally organized during the spring of 1892. Particularly in the South and Middle West, the Populists mounted a worrisome threat to the political parties both in state elections—where they controlled states such as Colorado and North Carolina—and in the presidential election of 1892. Although the Populists joined with the Democrats in the nomination of William Jennings Bryan in 1896, they began to lose their identity and intensity after that year. By 1900, they were no longer a potent political force.

Political discontent was also evident in American cities. Many Americans, particularly of the middle class, were concerned about what they thought was the disintegration of the social fabric due to intermittent labor and class violence after 1873. The crisis seemed even more threatening during the

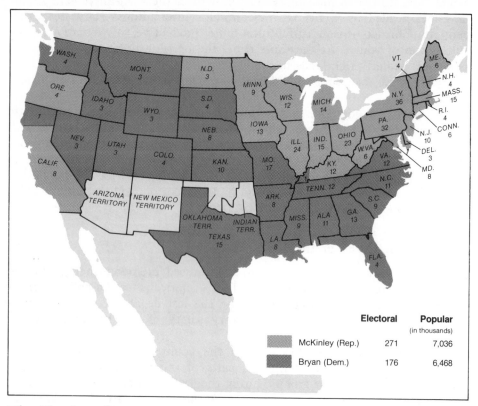

	Electoral	Popular
		(in thousands)
McKinley (Rep.)	271	7,036
Bryan (Dem.)	176	6,468

The Election of 1896

Panic of 1893. Unemployment became a national problem and—particularly in the march of Jacob S. Coxey's 500-strong "army" in Washington, D.C., in 1894—seemed to imperil social stability. By 1900, however, with the return of prosperity, the urban and rural threats—although very much on the minds of Americans—had receded.

2. THE CREATION OF AN INDUSTRIAL SOCIETY

The Rise of the City

By 1900, cities had begun to emerge as the dominant residential as well as cultural centers of the United States. Along with industrialization itself, urbanization—and the immigration of large numbers of people from the American countryside and Europe—brought the dimensions of modern society into sharp focus. The growth of the city thus appeared to undermine the traditional rural and homogeneous bases of society.

It is important to remember that, even in 1900, urbanization was a historical process whose full implications were not completely realized. In that year, most Americans did not inhabit large towns, much less big cities;

in fact, a majority did not even live in incorporated communities. Fewer than 14 per cent were born outside the United States, even with the massive immigration of Europeans at the end of the nineteenth century. Most Americans—about three quarters in 1900—also lived in the eastern half of the country.

Nonetheless, at the turn of the century, the full configuration of change —and its dramatic implications—were becoming clear. Population continued to migrate westward, although the frontier was officially declared to be at an end in 1890. Farmers migrated in large numbers to rich lands in Texas, the Plains states, and California. Many other farmers abandoned their vocation and moved to urban areas, particularly big cities. In 1910, the census recorded that 46 per cent of Americans lived in urban areas; ten years later, a majority of Americans lived in towns and cities.

The Process of Urban Growth

Since the colonial period, cities had been the commercial, political, and cultural hubs of the United States. Yet, during the last three decades of the nineteenth century, their status expanded in almost every respect. Not only did they grow in physical size and in absolute population at a dizzying rate, but their role in the national economy and in the emerging culture was also substantially altered.

Nineteenth-century Americans watched their cities change almost overnight. During the last part of the century, New York doubled its population to 3,400,000 people. By 1920, the nation possessed twenty-five cities with more than 250,000 people, most of them located in the industrial belts of the Middle West and Northeast. At the same time, new cities such as Birmingham, Atlanta, Denver, Los Angeles, and Seattle became major urban areas of the South and West. Meanwhile, small towns and cities— ranging in size from 2,500 to about 25,000 people—grew up at an equally staggering rate.

The shift from a predominantly rural to a predominantly urban nation was the result of several factors. Commercialization of manufacturing and agriculture in turn both depended on, and was the product of, concentrated centers of population and wealth. The revolution in transportation necessitated centers of marketing and trade; those cities which possessed strategic locations on railroad intersections or on rivers grew rapidly in wealth and population. By 1900, for example, westward-bound railroad traffic and the Great Lakes water traffic met at Chicago, and meat packing and the production of steel soon made the city one of the nation's largest metropolitan centers. Similar strategic locations, plus access to raw materials, made Pittsburgh and Birmingham centers of iron and steel production. The junction of two major railroad lines in western Virginia, along with the boom in the production of coal in the southwestern portions of the state, made Roanoke a booming financial and transportation center where a small village had existed before 1883. Commercialization of agriculture in the South and Middle West also stimulated the growth of large towns and cities, such as Des Moines, Dallas, and Wichita. Other urban areas specialized in the production of particular manufactured goods: Richmond produced cigarettes; Schenectady, electrical machinery; Fall River, Massachusetts, cotton textiles.

At the same time, as its population expanded, the physical layout of the American city underwent alteration. Older cities, such as Boston and Philadelphia, expanded outward because conveyances—first drawn by horses, then powered by steam and electricity—stimulated the growth of suburban areas. The widespread development of trolley systems permitted urbanites to live outside the "walking city," which had been about two and one-half miles in radius. Technological innovation in the design of bridges also made urban transportation systems more efficient. The most impressive example was the Brooklyn Bridge, completed in 1883, which spanned the East River and connected, in a length of 1,600 feet, Manhattan Island and Brooklyn. The Brooklyn Bridge was a model of a new type of steel suspension bridge designed to traverse large bodies of water.

Other innovations in the construction of buildings stimulated urban expansion. The availability of high quality and durable steel, which was in abundant supply by the end of the century, encouraged the construction of structures higher than ten stories. In 1885, William Jenny designed the Home Insurance Building in Chicago; it was the first building in the nation to use steel frames. Louis Sullivan, another Chicago-based architect, made further advances in the design of high-rise buildings with smooth functional lines, plain thin walls, and large glass windows. Beginning with the construction of the Tacoma Building in Chicago in 1888, Sullivan and his protégés—most notably Frank Lloyd Wright—established the architectural patterns of the American skyscraper.

Another important tendency in the physical growth of the American city was its increasing segregation. As the cities expanded, many residential areas, which had included homes, stores, and factories, became exclusively residential in character. The segregation of the work place from the home was also accompanied by the formation of class, ethnic, and racial lines. Increasingly, a new urban pattern emerged. In many cities, upper-income groups, generally white, lived on the periphery; lower-income groups, generally ethnic and black, resided in the center. This transformation, a departure from the generally homogeneous residential pattern, boded ill for the harmony of the major cities.

The Organizational Revolution

A subtle by-product of this social and economic transformation occurred in the patterns of social and economic interaction, and, by 1900, the very basis of social relations for most Americans had changed. The emergence of a modern industrial economy, in concert with the growth of cities, gave rise to an increasingly different style of human interaction. The intensely personal nature of American society, in turn, was to some degree replaced by an impersonal society in which bureaucratic organizations challenged the dominance of the age-old structures of family, community, and church.

The organizational revolution to a large extent followed the emergence of the modern corporation. The corporate mode of economic activity was not new; prior to the Civil War, it had existed in industries such as textiles, transportation, banking, and insurance. Those industrial firms which survived the intense competition and price cutting of the late nineteenth century did so through a hierarchical corporate structure. After 1850, railroads led the way in the creation of efficiently run managerial systems which assumed their day-to-day operation and long-range planning. Railroad and corporation managers, in turn, also possessed new professional attitudes toward their work; their primary responsibility was toward the organization and toward the impersonal bureaucracy which guided it.

After 1870, moreover, the organizational revolution not only spread through industry but also came to have an extensive influence on the social, cultural, and political organization of modern America. By 1900, the professions—the law, medicine, university teaching, and engineering—felt these effects. The professions, particularly the law and medicine, were relatively easy to enter in mid-nineteenth century America; in the law, for example, apprenticeship was the easiest way to begin one's profession, and, because of unrestricted access, by the Civil War, both professions had declined in status and standards. The history of the medical and legal professions is crucial, for, in both fields, leaders successfully reversed the status of their professions between 1870 and 1920. Medical and legal reformers used professional organizations—such as the American Medical Association (AMA) and the American Bar Association (ABA)—to restrict access to their professions. The AMA, which counted 70,000 members in 1910, pressed efforts to restrict the number of doctors graduated and to demand more stringent professional standards. Similarly, the National Education Association (NEA) was in the vanguard, on both state and national levels, for the improvement of the standards of teacher training as well as for increased appropriations for all levels of public education.

Many of these new professionals—what one historian has called the "new middle class"—saw organizations, often bureaucratic in structure, as the proper form of social organization. They believed fervently in an impersonal style of interaction; they therefore agreed that accreditation and university education was neutral and efficient. By the turn of the century, this new breed of professionals had not only permeated the professions, but also labor, business, and even agriculture. They would form the vanguard of the reform movements in government and society during the early twentieth century.

3. PLURALISM AND CONFLICT IN THE INDUSTRIAL STATE

The Beginnings of Ethnic, Racial, and Sexual Diversity

The social and economic transformation of America wrought other changes in social life. Because of the expansion of manufacturing—and its intensive demand for labor—diverse ethnic and racial groups peopled the cities of the twentieth century. The industrial revolution generated wealth and created opportunity for many Americans, yet it also began to fracture and fragment social homogeneity and cohesion in the cities as well as in the countryside.

The "New" Immigration

One of the most convulsive experiences in human history was the transfer of about 35,000,000 Europeans to the United States between 1830 and 1930. The vast majority of these immigrants traversed the Atlantic after 1860; during the last forty years of the nineteenth century, about 14,000,000 immigrants came to the United States, and, by 1915, another 14,500,000 had followed them. Yet, between 1880 and 1900, the basic nature of European immigration to the United States changed. In 1882, of the 648,000 Europeans who migrated to the United States, 530,000 were from Scandinavia, Great Britain, Germany, and Ireland, while the remainder, about 120,000, came from southern and eastern Europe. Twenty-five years later, when 1,200,000 Europeans moved to the United States—the all-time high—northern Europe sent only 200,000 immigrants. The remainder—the so-called "new" immigrants—came from southern and eastern Europe, and they were joined by increasing numbers of Asians and Mexicans. About 3,000,000 Italians immigrated between 1901 and 1915, most of them from south of Rome. Between 1880 and 1915, almost 6,000,000 Poles, Croatians, Slovaks, Ruthenians, South Serbs, and other peoples left the Russian and Austro-Hungarian empires.

The massive exodus of southern and eastern Europeans had various causes. The opportunity to make money and own property in the new world attracted many immigrants, particularly those from Italy, the Austro-Hungarian Empire, and Russia, where the collapse of feudal agriculture as well as overpopulation pushed many peasants to emigrate. The intensive worldwide increase in agricultural production depressed prices and made the vestiges of feudal agriculture obsolete. Many other artisanal laborers lost their livelihood —in textile production, for example—as a result of the triumph of the factory system. Other ethnic groups left their mother country because of religious persecution. Eastern European Jews, particularly in Russia, experienced systematic oppression during the last decade of the nineteenth century, and about 2,750,000 Ashkenazic Jews—whose strict religious practice and exclusiveness often resulted in clashes with the 250,000 German Jews already in the United States—migrated during this period.

At the same time, the "pull" of the American economy was strong. Promoters, relatives, and friends kept their countrymen at home well-informed about economic conditions in the United States, and, because of intensive competition among transatlantic steamship companies, they enjoyed fares as low as fifteen dollars from Naples to New York. The "new" immigrants often migrated in force into certain industries. In New York during the 1880s, eastern European Jews quickly took over the ranks of skilled laborers in the garment industry; by 1900, Jews virtually owned the industry. Italians, on the other hand, arrived as unskilled peasants and moved into the construction industry in major American cities. Poles, in contrast, filled the factories, particularly the steel mills of the industrial Middle West.

Ethnocultural Conflict and Immigration: Nativism and the Drive for Exclusion

The tremendous waves of immigrants who reached American shores by the end of the century—particularly the "new" immigrants—prompted an outburst of resentment on the part of old-stock Americans. "Nativism"—the hostility and prejudice of native citizens against new immigrants—had a long history in the United States, from the period of the anti-Catholic hysteria during the 1840s and 1850s to the tide of resentment which greeted refugees from Vietnam and Cuba during the 1980s. To Americans at the end of the nineteenth century, however, the infusion of so many immigrants of so radically different backgrounds appeared to create insuperable problems. Many persons believed that the poverty of the immigrant community was endemic to their culture; others were concerned about an aggravation of social problems. Still others worried that the unwillingness of many immigrants to abandon strong cultural traditions threatened the strength and homogeneity of the American republic.

A body of scientific and pseudoscientific scholarship, which attempted to demonstrate innate differences and gradations among and between races and cultures, gave intellectual respectability to these concerns. The vast majority of biologists, historians, anthropologists, and sociologists agreed that northern European civilization was superior to other cultures. Sociologists such as Franklin H. Giddings of Columbia University held that cultures developed and matured as did human beings; members of underdeveloped cultures, such as those from southern Europe, were thus innately inferior. Many other scholars and publicists—including the scholar Theodore Roosevelt—described a Darwinian struggle for racial supremacy which had raged throughout history and which the Anglo-Saxon civilization had won.

After 1880, the hostility of native Americans toward the recent immigrants stimulated the formation of many nativist organizations and, once again, prompted the infusion of nativism as a potent force in politics. Thus were created organizations such as the United Order of Deputies, the American League, and the Minute Men of 1886. The most influential of such groups was the American Protective Association (APA), formed in 1887 to wage the war to preserve old American values and to carry on the fight against Roman Catholicism. These organizations grew rapidly after the depression of the 1890s and influenced the political realignment of that decade.

At the same time, other groups—few as extreme as the APA—favored the restriction of immigration. Settlement-house workers, such as Jane Addams and Lillian D. Wald, favored restriction as a way to alleviate the social problems of the city. The conclusions of the Immigration Commission in 1911, which were written by progressives such as the economist W. Jett Lauck and the anthropologist Franz Boas, supported these conclusions. Other groups, such as organized labor, pressed hard for the adoption of a literacy test throughout the late 1890s and early 1900s. Facing such united support for exclusion legislation, Congress adopted a literacy measure three times, but Presidents Cleveland, Taft, and Wilson vetoed it each time, although Congress overrode Wilson's veto in 1917. After 1880, moreover, Congress enacted other measures which excluded "undesirable" immigrants. In 1882, it barred the immigration of convicts and the insane, and, in the same breath, excluded Chinese; subsequent legislation barred contract laborers, paupers, anarchists, and immigrants who had communicable diseases.

Immigrants in America: Victims or Victors?

In many respects, immigrants found a harsh greeting in the new world. Many of the jobs which they took in mining and manufacturing were low paying; in 1915, for example, the earnings of one third of workers in mining and one half in manufacturing were insufficient to house, feed, and clothe their families. Many others—despite the strength of old-world culture in American cities—found the cultural transition extremely difficult. As we have seen, old-stock Americans greeted the "new" immigrants with antagonism, suspicion, and often discrimination.

But the history of the "new" immigration defies easy generalization. Some immigrants, such as the Italians, came from a peasant culture; others, such as the Jews, were forbidden to own land in the old world and consequently came from an urban culture. The "new" immigrants were, in short, a diverse and disunited group. Some of the worst bigotry occurred between German Jews and eastern European Jews; the derogatory slur "kike," for example, was coined by German Jews of New York City to describe the recently arrived Jews who congregated in the lower East Side. Similar conflicts took place among Roman Catholic immigrants—Irish, Italians, and Poles—for control of the Church, which for the most part was dominated by the Irish.

The pace at which the "new" immigrants met success in the American economy depended on a variety of factors. Eastern European Jews placed a high priority on education, and they were able to enter the professions within two or three generations. Italians, on the other hand, valued income and more likely required their children to work. In general, as a result, their move up the occupational ladder occurred less rapidly, although they achieved more success after 1945. Nonetheless, the move of the "new" immigrants into a position of importance must be considered one of the most remarkable developments in American history. In large part, their success has been a result of the key part that they played in the development of an urban-industrial society; and, as critical components of the industrial revolution in the United States, they were among its leading beneficiaries.

Afro-Americans in the Industrial Society

Unlike the recent immigrants, the vast majority of black Americans lived outside the perimeters of the industrial society in 1900. During the last third of the nineteenth century, black freedmen did not migrate northward; 86.3 per cent of all American blacks in 1915 still resided south of the Mason-Dixon Line. Although many blacks moved to the new cities of the South during this period, most of them remained in the countryside, and, in 1910, only one southern black in five lived in a city.

Typically southern and typically rural, most blacks lived in an oppressive environment. Most confronted a strict and rigid caste system which forbade any expressions of racial equality. Moreover, particularly in cotton-producing areas of the Deep South, blacks—as well as poor whites—were part of an extensive and extremely productive system of plantation agriculture. Yet, unlike the antebellum system, plantation agriculture in the postwar period relied on the labor provided in the contractual relationships in tenant and sharecropper farming, in which freedmen and poor whites rented part of plantations either for shares of the crops that they produced or for a fixed annual rent. Often, sharecroppers and tenants were locked in an oppressive system of credit in which planters or merchants held them in virtual peonage. Share tenancy also tended to maximize the production of the staple crop (usually cotton) and to minimize food production; indeed, many parts of the cotton South lost their self-sufficiency in food after 1865. Between 1880 and 1910, share tenancy spread throughout the region at an alarming rate: to 50 per cent of all farmers in Georgia, Alabama, Mississippi, Louisiana, Texas, Arkansas, and South Carolina, and to over 40 per cent in North Carolina and Tennessee.

In spite of adversity, blacks had achieved substantial gains in their standard of living by 1900. Grinding poverty, poor health, and inadequate nutrition were basic components of life in the rural South, and yet they affected Southerners without much regard to race. In spite of the fact that the vast majority of southern blacks began emancipation with virtually no skills, land, or wealth, thirty-five years later they could boast a record of achievement in several areas. Although in 1865 about 95 per cent of southern blacks were illiterate, in 1900 about 45 per cent could read and write. The crop-lien and share-tenancy systems frustrated the aspirations of many blacks, but a significant number of them were able to acquire their own farms. In 1875, southern blacks, according to one estimate, owned about 3,000,000 acres of farmlands; twenty-five years later, that figure had increased to 12,000,000 acres.

The Beginnings of Sexual Change: The Status of Women

In the transformation of the sexual role and economic function of women, the American people were also remade by 1900. As the birthrate slowed by the middle of the century and as the size of the average family dropped sharply, women found more freedom from childbearing and child rearing. As in the case of immigrants and blacks, women became important members of the work force and, consequently, gained a new status and freedom.

The history of the last half of the nineteenth century is the story of the rapid entry of women into the work force. Some women entered the ranks of factory workers, particularly those industries which used power-driven machinery and required little heavy labor. In shoemaking and textiles—both industries which were heavily mechanized and organized in a factory system—women were employed in large numbers. In 1880, about 200,000 women constituted about 47 per cent of the labor force in textile mills. Moreover, between 1850 and 1900 the number of women working in manufacturing rose by 500 per cent. Women also penetrated into almost all occupations; women had become (albeit in small numbers) engineers, doctors, professors, and lawyers; by 1910, women comprised one fourth of all nonagricultural workers. In the professions, women particularly filled the ranks of teachers in public schools, and, by 1880, the substantial majority of all teachers (ranging from 80 to 90 per cent) were women.

The entrance of women into the work force, a long-term process with extensive implications for the family, was tempered by several factors. Few employers hid their main motivation in hiring women—that they could pay them substantially lower wages. At the end of the nineteenth century, for example, an experienced female factory worker earned on the average about five to six dollars for a sixty-hour work week, while unskilled and inexperienced males who performed the same work received about eight dollars per week. In some states, women were prevented by law from entering professions such as the law or medicine. As late as the 1920s, fully a third of the nation's medical schools refused to accept women. These restrictions were augmented by more subtle barriers. Even in 1900, the overwhelming proportion of women who worked were unmarried; in the age of the "separate spheres" of sexual roles, working was not considered consistent with marriage. In 1890, about 88 per cent of all working women were unmarried; thirty years later, the proportion had declined to 78 per cent. The proportion of working women who were married, however, tended to increase among the lower rungs of the socioeconomic and racial ladders; in Atlanta in 1896, for example, as many as 65 per cent of black wives worked.

Nonetheless, by the opening of the twentieth century, the status of women in American society had changed largely as a result of general industrialization. The need for unskilled labor opened up opportunities for factory work; the general concentration of population in the cities, in addition, made jobs as domestic servants available. Women's work was, in general, always lower paid; many women were denied access to many male-dominated jobs. Moreover, upon marriage most women either were expected or forced to leave work. Yet, women constituted an important part of the work force in 1900, and, by the beginning of the twentieth century, the die was cast for a much larger revolution in the nature of sexual roles.

The Triumph of Racism

For many blacks in the South and the North, emancipation was a bitter experience, for they faced a degree of racial prejudice and discrimination which insulted their dignity and obstructed their economic advancement. Actually, segregation and negrophobia had existed in northern states long before emancipation, and, although the Thirteenth, Fourteenth, and Fifteenth amendments wrote racial equality into the Constitution, racism persisted and even grew more virulent throughout the nation. If most Americans did not assume the innate inferiority of blacks, moreover, publicists and scholars were constantly reminding them of its scientific validity. Even more significant than the growth of prejudice was the increasing institutionalization of racism.

Before 1890, blacks in the South possessed the means to defend their civil rights. Intimidation—economic as well as political—made it certain that whites would hold the upper hand; yet, the pattern of racial antagonism was not fixed. Few states before 1890 had legislated the segregation of public facilities, but the postwar southern public school system—with the brief exception of schools in New Orleans during Reconstruction—was unquestionably segregated. Despite the supremacy of white-controlled governments in the South, blacks continued to vote in large numbers; as late as 1880, a majority of black voters participated in the presidential election in every state except two in the South.

Yet, the pattern of racial oppression—particularly the pattern of Jim Crow—had begun to emerge by the end of the nineteenth century. In many parts of the South, the final triumph of segregation awaited the exclusion of blacks from the political process, a development which occurred in state after state in the South—beginning in Mississippi in 1890—through devices such as the literacy test and the poll tax. Disfranchisement also insured the unquestioned authority of the Democratic party during the first half of the twentieth century. And, in spite of the much-heralded "grandfather" and "understanding" clauses, which were intended to permit indigent and illiterate whites to vote, disfranchisement also excluded significant numbers of whites, particularly former Republicans. In Louisiana, for example, black turnout declined by 93 per cent and white turnout by 46 per cent after disfranchisement.

The restriction of the franchise paved the way for the application of legally enforced segregation to all areas of southern life. Southern legislatures passed ordinances which required segregation in schools, restaurants, theaters, railway cars, and courtrooms. South Carolina went to the extreme length of mandating separate Bibles to swear in black witnesses.

The triumph of Jim Crow was possible because the champions of the freedmen had largely abandoned their cause by 1900. In 1883, the Supreme Court nullified the Civil Rights Act of 1875, which had barred segregation in public facilities. Thirteen years later, in a landmark decision, the Supreme Court ruled in Plessy v. Ferguson that segregation in transportation facilities was legal if they were "separate but equal." The dictum of Plessy not only gave legal sanction to an array of subsequent Jim Crow laws, but encouraged the enactment of a variety of new ones.

A tremendous increase in violence directed against blacks in the South also occurred around the turn of the century. In many parts of the South, lynching became a means of racial control. During the last sixteen years of the nineteenth century, more than 2,500 lynchings occurred, and an increasing number of the victims were black; during the first two years of the new century alone, 214 blacks were lynched. In the urban South, violent race riots took place in Wilmington, North Carolina, in 1898 and in Atlanta in 1906 in which mobs of whites indiscriminately attacked blacks and black-owned property.

Blacks reacted in various ways to the turn-of-the-century wave of racism. Booker T. Washington, a former slave, founded the Tuskegee Institute in Alabama during the 1880s; he promoted the principles of accommodation and self-help through "industrial" education. In public, Washington urged blacks to avoid political confrontation with whites and to postpone demands for social and political equality in favor of long-term goals of uplift; in private, he stressed that full equality was a long-term objective. Washington's accommodationist approach attracted considerable support from the rank and file of rural blacks; it also made him popular among northern philanthropists and southern white educators until his death in 1915.

Another tradition, largely in opposition to Washington, proposed that blacks confront racism and Jim Crow head-on. Unlike Washington, many of these leaders were college-educated and from the mulatto elite. William Monroe Trotter, a Harvard graduate and a Boston militant, was an ardent advocate of full racial equality. In November 1913 and 1914, he led delegations of black leaders to protest against federal segregation by the Wilson administration. William E. B. Du Bois attended Fisk University, a black college with strong ties to northern abolitionists, and he then completed graduate work at Harvard and the University of Berlin. The most prominent black scholar of his time, Du Bois became a leading opponent of Washington's approach when he published his searing attack on the Tuskegeean in 1903 in *The Souls of Black Folk*. Du Bois urged instead that blacks confront the system of segregation through the political process; blacks therefore urgently needed a "talented tenth," a college-educated elite.

4. THE EMERGENCE OF AN INDUSTRIAL CULTURE

The Creation of Leisure and the Transformation of Work

The transformation of American life at the end of the nineteenth century also involved a substantial reformulation and redefinition of American culture. The industrial revolution brought a startling change in the ways which Americans—and indeed most western Europeans—regarded their work. In preindustrial societies, work was seasonal and irregular; workers therefore performed their tasks with a combination of energy and sloth. The emergence of a modern economy during the nineteenth century revolutionized these attitudes. By 1900, this transformation also included the strict separation between work and leisure.

Industrial culture in the America of 1900, because of the regimentation of time necessary in the industrial system, involved the full development of the function of leisure and mass recreation. By the end of the nineteenth century, organized sports became crucially important to many Americans. Spectator sports, particularly baseball, as well as college football, became popular in major American cities. Wealthy and middle-class Americans flocked to new resorts in the mountains and beaches and even abroad. Even poor and lower middle-class Americans found leisure activities possible; by the turn of the century, the beach resort of Coney Island attracted New Yorkers of diverse socioeconomic and ethnic backgrounds.

The leaders of American culture saw organized leisure as one answer to the apparent social, ethnic, and racial fragmentation which was the result of industrial change. The regimentation of leisure—and its sharp segregation from work—involved a sort of moral rejuvenation of the value of work. Moreover, the strenuous life—what William James described as the "moral equivalent of war"—offered hope for the preservation of social harmony and cohesion.

Publishers and Publishing

A critical component of the industrial culture was a transformation in American book, magazine, and newspaper publishing between 1890 and 1920. It was a product of revolutionary changes in the technology of publishing—the invention of the power press during the 1830s, followed by innovations in typesetting in the latter part of the century—which greatly reduced the costs of production and hence the price. Publishers also found a receptive and voracious audience in the new urban middle classes.

Several giants dominated early twentieth-century newspaper publishing. Joseph Pulitzer, a Hungarian immigrant, became involved in journalism soon after his arrival in St. Louis in 1865. Pulitzer bought the *St. Louis Dispatch* in 1878; five years later, he purchased the New York *World* and moved his nascent empire there. With its attractive stories, cartoons, and editorials geared to a distinctly urban reader, the *World* established a pattern for modern American journalism. Similarly successful was William Randolph Hearst, who bought the New York *Journal* in 1895. Hearst went much further than Pulitzer in exploiting the sensational appeal to his readers; when his technique worked, Pulitzer adopted some, but not all, of Hearst's methods. Altogether, however, Pulitzer and Hearst created the modern style of journalism. Newspaper journalism, largely through expanded advertising revenues, became a big business. Chains also began to dominate; in 1914, Hearst controlled nine newspapers, and another conglomerate, headed by E. W. Scripps, owned thirty-four dailies. The publication of magazines also underwent substantial change during this period. Because of innovations in printing, high-quality weekly and monthly magazines could be produced inexpensively. Magazines such as *McClure's, Cosmopolitan, Saturday Evening Post,* and *Everybody's* were read by millions of Americans.

Main Trends in Literature

By 1900, the writing of fiction was in the midst of considerable change. Between 1865 and 1900, a new school of literary realists dominated American fiction. The realists, including William Dean Howells and Hamlin Garland, sought to portray life accurately; they reacted against the romanticism and stylized prose of antebellum fiction, and they tended to situate their novels in the locales of particular regions. Howells thus wrote about the effects of industrialization and the rise of the new rich in New England; Mary N. Murfree, about the country and mountain folk of eastern Tennessee; Mark Twain, the greatest novelist of his day, about the social environment of his boyhood in Missouri.

By the end of the nineteenth century, however, the basic contours of realism in fiction had changed. By this time, the influence of Darwinism was strong; the mild optimism and moral message of the realists began to disappear. The intellectual successor to realism, the naturalist school of fiction, continued to place fiction in a firmly rooted social and regional setting. Most of the naturalists were concerned with industrialization, particularly the social disintegration which it caused; they provided a frank picture of political, social, and economic problems. Naturalists, unlike realists, also presented a stark portrayal of human existence: even as people became more civilized, they still struggled against a Darwinian universe and lived in a deterministic environment. Just as Jack London's dog, Buck, had human characteristics in *The Call of the Wild* (1903), so humans were fundamentally animals governed by the dictates of animal instinct. Other naturalists, such as Stephen Crane in *The Red Badge of Courage* (1895), Ellen Glasgow in *Barren Ground* (1925), and Frank Norris in *McTeague* (1899), were equally pessimistic about human nature. The culmination of naturalism was Theodore Dreiser's *Sister Carrie* (1900), a novel about the reality and despair of prostitution.

Religious Life in the Industrial Age

The rapid changes wrought by industrialization, along with the glaring problems of social dislocation and human misery which accompanied it, also had a strong influence on American churches. The transformation of American culture affected religion perhaps more than any other aspect of social life, for it included a massive secularization. Churches were still an important influence—membership continued to increase steadily through the early twentieth century—and yet their role and function undeniably became less influential. Because professions such as university teaching, engineering, and the law tended to attract many of the young people who would have earlier entered the ministry—for example, Woodrow Wilson—church leaders did not exert as commanding a leadership over their flocks as before.

At the same time, American Protestantism faced other challenges. The publication of Charles Darwin's *Origin of Species* (1859) and the subsequent permeation of Darwinism into all aspects of cultural and intellectual life appeared to undermine the underpinnings of Christianity, for Darwin described a universe in which luck and physical strength, rather than divine plan, explained the evolution of nature and humankind. Moreover, the vast changes which Americans witnessed during the late nineteenth century appeared to support the validity of this world view.

A significant portion of the urban churches thus began to reformulate their entire approach to Christianity. As early as the 1870s, urban Protestant churches—in a movement known as the Social Gospel—began to attempt to alleviate social injustice. Largely influenced by the example of British Christian socialism, prominent advocates of the Social Gospel, such as Walter Rauschenbusch and Washington Gladden, advocated aggressive action by the churches to improve the lot of the poor and downtrodden. An army of ministers and priests, many of them trained in Social Gospel-dominated seminaries, were in the vanguard of reform.

Probably most American Christians knew little about the Social Gospel. In the South, most Protestant churches, with the exception of a few urban ones, were intensely other-worldly and had no interest in the betterment of humanity, aside from personal salvation. Nonetheless, the Social Gospel had a wide-ranging effect. Particularly in the seminaries, such as Union Theological Seminary of New York City, the intellectual leadership of the churches became firmly committed to social reform. The Roman Catholic Church—which largely ministered to urban immigrants—came foursquare behind social reform with the publication of Pope Leo XIII's pronouncement, *Rerum Novarum*, in 1891.

Educational Progress

By 1900, public education had begun to assume an increasingly important place as an institution in American culture. During the 1830s, Horace Mann had led a campaign to establish a publicly financed system of elementary, or common, schooling for all the children of Massachusetts. Most states had followed Mann's lead by the early twentieth century. Public schools in rural areas of the country—particularly in the South—tended to be badly funded, irregularly attended, and instructed by teachers who were barely better educated than their pupils.

Real innovation in public education, nonetheless, occurred during the late nineteenth century. Most of the leadership for professionalization of the teaching force and standardization of the schoolroom came from educators associated with the National Education Association. As early as the 1880s, these urban-oriented educators, such as William Torrey Harris, who was superintendent of schools in St. Louis, and Burke Aaron Hinsdale, who ran schools in Cleveland, established a pattern for educational reform during the early twentieth century in the institution, for example, of effective supervision and in the creation of a system of high schools.

An equally significant development was the transformation of American higher education. Before 1870, most American colleges trained students in a single classical course, which provided a general education and emphasized moral training and character. Led by Charles William Eliot, president of Harvard University, American colleges began to broaden their curriculum after the 1870s; by the end of the century, the curriculum of the typical American college resembled that of our own day. Professional graduate training also emerged and spread in the United States during this period. The Johns Hopkins University, founded in 1876, was the first modern university in the United States, and it was the unquestioned leader in American higher education during the next twenty-five years. Other universities, such as Harvard and the University of Wisconsin, became centers of research and promoters of the "new" social sciences—economics, sociology, and political science. After the establishment of a system of land-grant colleges of agriculture and engineering, financed by the Morrill Act of 1862, state-supported institutions proliferated throughout the nation.

The growth of universities provided added impetus for the uplift of public education. University presidents—such as Eliot; James McCosh, president of Princeton; and Edwin Anderson Alderman, president of the University of North Carolina and then of the University of Virginia—became ardent advocates of secondary education. High schools were typically confined to towns and cities, and in 1900 only about 500,000 American children attended secondary schools; colleges and universities at the same time enrolled only 100,000. Nonetheless, both secondary schools and higher education—as well as the entirety of public education—stood on the threshold of a great expansion.

SUGGESTED READINGS

Three works which explore the general context of change at the turn of the twentieth century are Robert H. Wiebe, *The Search for Order, 1877–1920* (1967); Samuel P. Hays, *The Response to Industrialism, 1885–1914* (1957); and John W. Chambers III, *The Tyranny of Change* (1980). Several important studies about late nineteenth-century America are useful, particularly Morton Keller, *Affairs of State: Public Life in Late Nineteenth Century America* (1977), and John A. Garraty, *The New Commonwealth* (1968).

Sam B. Warner, Jr., *The Urban Wilderness: A History of the American City* (1972), provides a good description of the physical development of American cities, while Arthur M. Schlesinger, Sr., *The Rise of the City,*

1878–1898 (1933), remains useful as an introduction to the urban history of the period. Glenn Porter, *The Rise of Big Business, 1860–1920* (1973), is a good introduction to the subject, but it should be supplemented by Alfred D. Chandler, Jr., *The Visible Hand: The Managerial Revolution in American Business* (1977).

Recent scholarship has focused on the social and cultural history of the United States. Among these works are Stephan Thernstrom and Richard Sennett, eds., *Nineteenth Century Cities: Essays in the New Urban History* (1969); Thernstrom, *The Other Bostonians: Poverty and Progress in the American Metropolis* (1973); Sennett, *Families against the City* (1970); Michael Frisch,

Town into City: Springfield, Massachusetts, and the Meaning Of Community, 1840–1880 (1972); and Clyde Griffen and Sally Griffen, *Natives and Newcomers: The Ordering of Opportunity in Mid-Nineteenth Century Poughkeepsie* (1977). An excellent introduction to the history of American labor is available in Melvyn Dubofsky, *Industrialism and the American Worker, 1865–1920* (1975). More specific studies are David Brody, *Steelworkers in America: The Nonunion Period* (1960) and Daniel T. Nelson, *Managers and Workers: Origins of the New Factory System in the United States, 1880–1920* (1975). The new urban culture is explored in John F. Kasson, *Amusing the Million: Coney Island at the Turn of the Century* (1978); Daniel T. Rodgers, *The Work Ethic in Industrial America, 1850–1920* (1978); and T. J. Jackson Lears, *No Place of Grace: Antimodernism and the Transformation of American Culture, 1880–1920* (1981).

A pioneering study of the experience of immigrants in the United States is W. I. Thomas and Florian Znaniecki, *The Polish Peasant in America* (1918). The best general survey is Glenn C. Altschuler, *Race, Ethnicity, and Class in American Social Thought, 1865–1919* (1982). A notable book, Oscar Handlin, *The Uprooted* (1951), has been subjected to serious criticism by later works, which have focused on immigrants and immigrant families in particular cities. Among these are Josef Barton, *Peasants and Strangers: Italians, Rumanians, and Slovaks in an American City, 1890–1930* (1977); Virginia Yans-McLaughlin, *Family and Community: Italian Immigrants in Buffalo, 1880–1930* (1977); and Thomas Kessner, *The Golden Door: Italian and Jewish Immigrant Mobility* (1977). John Higham, *Strangers in the Land: Patterns of Nativism, 1860–1925* (1955), remains the standard treatment of that subject. James Stuart Olson, *The Ethnic Dimension in American History* (1979), is a useful survey of various ethnic groups in America.

The role of religious organizations in dealing with social problems of urban-industrial America is discussed in Charles H. Hopkins, *The Rise of the Social Gospel in American Protestantism, 1865–1915* (1940); Henry F. May, *Protestant Churches and Industrial America* (1949); and Aaron I. Abell, *American Catholicism and Social Action: A Search for Social Justice, 1865–1950* (1960).

The Afro-American encounter with institutionalized racism in the late nineteenth century has been the subject of considerable research. John Hope Franklin, *From Slavery to Freedom*, 5th ed. (1980), and August Meier

and Elliott M. Rudwick, *From Plantation to Ghetto* (1966), are good introductions to the subject. The rise of *de jure* segregation is discussed in a classic study, C. Vann Woodward, *The Strange Career of Jim Crow*, 3rd ed. (1974), although some of its conclusions are challenged in Joel Williamson, *After Slavery: The Negro in South Carolina during Reconstruction, 1861–1877* (1965). The standard account of disfranchisement is J. Morgan Kousser, *The Shaping of Southern Politics: Suffrage Restriction and the Establishment of the One-Party South, 1880–1910* (1974). Booker T. Washington's early career is examined in the first volume of a projected multivolume biography: Louis R. Harlan, *Booker T. Washington: The Making of a Black Leader, 1856–1901* (1972).

The most informative works on the history of public education in the early twentieth century are Lawrence A. Cremin, *The Transformation of the School: Progressivism in American Education, 1876–1957* (1961) and David B. Tyack, *"The One-Best System": A History of American Urban Education* (1974). For a thorough treatment of the movement to extend education beyond the classroom, see Robert O. Case and Victoria Case, *We Called It Culture: The Story of Chautauqua* (1958). On higher education, see especially Lawrence R. Veysey, *The Emergence of the American University* (1965), and Richard Hofstadter and Walter Metzger, *The Development of Academic Freedom in the United States* (1955).

On art and architecture see Lewis Mumford, *The Brown Decades: A Study of the Arts in America, 1865–1895* (1931); Oliver W. Larkin, *Art and Life in America* (1949); Wayne Andrews, *Architecture, Ambition, and Americans* (1955); and John E. Burchard and Albert Bush-Brown, *The Architecture of America* (1961).

In addition to the general surveys of literary history already cited, a good survey of the period is Lazer Ziff, *The American 1890s: Life and Times of a Lost Generation* (1966). A good brief account is also found in Alfred Kazin, *On Native Grounds* (1942). Van Wyck Brooks, *New England: Indian Summer, 1865–1915* (1940), is a fine regional study. Everett Carter, *Howells and the Age of Realism* (1954), traces Howells' influence. The best treatment of Henry Adams is Ernest Samuels, *Henry Adams: The Middle Years* (1958) and *Henry Adams: The Major Phase* (1964). Justin Kaplan, *Mr. Clemens and Mark Twain* (1966), is a generally satisfactory biography, but it should be supplemented by James M. Cox, *Mark Twain: The Fate of Humor* (1966). The greatest work on an American writer of this period is Leon J. Edel, *Henry James*, 5 vols. (1953–1972).

CHAPTER 2
THE REFORM
IMPULSE

1. ORIGINS OF PROGRESSIVISM

Reform and Reconstruction

When Theodore Roosevelt succeeded President William McKinley in September 1901, the United States had already entered the first stages of the social and political eruption which historians call the progressive movement. In essence, progressivism was the most prominent response of Americans to the transformation of life, and the problems which accompanied it, at the end of the nineteenth century. Above all, progressives were modernizers, vigorous advocates of the changes which industrialization wrought. Nonetheless, they were deeply disturbed by many of its consequences: the breakdown of responsible democratic government in city and state; the spread of slums, crime, and poverty in the large cities; the exploitation of workers, especially women and children; and the emergence of large economic interests —railroads, great corporations, and banking empires —which had the power to affect profoundly the destinies of the people and yet remained beyond popular control. Even so, progressivism was not a unified national crusade but an enormously varied and sometimes mutually antagonistic aggregation of many movements for social, economic, and political reform.

Progressivism contained two broad currents. Some progressives belonged to the Mugwump tradition of reform, which, since the 1870s, had worked for honest, good, and efficient government without any important reconstruction of political or economic life.

Proponents of businesslike and reduced administration of government, they regarded the income tax as a pernicious class measure. Others advocated both reform and reconstruction through concerted and purposeful governmental action. These political and economic reconstructionists were the growing, dominant element among progressives after the Panic of 1893.

Reform in the 1890s

All of progressivism's major components originated as recognizable movements in the 1890s. They were among the immediate responses to the economic distress caused by both the agrarian depression of that period and the industrial depression which followed the Panic of 1893. It is more difficult to explain why the movement gained its greatest momentum and achieved its most important triumphs between 1897 and 1920—a period of expanding prosperity and national contentment. An understanding of this phenomenon requires study of the great variety of people involved in various aspects of progressive reform, their different objectives, and the many forms which their participation took.

Progressivism's roots lay deep in American traditions, but early twentieth-century reform was tied to a series of disconnected movements during the 1890s:

1. The most obvious was Populism. The Populists, and then Bryan in 1896, failed to win national power because they remained essentially southern and western agrarian spokesmen and never won the support of either industrial labor or the urban middle classes, the groups which provided most of the motivating force, leadership, and constituency of progressivism. Populism and Bryanism shook the political foundations and were part of a major political realignment. Although many future progressives strenuously opposed Populism in the 1890s, agrarian protesters publicized widespread distress and discontent with the industrial system; they also successfully promoted the concept of a "cooperative commonwealth" in which the state insured social stability and economic well-being. In addition, the Populists' emphasis upon greater popular participation in and control of the political machinery paved the way for sweeping institutional reforms in the near future.

2. The suffering connected with the depression of the 1890s stimulated enormously the two movements which furnished much of the moral zeal for progressivism—the Social Gospel and the movement for social justice. For increasing numbers of urban Americans, the sharp intensification of human distress after the Panic of 1893 dramatized the wide contrast between the privileged position of the well-to-do and the plight of the poor. The impact was heaviest on the ministers, priests, and social workers who worked in the slums of the great cities. When Walter Rauschenbusch saw poverty in a New York settlement house during the depression of the 1890s, he remarked that the underprivileged "wore down our threshold, and they wore away our hearts. . . . One could hear human virtue cracking and crumbling all around." Although the depression which began in 1893 was much less severe in the United States than the economic catastrophe of the 1930s, a larger proportion of the population lived at the subsistence level in 1893 than in 1929. For this reason, temporary unemployment had more serious consequences.

3. Americans in the 1890s, already convulsed by the hard-hitting indictments of the Populists and Bryan, were further agitated by a growing literature of exposure. It began with Henry George's *Progress and Poverty* (1879), gained momentum with the publication of Edward Bellamy's utopian socialist novel, *Looking Backward* (1888), and came to fully developed form in Henry Demarest Lloyd's scathing indictment of the Standard Oil Trust, *Wealth Against Commonwealth* (1894). From 1894 onward, arraignment and exposure were the order of the day in American journalism. The introduction of the inexpensive magazine in the 1890s provided a new medium of vast circulation. Soon the widely read magazines, such as *McClure's, Everybody's,* and *The American Magazine,* and the so-called muckrakers, such as Lincoln Steffens, Ida M. Tarbell, Ray Stannard Baker, and Burton J. Hendrick, were exploring and exposing every dark corner of American life. The muckrakers did not set off the progressive movement. However, they fired the moral indignation of the middle classes by exposing the misery and corruption in American society and helped to make the progressive movement in the early 1900s a national uprising instead of a series of disconnected campaigns.

4. By 1900, economists, political scientists, sociologists, and other publicists had begun to challenge the intellectual foundations of the laissez-faire state—social Darwinism and classical economics—and the whole cluster of ideals associated with rugged individualism. Leaders of this revolt against laissez faire were young economists, such as Richard T. Ely and Thorstein Veblen, and sociologists, such as Lester F. Ward and Edward A. Ross. After 1900, their ranks swelled. The psychologists G. Stanley Hall and Charles Horton Cooley stressed the role of welfare agencies and the state in the nurture and development of children and adolescents. Herbert Croly's *The Promise of American Life* (1909), Walter Weyl's *The New Democracy* (1912), and Walter Lippmann's *Preface to Politics* (1913) worked out a sophisticated justification for the activistic welfare state. Charles A. Beard, another muckraking historian, destroyed the halos around the Founding Fathers in his *An Economic Interpretation of the Constitution* (1913). Oliver Wendell Holmes promoted legal realism, the belief that the law rested not on an unchanging or fixed set of rules but on the needs and realities of contemporary society. Roscoe Pound and Louis D. Brandeis pioneered sociological jurisprudence, a legal system which included economic and social data as well as abstract legal theories.

5. The growth of the urban middle classes gave impetus to these movements and to the development of certain tendencies within them. The urban middle classes were profoundly changed in several important ways during the 1890s and early 1900s. By 1900, they had grown so rapidly because of industrial expansion that they wielded the balance of political power in many sections of the country. Many of the leaders of these classes, who valued university education, specialized training, and professional standards and affiliations, insisted on impersonal, bureaucratic, and efficient administration in public affairs. Avid readers of muckraking periodicals, people in the urban middle classes were deeply affected by the exposures of corruption and accounts of economic and social distress. By the late 1890s, they were building up a full head of steam of moral indignation; the boiler soon exploded with significant political repercussions.

2. URBAN PROGRESSIVISM

The Municipal Reformers

The crusade for municipal reform marked the beginning, chronologically speaking, of progressivism as a *political* movement. It began sporadically in the early 1890s and became a widespread revolt about 1896–1897. Hazen S. Pingree, elected mayor of Detroit in 1889, led the way by battling and subduing that city's trolley, gas, and telephone companies. Then an uprising occurred in Chicago against a corrupt city council which was busy selling franchises to Charles T. Yerkes, a utilities magnate. A Municipal Voters' League, organized by civic-minded businessmen, clergymen, and professional leaders, won control of the city council in 1896–1897 and helped to elect a reform mayor, Carter Harrison. Similar citizens' groups overthrew a notoriously corrupt administration in Minneapolis.

The dominant pattern of municipal reform, however, was redemption through the work of a single colorful and dynamic leader. There was a host of such city reformers, and only a few of them can be mentioned. Mark M. Fagan, elected mayor of Jersey City in 1901, fought for, and won, more equitable taxation of railroads and public utilities in order to pay for his program of expanded social services and better schools. Also notable were Samuel M. ("Golden Rule") Jones and Brand Whitlock in Toledo.

The most successful municipal reformer of this era was Tom L. Johnson of Cleveland. Johnson, elected mayor of that city in 1901, gathered around him some of the brightest young municipal administrators in the country. He made Cleveland, as Lincoln Steffens put it, the best-governed city in the United States. Johnson gained a national reputation for his fight against the Cleveland street railways. But he made his greatest contributions by reorganizing and streamlining the government of Cleveland and by proving that it could efficiently expand its services. Perhaps the most notable thing about Johnson was that he also won the support of the "new" immigrants and big-city masses.

A New Basis for City Government

All municipal reformers fought political officials—often the political machine —allied with privileged business elements and the underworld. In addition, they all fought for efficient government, equitable taxation of the property of railroads and corporations, regulation of public-service corporations, and better education and expanded social services for the poor. But the reformers soon learned that their victories would never be secure so long as the established leaders continued to control the party structures. Hence progressives in the cities joined hands with other groups to obtain new machinery to assure their control of the political process. This machinery included the direct primary for nominating candidates, the short ballot, and the initiative, referendum, and recall. These campaigns were carried out on the state level, and they will be discussed in connection with the progressive movement in the states.

In many areas, cities were governed only with the consent of the state government, and urban machines—usually powerful arms of state organizations—were often able to hobble the urban progressives by voting down their reforms in the legislature. Municipal reformers therefore supported home rule to end legislative interference in city administration. But the state legislatures, many of which rural and small-town representatives dominated, did not relinquish governance of the cities easily. Missouri, California, Washington, and Minnesota had granted home rule by 1900 and, although eight other states followed suit between 1900 and 1914, only two of them—Ohio and Michigan—had cities of any size.

As it turned out, the most successful institutional changes which progressives supported were two new forms of city government. The commission form, which political scientists conceived in the 1890s, was instituted in Galveston, Texas, in 1900, after a tidal wave inundated the city and the old administration of mayor and aldermen proved utterly unable to cope with the emergency. After 1903, city government was vested in five commissioners chosen by popular election.

The commission form was so successful in Galveston that Houston, Dallas, Fort Worth, Austin, and El Paso soon adopted it. It spread rapidly, particularly after the Iowa legislature adopted a more elaborate version of the Texas model in 1907. The Iowa Plan, or Des Moines Idea (so-called because Des Moines instituted the plan in 1908), provided for the election of five commissioners in a nonpartisan canvass. Each commissioner was responsible for a single administrative department, such as finance, public health, or public works. In addition, the Iowa Plan incorporated the initiative, referendum, and recall as part of the machinery of city politics. By 1914, some 400 municipalities had adopted the commission form. Between 1908 and 1912, progressives refined a new idea—government by an expert city manager appointed by and responsible to a popularly elected city council. The city-manager plan, first adopted in its complete form by Dayton, Ohio, in 1913, after a disastrous flood, spread rapidly. More than 300 cities had adopted it by 1923. It should be noted that only small- and medium-sized cities adopted the commission and city-manager plans; all of the large cities continued to govern themselves through mayors and aldermen.

Even so, the commission and city-manager forms and their spread across the country constituted a substantial change from the system of government by a mayor and board of aldermen. One of the urban reformers' most important objectives was to modernize city government to square it with the realities of industrial life. They thus abolished the ward system and lodged control in a small body of professionally trained experts. But commission government also made politics less personal and, as some historians have suggested, even less democratic. However, the commission and city-manager forms made possible further progressive changes in other areas of city government and insured that reformers would play a larger role in the future of the American city.

It would be a gross exaggeration to say that the municipal progressives were successful in all American cities before the outbreak of the First World War. But the legacy of the municipal crusaders was significant and, in most cases, left a permanent imprint on the American city. The era of flagrant nationwide corruption was over. Those old-fashioned organizations, such as Tammany Hall in New York City, survived the progressive onslaught because its leaders, such as Charles F. Murphy, Alfred E. Smith, and Robert F. Wagner, to a large extent became progressives. Cities not only were being governed more efficiently; they were also beginning to grapple successfully with economic and social problems. Moreover, a whole new generation of professional municipal administrators was trained across the country in the science of city government.

3. PROGRESSIVISM IN THE STATES

The Nineteenth-Century Polity

Progressives faced similar difficulties in the state governments, where special-interest groups, often corrupt, reactionary, and blind in many respects to the welfare of the people, controlled the governments of most states. Like city machines, state political organizations governed behind the facade of the formal structure. The so-called System worked usually with relentless efficiency.

Missouri and New Jersey offer vivid, if somewhat exaggerated, examples of the System in operation. In the former, the real power in the state capital was a lobby which represented certain railroad and business interests. This nonpartisan lobby governed through the party caucuses and controlled them by bribery and favors. In New Jersey, the System worked through a corporation-machine alliance in which the corporate, railroad, and financial interests furnished the leadership—called the Board of Guardians—of the dominant Republican party. The railroad lobby, for example, in 1903 provided the chief justice of the state, the attorney general, the state comptroller, the commissioner of banking and insurance, and one of the members of the state board of taxation. Railroads in New Jersey, needless to say, paid very low taxes.

Beginnings of Revolt

The progressive revolt in the states was the product of earlier reform movements, both urban and rural. In the South and the West, agrarian radicalism gave way to progressivism after 1896, as urban spokesmen took leadership in the fight against railroad and corporation dominance. The Middle West, where conservative Republicans were firmly in the saddle until near the end of the century, was swept by a series of spectacular state revolts from about 1900 to 1908. Insurgent antiorganization Republicans such as Robert M. La Follette of Wisconsin, Albert B. Cummins of Iowa, and Joseph H. Bristow of Kansas transformed the Middle West from a bastion of conservative Republican power into a center of progressivism in the states.

State progressive movements in the East were more often the culmination of earlier municipal movements, but they were no less important than those in other sections. New York progressives came to power in Albany under the governorship of Charles Evans Hughes from 1907 to 1910. Woodrow Wilson's election as governor of New Jersey in 1910 was the climax of a movement begun largely by Republican progressives. In Ohio, progressivism won its most sweeping triumph with the adoption of a new constitution and the election of a Democratic progressive, James M. Cox, in 1912. The successful campaigns of reformers such as William S. U'Ren in Oregon and Hiram W. Johnson in California equally convulsed politics on the West Coast.

The progressive revolt profoundly affected American politics. The rebellion shattered the structure and organization of nineteenth-century politics, brought new, reform-minded leadership to power, and, in many states, transformed the role of the state government. The most important cause of this upheaval, in the cities as well as in the states, was the sudden growth and maturation of the urban middle classes. Their spokesmen were quick to articulate and fight for their interests.

Political Restructuring

That fight proceeded first on the political front, in an effort to make institutions of government more susceptible to public control and less dominated by party organizations. Indeed, progressives viewed the nineteenth-century party system as inimical to democracy. Representative government had collapsed, progressives charged, because old forms either had broken down under the stress of socioeconomic change or were too easily controlled by self-serving politicians. Hence new forms had to be found to help restore democracy. One such device was the direct primary, in which voters themselves, rather than professional politicians in caucuses and conventions, nominated party candidates. Mississippi, in 1902, was the first state to require nominations by the direct primary. The following year, Governor La Follette persuaded the legislature of Wisconsin to enact a similar law, and the direct primary was widely adopted after this date. By 1916, only Rhode Island, Connecticut, and New Mexico still used the convention system for nominations.

The direct primary was merely a first step in the progressive transformation of government. Another was the short ballot, which, reformers contended, enabled voters to hold a fewer number of officeholders to accountability, but which, in practice, made more offices appointive and thus struck a telling blow at the patronage system. It was adopted most widely by cities in connection with the commission and city-manager forms of government. Still another was stringent corrupt-practices legislation which limited campaign contributions and expenditures. Progressives also obtained the direct election of United States senators by the people instead of by the state legislatures.

The demand for the direct election of senators had originated with the Populists. It was further excited by the muckrakers, particularly by David Graham Phillips' "The Treason of the Senate," published in *Cosmopolitan* in 1906. This series portrayed the upper house as the nerve center of the System in the United States. The Senate resisted the demand for popular election for many years, and state after state adopted the plan of permitting the voters to indicate their choice of a senatorial candidate in primary elections. By 1910, more than enough states to ratify a federal amendment had already instituted this indirect method of the direct election of senators. After a scandal in the senatorial election of William Lorimer, Republican boss of Illinois in that state's legislature, the Senate finally yielded in 1912 and approved the Seventeenth Amendment for the direct election of senators. It was ratified in record time in 1913. Another innovation—the presidential preferential primary—enabled voters to express their choice for presidential candidates. It was first adopted by Oregon in 1910; a dozen states used it in 1912.

Finally, progressives championed measures which struck at the traditional political system. Two such measures were the initiative and referendum, which enabled a certain percentage of the voters to initiate and submit legislation to the general electorate if the legislature refused to adopt it (the initiative), and to demand a special election which enabled voters to repeal legislation enacted by the legislature (the referendum). Some twenty-one states had adopted the initiative and referendum by 1915. A further measure was the recall, which enabled voters to unseat unpopular or dishonest officials, including judges. It was adopted most widely in cities with the commission and city-manager forms, but nine states, most of them in the West, made state as well as local officials subject to the recall.

Experience soon confirmed the sweeping changes which the progressive institutional reforms produced. By 1920, government in the cities and states was less under the grip of the once powerful political machines. Indeed, largely as a result of progressive reform, party government as it had existed in the nineteenth century—with the accoutrements of torchlight parades, high voter turnout, as well as pervasive corruption—had begun an irreversible decline. At the same time, government became more responsive to popular pressure, particularly pressure from well-organized interest groups. To a significant extent, the political world in which we live today is a product of progressive reform.

4. MOVEMENTS FOR SOCIAL AND SEXUAL JUSTICE

Social Reform

Progressives must be judged not so much by the institutional changes which they wrought, but on the basis of what they did with the political power which they won. Their achievement in modernizing the administrative structures of city and state governments was far-reaching in itself. Even more impressive were their accomplishments in social and economic reform. By 1914, every state but one had established minimum-age limits for child workers who ranged from fourteen to sixteen. By 1917, some thirty-nine states had attempted to protect women workers by limiting the number of hours which they might work. The Supreme Court, in Muller v. Oregon, in 1908 had upheld the constitutionality of this legislation. Various investigations revealed that numerous women received wages entirely inadequate to maintain a decent standard of living. Beginning with Massachusetts in 1912, some fifteen states by 1923 had enacted some form of minimum-wage legislation for women. In the latter year, the Supreme Court declared all such laws unconstitutional. Between 1911 and 1916, some thirty states established accident-insurance systems for industrial workers and thus removed the burden of industrial accidents and deaths from the backs of both workers and employers. Under the leadership of the Women's Christian Temperance Union, the Anti-Saloon League, and the Methodist, Presbyterian, Baptist, and Congregational churches, state after state, particularly in the South and West, prohibited the manufacture and sale of intoxicating beverages. Three fourths of the American people lived in dry counties by 1917, while two thirds of the states had adopted prohibition. Although many Americans did not consider prohibition either progressive or a reform, the leaders of the movement were sincerely trying to improve the quality of American life. Most states which did not have them by the beginning of the progressive era established railroad and public-utility commissions to regulate rates and services. So effective had state regulation of railroads become by 1914 that the railroad managers were then begging Congress to save them from too harsh controls by state commissions.

Progressives, despite all their concern for vital democratic government, on the whole ignored America's greatest problem—the plight of the one tenth of Americans who were black. As has been said, blacks remained economically submerged, socially ostracized, and, in large sections of the South, disfranchised as well. Faint glimmerings of hope did appear for black Americans. A small group of black intellectuals, led by Du Bois, organized the Niagara Movement in 1905 to work for the advancement of blacks. But Du Bois' movement became mired in constant controversy with the blacks and whites who looked to Booker T. Washington. In any event, it was largely in protest against Washington's program of accommodation that a group of black and white educators, editors, clergymen, and social workers organized the National Association for the Advancement of Colored People (NAACP) in 1909, the year after a race riot in Springfield, Illinois. The NAACP kept the American democratic conscience alive, in part through its journal, *The Crisis*, which Du Bois edited; but it represented only a tiny minority even as late as the outbreak of the First World War.

In addition, a group of white and black social workers, sociologists, and philanthropists organized the National Urban League in New York in 1911. It worked with increasing effectiveness to find jobs for blacks and to improve their living standards in the large northern cities. Indeed, the National Urban League played an indispensable role after the migration of hundreds of thousands of blacks from the South to northern and midwestern urban areas began in 1915.

Progressivism—Southern Style

The region which contained the vast majority of the nation's blacks—the South—was the scene of extensive progressive reform. Despite La Follette's assertion in 1912 that progressivism had never taken root in the region, reformers there had an active hand, like progressives elsewhere, in reshaping the nature of political institutions and the role of government in society.

Southern reform in many respects reflected the darker side both of progressivism writ large and of the peculiarities of southern life. As has been said, in the South reform was often associated with a degree of political and racial oppression. The era of Jim Crow in the South also spawned a type of southern politician—men such as James K. Vardaman and Theodore G. Bilbo of Mississippi and Benjamin R. Tillman and "Cotton Ed" Smith of South Carolina—who combined a blatantly racist rhetoric with an advocacy of progressive reform.

At the same time, like their northern counterparts, southern progressives were responsible for the modernization of their region's political, economic, and social institutions; unlike industrial America, however, southern institutions were the product of *under*development and not of rapid economic growth. Hence southern progressives centered not only on political reform but also on an effort to bring the South into modernity. Between 1900 and 1920, a series of progressive governors in the South—for example, Charles B. Aycock of North Carolina, Andrew J. Montague and Claude A. Swanson of Virginia, and Braxton B. Comer of Alabama—transformed their state governments into active agencies for modernization in three major ways. By 1920, most of the South had established governmental responsibility for public health, a position entrenched by the dramatic success of the campaign (funded and organized with the philanthropic agents of John D. Rockefeller, Jr.) to eradicate hookworm infestation. Southern state governments also assumed responsibility for the expansion of a state-funded highway system, which, after 1920, made substantial progress in eliminating the extreme isolation of the rural South.

The most dramatic accomplishment of the southern progressives was the expansion of the states' educational systems. Southern progressives worked with an assortment of Northerners interested in southern uplift—men such as Rockefeller and Robert Curtis Ogden, department-store magnate of New York City—who worked together in intersectional organizations such as the Southern Education Board, founded in 1901, and the General Education Board, begun a year later. The accomplishments of the educators and reformers were considerable. Southern schools came under the control and scrutiny of the state governments; new facilities for teacher training were created; a system of secondary education was begun; and vocational—especially agricultural—education began in earnest.

All in all, the most significant result of southern progressivism was the increase in the scale of the government's role in society. Through active interference, state governments became committed, moreover, to the uplift and modernization of the region as a whole.

Women and Reform

Much of the generative power of progressivism came from what has to be called one of the most remarkable generations of women in American history. Middle-class women began to go in large numbers to college, particularly to the women's colleges which were founded during the last four decades of the nineteenth century (for example, Vassar, 1861; Smith, 1871; Bryn Mawr, 1885; Agnes Scott, 1889; Randolph-Macon College for Women, 1893). Some 2,500 women were graduated from college in 1890; that number had increased to nearly 8,500 by 1910.

A few brave women almost literally fought their way into graduate and professional schools, but they were rare exceptions. Many female college graduates, of course, went into elementary and secondary school teaching. Most of them married and devoted themselves full-time to their families, but a large number were filled with a zeal for social service and reform. Of this latter group, some took leadership in establishing settlement houses—social centers built in the midst of the slums of great cities which provided day-care services for children, classes for immigrants, and a wide variety of social services. To mention only two, Jane Addams founded Hull House in Chicago in 1889 and became in the eyes of many persons the greatest woman of her generation. Lillian D. Wald founded the Henry Street Settlement in New York in 1895; she was also active in many other reform causes. Numerous women went into the new profession of social work. Others, such as Frances Willard, who founded the Women's Christian Temperance Union in 1874, led the fight against the saloon. Still others worked for child-labor legislation and the regulation of the hours and wages of women and helped to organize female workers in the garment workshops. Margaret Drier Robins and Mary McDowell were the driving forces in the National Women's Trade Union League, founded in 1903. Josephine Goldmark organized the National Consumers' League in 1899 to work on behalf of saleswomen in department stores. Florence Kelley and Goldmark also assembled the data which Brandeis used in his brief in the case of Muller v. Oregon. Julia Lathrop became, in 1912, the first head of the United States Children's Bureau. These are only a few representatives of thousands of women who were in the forefront of the movement for social justice. That movement could not have succeeded without their energy, zeal, and moral commitment.

Woman Suffrage

The movement for woman suffrage, begun so bravely at the Seneca Falls convention of July 1848 by Lucretia Mott and Elizabeth Cady Stanton, did not prosper during the Victorian period because of that era's emphasis on male supremacy, separate sexual spheres, and the "proper" role of women. Stanton

Woman Suffrage before 1920

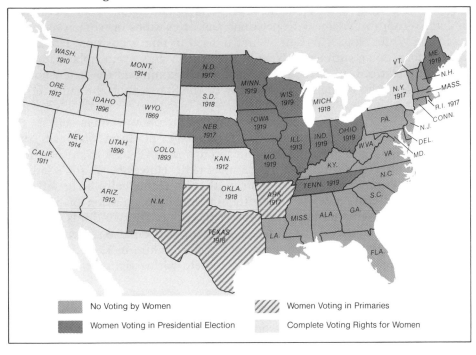

No Voting by Women	Women Voting in Primaries
Women Voting in Presidential Election	Complete Voting Rights for Women

and a younger recruit, Susan Brownell Anthony, organized the National Woman Suffrage Association in 1869 to secure a Sixteenth Amendment; it was reorganized in 1890 as the National American Woman Suffrage Association (NAWSA). But woman suffrage reformers met abuse and ridicule, not only from men, but also from many Victorian women, who thought that political equality would lead to the destruction of the home and what women's magazines called the redeeming feminine influence. The real power and momentum of the campaign for female suffrage had to await the emergence of the new middle-class generation of women. By 1900, only Wyoming (1890), Colorado (1893), and Idaho and Utah (1896) had granted suffrage to women, because the groups working for law and order needed women's votes to tame the frontier.

What had been a seemingly hopeless cause began to turn into a crusade with the election of Carrie Clinton Lane Chapman Catt as president of the NAWSA in 1900 and of Dr. Anna Howard Shaw to the same position in 1904. They turned the NAWSA from propaganda work to political action. Washington (1910), California (1911), Arizona, Kansas, and Oregon (all in 1912), and Montana and Nevada (1914) fell into line; and Illinois, in 1913, permitted women to vote in presidential elections. But resistance remained formidable, both from women and men in the South and the East. New Jersey, New York, Massachusetts, and Pennsylvania rejected woman suffrage in 1915. Moreover, the ranks of woman reformers divided when a militant group, led by Alice Paul, broke away from the NAWSA in 1914 and formed the Congressional Union (later the National Woman's party). Paul and her associates announced that they had only one objective and would oppose *any* candidate who would not promise to vote for a federal woman suffrage amendment.

The Progressive platform of 1912 contained a plank vaguely favoring woman suffrage; the Democrats and Republicans were silent on the issue in that year. But this did not daunt Catt, Shaw, and Paul. They began to bombard Woodrow Wilson with petitions and delegations of women once he was in the White House. Wilson at first refused to take a position. However, he voted for woman suffrage in New Jersey in 1915 and wrote a plank for the Democratic platform of 1916 which read: "We recommend the extension of the franchise to the women of the country by the States upon the same terms as to men."

Wilson seems to have become committed in principle to woman suffrage in 1916. He would not go beyond the Democratic platform plank in the campaign of 1916, although his Republican opponent, Charles Evans Hughes, came out in favor of a federal suffrage amendment. However, Wilson's letters and speeches during the campaign indicate that he deeply believed in suffrage for women and that, now, it was with him merely a question of political strategy—that is, whether he could muster the necessary two-thirds votes in both houses of Congress for a federal amendment. Wilson also recognized and was grateful for the votes of women which reelected him in 1916. He carried ten of the eleven states which granted complete voting rights to women by 1916.

For whatever reason, Wilson became a leading advocate of woman suffrage from this time forward and worked in close cooperation with Shaw and Catt. Women rallied to the war effort once the United States entered the First World War. Wilson said that they had earned the suffrage by their heroic sacrifices; but he also insisted that woman suffrage was "an act of right and justice." Wilson was also influenced by Paul and other members of the National Woman's party when they picketed the White House in 1917 and were arrested and sent to the District workhouse. Paul and others further dramatized, by widely publicized hunger strikes, the anomaly of fighting to make the world safe for democracy while refusing to give basic civil rights to women.

Under Wilson's pressure, the House of Representatives approved a woman suffrage amendment on January 10, 1918. Prospects for approval by the Senate seemed bleak, but Wilson only redoubled his campaign. When it seemed certain that the Senate would reject the amendment, Wilson went before that body on September 30, 1918, and eloquently appealed for its approval. It was the only time in American history that a President has ever addressed either house of Congress on behalf of a constitutional amendment. The Senate rejected the amendment on October 1, but Wilson would not give up. He twisted the arms of his personal friends in the upper house and sent a special message to Congress from the Paris Peace Conference on May 20, 1919. The Senate yielded on June 4—with no votes to spare. Wilson worked as hard for ratification as he had for congressional approval of what was now the Nineteenth Amendment. It was owing entirely to his influence that Tennessee ratified the amendment on August 21, 1919, and made it a part of the Constitution.

The Nineteenth Amendment was one of the crowning achievements of the progressive era. It did not bring the millennium for women in the United States. They continued for decades to run into stone walls when they tried to enter the professions, particularly the medical and legal professions. They also continued (and still continue) to suffer discrimination in numerous ways. But the Nineteenth Amendment was *the* necessary beginning and the cornerstone of what would eventually become a powerful movement to recognize the dignity and simple human rights of more than one half of the American people.

5. ORGANIZED LABOR AND SOCIALISM

The Emergence of Socialism

The spectacular growth of socialism after 1900 gave revealing and, to many persons, alarming proof of the extent of discontent. Socialists united in the 1890s to form the Socialist Labor party under the dogmatic Marxian theorist Daniel De Leon. They remained, however, a small minority of little influence. A new era began when the midwestern labor leader Eugene V. Debs founded the Social Democratic party in 1896. The anti-De Leon group in the Socialist Labor party, led by Morris Hillquit of New York and Victor Berger of Milwaukee, joined Debs to launch the Socialist Party of America in 1901.

The new party was torn by dissension until it finally divided between Communists and Socialists in 1919. On one side were doctrinaire Marxists and radical labor leaders, such as William D. Haywood of the Industrial Workers of the World (IWW). They wanted to work for revolution and a proletarian commonwealth. On the other side stood moderates, such as

Hillquit and Berger, who advocated working through democratic processes to achieve a limited socialistic economy. The moderates triumphed, at least temporarily. In 1912, they obtained the adoption of a resolution by the Socialist national convention which expelled advocates of crime, violence, and sabotage.

Meanwhile, the party's increasing commitment to democratic gradualism had attracted to its ranks a large number of clergymen, writers, and others who believed that thoroughgoing reform was impossible through the major parties. The Socialist party's membership of 58,000 in 1908 had increased to 126,000 by 1912. By 1912, Socialist mayors held office in Milwaukee, Schenectady, and Berkeley, California. One Socialist sat in the United States House of Representatives, and another soon would join him. In the presidential election of 1912, the Socialist candidate, Debs, won 900,000 votes.

As the advanced guard, or left wing, of progressivism, socialism posed a real challenge to the two major parties. Moreover, moderate, or reform, socialistic ideas had a close relationship with left-wing progressivism. Marxism had strongly influenced leading American social scientists, particularly the economists. The most important among them avoided any open avowal of Marxist beliefs because the public tended to associate Marxism with anarchism and revolution. However, the founders of modern American social science—among them, Richard T. Ely, Henry Carter Adams, John R. Commons, Thorstein Veblen, and Woodrow Wilson—were all profoundly affected by socialistic ideas. So also was the Social Gospel; its chief propounder was Walter Rauschenbusch, a Socialist.

For another thing, Americans have in general stubbornly refused to lie on any ideological Procrustean bed. One of their responses during the progressive era to the problem of controlling the things which affected them most vitally—utilities—was to institute public ownership. By 1915, 3,045 cities owned their own waterworks, as compared with 1,355 cities which had privately owned facilities. In 1917, 2,318 cities owned their own central electrical power stations—nearly half the number which used the services of private companies. St. Paul, Minnesota, established a municipal bank in 1913; North Dakota opened a large state bank—the Bank of North Dakota—in 1919. San Francisco took over ownership of its streetcar lines in 1912; Seattle, in 1919; Detroit, in 1922. Other cities established municipal fuel yards, ice plants, ports, piers, and terminals, printing plants, markets, ferries, and so on. Not only this, but the trend toward municipal ownership greatly accelerated between 1890 and 1920. One conclusion can surely be drawn from these facts: the American people were not so wedded to the idea of private ownership that they were unwilling to undertake public ownership whenever they concluded that the latter would furnish essential services more efficiently and more cheaply than private companies.

Yet, by 1920, socialism was defunct as a political force in the United States. The immediate cause of its decline was the outbreak of the First World War, which brought its latent ambivalences and tensions into the open. Also, when the United States entered the war in 1917, the federal government arrested and secured the conviction of many radical Socialists for obstructing the war effort. Larger and longer-term factors also had a debilitating effect. The United States lacked a strong tradition of unified class consciousness; the working class, as such, was divided often by ethnicity, region, and race.

Most American workers, particularly artisans, considered themselves capitalist entrepreneurs; most workers strongly subscribed to a "work ethic," even during the very time that they were losing control over the nature of their work.

Unions and Labor Strife

The prevalence of labor unrest, particularly among the ranks of unskilled and exploited workers, was a further sign of social ferment. By 1914, the American Federation of Labor (AFL), which was founded in 1886 by Adolph Strasser and Samuel P. Gompers, had organized about 2,000,000 skilled workers. But the AFL was constantly thwarted by employers when it tried to organize the mass of industrial workers. Efforts in 1901 and 1909 to organize the steel industry resulted not only in failure, but also in the destruction of the steelworkers' union. The United Mine Workers, an AFL affiliate, succeeded in organizing the older coal areas, but it failed in West Virginia in 1912–1913 and in Colorado during 1913–1914. Violence, even open warfare, broke out in these states. The worst episode was the so-called Ludlow Massacre in Colorado, when National Guard troops attacked a miners' tent colony on April 29, 1914, and accidentally killed eleven women and two children.

The most eloquent and frankly revolutionary voice of labor discontent was the IWW, which worked largely among western lumbermen and miners. In the East it organized unskilled workers, especially in the textile industry. The IWW seemed to be gaining strength just before the First World War, in spite of its advocacy of violence and sabotage when necessary in labor disputes.

The most important challenge to progressive leaders during this era, in addition to the plight of blacks, was the struggle for economic justice by millions of impoverished workers. Progressives were divided in their response. Most urban middle-class progressives remained either unconcerned or unsympathetic for various reasons, but they supported measures such as those for minimum wages, factory inspection, and workmen's compensation in the hope that these measures would prevent the spread of socialism and labor radicalism. Others, particularly leaders of the social-justice movement, warned that American democracy could not survive if a large element of workers felt disinherited and powerless to shape their own destinies. These progressives asserted that the labor movement was the hope of the future, and that governments, state and federal, should encourage labor drives for unionization and collective bargaining. Leaders in Washington heeded their warnings to some degree during the Wilson administration and much more extensively during the New Deal of the 1930s.

SUGGESTED READINGS

Among the general works on the progressive movement, Richard Hofstadter, *The Age of Reform: From Bryan to F.D.R.* (1955), is the book most often read by students and also most often criticized by specialists in the period. A new synthesis is provided in Arthur S. Link and Richard L. McCormick, *Progressivism* (1983). Three fine overviews, already cited, are Wiebe, *The Search for Order,* Hays, *The Response to Industrialism,* and Chambers, *The Tyranny of Change.* Wiebe, *Businessmen and Reform* (1962), and Gabriel

Kolko, *The Triumph of Conservatism* (1963), emphasize the role which businessmen played, although it must be said that the latter book is badly flawed. Excellent general works are Sidney Fine, *Laissez Faire and the General Welfare State* (1964); Eric F. Goldman, *Rendezvous with Destiny* (1953); John D. Buenker, *Urban Liberalism and Progressive Reform* (1973); James T. Timberlake, *Prohibition and the Progressive Movement* (1963); Russell B. Nye, *Midwestern Progressive Politics* (1951); and, for the South, Woodward, *Origins of the New South, 1877–1913* (1951).

Most of the works mentioned on reform movements in Suggested Readings for Chapter One are relevant here. Among the most significant specialized works are Morton White, *Social Thought in America: The Revolt against Formalism* (1949); Daniel Aaron, *Men of Good Hope* (1951); David W. Noble, *The Paradox of Progressive Thought* (1958); and Henry May, *The End of American Innocence* (1959). The best work on the muckrakers is David M. Chalmers, *The Social and Political Ideas of the Muckrakers* (1964), but there is no substitute for the writings of the muckrakers themselves, particularly Lincoln Steffens, *The Shame of the Cities* (1904) and *The Struggle for Self-Government* (1906).

The best state study on progressivism is David P. Thelen, *The New Citizenship: Origins of Progressivism in Wisconsin, 1885–1900* (1972). Other good local and state studies are Ransom E. Noble, Jr., *New Jersey Progressivism Before Wilson* (1946); George E. Mowry, *The California Progressives* (1951), which should, however, be supplemented by Spencer C. Olin, Jr., *California's Prodigal Sons* (1968); James B. Crooks, *Politics & Progress: The Rise of Urban Progressivism in Baltimore* (1968); Zane L. Miller, *Boss Cox's Cincinnati* (1968); Melvin G. Holli, *Reform in Detroit: Hazen S. Pingree and Urban Politics* (1969); and Richard L. McCormick, *From Realignment to Reform: Political Change in New York State, 1893–1910* (1981). A study of broad significance is David C. Hammack, *Power and Society in Greater New York, 1886–1903* (1982).

There is now a growing literature on the movement for social justice. Robert H. Bremner, *From the Depths: The Discovery of Poverty in the United States* (1956), is the best general study. Excellent also are Allen F. Davis, *Spearheads for Reform: The Social Settlements and the Progressive Movement* (1967); Walter I. Trattner, *Crusade for Children* (1970); and Roy Lubove, *The Struggle for Social Security* (1968). For the contributions of women, see John C. Farrell, *Beloved Lady* (1967), on Jane Addams, and Josephine C. Goldmark, *Impatient Crusader: Florence Kelley's Life Story* (1953).

There is a rich literature on the struggle for women's rights; some of the most important works on this subject are Eleanor Flexner, *Century of Struggle: The Woman's Rights Movement in the United States* (1975); Aileen S. Kraditor, *The Ideas of the Woman Suffrage Movement, 1890–1920* (1965); and Anne Firor Scott, *The Southern Lady: From Pedestal to Politics, 1830–1930* (1971).

For socialism and left-wing unionism during the progressive era, see David A. Shannon, *The Socialist Party of America: A History* (1955); John P. Diggins, *The American Left in the Twentieth Century* (1973); Howard Quint, *The Forging of American Socialism* (1953); Ira Kipnis, *The American Socialist Movement, 1897–1912* (1952); James Weinstein, *The Decline of Socialism in America, 1912–1925* (1967); and Melvyn Dubofsky, *We Shall Be All: A History of the Industrial Workers of the World* (1969).

CHAPTER 3
ROOSEVELT, TAFT, AND THE POLITICS OF PROGRESSIVISM, 1900–1912

1. TR AND THE CORPORATE ECONOMY

Roosevelt and Reform

Theodore Roosevelt, only forty-three years old when elevated to the presidency by an assassin's bullet, was born in New York City on October 27, 1858. His parents united northern and southern aristocratic traditions. His father was from a wealthy Knickerbocker family, his mother a member of a prominent Georgia family. After graduation from Harvard in 1880, Roosevelt spent two strenuous years on a ranch in North Dakota to rebuild his health. He denounced his genteel friends who refused to dirty their hands with political affairs, and he decided to make politics his profession. Theodore served successively in the New York state legislature, on the national Civil Service Commission, and as president of the Police Board of New York City. He demonstrated independence from the other Republican reformers of his day by spurning the Mugwump revolt and supporting the allegedly corrupt James G. Blaine for the presidency in 1884. Thirteen years later, McKinley appointed Roosevelt to be Assistant Secretary of the Navy, but he soon resigned to help organize the Rough Rider regiment in the Spanish-American War. With the help of publicity about his battlefield heroics, Roosevelt won election as governor of New York in 1898. He was then nominated for the vice-presidency in 1900 at the insistence of the New York Republican boss, Thomas C. Platt, who was eager to speed Roosevelt's exit from the state.

Dynamic energy is the key to understanding Roosevelt's character from boyhood onward. The variety of his interests, activities, and accomplishments was incredible. Although not a professional historian, he wrote what is still the authoritative history of the naval war of 1812. He was a distinguished amateur naturalist and an accomplished explorer and big-game hunter. Although born to wealth, he chose his friends from all walks of life: cowboys, ambassadors, labor leaders, senators, clergymen, prize fighters, and journalists. People from widely different backgrounds were likely to meet one another in the reception room of the White House or to sit down at Roosevelt's table.

A Plebiscitory President

It would have been difficult for a man of Roosevelt's intelligence, interests, and energy to have continued the recent tradition of passive presidents. He broke tradition with the succession of weak chief executives from Andrew Johnson to William McKinley and set a new pattern of strong presidential leadership. More than that, Roosevelt was what Arthur M. Schlesinger, Jr., has called the plebiscitory President. Such presidents (Andrew Jackson and Richard M. Nixon are two other striking examples) believe that they derive their sovereignty directly from the people and that they possess all executive power not explicitly denied them by the Constitution. When he encountered opposition from Congress in domestic and foreign affairs, Roosevelt ruled by executive orders at home and executive agreements abroad. In fact, Roosevelt began the practice of using executive agreements to bypass the Senate. He laid the foundations for what has been called the imperial presidency. He also soon took over leadership of the progressive movement in national politics and became the best publicity agent for the progressive crusade.

Antitrust

Circumstances would probably have required a person of Roosevelt's temperament to play the role of a plebiscitory President in any event, because he found obstacles in every path that he took toward reform in his early years in the White House. The Republican party, which elected every President except Cleveland after Reconstruction, was dominated by a strong internal organization which mere bugle blasts could not topple. Commonly known as the Old Guard, this organization controlled the Senate through men such as Senators Mark A. Hanna of Ohio, Nelson W. Aldrich of Rhode Island, and William B. Allison of Iowa. A somewhat different Old Guard coalition, oriented more toward local business interests, was almost as firmly entrenched in the House of Representatives. It ruled there with the help of the enormous power exercised by Speaker Joseph G. Cannon of Illinois. Unable to destroy the Old Guard, Roosevelt decided to work with it; meanwhile, he undermined its power and gained personal control of the GOP.

Roosevelt was nonetheless keenly responsive to popular opinion. Americans in 1901 were alarmed about the rapid spread of industrial consolidations popularly called "trusts." The return to prosperity and business confidence in 1897 had prompted an extraordinary outburst of industrial and financial combinations, and the public outcry was loud, especially throughout the

Middle West. Roosevelt, in fact, had a fairly sophisticated understanding of the economic causes for the concentration movement; he never opposed giant corporations simply because of their size. Rather, he tended to apply subjective moral standards to differentiate between good corporations and bad ones. But he stood foursquare against monopoly in industry, and he believed that great corporations should be subjected to considerable regulation. In December 1901, Roosevelt declared in his first Annual Message to Congress that corporations engaged in interstate commerce should submit to full investigations of their business practices.

The financial community was startled a few weeks later to discover that the new President seemed to mean what he said. In February 1902, Roosevelt instructed Attorney General Philander C. Knox to bring suit under the Sherman Act for dissolution of the Northern Securities Company, which J. Pierpont Morgan had recently formed as a holding company to control the Northern Pacific and Great Northern railroads. James J. Hill, who controlled the Northern Pacific, had organized the combination in order to protect the securities of the two lines from the raids of Wall Street speculators, not to monopolize the traffic of the Northwest. But the federal court in St. Paul ordered dissolution of the Northern Securities Company in 1903, and the Supreme Court upheld the decision by a five-to-four vote in 1904.

The government's action in this case actually was more significant in its promise for the future than for its immediate practical accomplishments. It symbolized Roosevelt's determination to assert the nation's sovereignty over large concentrations of wealth, and it promised the beginning of a vigorous antitrust crusade on several fronts. Only a few months after the institution of the Northern Securities suit, Roosevelt began the activation of the Sherman Act against industrial corporations. The campaign opened with a suit against the so-called Beef Trust in late 1902 and reached its culmination with suits against the Standard Oil Company in 1907 and the American Tobacco Company in 1908. All told, the Justice Department during the Roosevelt administration instituted eighteen proceedings in equity and obtained twenty-five indictments under the Sherman Act. The Supreme Court supported the government in every case; it even went so far in the oil and tobacco cases in 1911 as to reverse the Knight decision* and to rule that the Sherman Act did outlaw monopolies in manufacturing.

Meanwhile, in the early months of 1903, Roosevelt moved on another front. He demanded enactment of a bill to create a Bureau of Corporations to investigate all business practices and advise the Justice Department on antitrust proceedings. Immense opposition developed from big business interests, but Roosevelt won his measure by appealing over the head of Congress to public opinion. The Bureau of Corporations' reports on the Beef Trust (1905); the Standard Oil Company (1906–1907); the Tobacco Trust (1909–1916); the steel industry (1911–1913); and the International Harvester Company (1913), furnished exhaustive details for future antitrust proceedings.

These forays alarmed conservatives, who from the beginning had wondered whether Roosevelt could be trusted to carry on the McKinley policies. Hanna

---

*E. C. Knight *v.* the United States (1895), which ruled that manufacturing was local in nature and hence not subject to federal control.

had allegedly retorted, when Platt insisted upon Roosevelt's nomination for the vice-presidency, "Don't any of you realize that there's only one life between that madman and the White House?" But for every enemy that Roosevelt made in Wall Street or among the lobbies in Washington, he attracted thousands of devoted followers among the people at large. His declaration that government had to be "the senior partner in every business" was hailed as a warning that no business interest would be permitted to defy the law.

Labor and Capital

Roosevelt again asserted his leadership dramatically in the same year in which he opened his antitrust crusade. Nearly 150,000 anthracite coal miners in Pennsylvania began a strike on May 14, 1902. John Mitchell, president of the United Mine Workers, tried in vain to persuade the mine operators to hear the workers' grievances or to submit their complaints to arbitration. The strike dragged on through the summer and into the autumn. Anthracite was the fuel used for heating most eastern homes, and its price rose from five dollars to thirty dollars a ton for those fortunate enough to find any. To Roosevelt, the situation was intolerable, and he decided to intervene in a typically Rooseveltian way.

On October 3, Roosevelt summoned Mitchell and the mine operators to the White House. Let the miners go back to work at once, he demanded. Meanwhile, he would appoint an arbitral commission to investigate and recommend a settlement. Mitchell sprang to his feet and accepted the plan, but the operators flatly refused; they insisted that there was nothing to arbitrate. George F. Baer, president of the Reading Railroad, which controlled a large number of coal mines, had earlier been reported to have written that the interests of the miners would be protected, "not by the labor agitators, but by the Christian men to whom God, in His infinite wisdom, has given control of the property interests of the country."

To an imperial President, the operators' refusal was nothing less than defiance of presidential authority and the national interest. In an action unprecedented in peacetime, he issued secret orders to the army to move 10,000 troops into the anthracite region, seize the mines, and operate them for the government. Next he sent Secretary of War Elihu Root to New York City to warn J. P. Morgan, who had large investments in the coal companies and great influence with the operators, of the impending seizure. Morgan and Root worked out a plan of mediation. The operators accepted it on the condition that Roosevelt would not name a labor leader to the arbitral commission. Mitchell accepted the plan but insisted that the President be free to name any arbiters he might choose. Roosevelt cooly named a former railway union official to the commission as a "sociologist." He greatly enjoyed the joke which he had played upon the operators.

The miners returned to work on October 23, 1902. A short time later, the arbitral commission awarded them a nine-hour day, a 10 per cent wage increase, the right to check on the weighing of coal, and a permanent board of conciliation. But the significance of the affair went far beyond miners' immediate gains. For the first time in American history, the federal government had intervened in a labor dispute without automatically taking the side of management. More important, a President had used the threat of force to impose *his* solution in a labor dispute.

2. BEGINNINGS OF CONSERVATIONISM

Origins

Roosevelt came to the presidency with a concern, born during the years which he had spent in the West, for the conservation of America's enormous but dwindling supply of natural resources. His education as a conservationist was advanced by his friend and favorite White House boxing partner, Gifford Pinchot, chief of the Forestry Service in the Department of Agriculture. Pinchot had taken up the task of forest preservation in the same spirit which brought other wealthy progressive reformers into social work and the reform of city administration.

Roosevelt discussed the various aspects of conservation in his first Annual Message to Congress in 1901. The government had disposed of most of its unoccupied lands, he pointed out, in an era when few persons seriously considered the possibility that the supply might not be endless. Americans had wasted natural resources by the careless mining of coal, reckless cutting of forests, and shortsighted farming of semiarid land. It seemed clear, Roosevelt concluded, that posterity would enjoy America's natural riches only if the present generation acted more responsibly. With aid from Pinchot and others, Roosevelt promoted a program of conservation with four main objectives. First, national forests should be enlarged, protected, and used carefully in order to guarantee a perpetual yield. Second, irrigation projects should be launched to reclaim arid lands. Third, internal waterways should be improved and extended. Fourth, state governments should work in close partnership with the national government in conservation programs.

Congress, in the Forest Reserve Act of 1891, had given the President power over "public lands wholly or in part covered with timber." He could withdraw these lands from sale and homesteading and establish them as forest reserves. Cleveland set aside the San Joaquin forest of 25,000,000 acres in California as a national forest. However, the total combined area of lands reserved by Harrison, Cleveland, and McKinley was less than 50,000,000 acres. Roosevelt added 148,000,000 acres. He also withdrew from the public domain more than 80,000,000 acres of mineral lands and 1,500,000 acres of water-power sites. In 1905, he transferred control over the government's forest lands from the Public Land Office to Pinchot's Forestry Service. All these actions he took by executive order, without the sanction of law.

The Carey Act of 1894 had authorized the President to allot to states with large areas of public lands within their borders 1,000,000 acres each for irrigation and reclamation. But little was done, since the public-land states lacked the financial resources to launch large-scale projects. Roosevelt inaugurated a new era of federal participation with the adoption of the National Reclamation, or Newlands, Act of 1902. Its generous provisions awarded almost all the proceeds from the sale of public lands in sixteen western states to finance irrigation projects. The irrigated lands were to be sold to settlers at reasonable prices on a ten-year installment plan. The proceeds constantly renewed the fund. The acreage of irrigated land, less than 1,000,000 in 1880, had increased to more than 20,000,000 by 1920. Arid land, formerly worth only a cent or two an acre for grazing, became worth hundreds of dollars an acre for agriculture. Fruits and vegetables came to eastern markets from Arizona and California farms which, a few years earlier, had been sandy wastes. Almost 10 per cent of the population of Mexico crossed the border and provided the labor which made this transformation possible. The great Roosevelt Dam on the Salt River in Arizona, completed in 1911, stands as a monument to the man who gave the greatest impetus to such projects. It was the forerunner of the huge flood-control and power projects constructed later on the Tennessee, Colorado, Missouri, and Columbia rivers.

A related aspect of the conservation movement was the improvement of transportation over the 26,500 miles of navigable rivers and canals in the United States. The rapid spread of the railroad network had condemned most canals to decay and reduced the importance of rivers as commerce carriers. Again, natural resources were being wasted. Roosevelt, in 1907, appointed an Inland Waterways Commission to study the possibility of developing rivers and canals into a great arterial system.

Conservation as a National Movement

The White House, Roosevelt said, was a "bully pulpit," and he used it to arouse public support for his policies. He used the "bully pulpit" with particular success in his campaign for conservation. The high point of that campaign occurred when he summoned the Conservation Conference to the White House in May 1908. So dramatic was Roosevelt's invitation that the meeting room was crowded with thirty-four governors, members of the cabinet and of the Supreme Court, congressmen, influential businessmen, labor leaders, and delegates from sixty-eight conservation organizations. For days the conference monopolized the front pages of newspapers throughout the country. It resulted in the appointment of a National Conservation Commission, headed by Pinchot, and forty-one state conservation commissions. Private citizens also organized a National Conservation Association in 1909 to further the work of public education. It soon became one of the most powerful special-interest groups in the United States.

These programs, policies, and organizations laid the foundations for a great, coordinated national conservation effort. Further development of national policy beyond Roosevelt's achievement was delayed during the Taft and Wilson administrations by fierce public controversies over whether private capital should be permitted to develop resources in the public domain, and on what terms. But the adoption of the General Leasing Act and the Water Power Act in 1920 finally resolved these issues. The former kept large oil reserves from private exploitation but permitted the Secretary of the Interior to lease other public lands, which contained mineral and oil deposits, to private parties on terms that safeguarded the public interest. The Water Power Act established the Federal Power Commission, which was authorized to license the building and operation of dams and hydroelectric plants on navigable rivers and nonnavigable rivers within the public domain.

3. A NEW WORLD POWER EMERGES

Overseas Empire

By the time that Roosevelt entered office, the United States had acquired a far-flung colonial empire. The Spanish-American War, fought in 1898 initially over the issue of Cuban independence, had resulted in a smashing and quick American victory. In the Caribbean, Cuba gained its independence under American suzerainty. After a brief period of occupation by American military forces, General Leonard Wood supervised with considerable success the reconstruction of the war-torn island. During the summer of 1900, the Cubans wrote a constitution patterned on that of the United States, but it went into effect only after the Cubans had accepted terms conceived by Secretary of War Elihu Root and Senator Orville H. Platt of Connecticut. These terms, which were embodied in the Platt Amendment to the Army Appropriations Act of 1901, permitted Americans to withdraw from the island once Cuba had agreed to provide naval bases and coaling stations to the United States, to make no treaties with other powers which impaired its independence, to contract no debts which could not be paid out of current revenues, and, most important, to recognize the right of the United States to intervene whenever it thought such intervention was necessary or appropriate. Having no alternative, the Cubans agreed and embodied these severe restrictions on their sovereignty in a treaty in 1903.

In the years that followed, American presidents frequently intervened under the provisions of the Platt Amendment, in all cases to protect the interests of the Cuban upper and middle classes. After a revolution broke out in 1906 on the reelection of President Estrada Palma, the American army intervened to restore order and ruled the island for three years. In 1912 and in 1917, American marines landed to forestall civil war, and, four years later, American troops supervised Cuban elections.

The Treaty of Paris with Spain also brought the United States explicit colonial responsibilities. Puerto Rico came under American control in a status (established by the Foraker Act of 1900) as something between a colony and a territory. Under the Jones Act of 1917, the island acquired full territorial status and American citizenship for its inhabitants; Puerto Ricans also were given control of both houses of the territorial legislature. In 1952, Congress approved a new constitution which made Puerto Rico a self-governing commonwealth, free to choose independence at any time.

Governance of the Philippines was the hardest test of American abilities at colonial administration. An archipelago of 8,000,000 people, which was nearly 7,000 miles from the shores of the United States, had been turned over to American rule against the consent of the inhabitants of the islands. Like the Cubans, the Filipinos, led by Emilio Aguinaldo, had been in revolt against Spain, and, on June 12, 1898, the rebels had proclaimed a provisional republic with Aguinaldo as its President. By early 1899, however, it had become clear that the United States was preparing to rule the Philippines as a colony. Only after a large and bloody guerrilla war, which cost the United States 1,000 lives and $135 million, did the last rebel surrender in 1902. In the absence of congressional legislation, President McKinley, as commander in chief, exercised full power over the Philippines. He delegated this power in 1900 to a commission of five members, headed by Judge William Howard Taft of Ohio. The commission proceeded at once to build a civil government and an educational system.

The Spooner Amendment of 1901 gave the President of the United States as absolute a power over the Philippines as any proconsul ever exercised over a distant province of the Roman Empire. The President then appointed Taft as governor of the islands. The Philippine Government Act, approved on July 1, 1902, provided for the faint beginnings of self-government. The act called for the appointment of a civilian Philippine Commission, to be headed by a civilian governor-general. The commission should take a census of the islands as soon as the insurrection was declared officially to be at an end. Two years later, the commission was to hold elections in the Christian provinces for a Philippine assembly. The commission would be the upper house of the Philippine legislature; the assembly, the lower house. The right to vote was to be given to all males who were twenty-three years of age or over and had held municipal office, or possessed property, or paid taxes of a certain amount, or were literate in either the Spanish or English languages. The literacy test disfranchised a majority of male Filipinos, who were literate in their native languages but were not literate in Spanish or English.

Elections held in 1907 resulted in the choice of an assembly of eighty-one members. About three fourths of these were Nationalists, or supporters of Philippine independence. Meanwhile, ex-Governor Taft had won great popularity by his fair, friendly, and forward-looking administration. He went to Manila in person (he was now the Secretary of War) to open the first session of the new assembly in October 1907. Congress had already, in 1902, permitted Philippine products to enter the United States at a reduction of 25 per cent from prevailing tariff rates. Free trade between the Philippines and the United States was established by the Underwood-Simmons Tariff Act of 1913.

Although both the Republican and Democratic parties were committed to eventual independence for the Philippines during this period, the Democrats were more honest in their promises. President Woodrow Wilson was able partially to redeem these promises in the Jones Act, or new Organic Act, of 1916. Although the Jones Act reserved ultimate sovereignty to the United States, it created an elected Senate to supplant the commission as the upper house of the Philippine legislature. It lowered suffrage requirements and required the American governor-general to appoint most heads of executive departments with the consent of the Philippine Senate. Filipinos were far along the road to full self-government by the end of the Wilson administration in 1921; indeed, it was obvious by then that independence could not be long postponed.

TR and the World Order

Both as historian and as Assistant Secretary of the Navy, Roosevelt had long been an ardent proponent of an American colonial empire. He had, moreover, decided that far-flung American interests necessitated even more forceful participation in world politics. He took part increasingly, with the same vigor and adventurism which he showed in domestic affairs, and he justified his actions with what he said was an old African proverb: "Speak softly and carry a big stick, and you will go far." Roosevelt carried a big stick, but he did not always speak softly during his first years as President. Experience alone could teach him that force must be tempered with wisdom and used with restraint.

Toward an Isthmian Canal

Americans had dreamed for at least half a century of uniting the Atlantic and Pacific oceans by an interoceanic canal. In 1878, a French company headed by Ferdinand de Lesseps, builder of the Suez Canal, obtained from Colombia the right to dig a canal across the Colombian province of Panama. But disease and engineering obstacles ruined De Lesseps' hopes. The French company declared bankruptcy and abandoned work.

The Spanish-American War revived American interest in connecting the two oceans. The dramatic 14,000-mile voyage of U.S.S. *Oregon* from the Pacific Ocean to Cuban waters emphasized the strategic necessity of a canal in wartime. Also, the development of the West Coast, anticipation of a large far eastern trade, and acquisition of distant Pacific colonies highlighted the economic and strategic needs. Congress, only a month after ratification of the Treaty of Paris, therefore, created an Isthmian Canal Commission and directed it to investigate the comparative advantages of routes through Nicaragua and Panama.

One diplomatic obstacle blocked the execution of any plans—the Clayton-Bulwer Treaty of 1850, by which both Great Britain and the United States had promised not to build a canal without the other's participation. The British government, eager to win American friendship, abandoned its rights under the Clayton-Bulwer Treaty in the first Hay-Pauncefote Treaty (1900), on the condition that the United States should never fortify the canal. The Senate refused to accept the condition. Then the British, in the second Hay-Pauncefote Treaty (1901), withdrew their objection to fortification.

Discussion now focused on the best route. Roosevelt and the Isthmian Canal Commission favored a Nicaraguan route, and the House of Representatives concurred on January 9, 1902. Meanwhile, agents of the New Panama Canal Company (which owned the rights and property of the old French company) had been working desperately for the Panamanian route. They hastily cut their price from $109 million to $40 million. Roosevelt and the commission thought that this was a good bargain. Congress, in the Spooner Act of June 1902, authorized use of the Panamanian route, provided that the President could obtain a right of way from Colombia within a reasonable time. If not, he should use the Nicaraguan route.

TR and Revolution in Panama

There remained only the necessity of coming to agreement with Colombia. Secretary of State John Hay concluded a treaty with the Colombian Chargé, Tomás Herrán, on January 22, 1903. The United States agreed to pay Colombia $10 million at once and an annual sum of $250 thousand beginning nine years after ratification of the treaty. In return, Colombia leased to the United States forever a strip of land six miles across the Isthmus of Panama. Colombia also promised not to conduct independent negotiations with the

New Panama Canal Company; in other words, Colombia would not attempt to gain a share of the $40 million to be paid to that company.

The Colombian government rejected the treaty, chiefly because the rights of the French company would expire within a year, and Colombia could then demand payment to itself of the $40 million. Roosevelt was outraged. It was, he said, as if "a road agent had tried to hold up a man." Colombians were entitled "to precisely the amount of sympathy we extend to other inefficient bandits." Infuriated, Roosevelt made plans to seize the isthmus by force.

New and somewhat melodramatic events soon made unnecessary direct violent action by Roosevelt. Panamanian leaders, inspired and financed by Philippe Bunau-Varilla (chief agent of the New Panama Canal Company in the United States), set plans in motion for a revolution. Roosevelt and Hay knew about the plot. They did not openly encourage it, but Bunau-Varilla received the impression that the United States Government would not permit a Panamanian revolution to fail.

The "revolution" took place in Panama City on schedule on November 3, 1903. To prevent it, some 400 Colombian troops had already been landed at Colón, on the Atlantic side of the isthmus. But U.S.S. *Nashville* had, quite providentially, arrived at Colón on the preceding day. Its commander, under instructions from Washington, landed troops and forbade the Colombian general to march his troops across the isthmus. The Colombians reembarked two days later and returned to Cartagena.

The United States recognized the independence of Panama on the next day, November 6. Bunau-Varilla, a *French* citizen, hastened to Washington as Panamanian Minister to the United States. On November 18, he signed with Hay a duplicate of the Hay-Herrán Treaty—except that the strip of land was widened to ten miles, and the United States obtained the right to intervene at any time in order to protect Panama City and Colón.

The Senate approved the Hay-Bunau-Varilla Treaty with great enthusiasm, but Americans gradually developed a very guilty conscience about the affair, and a committee of the House of Representatives in 1912 virtually accused Roosevelt of wrongdoing. Roosevelt never seemed to have any regrets. In a special message to Congress on January 4, 1904, he declared: "No one connected with this government had any part in preparing, inciting, or encouraging the late revolution of the Isthmus of Panama." Every action of his administration in the affair, he later wrote, had been "in accordance with the highest, finest, and nicest standards of public and governmental ethics." But Roosevelt finally told the truth when he blurted out in 1911: "I took the Canal Zone and let Congress debate, and while the debate goes on the Canal does also."

Actually, work was held up while Colonel William C. Gorgas and his assistants cleaned up the isthmus and destroyed the mosquitoes which carried yellow fever. Construction began under Colonel George W. Goethals and the Army Engineers in 1907. The first ship passed through the canal on January 7, 1914. It soon proved a tremendous boon to world trade, as well as a vital link in American national security. Whether the good accomplished justified the American government's aggression against Colombia remains a very doubtful question.

Controversies with Europe

Roosevelt used the "big stick" impartially against large as well as small nations during the early years of his presidency. A sharp dispute among the United States, Canada, and Great Britain broke out at the end of the nineteenth century over the boundary of the long finger of Alaska that runs from Alaska proper down the Pacific coast to the latitude 54°40'. The State Department knew that arbitrators tend to split the difference in boundary disputes and refused to submit the dispute to arbitration. Roosevelt was sincerely convinced that the American claim was absolutely sound; he insisted that the matter be settled by an Anglo-American-Canadian tribunal. The British expressed willingness, and the tribunal, consisting of three Americans, two Canadians, and the Lord Chief Justice of England, met in London in September 1903. While the tribunal deliberated, Roosevelt sent word to friends in the British government that he would ask Congress for authority to determine the boundary line himself if the tribunal did not support the American position. This threat could not have failed to intimidate the British government; the Lord Chief Justice voted with the American members to uphold the American claim; and Canadians felt, justly, betrayed.

In that same year, 1903, Roosevelt spoke nearly as harshly to the arrogant and reckless German Emperor, William II. Britain, Germany, and Italy had instituted a blockade of Venezuela in December 1902 after that country's dictator, Cipriano Castro, had refused to pay Venezuela's debts to European creditors. Castro offered to submit the matter to the Hague Tribunal (a world agency created by the First Hague Conference in 1899), but the Germans replied by bombarding a Venezuelan fort and destroying the adjacent town. Roosevelt called the German ambassador to the White House in February 1903 and told him that he had sent the Atlantic Fleet under Admiral Dewey to the West Indies for its annual maneuvers. American opinion was so aroused against the German action, Roosevelt continued, that, "regretfully," he would have to use force against the Germans if they tried to seize territory in Venezuela or anywhere else in the Caribbean area. The German government probably had no such intention, but it and the British government quickly agreed to arbitration of the Venezuelan debt issue.

Reshaping the Monroe Doctrine

In its ruling on the Venezuelan debt controversy in 1903, the Hague Tribunal awarded first claim on Venezuela's debt payments to Germany, Britain, and Italy—the very countries which had used force to attempt to collect the debts. The ruling, therefore, seemed to suggest that the application of military force was the surest guarantee of collection of debts against Latin American countries. Roosevelt agreed that European creditors were entitled to the payment of just debts, but he believed that the American people would never again tolerate armed intervention by a European power in Latin America.

The problem of how to satisfy both European creditors and American public opinion faced Roosevelt in 1904, when the Dominican Republic defaulted on its foreign debt of $32 million. Roosevelt desired neither to annex the war-torn island republic nor to assume responsibility for its finances. To prevent European intervention, he established (with full Dominican approval) an American receivership of the Dominican customs. When the Senate, in 1905, refused to approve the treaty which established the receivership, Roosevelt continued it by executive agreement until the Senate yielded in 1907 and approved the treaty. American control of the main source of Dominican revenues removed the financial incentive to revolution, and the island prospered for a decade under American guidance.

By now Roosevelt was convinced that American sensitivity over armed European intervention in Latin America and concern for the defense of the Panama Canal demanded absolute American naval supremacy in the Caribbean. Partly to achieve this objective, in 1904, he announced a new policy, soon known as the Roosevelt Corollary to the Monroe Doctrine. Since the Monroe Doctrine, Roosevelt stated, prohibited European intervention by the use of force in the new world, the United States would itself guarantee that Latin American nations paid their debts and performed their international responsibilities. The Roosevelt Corollary was based upon a gross distortion of history; no one ever before had suggested that the Monroe Doctrine precluded temporary European interventions. Nor was it clear that the United States possessed any right, other than that derived from superior military power, to collect the debts of Latin American countries and supervise their payments.

4. A PROGRESSIVE TRIBUNE, 1904–1908

The Election of 1904

Four vice-presidents had succeeded to the presidency during the nineteenth century, but none had been able to win nomination for a full presidential term. Wall Street and other big business interests eagerly sought Roosevelt's retirement in 1904. They preferred Senator Hanna, and Hanna seemed willing enough. At least he opposed a resolution of the Ohio Republican convention of 1903 which endorsed Roosevelt for nomination in 1904. But Hanna died on February 15, 1904, and no other prominent Republican dared to challenge Roosevelt's claim. In fact, Roosevelt had been using patronage quietly but very effectively to gain control of the Republican state organizations. By early 1904, he had so completely mastered the GOP organizations and so mesmerized the rank and file of Republican voters that even Hanna could not possibly have prevented his nomination. The Republican national convention named Roosevelt by acclamation. For his running mate, Roosevelt chose Charles W. Fairbanks of Indiana.

The Democrats hoped to capitalize on conservative opposition to Roosevelt and nominated a colorless nonentity, Judge Alton B. Parker of New York. At Parker's insistence, the convention incorporated a plank in the Democratic platform which favored the gold standard. But the platform also denounced the "trusts" and called for more effective federal regulation of the railroads.

A dull campaign followed, which was enlivened only by Parker's charge, near the end of the campaign, that Roosevelt had blackmailed Wall Street into financing his campaign. Roosevelt blackmailed no one, but J. P. Morgan and other railroad, financial, and industrial leaders did contribute generously to the Republican war chest. Then Roosevelt began to suspect that other Wall Street interests were pouring money into the Democratic coffers, and he actually feared defeat. In the end, the voters gave Roosevelt the largest popular majority awarded a presidential candidate to that time. He won 7,629,000 popular and 336 electoral votes, to 5,084,000 popular and 140 electoral votes for Parker, and 402,000 popular votes for Debs, the Socialist candidate.

Roosevelt the Reformer

The size of the popular mandate momentarily stunned Roosevelt, but he quickly grasped the significance of his victory. Progressivism and insurgency—a revolt against conservative policies—were sweeping the country. Roosevelt responded by taking leadership of the nationwide reform movement.

He began with a speech in January 1905 before the Union League Club of Philadelphia, a bastion of the Old Guard. Great corporations, railroads, and financial institutions had to submit to public control, Roosevelt warned. The people particularly demanded effective control of the railroads, and he would see to it that this control was obtained. Roosevelt followed this blast by ordering the Bureau of Corporations to make a thoroughgoing investigation of the meat-packing industry.

The fight began in earnest when the Fifty-ninth Congress assembled in December 1905, for Roosevelt demanded a new railroad-regulation law, pure-food and drug legislation, and other reforms. The fight for railroad legislation was long and hard, and Roosevelt had to make some minor compromises. Nevertheless, he won all his essential objectives in the Hepburn Act, which he signed on June 29, 1906. The act increased the membership of the Interstate Commerce Commission (ICC) from five to seven; extended the ICC's authority to express companies, sleeping car companies, oil pipelines, bridges, ferries, and terminals; and tightened the provisions of the Elkins Act of 1903 against rebating. Other provisions required advance notice of any change in rates and obliged railroad companies to open their books to inspection by the ICC. Most important, the act gave the ICC power to reduce unreasonable rates on the complaint of shippers, subject to the review of federal courts. The Hepburn Act, in short, gave the ICC really effective power for the first time since its creation in 1887. Ultimate control over rates was taken from private hands and given to a governmental agency.

Roosevelt passed on other fronts and won passage of three other reform measures. A Meat Inspection Act gave federal officials authority to see that all meat shipped in interstate commerce came from healthy animals and was packed under sanitary conditions. Passage of this measure was helped by the publication, a few months earlier, of a novel, *The Jungle*, by the muckraking novelist Upton Sinclair. Sinclair wrote the novel as a plea for socialism. Yet, as he declared later, *The Jungle* appealed to the stomachs of the American people and not to their hearts, for it revealed in revolting detail the insanitary conditions in the Chicago stockyards and meat-packing plants. The Food and Drug Act forbade the manufacture and sale of adulterated or poisonous foods, drugs, and liquors. Labels on patent medicines were required to show what the contents actually were. Finally, the Employers' Liability Act of 1906 established a system of accident insurance for workers in the District of Columbia and on interstate railroads.

Economic Crisis and Renewed Reform

A sharp decline on the New York Stock Exchange began in March 1907, continued into the summer, and resulted in an increase in business failures, much public alarm, and runs on banks which caused a dangerous financial stringency (particularly after the closing of the Knickerbocker Trust Company of New York). For a brief period, Roosevelt relaxed his reform energies; during the worst of the panic, he permitted the United States Steel Corporation to purchase a large competitor in the South, the Tennessee Coal and Iron Company. He ignored this violation of the Sherman Act in order to forestall a dumping of the Tennessee Company's shares on the market and a deepening of the stock market decline. And, in any event, Roosevelt considered United States Steel to be a "good trust."

The panic produced one immediate legislative result—adoption in May 1908 of the Aldrich-Vreeland Act. This temporary measure enabled banks to obtain additional currency during financial emergencies; it also provided for the appointment of a National Monetary Commission to study American banking and currency needs. The commission, headed by Senator Aldrich, worked diligently until 1912, and its investigations and recommendations provided a starting point for the Wilson administration when it turned to the problem of new banking legislation.

Business confidence and prosperity returned rapidly in 1908, and Roosevelt energetically resumed his drive for reform. He obtained little legislation from Congress during his last year in office, but, in a series of messages, he advocated an income and estate tax, reduction of the tariff, and more effective governmental control of business. "The nation," he warned, "will not tolerate an utter lack of control over very wealthy men of enormous power in the industrial, and, therefore, in the social, lives of all our people." He was in fact laying the foundations of a new, advanced progressive program of his own, which he would call the New Nationalism.

Hindsight makes it clear that Roosevelt was not a radical and certainly not a socialist, as his more violent critics charged. He had no compassion for the poor and down and out and thought that the strength of the United States lay in the upwardly mobile middle class. A fervent believer in the free enterprise system, he wanted to make it work more efficiently and to extend its benefits to more Americans. In more ways than one, Roosevelt embodied the progressive spirit of the early twentieth century. Through the office of the presidency, he enlarged the role of the federal government in the social and economic lives of Americans to an unprecedented extent. Above all, he gave the first successful leadership to the progressive movement from the "bully pulpit" of the White House.

5. THE DIPLOMACY OF IMPERIALISM

The United States and the Far East

During his second term, Theodore Roosevelt was a different kind of diplomatist. Some historians say that the change was due to the wise influence of Elihu Root, who became Secretary of State in 1905 after Hay's death. Others say that experience made Roosevelt wiser and more cautious. Others point to the fact that events in the Far East forced Roosevelt to realize the limits of American power on the world stage. Whatever the cause, a visible change occurred. Gone were most of the bluster and arrogant chauvinism. Now Roosevelt revealed some tact and restraint in the use of power, even as he emerged as a principal actor on the stage of world affairs.

This new style was first revealed when Roosevelt mediated the Russo-Japanese War. Japan had gone to war with Russia in 1904 to block Russian expansion into Korea and Manchuria—areas in which Japanese leaders hoped that their nation would obtain special economic, if not political, influence. The Japanese were victorious everywhere by 1905, but they were also financially exhausted, and the Japanese government appealed to the American President in April 1905 to mediate the conflict. Roosevelt earlier had supported the Japanese, even to the extent that he warned Germany and France that he would not sit idly by if they went to Russia's assistance.

But Roosevelt refused to mediate until the Japanese returned the captured province of Manchuria to Chinese sovereignty and accepted the policy of the Open Door. The Open Door, which Secretary of State Hay had declared as a cornerstone of American far eastern policy in separate diplomatic notes in 1899 and 1900, maintained that foreign powers should not interfere with the freedom of other powers to trade in all parts of China. For the most part, the European governments publicly accepted the Open Door in China, yet in practice they systematically divided the country into separate spheres of economic and political interests. The Japanese finally consented to this condition, and, in August 1905, Roosevelt invited Japanese and Russian delegates to a peace conference at Portsmouth, New Hampshire. For his part in ending the conflict, Roosevelt was awarded the Nobel Peace Prize in 1906.

Crisis in Morocco

Meanwhile, an even more dangerous situation was brewing in Europe. The German government deeply resented France's expanding control over the North African state of Morocco, which endangered German commercial interests. The Germans seized the opportunity to force the issue when France's ally, Russia, was embroiled in war with Japan. The Germans demanded an international conference to guarantee free access to Morocco. When the French refused, it seemed certain that war would ensue. Then the German Emperor appealed to Roosevelt to put pressure on the French to yield. Roosevelt supported the Emperor reluctantly and only because he feared that the United States could not avoid entanglement in a major western European conflict. The French yielded, and, in early 1906, a conference of the major powers, including the United States, met in Algeciras, in southern Spain. The conference reached an agreement which averted war but did not prevent the French from closing the door in Morocco. But German leaders realized that world political and economic power commensurate with their nation's relative wealth and military might was only possible by force of arms.

Japan: Conflict and Reconciliation

Roosevelt greatly admired the Japanese for their industry and progress in modernization. He looked to the island empire as a buffer against Russian aggression in the Far East. To cement good relations, in July 1905 he negotiated an executive agreement with the Japanese government—the Taft-Katsura Agreement—which acknowledged Japan's supremacy in Korea and confirmed American sovereignty over the Philippines.

Only a year later, this good beginning was rudely interrupted. Since the 1890s, Japanese laborers had arrived in California at the rate of about 1,000 a year, and Californians were becoming greatly agitated by fearful predictions of a "Yellow Peril." In the autumn of 1906, the San Francisco school board ordered the segregation of all Oriental school children. It was an open insult to a proud and hitherto friendly people, and much demagogic war talk ensued in both countries. Roosevelt, however, threatened to use the army if necessary to compel the school board to rescind its order; it mattered not that he had no constitutional authority for this threat. Such a drastic remedy was forestalled when Roosevelt summoned the members of the school board to Washington and persuaded them to revoke the segregation order. In return, the State Department negotiated a "Gentlemen's Agreement" with the Japanese government—an informal understanding that the Tokyo government would issue no more passports to peasants or workers who intended to go to the continental United States. Thus, Roosevelt reached amicable agreement with the Japanese and, at the same time, removed the chief cause of the fear of Californians.

Naval Power and a World Tour

Roosevelt was neurotic about "manhood" and any show of weakness. Partly to let the Japanese know that he had not acted out of fear, he decided in the summer of 1907 to send the main American battle fleet around the world. A fleet of twenty-eight vessels, including sixteen battleships, steamed out of Hampton Roads, Virginia, on December 16, 1907. The fleet circled the world by way of the Strait of Magellan, San Francisco, Hawaii, Australia, the Philippines, China, Japan, the Suez Canal, and the Mediterranean. The officers and men were received warmly at every port of call, and nowhere was there greater friendliness than at Yokohama and Tokyo. The Japanese government also responded warmly by instructing its ambassador in Washington to open negotiations for a comprehensive agreement with the American government. The outcome was the Root-Takahira Agreement of November 30, 1908—another executive agreement—in which both countries agreed to respect each other's territorial possessions and to cooperate in maintaining the Open Door in China and the territorial integrity of that country.

The fleet returned to Hampton Roads on February 22, 1909. As he looked back over his administration a few years later, Roosevelt wrote that sending the fleet on its 46,000-mile voyage had been his most important contribution to the cause of peace. Roosevelt exaggerated the voyage's effect, but it had become indelibly clear that the American navy was an efficient, well-disciplined, and highly mobile striking force—a power to be reckoned with in the councils of the world.

6. TAFT AND REPUBLICAN INSURGENCY

Roosevelt and Taft

After his election in 1904, Roosevelt had announced that he would not be a candidate again in 1908. As the national conventions of that year drew near, his friends and party leaders put enormous pressure on him to run again. But he stubbornly refused and said that, while he had enjoyed every minute in the White House and had tried to do everything possible to increase the powers of the presidency, he did not believe that one man should hold the office for more than a "limited time."

Roosevelt would have preferred to choose as his successor his brilliant Secretary of State, Elihu Root. Root's career as an attorney for major business firms, however, eliminated him as a candidate. Agitation against the "trusts" was so intense that any political opponent probably could have defeated Root simply by listing the huge corporations which he had represented. Roosevelt made overtures to Charles Evans Hughes, reform governor of New York, but Hughes coldly rebuffed the President's approaches. Roosevelt then turned to his Secretary of War, William Howard Taft, who accepted the candidacy. Taft was nominated on the first ballot by the Republican national convention.

The Democrats turned again to Bryan, who, in spite of his party's nomination of Parker in 1904, was still the popular party leader. The "Great Commoner" waged his campaign largely on the issues of the tariff and "trusts," but he also openly appealed for labor support by promising unions relief from injunctions. For the first time in the history of the American Federation of Labor, its president, Samuel Gompers, departed from the policy of nonpartisanship and entered the campaign for Bryan.

In the election, Taft received 7,675,000 popular and 321 electoral votes, to 6,412,000 popular and 162 electoral votes for Bryan, and 421,000 popular votes for Eugene V. Debs, the Socialist candidate. Yet, the election of Taft reflected Roosevelt's popularity rather than the dominance of the GOP. Bryan increased the Democratic vote by 1,330,000 over 1904, and Democratic governors were elected in several states which went for Taft. More significant for the near future was the marked increase of Republican insurgency in the Middle West. The midwestern progressive group in Congress, heretofore a small minority, would be a powerful force in both houses of the Sixty-first Congress.

The Taft Presidency

William Howard Taft, born in Cincinnati in 1857, educated at Yale and the Cincinnati Law College, had enjoyed a distinguished career in the public service since the 1880s. A fine lawyer and model administrator, Taft was also the largest man, physically speaking, ever to sit in the presidential chair; his good humor matched his weight, and it was sheer delight to see him laugh. His laugh, it was said, began in the folds of his stomach and slowly worked its way up to his face.

In a normally quiet period of political life, Taft would have been a successful and beloved President. Unhappily for this man who wanted only to do well, he became President in a highly abnormal period. The country simmered in political revolt, and the Republican party was split between the rising insurgents and the Old Guard. Had Roosevelt been in Taft's place, he might have kept the GOP together by bringing the insurgents under his control. But for various reasons, Taft not only was unable to keep peace within the party, he also contributed to its disruption. The new President considered himself progressive, and in many ways he was. Taft believed in tariff and tax reform, he pursued Roosevelt's conservation policy by enlarging the forest reserves and setting aside additional mineral lands, and he pressed the antitrust crusade by instituting forty-six suits for dissolution, which included cases against the United States Steel and International Harvester companies.

Taft ran into increasingly grave difficulties for several reasons. One of his problems was acute obesity. Carrying his 300-odd pounds required so much energy that Taft had little left over for affairs of state. He was consequently slow-moving and gave the appearance of laziness; in short, he did not have the physical strength to act decisively at a time when the public demanded vigorous leadership. In addition, Taft was a poor leader and inept politician. Several failures could have been avoided if he had only given decisive leadership to his party in Congress. But his intervention was always too little and too late, and frequently misguided as well. Taft's judicial temperament also controlled his style of leadership. He had grave doubts about the wisdom of many advanced progressive measures, particularly those which established governmental regulation by administrative commissions. He favored review of business activities by the courts, with their careful examination of the evidence in each case. Finally, Taft could not get on with the new insurgent leaders in his own party. He disliked and distrusted them; to him, they seemed fanatics and demagogues. Taft much preferred the company of the Old Guard and inevitably drifted toward the political attitudes of his conservative friends.

Early Difficulties

The Republican platform of 1908 pledged the new administration to revise the highly protective Dingley Tariff Act of 1897. The cost of living had increased some 40 per cent between 1897 and 1909, and most people incorrectly assumed that high tariff rates were responsible for the increase. To honor the platform pledge, and also because he believed sincerely in tariff reform, Taft called Congress into special session in March 1909 with the admonition, "The successful party in the late election is pledged to a revision of the tariff." Sereno E. Payne of New York, chairman of the Ways and Means Committee, introduced the administration's bill in the House of Representatives. The Payne bill fulfilled the Republican party's pledge by enlarging the free list and substantially reducing rates on iron and steel products, sugar, agricultural implements, and lumber. It also included a new federal estate tax ranging from 1 to 5 per cent.

The Payne bill had easy sailing in the House and passed that body by a large majority. However, it was a different story in the Senate. The Finance Committee, headed by Senator Aldrich, simply collapsed under the pressure of various lobbies. The committee reported the Payne bill to the Senate with

847 amendments, more than 600 of which increased rates, and it eliminated the provision for the estate tax. A wave of indignation swept the country, particularly after a group of midwestern insurgent Republican senators took leadership in the fight against the Aldrich bill. Their efforts failed, and the measure, now known as the Payne-Aldrich bill, passed both houses. Taft signed it in August 1909.

The Payne-Aldrich Act was a plain betrayal of party pledges. Yet, until the very end of the fight in Congress, Taft made no attempt to prevent special-interest lobbyists from making the bill a mockery of those pledges. He did persuade the conference committee to lower some rates, and he obtained a promise of support from Aldrich for the submission of an income tax amendment—the Sixteenth Amendment—to the states. Congress approved it on July 12, 1909, and it was ratified in 1913.

In a speech in September 1909 in Winona, Minnesota, a center of insurgency, Taft foolishly called the Payne-Aldrich Act the best tariff measure that the Republican party had ever passed. However, angry public opinion disagreed. Even Republican newspapers published fiery editorials about the tariff "betrayal," and insurgent Republican leaders wondered whether Taft had deserted to the Old Guard.

The so-called Ballinger affair, which followed immediately afterward, turned a bad start into a debacle. An investigator in the Interior Department told Gifford Pinchot that Richard A. Ballinger, Secretary of the Interior, was showing favoritism to a private syndicate which had been formed to develop coal properties in Alaska. Pinchot urged the investigator to go directly to the President. He did so, but Taft accepted Ballinger's explanation and dismissed the investigator. Then Pinchot entered the controversy publicly with accusations against Ballinger; Taft at once dismissed Pinchot. A congressional committee later cleared Ballinger of wrongdoing, but the committee's investigation revealed that the Secretary was openly antagonistic to conservation. The affair widened the breach between Taft and the progressives, particularly the conservationists.

Everything seemed to go wrong during the regular session of Congress which opened in December 1909. Insurgents were angered when Taft did not help them in their successful attempt, led by Representative George W. Norris of Nebraska, to shear Speaker Cannon of his dictatorial powers over the House of Representatives. Progressives accused Taft of working hand in glove with Wall Street bankers in the passage of a bill to establish postal savings banks in 1910. They also accused Taft of favoring the railroads during discussion of a measure to increase the powers of the ICC. The outcome, the Mann-Elkins Act of 1910, was in fact a great victory for the progressives, rather than for Taft. It empowered the ICC to suspend rate increases or to reduce rates on its own initiative. The act also strengthened old prohibitions against charging more for a short haul than for a long one, and forbade railroads to acquire competing lines.

Taft was convinced early in 1910 that the insurgents planned to prevent his renomination, even if it meant the disruption of the Republican party. The President therefore joined with Aldrich, Cannon, and other leaders of the Old Guard in a nationwide campaign to defeat the insurgents in the mid-term Republican primaries. But the flames of insurgency continued to rage across the country, and the administration's candidates went down to defeat everywhere. By the summer of 1910, Republican insurgents were talking about organizing a new party if Taft won renomination in 1912.

The Diplomacy of the Dollar

The years from 1909 to 1913 were a time of increasing tension in Europe. Unlike his predecessor, Taft had neither the will nor the ability to play a leading role in world affairs. He and his Secretary of State, Philander C. Knox, were notably unsuccessful in their limited undertakings in foreign policy.

The most important new departure was "dollar diplomacy." Above all, Taft and Knox desired to increase American security and influence in the Caribbean area; they therefore attempted to persuade American bankers to displace European creditors in that region. Taft explained the motivation behind "dollar diplomacy" in idealistic terms: "The diplomacy of the present administration has sought to respond to modern ideas of commercial intercourse. This policy had been characterized as substituting dollars for bullets. It is one that appeals alike to idealistic humanitarian sentiments, to the dictates of sound policy and strategy, and to legitimate commercial aims." However, implementing "dollar diplomacy" led, among other things, to American participation in a civil war in Nicaragua and the victory of the conservative party of that country. Equally ill-fated was the Washington government's proposal in 1909 for the internationalization of the railroads in Manchuria, a move which drove Russia and Japan together in order to ward off American influence. Taft succeeded in forcing an international group, formed for the purpose of lending money to China, to admit American bankers, but one of his successor's first actions was to withdraw American bankers from this consortium on the ground that the loan agreement seriously infringed on Chinese sovereignty.

Indeed, it seemed that Taft and Knox could not succeed even when they advocated statesmanlike policies. They negotiated treaties with Britain and France in 1911 for the arbitration of virtually all disputes, but the Senate so emasculated the treaties in consenting to their ratification that Taft withdrew them in disgust. During the same year, the State Department negotiated a reciprocity agreement with Canada which would have enormously benefited both countries. Taft finally roused himself, fought hard, and won congressional approval—only to see the treaty killed by Canadian voters frightened by talk that the United States would annex Canada.

The Failure of Taft

The revolt against the administration reached its first culmination in the mid-term elections of 1910. So great was public indignation against the Payne-Aldrich Tariff Act, Pinchot's dismissal, and "dollar diplomacy" that repudiation of the Taft policies seemed inevitable. Taft tried to make peace with the midwestern insurgents, but to no avail. He blundered again by alienating Theodore Roosevelt.

Actually, that alienation had begun much earlier. Roosevelt, after Taft's inauguration, departed for Africa to hunt lions, and en route made a triumphal tour through Egypt, Italy, Austria, Germany, France, Holland, and England. But he also followed events at home with a careful eye and with the aid of messages from friends like Pinchot. He returned to New York on June 18, 1910, convinced that Taft's betrayal of his policies had made a division in the Republican party inevitable. Although Roosevelt was eager to do what he could to heal party wounds, Taft rebuffed his efforts at mediation. Roosevelt then set out upon a speaking tour in the summer, climaxed by a speech at Osawatomie, Kansas, on August 31. In this series of speeches, Roosevelt expounded his now fully matured advanced progressivism—the New Nationalism. He advocated strict regulation of large corporations, publicity of campaign funds, income and estate taxes, workmen's compensation laws, legislation to protect women and children in industry, and all the measures for the reform of political institutions that progressives were then championing. Above all, Roosevelt called for a powerful federal government to work not only on its own initiative but also in partnership with the cities and states.

Roosevelt's eloquent articulation of an advanced progressive program only emphasized the wide gulf between the insurgents and the Taft administration. It also contributed to the emphatic repudiation of Taft and the Old Guard which occurred on November 8, 1910, when the Democrats won control of the House of Representatives for the first time since 1892. Old Guard strength in the Senate was so greatly reduced that a coalition of Democrats and progressive Republicans would control that body from 1911 to 1913. Democrats, moreover, elected twenty-six governors, including governors in the traditionally Republican states of Massachusetts, New York, New Jersey, and Ohio.

SUGGESTED READINGS

The best introduction to this period is George E. Mowry, *The Era of Theodore Roosevelt* (1958) and *Theodore Roosevelt and the Progressive Movement* (1947). But see also Horace S. and Marion G. Merrill, *The Republican High Command, 1897–1913* (1971).

Samuel P. Hays, *Conservation and the Gospel of Efficiency: The Progressive Conservation Movement, 1890–1920* (1959); Elmo P. Richardson, *The Politics of Conservation . . . 1897–1913* (1962); Frank W. Taussig, *Tariff History of the United States* (1931); Sidney Ratner, *Taxation and Democracy in America* (1967); and Hans Thorelli, *The Federal Antitrust Policy* (1954), are the standard works on these subjects. Albro Martin, *Enterprise Denied: Origins of the Decline of American Railroads, 1897–1917* (1971), argues convincingly that overregulation nearly destroyed the solvency of American railroads.

The biographical literature on the political leaders of this period grows increasingly richer. William H. Harbaugh, *The Life and Times of Theodore Roosevelt* (1963), is the best one-volume biography; but see also

John M. Blum, *The Republican Roosevelt*, 2nd ed. (1977). Henry F. Pringle, *The Life and Times of William Howard Taft*, 2 vols. (1938), is uncritical. Compare its treatment of the Taft presidency with Mowry, *Theodore Roosevelt and the Progressive Movement*, and Alpheus T. Mason, *Brandeis: A Free Man's Life* (1946). Richard W. Leopold, *Elihu Root and the Conservative Tradition* (1954); Merlo J. Pusey, *Charles Evans Hughes*, 2 vols. (1951); and John A. Garraty, *Henry Cabot Lodge* (1953), are all excellent biographies of distinguished Republican leaders.

For the diplomacy of the Roosevelt and Taft administrations, see Howard K. Beale, *Theodore Roosevelt and the Rise of America to World Power* (1961); A. Whitney Griswold, *The Far Eastern Policy of the United States* (1938); Dexter Perkins, *The Monroe Doctrine, 1867–1907* (1937); and Dana G. Munro, *Intervention and Dollar Diplomacy in the Caribbean, 1900–1920* (1964). A thoughtful, if uncritical, reevaluation of Roosevelt's diplomacy is Frederick W. Marks III, *Velvet on Iron: The Diplomacy of Theodore Roosevelt* (1979).

CHAPTER 4
WOODROW WILSON: FROM NEW FREEDOM TO NEW NATIONALISM

1. INSURGENT REPUBLICANS AND PROGRESSIVE DEMOCRATS, 1910–1912

The Old Guard and the Insurgent Challenge

Republican insurgents did not wait long after the elections of 1910 to organize a fight for control of their party. Their leaders met at Senator La Follette's home in Washington, D.C., in January 1911, formed the National Republican Progressive League, and adopted La Follette's "Declaration of Principles." Later, in the autumn of 1911, a conference of about 300 progressives, most of them Republicans, met in Chicago. The group endorsed La Follette as "the logical candidate for the Presidency of the United States."

The great enigma in the Republican situation was Theodore Roosevelt. He warmly supported the insurgents, but he was not at all certain about what he should do. Republican progressives were putting heavy pressure on him to enter the race against Taft for the presidential nomination. They admired La Follette for his courage and devotion to progressivism, but they admired Roosevelt even more, and they knew that only he could unseat an incumbent President. Roosevelt, by his hesitation, was not simply playing hard to get. He hated the thought of a personal battle against his old colleague, Taft. Moreover, Roosevelt despised the Democrats and did not want to destroy the Republican unity so essential to victory in 1912.

Roosevelt finally yielded to the pleadings of his friends, mainly because he was convinced that Taft's renomination would wreck the GOP and lead to

Democratic victory in 1912. The mass of Republican voters rallied to Roosevelt, as he won smashing victories in most of the states which held presidential primaries. Roosevelt defeated Taft even in his home state of Ohio and amassed a total of 1,157,397 primary votes to 761,716 for the President. Yet, by the end of the Republican preconvention campaign, the issue was still very much in doubt. Roosevelt had barely missed winning a majority of the delegates. Taft had collected about one third, many of whom were southern officeholders who owed fealty to the President; the rest of the Taft delegates were from northern states controlled by conservative organizations. The outcome of the convention, and the fate of the Republican party in 1912, depended on the selection of 254 contested delegates in Chicago in early June.

As it turned out, Taft and the Old Guard controlled the Republican National Committee. Its credentials committee awarded nineteen of the contested delegates to Roosevelt and 235 to Taft—just enough to insure a majority for Taft. With the aid of these delegates, the Taft managers were able to organize the convention, beat down all attempts to seat the Roosevelt delegates, and, finally, barely renominate Taft.

Meanwhile, Roosevelt had come to Chicago to take personal charge of his forces. He was convinced that the bosses had stolen the nomination and was angrier than ever before in his political career. Immediately after the Republican convention, Roosevelt agreed to accept nomination on a third-party ticket. The rebels returned to Chicago on August 5, organized the Progressive party, and nominated Roosevelt and Governor Hiram W. Johnson of California to head their ticket. The delegates acted as if they were at a camp meeting rather than at a political convention. They sang the Doxology and "Onward Christian Soldiers" and listened, enraptured, as Roosevelt announced in his acceptance speech—his "Confession of Faith"—that they stood at Armageddon and battled for the Lord. Roosevelt also said that he felt as strong as a bull moose.

The Rise of Woodrow Wilson

It seemed obvious after the elections of 1910 that, with new leadership, the Democratic party could be reconstructed and win the presidency in 1912. Bryan admitted as much by announcing immediately after the elections of 1910 that he would not be a candidate. Party leadership and a chance for the highest office were open, therefore, and an all-out struggle for control followed. This struggle was not as colorful as the one taking place within the Republican party, but it proved more decisive.

Woodrow Wilson had made a brilliant campaign for the governorship of New Jersey during the autumn of 1910. Then he had pushed a series of important reform laws through the state legislature in the first months of 1911. Wilson quickly emerged as the leading Democratic contender. Bold and aggressive, he was rapidly transforming himself into a true progressive. Furthermore, he was a new type of politician—a man who had stepped from the presidency of Princeton University into leadership in politics. Wilson began an exhaustive campaign in the spring of 1911 for the Democratic presidential nomination. He was so successful that, by the end of the year, it seemed that he would meet no serious resistance.

Strong opposition developed suddenly during the early months of 1912 in the candidacy of Champ Clark of Missouri, Speaker of the House of Representatives. He was a devoted follower of Bryan who had served without distinction in the House of Representatives since the 1890s. Clark was also completely mediocre. He was the only serious contender for the presidency ever publicly to endorse a patent medicine—a product called Electric Bitters—which he probably liked because of its high alcoholic content. Wilson campaigned widely but would make absolutely no promises to conservative state organizations. Clark remained in Washington and lined up the support of many state leaders and of William Randolph Hearst, the demagogic newspaper and magazine publisher, who was powerful in the Democratic party.

Clark was far ahead of Wilson in the race for delegates by the end of the preconvention campaign. To make matters worse for Wilson, Oscar W. Underwood of Alabama, the leader of the Democrats in the House of Representatives, also entered the contest. Underwood drew off support in the South which, otherwise, probably would have gone to Wilson.

The Wilson cause, in fact, seemed hopeless when the Democrats assembled in their national convention in Baltimore on June 25, 1912. Clark won a majority, but not the two thirds then necessary for nomination, on the tenth ballot. The Wilson and Underwood delegates stood firm, and Bryan switched his vote from Clark to Wilson on the fourteenth ballot because Tammany Hall had thrown the votes of New York to Clark. Then there followed a long and harrowing battle in which the Wilson managers gradually wore away Clark's strength, much of which was superficial. Finally, Underwood's supporters threw their votes to Wilson, and the nomination went to the New Jersey governor on the forty-sixth ballot. He chose Governor Thomas R. Marshall of Indiana as his running mate.

Two Political Philosophies

Taft was never in the running; he was a candidate only in order to keep Roosevelt out of the White House. The Socialist candidate, Eugene V. Debs, made a hard fight and had some impact, but he never had a chance. However, the two serious contenders—Roosevelt and Wilson—were candidates of superb intelligence, great capacity for leadership, and boldness of vision. Both men called themselves progressives, but important differences separated them. The campaign revealed, for the first time, a deep cleavage which had developed in national progressivism.

The Democratic platform of 1912, drafted largely by Bryan, approved or demanded most of the then popular measures for political and economic reform, such as the direct election of senators, the adoption of a federal income tax, the strengthening of the Sherman Act, and immediate and drastic tariff reduction. On the great issue of 1912—how far the federal government should go in promoting human welfare—the Democratic platform was vague and evasive. It gave scant encouragement to various groups who were working for economic and social justice. Indeed, its silence on specific social and economic welfare legislation indicated that the party still adhered to its traditional state-rights doctrines and a general policy of modified laissez faire on the federal level.

Wilson, following his party's platform, began by highlighting the tariff issue. But this thrust drew only an indifferent popular response. While he searched for a more dramatic issue, Wilson met Louis D. Brandeis, the "people's lawyer" of Boston, in August 1912. Brandeis quickly persuaded Wilson that the most important national problem was the destruction and prevention of industrial and financial monopoly. Wilson then highlighted the program which he called the New Freedom. He would unleash American economic energies through destruction of special privileges and the preservation of competition in the business world. And he would accomplish this goal by reducing the tariff, reforming the banking and currency systems, and strengthening the Sherman Act.

Theodore Roosevelt responded with what he called the New Nationalism. It was embodied in the platform of the Progressive party, in Roosevelt's "Confession of Faith," and in other campaign speeches. The New Nationalism expressed advanced American political and socioeconomic thinking. It included all the various proposals then advanced for the reform of political institutions and practices. It embodied, moreover, Roosevelt's more recent thinking about the most effective way to deal with big business. Great corporations were here to stay, Roosevelt asserted, and they should be subjected to sweeping regulation by a federal trade commission. Finally, the New Nationalism demanded a graduated federal income and estate tax, a national child-labor law, and other measures to erect strong safeguards between workers and farmers and the interests that allegedly exploited them.

The Election of 1912

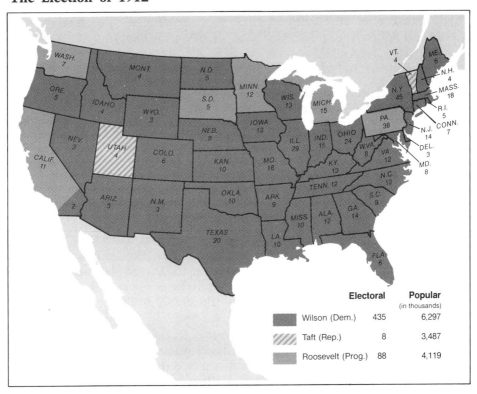

		Electoral	Popular (in thousands)
	Wilson (Dem.)	435	6,297
	Taft (Rep.)	8	3,487
	Roosevelt (Prog.)	88	4,119

The debate between Wilson and Roosevelt only emphasized the wide ideological gulf between the New Freedom and the New Nationalism. Wilson charged that the New Nationalism would end in acceptance of monopoly by the federal government, domination of that government by big business, and, finally, enslavement of the American people by a paternalistic government dominated by large economic interests. Roosevelt replied with equal vigor. He asserted that the New Freedom was based on a state-rights philosophy and embodied a rural Toryism oblivious to the social and economic challenges of the time.

Wilson and the Democrats swept the country on election day, November 2, 1912. The Democratic candidate carried forty states and received more electoral votes (435) than any previous presidential contender. For the first time in American history, many blacks, including Du Bois, supported a Democrat for President because of Wilson's promises of fair treatment and recognition. The Democrats also won control of the Sixty-third Congress, which would sit from 1913 to 1915, and elected governors in twenty-one of the thirty-five states which had gubernatorial elections in 1912.

But the election returns also provided the President-elect with material for sober thought. He had won slightly less than 42 per cent of the popular vote and would, in fact, be a minority President. He, and other Democrats as well, had won only because the Republicans were divided and because Roosevelt had failed to unite progressives of both parties in a majority reform coalition. Perhaps even more unsettling was the spectacular increase in the Socialist presidential vote to nearly 900,090, or about 6.5 per cent of the total, despite the fact that there were two other strong reform candidates on the ballot.

2. THE DEMOCRATIC PARTY AND NATIONAL REFORM

Woodrow Wilson and the Progressive Movement

Despite their differences during the presidential campaign, a great deal of continuity existed between the administrations of Roosevelt and Woodrow Wilson. Like Roosevelt, Wilson established the basic pattern of governmental involvement in the economy. To a large extent, indeed, the most significant reforms of the Wilson administration embodied more of the New Nationalism than of the New Freedom. Wilson also continued Roosevelt's reconstruction of the presidency into the powerful office that it is today.

Thomas Woodrow Wilson was born in Staunton, Virginia, on December 29, 1856. He grew up in Georgia and South Carolina during the Civil War and Reconstruction, but from his youth he was an American nationalist, grateful for the abolition of slavery and the preservation of the Union. He early showed evidence of the quick, keen intelligence and incredible self-discipline which later would set him apart from other politicians. He attended Davidson College in North Carolina for one year and transferred to Princeton University, where he was graduated in 1879. He studied law at the University of Virginia and practiced for a year in Atlanta. He then went to the newly founded Johns Hopkins University in Baltimore for graduate work in history, political science, and economics, where he received the Ph.D. degree in 1886. He taught, successively, at Bryn Mawr College, Wesleyan University, and

Princeton University between 1885 and 1902. He was elected president of Princeton in 1902 and soon earned a national reputation as a pioneer in the field of higher education.

During all his adult life, Wilson was obsessed with the study of how leadership could make democracy work more effectively. He believed for many years that the chief, almost fatal, defect of the American constitutional system was the division of responsibility between Congress and the President, a separation which, he thought, made responsible leadership impossible. His remedy—elaborated in his most famous work, *Congressional Government* (1885)—was some form of adaptation of the British cabinet system, which concentrates all responsibility in a ministry responsible directly to the national legislature. But the Spanish-American War and, particularly, Roosevelt's revivification of the presidential office, prompted Wilson to change his view of the presidency. The President, Wilson wrote in *Constitutional Government in the United States* (1908), "is ... the political leader of the nation, or has it in his choice to be. The nation as a whole has chosen him, and is conscious that it has no other political spokesman. His is the only national voice in affairs. Let him once win the admiration and confidence of the country, and no other single force can withstand him, no combination of forces will easily overpower him. ... If he rightly interprets the national thought and boldly insists upon it, he is irresistible."

Wilson was himself so nearly irresistible in leadership that he literally transformed the presidency. Politicians since his day have studied his methods and profited from his example. Wilson succeeded, first, because he was a strong-willed activist, determined to be a strong leader. He took control of his party in Congress and became, in effect, its prime minister. But he led and did not drive his forces in Congress. And he succeeded mainly because he was a person of complete integrity, who insisted only that congressmen and senators fulfill their promises to the people. Wilson succeeded, finally, because he was deeply immersed in the democratic, Judeo-Christian traditions which underlay the progressive movement, and, most of all, because he was able to express these traditions in speeches of unrivaled eloquence.

Tariff Reform

At his inauguration on a bright March 4, 1913, Wilson announced the purposes of his presidency. The first item on Wilson's schedule was tariff reform, because the integrity and success of the Democratic party and the new administration depended upon revision of the Payne-Aldrich Act—that glaring symbol of the power of special-interest groups. Therefore, Wilson, on the very day that he was inaugurated, called Congress into special session. When it met, he went in person on April 8, 1913, to deliver a brief and forceful address. Thus, at the very beginning of his administration, he asserted his leadership in legislation; he also deliberately focused public attention on Congress. It was the first time since John Adams that a President had addressed a joint session of Congress.

The administration's bill, drafted under Wilson's supervision by Oscar W. Underwood and the Ways and Means Committee, fulfilled all the Democratic party's promises of tariff reform. It reduced duties on hundreds of articles and put sugar, wool, iron and steel products, shoes, agricultural implements, and other products on the free list. It included a provision for an income tax, which ranged from 1 to 4 per cent. The measure encountered no difficulties and passed the House of Representatives by a vote of 281 to 139 on May 8.

Many times earlier, the House had enacted sweeping tariff reductions, only to see its work wrecked by a Senate which yielded to tariff lobbies. That danger was particularly acute in 1913, for hundreds of lobbyists descended upon Washington to put pressure on the Senate Finance Committee, which would consider the Underwood bill. Furthermore, Wilson, by his insistence upon free sugar and free wool, had antagonized Democratic senators from the states which produced these commodities. Without their votes, the Underwood bill would fail, just as the Payne bill had failed in 1909. Wilson struck back by denouncing the lobbyists who, he said, infested Washington. Wilson, moreover, put such heavy personal pressure on wavering Democratic senators that all but two of them fell into line. Wilson also had loyal support from the chairman of the Finance Committee, Furnifold M. Simmons of North Carolina.

The bill which the Finance Committee reported and the Senate approved on September 9 actually *reduced* the rates of the Underwood bill. The Senate committee reduced average rates to about 29 per cent, as compared to the Payne-Aldrich Act's average of about 40 per cent. The Senate committee, in addition, *increased* the maximum income tax to 7 per cent. Both houses approved this version, and Wilson signed the bill on October 3, 1913.

The First World War broke out before the effects of the new rates could be felt significantly, but the Underwood-Simmons Act had a crucial political significance. Defeat in this first test of leadership would have been fatal to the new President. Instead, Wilson's victory fastened his control over the Democratic forces in Congress and won the confidence of people still skeptical about the Democratic party's ability to fulfill its campaign promises.

Banking and Currency Reform

Wilson went to the Capitol again on June 23, 1913, to demand thoroughgoing banking and currency reform. Scholars, public leaders, and bankers had been seeking solutions since the 1890s. The Panic of 1907 had revealed two major flaws—the absence of a central bank to mobilize reserves and move them where needed in emergencies, and a currency based upon inflexible supplies of gold and the bonded indebtedness of the United States (the basis for National Bank notes), rather than upon the real wealth of the country.

The National Monetary Commission had drafted a bill which Senator Aldrich, its chairman, introduced in 1912. It proposed a single central bank, with branches, which would hold banking reserves and issue currency against gold and commercial assets. It would be owned and controlled by private banks, and its currency would not be an obligation of the United States Government. Both the Democratic and Progressive platforms of 1912 denounced the Aldrich bill. Furthermore, popular fear of Wall Street increased early in 1913, when a committee of the House of Representatives revealed that the House of Morgan and its allies exerted powerful influence over the national economy and that a "money trust" might exist.

Wilson moved quietly but effectively and made the final decisions about the banking and currency measure called the federal reserve bill. Under its provisions, private banks owned and largely controlled a decentralized system of Federal Reserve Banks which mobilized reserves and performed other central banking functions. These Federal Reserve Banks could issue a new currency—Federal Reserve notes—which was based on gold and commercial and agricultural paper, in accordance with fluctuating needs, and which was the obligation of the United States Government. A Federal Reserve Board, composed entirely of presidential appointees, was, as Wilson put it, the "capstone" of the Federal Reserve System. It could shift banking reserves from one section of the country when needed, set interest rates, and, in general, determine the volume of currency in circulation.

Carter Glass of Virginia, chairman of the Banking Committee of the House of Representatives, introduced the federal reserve bill on September 9, and the House approved it by a huge majority only nine days later. The fight in the Senate, in contrast, was long and harrowing on account of the frantic opposition of certain big-city banking interests. But Wilson would not yield on any major point and maintained relentless pressure on the Senate. He got his federal reserve bill, exactly as he wanted it on December 23, and signed it on the following day. "I cannot say with what deep emotions of gratitude I feel," he declared as he signed the bill, "that I have had a part in completing a work which I think will be of lasting benefit to the business of the country."

Wilson did not exaggerate the significance of the Federal Reserve Act, for it was his crowning domestic achievement. The Federal Reserve System, with twelve regional banks united by the Federal Reserve Board, went into operation in 1914. It was a success from the outset, and, soon, the very bankers who had condemned the bill most violently were its strongest supporters. As a result of the collapse of the American banking system in the early 1930s, the Federal Reserve Board was reorganized and its powers were greatly enlarged in 1935. But, in essence, Wilsonian legislation established our present-day banking and currency structures.

Wilson and Antitrust

The last major item on the New Freedom schedule was legislation to strengthen the Sherman Antitrust Act. When Wilson went before Congress to ask for new antitrust legislation in January 1914, nearly as much controversy surrounded it as had encompassed banking and currency legislation.

Wilson reaffirmed the stand which he had taken during the campaign of 1912 and came out firmly on the side of those who wanted merely to strengthen and clarify the Sherman Act. The original administration program consisted of three measures: first, an antitrust bill, which Representative Henry D. Clayton of Alabama introduced and which was aimed at industrial and financial interlocking directorates and practices used to suppress competition; second, a bill introduced by Representative James H. Covington of Maryland, which established an interstate trade commission without any regulatory authority; and, third, a railway-securities bill, written largely by Brandeis, which gave the ICC authority over the issuance of new securities by railroads. The House of Representatives approved all three bills on June 5, 1914.

House approval only intensified the public furor. Businessmen, small and large, were up in arms against the draconian features of the Clayton bill. It also seemed impossible to define and prohibit, by statute, every conceivable means of restraining trade. Meanwhile, a close friend of Brandeis, Representative Raymond B. Stevens of New Hampshire, had introduced a bill to establish a strong federal trade commission. It could order businessmen to "cease and desist" from committing so-called unfair trade practices. At Brandeis' urging, Wilson shifted ground, took up the Stevens bill, and made it the cornerstone of his antitrust program. Wilson signed the Federal Trade Commission Act on September 26, 1914.

Meanwhile, Wilson and his lieutenants had rewritten the Clayton bill. They softened somewhat its severest provisions. Even so, the measure which Wilson signed on October 15, 1913, greatly strengthened the antitrust powers of the government; moreover, it made businessmen, personally, criminally liable for infractions. In addition, one provision of the Clayton Act explicitly declared that labor unions and farm organizations were not conspiracies in restraint of trade; and it also provided substantial relief from indiscriminate court injunctions against unions engaged in strikes.

The Federal Trade Commission Act signaled an important new departure in antitrust policy. The federal government now had an agency—the Federal Trade Commission—whose business it was to protect competition and deter would-be monopolists before, rather than after, they had crushed competitors. The act also evidenced an important shift in the philosophy of the Wilson administration. Wilson had adopted much the same program for the regulation of business which he had condemned when it was advanced by Theodore Roosevelt in 1912. Wilson was soon to demonstrate flexibility in other areas of domestic and foreign policy.

3. WOODROW WILSON AND THE AMERICAN IMPERIUM

Wilson Diplomacy: Main Elements

Wilson, of course, had had no practical training in diplomacy before 1913, and yet, from the very outset of his administration, he was deeply involved in foreign affairs. In the conduct of foreign relations, Wilson—like Roosevelt—was an advocate of a strong presidential role. He believed that the people had vested their sovereignty in foreign affairs in him. Although he made some mistakes at the beginning, he quickly learned not only the skills of diplomacy but also how to use power wisely and with restraint. By 1916, his was a major voice in world affairs.

The New Freedom in the World

Wilson was, in many respects, the pivot of democratic foreign policy of the twentieth century. He was the first effective decolonizer among statesmen of the twentieth century. As has been noted, the Jones Act of 1916, which Wilson sponsored, gave self-government and promised early independence to the Philippine Islands. His mandate system, embodied in the covenant of the League of Nations, promised eventual independence for many of the former German and Turkish colonies.

Wilson was the most effective and certainly the most eloquent champion of human rights among all the statesmen of the twentieth century. As we will see, he used the power of the United States, wherever he could effectively do so, to protect weak nations against aggression by stronger powers. He was also the most effective champion of self-determination, that is, of the right of peoples with a common language, culture, and history to govern themselves.

Wilson was also the first effective antiimperialist statesman of the twentieth century. He believed strongly in the free-enterprise system and in a world united by trade and commerce. But he believed even more strongly that it was morally wrong for rich powers to exploit underdeveloped countries and colonies. As he once said, he would never permit dollars to be used to purchase other people's liberties. Almost single-handedly, Wilson destroyed the imperialist system in Mexico.

Finally, Wilson was the most ardent champion of peace and world unity among all the leaders of the twentieth century. He hated war and the use of force in international relations, although he did have to use force himself. He promoted vigorously, although unsuccessfully, a Pan-American pact to mutualize the Monroe Doctrine. And he was of course the chief architect of the League of Nations—the first organization in the history of the world devoted to the advancement of world unity and the prevention of war.

Wilson appointed William Jennings Bryan as his Secretary of State mainly because it was safer to have the "Great Commoner" inside the administration than on the outside. Actually, both Wilson and Bryan were Christian moralists who shared common assumptions about the proper goals of foreign policy. They embarked, therefore, upon various programs to further peace, restore the integrity of the United States in the eyes of the world, and advance the cause of human rights.

With Wilson's blessing, Bryan negotiated conciliation (not arbitration) treaties with thirty nations. These provided for a "cooling-off" period of six months or a year and an investigation of any disputes before nations in controversy could resort to war. Whether the treaties did much good is doubtful, but they were evidence of the dedication of the administration to the cause of world peace. Other policies were of more immediate personal significance.

The administration tried to make honorable amends for Roosevelt's aggression against Colombia in a treaty signed in Bogotá on April 6, 1914. The United States expressed "sincere regret" that anything should have happened to mar good relations between the two countries and agreed to pay Colombia $25 million for the loss of Panama. Publication of the treaty evoked a roar of rage from Roosevelt, and his friends in the Senate prevented approval of the treaty. But, in April 1921, after Roosevelt's death, a Republican Senate approved the treaty—with the expression of "sincere regret" omitted.

Wilson withdrew American bankers from the international group formed to lend money to China because he believed, correctly, that the loan agreement was a blatant instrument of "dollar diplomacy." He also recognized the new Republic of China in 1913, without insistence upon the concessions which the other great powers had laid down as the price of recognition. Furthermore, in 1915, when Japan tried to make China a virtual protectorate by imposing certain "demands" upon her, Wilson intervened so strongly in China's behalf that the Japanese withdrew them.

Wilson also settled a potentially serious dispute with Great Britain. In 1912, Congress had adopted a law which exempted American coastwise shipping from payment of tolls for use of the Panama Canal. The British government, in a formal protest, asserted that this exemption violated the Hay-Pauncefote Treaty, which promised that the canal would be open to the ships of all nations on equal terms. In 1914, Wilson delivered a special address before Congress in which he admitted that the United States had possibly violated the treaty and demanded repeal of the tolls exemption. Although he realized that he was jeopardizing his leadership of the Democratic party in Congress, Wilson won repeal after a hard struggle; actually, his victory strengthened his leadership of congressional Democrats.

Wilson also moved forcefully in the spring of 1913, when the California legislature debated a bill to deny aliens "ineligible to citizenship"—in other words, Orientals—the right to own land in the state. The Japanese government protested against what it said was invidious discrimination and an open insult to the Japanese people. Wilson sent Bryan to Sacramento to plead against adoption of the bill. He failed, and the Japanese government delivered a strong formal protest. Sensationalist newspapers, both in Japan and the United States, fanned ill feeling, and American naval leaders began to talk about the danger of war with Japan. Wilson sternly suppressed such discussions in official circles and kept the dispute on a diplomatic level. Since California had a good legal case, Wilson was severely hampered in negotiations. The California legislation explicitly stated that any of its provisions contrary to the treaty obligations of the United States would be null and void. Actually, the California law did not violate any Japanese-American treaty. Moreover, Japanese law forbade aliens to own land in Japan.

Caribbean Troubles

The results of the policies of Wilson and Bryan in certain Caribbean and Central American republics reveal that good intentions do not always produce anticipated results. Wilson and Bryan carried on active diplomacy in the Caribbean region partly because of their concern to protect the Panama Canal. Hence the Wilson administration not only supported the conservative government of Nicaragua which Secretary Knox had helped to install, but it also negotiated a treaty with Nicaragua for a right-of-way for a canal in Nicaragua, in return for payment of $3 million. The treaty also empowered the United States to intervene in Nicaragua, if necessary, to protect order, property, and Nicaraguan independence—a provision which was added at the strong urging of the conservative Nicaraguan government.

But the main objectives of the policies of Wilson and Bryan in the Caribbean area and Central America were the maintenance of peace and the development of orderly, democratic governments. Wilson and Bryan were, so to speak, missionaries of democracy who sincerely desired to help other people.

An important—and somewhat inadvertent—result of missionary diplomacy was that Wilson and Bryan sank in a quagmire of local factional politics in the Dominican Republic, and Wilson occupied the country in 1916 in order to

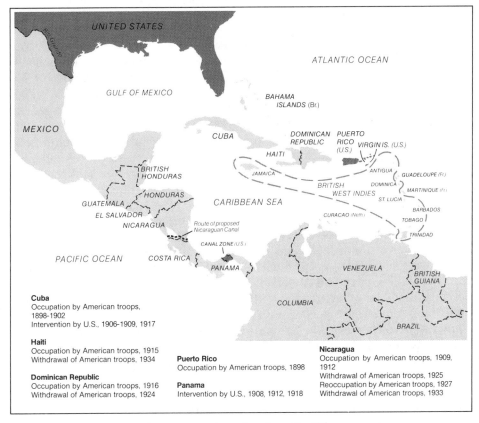

Cuba
Occupation by American troops,
1898-1902
Intervention by U.S., 1906-1909, 1917

Haiti
Occupation by American troops, 1915
Withdrawal of American troops, 1934

Dominican Republic
Occupation by American troops, 1916
Withdrawal of American troops, 1924

Puerto Rico
Occupation by American troops, 1898

Panama
Intervention by U.S., 1908, 1912, 1918

Nicaragua
Occupation by American troops, 1909,
1912
Withdrawal of American troops, 1925
Reoccupation by American troops, 1927
Withdrawal of American troops, 1933

United States Armed Intervention in the Caribbean

prevent anarchy. In a rescue operation, undertaken reluctantly, Wilson also occupied Haiti in 1915. The irony of this situation was that, as Wilson discovered, the spread of democracy in Haiti and the Dominican Republic seemed possible only in repression and in the violation of these nations' sovereignty. Moreover, "missionary diplomacy" did not succeed in the long run. In the Dominican Republic, Haiti, and Nicaragua, American administrators and diplomats did not try to train the peoples involved for effective self-government, and, once American forces were withdrawn from these countries in the 1920s, military dictators again seized power.

Wilson and the Mexican Revolution

The acid test of Wilson's sincerity about promoting human rights abroad was the long, nagging problem of Mexico, where the first authentic sociopolitical revolution of the twentieth century broke out in 1911. The United States was vitally concerned, not only because Mexico was its nearest southern neighbor, but also because Americans had invested nearly $1 billion in Mexican mines, oil properties, ranches, railroads, and public utilities. Some 40,000 to 50,000 Americans resided in Mexico. Increasingly, there were threats to these property interests and people as the revolution moved from one bloody stage to even more violent ones.

The revolution began hopefully when the middle-class reformer, Francisco I. Madero, overthrew the aged dictator, Porfirio Díaz, and was elected President of Mexico in 1911. Then, in February 1913, a cruel but able general, Victoriano Huerta, proclaimed himself President and had Madero and his Vice-President murdered. Huerta promised to accord full protection to foreign property, and Japan and the major European powers hastened to recognize his government. Business interests put great pressure on Wilson to grant recognition to Huerta. The American ambassador in Mexico City, Henry Lane Wilson—who had helped to arrange Madero's overthrow—strongly endorsed their advice. But President Wilson hesitated; he would not, he said privately, recognize a "government of butchers." Moreover, in a public statement he declared: "We can have no sympathy with those who seek to seize the power of government to advance their own political interests or ambition."

Wilson announced his policy in mid-June 1913. He offered to mediate between Huerta and the followers of Madero, the Constitutionalists, who had begun the revolution anew under Venustiano Carranza, governor of a northern state. Under Wilson's plan, Mexico would hold early constitutional elections, and, in order to insure the possibility of a fair election, Huerta would not run for the presidency.

Huerta, encouraged by the British—whose subjects had large oil and other interests in Mexico—replied with the dispersion of the Mexican Congress and the establishment of a military dictatorship. Wilson then went into action with grim determination. First, he virtually compelled the British to withdraw support from Huerta by making it clear that they faced a choice between American friendship or ties with Huerta. Second, Wilson became emotionally committed to the cause of the Mexican Revolution, which he compared with the French Revolution as the struggle of an oppressed people for land and liberty. He therefore threw his support to the Constitutionalists and, in early 1914, permitted them to purchase arms in the United States.

But by the spring of 1914, when Huerta had consolidated his power, Wilson resorted to military force. He found an excuse in a petty incident which occurred in Tampico. When Huerta refused to yield to Wilson's extreme demands, Wilson sent marines and sailors into Veracruz and seized that port on April 22, 1914. Wilson had expected the operation to be bloodless; indeed, he did not give the order for the occupation until the Mexican general at Veracruz had agreed to withdraw his troops to Mexico City. Fighting nonetheless broke out when cadets at the Mexican Naval Academy resisted the invaders; heavy casualties were incurred, particularly on the Mexican side. Wilson was appalled and quickly accepted an offer of mediation of the dispute by the ambassadors to the United States of Argentina, Brazil, and Chile. Throughout the mediation, Wilson's primary goal was the triumph of the revolution. Huerta, greatly weakened by the loss of revenues from Veracruz and hard pressed by the Constitutionalists, fled to Spain in July 1914.

Armed Conflict with Mexico

Carranza's entry into Mexico City on August 20, 1914, seemed to mark the triumph of the revolution. However, even worse difficulties were brewing at that very time. Francisco (Pancho) Villa, Carranza's most colorful general, began a new revolt only a few weeks after Carranza entered the Mexican capital. Another terrible civil war raged for more than a year. Carranza rapidly emerged as the head of the more democratic, modernizing forces in the revolution; Villa, as leader of its chaotic and corrupt elements. But Villa shrewdly appealed for American support by promising to protect American property interests in Mexico. The State Department actually made plans for American military intervention in order to assure the victory of Villa's army. Wilson had learned his lesson at Veracruz, however, and he would not intervene in any way. The Mexicans, he said in rejecting the State Department's plan, were entitled to settle their problems in their own way. And, after Carranza had dealt Villa several crushing defeats, Wilson extended de facto recognition to the Carranza regime in October 1915.

Mexican-American relations were unusually friendly during the following months. Then, on March 9, 1916, Villa, partly to provoke war between the United States and the Carranza regime, swooped down on the border town of Columbus, New Mexico, where he burned the town and killed nineteen inhabitants. Under tremendous pressure at home, Wilson sent a punitive expedition, under General John J. Pershing, into Mexican territory to apprehend Villa. Villa cleverly drew Pershing deeper and deeper into Mexico until, by April, Pershing had advanced 300 miles below the border. Fighting broke out between Carranza's forces and American troops at Parral on April 12, 1916, and Carranza demanded the immediate withdrawal of Pershing's command from Mexican soil. The American government replied in a stinging rebuke, and Wilson mobilized most of the National Guard and sent it to the Mexican border. Another sharp engagement between Mexican and American troops occurred at Carrizal, in northern Mexico, on June 21. The American officer in command was clearly the aggressor in this incident, but, without waiting for an accurate report, Wilson assumed that the Mexicans were responsible. He sent an ultimatum which demanded the immediate return of Americans taken prisoner at Carrizal. He also drafted a message which requested authority from Congress for him to occupy northern Mexico.

Both nations recoiled from the thought of war just as it seemed inevitable. Wilson, in an address at the height of the crisis, asked whether there would be any glory in conquering a poor people who were struggling for liberty. Carranza responded with a suggestion to appoint a joint high commission to try to settle Mexican-American differences, and Wilson accepted the suggestion at once. The commission met off and on during the summer and autumn of 1916 but failed because Wilson would not yield to Carranza's demand for complete and immediate withdrawal of American troops from Mexican territory. However, once Carranza had succeeded in decimating Villa's forces, Wilson withdrew Pershing in January 1917 and accorded recognition to Carranza's new constitutional regime on April 21, 1917.

Wilson made many mistakes in his relations with Mexico. Most particularly, he tried, at least at first, to impose his own solution upon Mexico, and he permitted Pershing to go too far and stay too long. But Wilson was a sincere, even dedicated, friend of the Mexican Revolution. He prevented Huerta from consolidating his regime with European support, and he helped the Constitutionalists to overthrow the dictator. Wilson also supported Carranza at a critical time. He never permitted American interests with property in Mexico to swerve him from support of the revolution. Finally, during the dark days after Carrizal, when war seemed inevitable, Wilson never lost control of events. Along with the patient Carranza, Wilson preserved the peace until Mexican-American friendship could be built on solid foundations.

4. WILSON AND NATIONAL PROGRESSIVISM

Wilson and Reform

As we have said, the dilemma of national progressivism was the question of how far the federal government should go to promote economic security and social welfare. More cautious progressives argued that the federal government should never favor any class or classes—whether workers, farmers, or businessmen. Advanced progressives and spokesmen for workers and farmers replied that the national government should help to correct the injustices which it had helped to create by giving special protection now to the helpless, disadvantaged, and exploited. For example, farmers wanted the federal government to subsidize long-term loans to them. Labor leaders and many social workers demanded some form of restriction of immigration. Advocates of social justice pressed hard for federal child-labor legislation and a new workmen's-compensation act for federal employees.

Yet, Wilson resisted these demands during the first two years of his administration. He threatened to veto a bill which provided for federal operation and subsidy of a system of rural credits. In 1915, Wilson vetoed the Burnett bill, which provided for restriction of immigration by the imposition of a literacy test. It should be said that social-justice leaders were deeply divided on this measure and that many of them applauded Wilson's eloquent veto message. The Burnett bill was passed over Wilson's veto in 1917. Wilson refused to fight for the passage of a child-labor bill, on the ground that it was unconstitutional, even after the House of Representatives had approved it by a huge majority in 1914. He did sign the Seamen's Act, which freed American seamen from bondage to their labor contracts, in 1915, but only because he decided that the measure conferred no special privileges. In the area of race relations, Wilson did little to combat the rising tide of Jim Crow in the federal government. He even permitted his Secretary of the Treasury and Postmaster General to segregate some of their black and white employees in 1913, an action which provoked a storm of protest.

The first clear sign that Wilson was beginning to doubt that a limited progressivism would either satisfy public opinion or meet the problems of the modern age came when he accepted the proposal for a strong Federal Trade Commission. His switch revealed that his mind was open to new suggestions and that, in the future, he might not adhere rigidly to the ideology of the New Freedom.

New Nationalism Triumphs

Wilson became a convert to the New Nationalism in 1916. The longer he served as President, the more he became convinced that the federal government had to take leadership in social and economic reform. Moreover, by the summer of 1914, the Mexican Revolution and the Colorado coal strike had considerably radicalized him. The strike in Colorado had a particularly heavy impact on Wilson, on account of the refusal of the mine owners to accept his mediation. He also knew that he faced defeat in the coming presidential election unless he came out wholeheartedly for advanced reform. The Progressive party had virtually disintegrated by the early months of 1916. The Democrats were still a minority party, and Wilson realized that his only hope of reelection lay in attracting the support of a large number of Roosevelt's former followers.

Wilson signaled his new departure by appointing Brandeis, perhaps the foremost champion of social justice in the country, to the Supreme Court on January 28, 1916. The Senate confirmed Brandeis, but only after a long and bitter battle in which Wilson backed his nominee with all of his influence as leader of the Democratic party.

Next, Wilson came out in support of the same rural-credits bill which he had earlier threatened to veto. Adopted in July 1916, it established twelve Federal Land Banks and stipulated that the government should furnish funds for loans to farmers if private investors refused to buy the Federal Land Banks' bonds. At the same time, he pushed the federal child-labor and workmen's-compensation bills through Congress. The former (depending upon the products involved) forbade shipment in interstate commerce of goods manufactured in whole or in part by children under fourteen or sixteen. It was one of the most important pieces of legislation of the twentieth century. It marked the first effort by Congress to regulate conditions of labor *within the states* by use of its control over interstate commerce, and as such, was the forerunner of all such legislation in the 1930s and afterward.

To avert a nationwide railroad strike, Wilson, in September 1916, persuaded Congress to adopt the Adamson Act, which established the eight-hour day as the standard for workers on interstate railroads. Finally, a few days after he approved the Adamson Act, Wilson signed a tax bill which greatly increased the income tax and imposed a new federal estate tax and taxes on excess profits, corporation income, and munitions manufacturers. It marked the triumph of Populist tax policy and was the first serious effort in American history to effect some redistribution of wealth through taxation.

SUGGESTED READINGS

The basic source for Wilson and his era is Arthur S. Link et al., eds., *The Papers of Woodrow Wilson,* 39 vols. to date (1966–). The only general works on the Wilson era are Arthur S. Link, *Woodrow Wilson and the Progressive Era* (1954), and Frederick L. Paxson, *The American Democracy and the World War,* 3 vols. (1936–1948). The richest literature on Wilson's first administration is in the form of biographies. Arthur S. Link, *Wilson,* 5 vols. to date (1947–), covers Wilson's rise to political prominence, the campaign of 1912, and the first Wilson administration in great detail. Arthur Walworth,

Woodrow Wilson, 2 vols. (1958), is a good personal biography. Edwin A. Weinstein, *Woodrow Wilson: A Medical and Psychological Biography* (1981), is indispensable to an understanding of Wilson's personality and career. See also Charles Seymour, ed., *The Intimate Papers of Colonel House,* 4 vols. (1926–1928); Frank Freidel, *Franklin D. Roosevelt: The Apprenticeship* (1952); Paolo E. Coletta, *William Jennings Bryan: Progressive Politician and Moral Statesman, 1909–1915* (1969); and Richard Lowitt, *George W. Norris: The Persistence of a Progressive* (1971).

For specialized studies, see Henry P. Willis, *The Federal Reserve System* (1923); John D. Clark, *The Federal Trust Policy* (1931); Stephen Wood, *Constitutional Politics in the Progressive Era: Child Labor and the Law* (1968); and George B. Tindall, *The Emergence of the New South, 1913 – 1945* (1967).

For a general overview of Wilson as a maker and practitioner of foreign policy, see Link, *Woodrow Wilson: Revolution, War, and Peace* (1979), and Link, ed., *Woodrow Wilson and a Revolutionary World, 1913 – 1921* (1982), a collection of essays by leading scholars of Wilson's foreign policies. The second, third, fourth, and fifth volumes of Link's biography cover Wilson's Caribbean, Mexican, Latin American, and Far Eastern policies from 1913 to 1917 in detail. However, the following specialized works are extremely helpful: Munro, *Intervention and Dollar Diplomacy in the Caribbean, 1900 – 1920,* cited earlier; Kenneth J. Grieb, *The United States and Huerta* (1969); Robert E. Quirk, *An Affair of Honor: Woodrow Wilson and the Occupation of Veracruz* (1962) and *The Mexican Revolution, 1914 – 1915* (1960); and Friedrich Katz, *The Secret War in Mexico: Europe, the United States and the Mexican Revolution* (1981).

CHAPTER 5
THE UNITED STATES AND THE FIRST WORLD WAR, 1914–1920

1. AMERICAN NEUTRALITY

The War Begins

The First World War changed the course of human history, or at least greatly hastened events which might not have occurred for generations. It destroyed three mighty European empires, terribly weakened the economic and political foundations of western Europe, and unleashed forces which would continue to threaten the order and stability of the world for decades to come. The war, caused by the same western European military power and aggressiveness which had created the European world empires, now accelerated the erosion of that western domination.

Even the immediate origins of such great events are always deep and complex. It is clear, nevertheless, that conflicts over national boundaries, colonies, and markets had produced arms races and led to a number of incidents that threatened general war. By 1914, Europe was divided into armed camps. On one side stood the Triple Entente, composed of Great Britain, France, and Russia. On the other side stood the Triple Alliance, composed of Germany, Austria-Hungary, and Italy. So tightly knit were both alliances that it was almost impossible for a member of one to become involved in conflict with a member of the other without plunging all the major European powers into war.

The fuse that detonated the powder keg was the assassination of the Archduke Franz Ferdinand, heir to the Austrian and Hungarian thrones, on June 28, 1914. A Serbian nationalist shot him and his wife while they

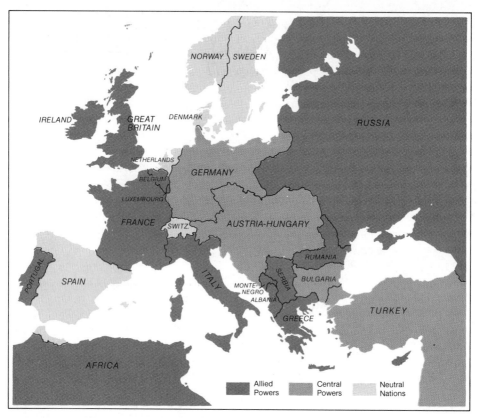

European Alliances in World War I

were driving through the streets of Sarajevo in the Austrian province of Bosnia. Serbians hoped to add Bosnia to their kingdom and feared that the popular Archduke might defeat their ambitions. Austria-Hungary claimed that Serbian revolutionary societies were responsible for the murders and issued an ultimatum. Serbia, strongly supported by Russia, refused to yield to the severe Austrian terms. The German government, eager for a preventive war against Russia, meanwhile egged on its Austro-Hungarian ally. Austria-Hungary declared war on Serbia and marched upon Belgrade on July 28.

The war might still have been localized if the other powers had not proceeded to mobilize their armed forces and to move them into positions according to long-standing war plans. Each nation feared that, unless it struck first, its enemies might gain a decisive early advantage. While the Russians prepared to march against Austria-Hungary, Germany struck first and declared war on Russia on August 1. Meanwhile, Russia's ally, France, was preparing to meet its commitments when Germany declared war on France two days later. British leaders had secretly promised to come to France's aid; they needed some dramatic incident to arouse their nation, an incident which Germany provided when it sent its armies across Belgium. Since England was committed by treaty to defend the neutrality of Belgium, Parliament declared war on Germany on August 4.

The system of alliances was now operating automatically. Bulgaria and Turkey joined Germany and Austria-Hungary—the Central Powers; Japan and Italy were lured to the side of the Entente—or Allies—by promises of territory. Eventually, in all of Europe, only Norway, Sweden, Denmark, Holland, Spain, and Switzerland were fortunate enough to avoid involvement.

Defining Neutrality

Most Americans recoiled in horror and disbelief and could not understand why Europeans had set out to slaughter each other. The brutal German invasion of Belgium particularly outraged many Americans. Probably a majority of Americans, influenced to some degree by British propaganda, were pro-Allied in sentiment and remained so until the United States entered the war. However, the Germans also conducted a skillful propaganda campaign in the United States and had many defenders among the large German-American and Irish-American elements. Most thoughtful Americans, however, realized that the causes of the war were complex and that no single nation was to blame, a view which President Wilson shared. Americans in general, whomever they blamed for the onset of the war, remained doggedly neutralist and were determined to avoid entanglement if at all possible.

In the light of this widespread determination and Wilson's own passion for peace, any course others than neutrality was unthinkable for the United States. Wilson issued a proclamation of neutrality on August 4. Two weeks later, he added a personal appeal to his fellow citizens to be "neutral in fact as well as in name" and "impartial in thought as well as in action."

It was easy to set the ordinary machinery of neutrality in motion, but it was extremely difficult for the administration to work out the rules in complicated situations. Neutrality meant doing nothing which would give an undue advantage to either side. It also meant respect of legitimate belligerent rights—for example, the right of blockade. The Wilson administration always tried to be fair. It steadfastly resisted demands by German Americans and others for an arms embargo, because such an embargo would have denied to the British the advantage of access to American markets which their dominant sea power gave them. The administration did discourage American loans to the belligerents during the early months of the war. But it quietly reversed this policy before the end of 1914 and openly repudiated it when the British and French governments sought to float a public loan in the United States during the summer of 1915. To have denied any belligerent access to private credit markets would have been as unneutral as to deny any belligerent access to American commercial markets.

British Challenges

The British naturally were determined to use their great fleet to cut off the flow of vital materials from the United States to the Central Powers. Wilson and his administration were equally determined to preserve as much freedom of trade as possible for American producers and merchants.

On the matter of the shipment to Germany of absolute contraband—munitions and articles destined for military use—there was no difference between the British and American governments. It was well established in international law that a belligerent had the right to seize and confiscate absolute contraband which was going to its enemy. But there were innumerable controversies over conditional contraband—articles which *might* be used by armed forces—and so-called innocent goods, destined for use by civilians. Controversies occurred also over certain British blockade policies. For example, the British established a long-range blockade of Germany instead of following the traditional policy of maintaining cruisers outside enemy ports. The British also forbade so-called broken voyages, that is, the shipment of contraband to the Central Powers by way of an intermediary neutral port.

The American government sent strong protests to London, but Anglo-American differences over the blockade were never acute, at least not before 1916, for a number of reasons. The British instituted their controls over American trade gradually and usually with a keen regard for American property rights and interests. Not until the Germans had declared an unprecedented submarine blockade did the British forbid all trade with the Central Powers. The British government also argued convincingly that it was impossible to distinguish between types of contraband during total war, since food destined for civilian populations, for example, was as essential to a war economy as guns and bullets. The British, moreover, were careful to avoid any open affronts to American sovereignty, at least before 1916. Finally, the British could say, quite accurately, that they, in their own extension of blockade practices, were simply following precedents established by the United States during the Civil War.

Submarine Warfare

So long as the British controlled the seas and the Germans dominated the heartland of Europe, the American task of neutrality was relatively simple—to pursue the most impartial policies within this framework of power. But Wilson faced an entirely new situation when the Germans decided in early 1915 to challenge British control of the seas by using an untried weapon—the submarine. The German Admiralty announced on February 4, 1915, that all enemy vessels would be torpedoed without warning in a broad area around the British Isles, and that even neutral vessels would not be safe. Wilson responded quickly on February 10 that the United States would hold Germany to a "strict accountability" (a conventional diplomatic term) for illegal destruction of *American* ships and lives. The German government soon retreated from its threat against American ships, and submarine attacks against them were not a matter of serious dispute between the two governments before 1917.

Much more complex and difficult questions were involved when the Germans sank Allied ships on which Americans were traveling or working, and especially when these ships were armed. Wilson rarely adopted an inflexible position against the German undersea campaign. On the contrary, he did not desire to deprive the Germans of the advantage which came from the use of submarines, and he usually struggled hard to find policies of accommodation. Moreover, Wilson evolved his policies in response to particular situations; the result was that his policies toward submarine warfare underwent considerable change between 1915 and 1917.

The first German-American dispute involved the right of Americans to travel in safety on *unarmed* Allied *passenger* ships. It was first raised when a German submarine sank the British liner *Falaba* on March 28, 1915, and killed one American. Under strong pressure from Bryan, Wilson decided to make no protest at all. Then the German submarine *U20* sank the great British liner *Lusitania* without warning in the Irish Sea on May 7; nearly 1,200 persons, including 124 American citizens, perished. So overwhelming was the American revulsion against the deed that Wilson was no longer able to maintain silence. Most Americans were still opposed to intervention, and Wilson, who agreed ardently with them, chose to deal with the crisis by diplomacy. In a series of notes, he appealed to the German government to abandon its campaign of terror against *unarmed* passenger liners. The Berlin government responded evasively or negatively to each note from Washington. On August 19, 1915, a German submarine sank another British liner, *Arabic*, with loss of American lives. Wilson now made it plain that he would break diplomatic relations if Germany did not stop sinking unarmed passenger ships. The Germans had no alternative but to yield; they had so few submarines that it would have been foolish to have risked war with the United States over the issue.

One result of the *Lusitania* crisis was the loss by Wilson of Bryan as Secretary of State. The "Great Commoner" resigned on June 8, 1915, rather than sign the second *Lusitania* note to Germany, because he thought that it was not conciliatory enough. Bryan's successor was Robert Lansing, formerly Counselor of the State Department, an expert in international law and usage, whose views on foreign policy were a curious mixture of idealistic liberalism, conservatism, and legalism.

Preparedness

The major domestic repercussion of the *Lusitania* and *Arabic* crises was the strong stimulus which they gave to demands for the expansion of the armed forces of the United States. A small minority led by Theodore Roosevelt had been sounding dire alarms since the autumn of 1914. But Wilson, Congress, and the people did not respond until the submarine controversy had revealed that war with Germany was possible. When Congress met in December 1915, Wilson made preparedness the chief objective of his legislative program. He encountered bitter resistance from pacifists and progressives, who contended that money spent for defense would benefit only big business and Wall Street. Then Wilson went to the people to build support for his program. The outcome was a series of measures, some of which were compromises that pleased neither antiwar progressives nor Roosevelt and his friends.

The Army Reorganization Act of June 3, 1916, greatly expanded the National Guard forces of the states and brought them under strict federal control. The act also provided for large increases in the regular army and authorized the War Department to establish summer training programs for civilians. Congress followed, in August 1916, with an act which authorized huge increases in the navy during the next three years. A month later, Congress also created a United States Shipping Board and provided it with $50 million to build, purchase, or lease merchant ships. Wilson rounded out his preparedness program in October 1916 by appointing a Council of

National Defense to advise the administration on problems of economic mobilization, if war should come.

The Purchase of the Danish West Indies

One by-product of the increased concern for national security was the purchase of the Danish West Indies, or the Virgin Islands. Wilson took up the project with grim determination in 1915 after the American minister to Denmark warned him that Germany might absorb Denmark—and the Virgin Islands along with the mother country—if Germany won the war. The Danes asked the exorbitant price of $27 million, but Wilson was not inclined to haggle after his naval advisers said that the United States could not safely permit a potential enemy to acquire the islands with their fine sites for naval bases. A treaty, signed in New York on August 4, 1916, provided for the transfer of the islands to the United States at the slightly reduced price of $25 million. Both governments promptly ratified the treaty, and the United States took formal possession on March 31, 1917.

Between 1916 and 1931, St. Thomas, St. John, and St. Croix were governed by an American naval officer appointed by the President of the United States, and by local councils. The Interior Department administered the islands beginning in 1931; meanwhile, in 1927, the islanders had received American citizenship. An Organic Act in 1936 greatly enlarged the electorate and self-government of the American Virgin Islands but reserved final control over the affairs of the islands to the President and Congress of the United States.

2. WILSON AND PEACEMAKING, 1914–1916

Early Attempts at Peacemaking

No sooner had the fighting started in August 1914 than men began to talk of peace. Wilson offered American "good offices," or mediation, to the belligerents immediately after the outbreak of hostilities. A short time later, he tried to prevent Japan's entrance on the Allied side. Failure in these first overtures did not deflect the eager would-be peacemaker from his course; indeed, before 1917 all of his policies pursued one ultimate goal—his mediation of the war in Europe. Wilson sent his confidant, Colonel Edward M. House, to Europe in the early months of 1915 to explore further the possibilities of American mediation.

Up to this point, Wilson had been feeling his way. He moved more aggressively after the *Lusitania* and *Arabic* crises, because the British foreign secretary, Sir Edward Grey, indicated that his government might be willing to discuss peace terms with certain guarantees from the United States. Wilson sent Colonel House back to London in January 1916 to press for an Anglo-American plan for peace. Under the provisions of this plan, Great Britain and France would request the American President to call a peace conference. The United States would not only issue the invitation, but also would probably enter the war if Germany refused the call. If the peace conference met, the United States would cooperate with the Allies in demanding a reasonable settlement and the establishment of a league of nations to maintain peace in the future. If the Germans proved uncooperative at this point, the United

States, again, would probably enter the war on the Allied side.

House, in his discussions in London, made it very clear that Wilson, when he talked about a reasonable settlement, had in mind a peace of reconciliation accompanied by substantial disarmament and the establishment of a league of nations. The United States would support the restoration of Belgium, France's claim to Alsace-Lorraine, and certain other Allied war aims. But House insisted that Germany would have to be compensated also, and at no time did he promise that the United States would go to war to achieve any particular Allied war objective. This, precisely, was the rub, insofar as the British leaders were concerned. Grey initialed a memorandum which embodied the Wilson-House plan on February 22, 1916, but the foreign secretary carefully stipulated that the British and French governments would decide when the plan was to be implemented.

The Sussex Crisis

While House was in London negotiating what is known as the House-Grey Memorandum, Wilson and Lansing were beset by a host of difficulties at home. One of them was the problem of armed ships. Late in 1915, the Allies began to arm both passenger liners and merchantmen. The Germans argued that it would be very dangerous for submarine commanders to surface their frail craft in order to demand that armed merchant ships stop and submit to search. Lansing, with Wilson's approval, on January 18, 1916, proposed to the Allied governments that they disarm their merchantmen in return for a pledge by the Germans that they would not sink ships without warning. This proposal enraged the British leaders and seriously endangered the continuation of House's negotiations. Wilson thereupon withdrew the proposal and announced that the American government would defend the right of Americans to travel on ships which were armed *defensively* and did not threaten the security of an attacking submarine. Wilson's announcement set off a rebellion in the House of Representatives which threatened to take control of foreign policy out of his hands. A resolution, introduced by Representative Jeff McLemore of Texas, forbade Americans to travel on armed foreign ships. A furious fight ensued, and the McLemore Resolution seemed certain to pass; but Wilson finally obtained the tabling of the resolution, although only by reassuring Congress that he did not intend to go to war if the Germans sank a ship which had acted aggressively toward an attacking submarine.

The controversy with Germany came to a new and threatening head soon afterward, when a German U-boat torpedoed the unarmed French Channel packet *Sussex* on March 24 with heavy loss of life. Americans were aboard, but none died. In the belief that the British were eager to implement the House-Grey Memorandum, Wilson delivered an ultimatum to the German government. He declared that the United States would break diplomatic relations if German submarines did not cease their attacks against merchantmen without warning. The German leaders capitulated, but at the same time they stated their own views. They threatened to resume the unrestricted submarine campaign against Allied ships if the United States failed to force the British to observe international law in their blockade practices.

Mediation Fails

Wilson now lost no time in trying to put the House-Grey Memorandum in operation. In a speech in Washington on May 27, 1916, he announced that the United States was prepared to join a postwar league of nations. Next, Wilson and House began to put heavy pressure on the British government to give its consent to American mediation under the House-Grey Memorandum. The British, actually, had never taken that memorandum seriously. They would never accept Wilson's mediation so long as they thought that they had a chance to win. During protracted negotiations, the British revealed that they did not intend to submit to what they considered a risky American mediation.

The London government's negative replies convinced Wilson that the British were fighting for unworthy objectives. A series of events in 1916 confirmed Wilson's suspicion and caused him and many Americans to turn sharply against the Allies. One of these events was the British army's severe suppression of a rebellion by Irish freedom fighters which broke out in Dublin on Easter Sunday. In addition, the British began to censor American mail which went to Europe and forbade their subjects to deal with American firms which maintained any trade with the Central Powers. These latter measures seem trivial in retrospect, but Wilson and many Americans deeply resented them as flagrant violations of American sovereignty and national dignity. Anti-British feeling ran so high, in fact, that Congress, at Wilson's instigation, authorized the Chief Executive to take severe retaliatory measures against the British in certain circumstances.

The Election of 1916

Meanwhile, leaders in both parties had been laying plans for the presidential election. The Republicans were in a dire dilemma. They had to nominate a candidate acceptable to such conflicting groups within the party as former progressives, conservatives, the large antiwar midwestern Republican element, and advocates of a strong foreign policy against Germany. The Republican convention, which opened in Chicago on June 8, solved the problem by nominating Charles Evans Hughes, Associate Justice of the Supreme Court.

There never was any doubt that the Democrats would renominate Wilson, and the Democratic convention, which met at St. Louis, named him by acclamation on June 14. Wilson personally wrote the party's platform, which expressed the ideals and embodied the objectives of advanced progressives. The biggest surprise of the St. Louis convention was the numerous demonstrations for peace which followed every reference to Wilson's success in keeping the country out of war. Indeed, "He kept us out of war" was written into the Democratic platform as the slogan of the party.

Hughes stumped the country from New York to California and denounced the administration for its alleged bungling diplomacy, weak Mexican policy, and inefficiency. He repeatedly said that he stood for the "firm and unflinching maintenance of all the rights of American citizens on land and sea." But when asked what he would do if elected—whether he would compel Great Britain to relax its blockade, or go to war with Germany—he fell silent. Wilson conducted a "front-porch" campaign from his summer home in New Jersey. Wilson fully realized Hughes' dilemma and hit repeatedly on the issue of war or peace by implying that the Republicans would take the country into the war. Moreover, Wilson eloquently defended his administration's progressive achievements and frankly said that the Democrats had taken over the Progressive platform of 1912 and had enacted most of its planks into law. And when Hughes called the Adamson Act a cowardly surrender to organized labor, Wilson replied that the eight-hour day should be standard for *all* American workers. Labor and farm leaders, social-justice champions, social workers, and many former Progressives and Socialists responded by moving into the Wilson camp. The new democracy which Wilson had worked so hard to build was now in existence, and the two streams of progressivism which had hitherto diverged were now united, at least temporarily.

Even so, the United States was still very much a Republican country, and the election was the closest since the election of 1876. Before midnight of election day, November 7, it was clear that Hughes had carried virtually all eastern states, plus Indiana, Illinois, Michigan, and Wisconsin. The New York *World,* the leading Democratic newspaper in the country, conceded victory to Hughes. But Wilson's prospects grew brighter as returns began to come in from the western states early in the morning of November 8. By the following day, it was certain that Wilson had carried California by a slim margin, and therewith the election. The electoral vote was 277 for Wilson to 254 for Hughes; the popular vote, 9,129,000 to 8,538,000. Actually, Wilson's triumph was one of the greatest achievements in the history of the presidency. He increased his popular vote in 1916 by nearly 50 per cent over his popular vote in 1912. And in some states, such as California, Wilson nearly doubled his popular vote in 1916 over that of 1912.

3. AMERICAN INTERVENTION

Conflict with Germany

A shrewd analyst of public opinion, Wilson was convinced by the end of the election that the American people ardently desired to avoid involvement in war over disputes with Germany about the right of Americans to travel on Allied ships, whether armed or unarmed. But Wilson also knew that the European rivals were growing increasingly desperate and that they would so intensify the war on the seas that it might become impossible to avoid entanglement. Wilson also wanted to play what he believed was the noblest role given to a leader—that of peacemaker. In November 1916, he therefore set out upon a course of independent mediation.

Wilson's first step, taken on December 18, 1916, was to send a moving appeal to all the belligerents. He implored them to think about peace and asked that they state the terms upon which they would be willing to conclude a settlement. The Germans, who had already issued their own call for a peace conference, returned an evasive reply to Washington. The Allies, egged on secretly by Secretary Lansing, announced sweeping terms such as could be achieved only by a smashing military victory. Undisturbed, Wilson moved to the second stage of his plan. He opened secret negotiations with the British and German governments for a peace conference in the immediate future.

While he waited for replies from Berlin and London, Wilson appeared before the Senate on January 22, 1917. There he explained the conditions on which the United States would "give its formal and solemn adherence to a league of peace" to be formed to help to enforce the peace settlement which would be made. The present war had to be ended first, he announced, but it had to be ended by terms which would create a peace worth guaranteeing. First of all, it had to be "a peace without victory," for victory "would mean peace forced upon the loser, a victor's terms imposed upon the vanquished. It . . . would rest, not permanently, but only as upon quicksand." Only a "peace between equals" could last. Wilson went on to list what he thought should be the terms: limitation of armaments; freedom of the seas; self-determination for peoples under alien domination, particularly the Poles; and security against aggression for all nations.

These words not only raised the hopes of war-weary peoples all over Europe; they also drew favorable responses from leaders in Great Britain and Germany. The British government indicated that it might go to the peace table. But the German government could not return so positive a reply, for it had decided in early January to launch total submarine blockade against the British Isles and other areas. U-boats already were on their way to their stations.

So the Germans replied, first, by announcing that submarines would begin unrestricted operations on February 1. They would sink all ships—neutral as well as Allied—without warning. The Germans added that they would permit a limited number of American passenger ships to sail without danger; and they postponed attacks against American ships until mid-March. The Imperial German Chancellor, in a confidential message to the White House, also divulged some of the German peace terms, but not the most extreme ones, and begged Wilson to continue his efforts for peace.

Wilson broke diplomatic relations with the German Empire on February 3, mainly as a protest against the new German submarine decree. But Wilson made it clear, when he broke relations, that he would not go to war merely because the Germans sank Allied ships. He continued to hope and pray for peace. However, two events soon pushed him nearer to the brink of war. One was the disclosure by the British of a telegram (which British intelligence had intercepted) from the German foreign secretary, Arthur Zimmermann, to the German minister in Mexico. In the message, Zimmermann invited Mexico to attack the United States in the event of war between the United States and Germany. In return, Germany would pay Mexico handsomely in money and in the restoration of her "lost provinces" in the American Southwest. The other event was the near paralysis of American foreign trade which occurred when American shipowners refused to send their unarmed vessels into the blockaded area.

Wilson responded on February 26 by asking Congress for authority to arm American merchant ships and to take other measures to protect American commerce. Strong opposition to the proposal developed at once in the House of Representatives, whereupon the President gave the text of the Zimmermann telegram to the newspapers on February 28. It was published on the following day and aroused such anger across the nation that the House of Representatives approved an armed-ship bill at once. But in the Senate the measure met the stubborn resistance of about a dozen men, headed by La

Follette. They were not so much opposed to arming merchantmen as to giving the President power to wage what they feared would be an undeclared maritime war. They took advantage of the rule of unlimited debate to prevent the bill's passage until the mandatory adjournment of Congress on March 4. Wilson, then, on March 9, invoked the authority of an old piracy statute and instructed the Navy Department to put guns and gun crews on merchant vessels. The armed American liner *St. Louis* soon afterward left New York and passed safely through the submarine zone.

The Decision for War

Woodrow Wilson suffered intense agony during the first three weeks of March 1917 as he tried to decide between peace and war. In spite of everything that had happened, he still wanted desperately to avoid belligerency. He told a French philosopher that God would hold him personally responsible for the death of any Americans if the United States entered the war. He had no illusions about Allied war objectives; they were, he knew, punitive. He realized, too, that participation in a total war would cause grave damage to democracy at home. He would have preferred to follow a course of armed neutrality; but he felt drawn irresistibly to a decision for war, which he reached on about March 20, for the following reasons:

1. The Zimmermann telegram had caused Wilson to lose all faith in the German government. He believed that it proved that the military leaders were the true masters of Germany, and that these leaders had adopted policies which would inevitably bring the United States into the war.

2. Wilson concluded that armed neutrality could not protect American maritime rights against the German challenge. Armed neutrality did not provide sufficient protection to American merchantmen, and Wilson believed that it would eventually lead to declaration of war between the two countries.

3. Wilson was heartened by news of the Russian Revolution on March 15, which drove Nicholas II from his throne. It would be easier, Wilson thought, to make a lasting peace with a democratic Russian government involved in the peace conference.

4. German submarines on March 18 sank three American merchantmen, one with heavy losses of American lives. Demonstrations and demands for war swept the country. These signs of a growing national sentiment for war, however, merely reinforced a decision which Wilson made on other grounds.

5. Most important, Wilson was convinced that Europe could not endure its agony much longer. The war was in its final stages, and American belligerency would hasten its end. Moreover, Wilson knew that he would have much greater influence at the peace conference as a belligerent leader rather than as a neutral outsider.

Thus Wilson, on the evening of April 2, 1917, went before a joint session of Congress to ask it to recognize that a state of war existed between the United States and the German Empire. Wilson reviewed the series of acts which proved that the German autocracy was not and never could be the friend of the United States. He asserted that the American people had no quarrel with the German people. He insisted that America's motives should be "not revenge or the victorious assertion of the physical might of the nation, but only the vindication of human rights,'' and he ended with a statement of liberal war aims.

On that same evening, resolutions were introduced into both houses of Congress which acknowledged that a state of war already existed between Germany and the United States because of German aggressions. After a heated debate, the Senate adopted the resolution by a vote of eighty-two to six on April 4. The debate in the House lasted through the following day and night. Congressmen finally approved the resolution by a vote of 373 to fifty at 3 A.M. on the morning of April 6, and Wilson signed it on the same day. For the first time in more than a century, the United States was involved in a major European war, and, for the first time in their history, Americans were about to enter on the European stage as a military power.

4. THE FIRST WORLD WAR AND THE AMERICAN PEOPLE

American Involvement: The Military Effect

When they entered the war, most Americans, including Wilson and the members of his cabinet, believed that their contributions would be limited to naval cooperation and credit and supplies to the Allies. Credit was forthcoming in abundance (the Allies borrowed about $7 billion from the United States in 1917 and 1918) and saved the Allied war effort literally from collapse. However, British and French delegations, dispatched to Washington in April 1917, made it clear that the Allies were scraping the bottom of their manpower reserves and that American reinforcements were desperately needed. In response, Wilson obtained quick approval by Congress of a Selective Service Act to raise a huge national army in the shortest possible time. Eventually, the selective draft produced 2,810,296 men; by the end of the war, some 4,000,000 men and women were serving in the military forces.

General Pershing, commander of the American Expeditionary Force, arrived in Paris on June 14, 1917, and had some 14,500 men under his command by the autumn of that year. A series of events catastrophic to Allied fortunes emphasized the desperate need for rapid and massive American reinforcements. In October 1917, the Italians suffered a crushing defeat at the hands of a combined German-Austrian army. In the following month, the Bolsheviks seized control of the Russian government and sued for an armistice with the Germans. As a consequence, forty German divisions were freed to be thrown against Allied troops on the western front. There, in March 1918, the German army began a great offensive—the second Marne offensive—to break through the British and French lines and capture both the Channel ports and Paris before American men and munitions could turn the tide. Although the Germans conquered 3,000 square miles of territory and took 150,000 prisoners, they failed to achieve either of their main objectives.

The American navy was fully mobilized and prepared for instant action when Wilson signed the declaration of war. The gravest threat to the allies at this time was not on land, but on the seas, for it seemed that German U-boats might well succeed in reducing the British to starvation and surrender. The American government set aside plans for construction of battleships and large cruisers and concentrated upon the production of destroyers and other subchasers. Moreover, all available destroyers steamed to British waters to help the British navy to convoy merchantmen. This convoy system, introduced largely at Wilson's insistence, turned the tide against the submarines in the last months of 1917.

Some 112,000 Americans sacrificed their lives for the Allied-American victory, as compared to 1,700,000 Russians, 1,385,300 Frenchmen, and 900,000 Britons and men from the British dominions. The Italians and Serbs also suffered huge losses. But the American contribution came in the nick of time, both on the seas and on the western front. It turned the tide against what might have been, without American help, an irresistible German assault.

American troops participated heavily in the land fighting when the 1st Division captured the strongly fortified town of Cantigny on May 28, 1918, at the height of the second Battle of the Marne. Three days later, the 2nd Division and several regiments of marines helped the French to stop the Germans at Chateau-Thierry on the Marne River, only forty-two miles from Paris. By mid-July, the German drive had been checked at all points. Marshal Ferdinand Foch, the Supreme Allied Commander, then began a counteroffensive that lasted four months. The American army in France, now more than 1,000,000 strong, participated significantly in this drive which brought the war to an end in November 1918, one year earlier than the military leaders had anticipated.

Mobilization and the Home Front

It had been a long time since the American people had fought a total war, and the organization of the war effort during the Civil War had been so inefficient as to furnish few guidelines for Wilson in 1917. Roughly speaking, the government's efforts at economic mobilization during the First World War went through two stages. During the first, lasting from April 1917 to about the end of that year, the administration relied mainly, but not altogether,* on voluntary and cooperative efforts. During the second stage, after about December 1917, the administration moved firmly and relentlessly to establish sweeping and complete control over every important phase of economic life. During this second stage, Wilson acted under his emergency war powers and under the authority of the Overman Act of May 1918.

Farmers and housewives were mobilized by the Food Administration, headed by Herbert Hoover, who had already gained a reputation for efficiency as director of the Belgian Relief Commission. Adverse weather conditions hampered Hoover's efforts to increase the production of wheat, corn, and hogs, but his system of indirect rationing and voluntary reduction in home consumption of food was so successful that the United States was able to export three times as much food in 1918–1919 as in 1916.

In 1917, many American railroads were run-down largely because of the ICC's refusal to permit the railroads to increase their rates to meet rising

---

*For example, the administration, under the Army Reorganization Act of 1916, had complete control over the railroads. The Lever Food and Fuel Act of August 1917 gave the government control over the prices of foodstuffs and fuels. And the government controlled the prices which it paid when it purchased for itself or for the Allies such commodities as steel, copper, lumber, and cement.

costs. Wilson took over the railroads on December 26, 1917, and named Secretary of the Treasury William G. McAdoo as Director-General. McAdoo abolished competition, pooled terminals and rolling stock, poured more than $500 million into long-needed equipment and improvements, and created an efficient nationwide railway system.

The government moved in various directions to build a "bridge of ships" to western Europe. A Shipping Board was already in existence when the United States entered the war. It seized eighty-seven German ships in American ports; they totaled more than 500,000 tons. The Shipping Board also commandeered some 3,000,000 tons of merchant ships in process of construction, and later purchased about 500,000 tons of Dutch ships in American harbors. In addition, the Shipping Board's Emergency Fleet Corporation built ninety-four shipways designed to construct some 15,000,000 tons of new ships. However, these shipways had turned out only about 500,000 tons of ships because the war ended a year ahead of schedule.

All of the aforementioned efforts would have been in vain without a smoothly functioning and highly coordinated production of uniforms, guns, and all the other equipment needed by the armed forces. The administration tried hard all through the first months of the war to achieve industrial mobilization through the voluntary cooperation of businessmen and industrialists. These efforts collapsed in the face of a wild scramble for raw materials and goods, and Wilson, on March 4, 1918, gave sweeping new powers to the already established War Industries Board. The new head of the board, Bernard M. Baruch, soon brought order out of chaos, mainly by controlling prices and the allocation of scarce raw materials such as steel. By the spring of 1918, the enormous American industrial machine had been tightly harnessed for a victory effort.

Labor

Labor received consideration during the war such as it had never enjoyed before. Four million workers or potential workers were drained off into the armed forces, while immigration, which had totaled more than 1,000,000 in 1914, shrank to 110,000 in 1918. A million women new to the work force filled the gap to some extent, but a chronic shortage of labor was one of the difficulties with which the government had to wrestle. To prevent wasteful turnover in employment, the Department of Labor established a United States Employment Service which placed more than 3,700,000 workers in vital industries.

Organized labor rallied to the war effort, and the AFL agreed not to engage in strikes during the war. But strikes did occur, sometimes because employers would not recognize the AFL as a bargaining agent, sometimes because workers would not accept the terms which employers offered. Hence Wilson established a National War Labor Board in April 1918 to serve as a court of arbitration in labor disputes. Some 1,500 cases were submitted to the National War Labor Board, and almost all of them were successfully arbitrated. In the few cases in which labor or management refused to accept the decision, Wilson commandeered the plants involved. Labor was held to its promise not to strike; but employers were forbidden to discharge workers for union activities and were encouraged to lower the hours of labor. As a consequence, total union membership grew from 2,722,000 in 1916 to 4,046,000 in 1919; and hours of labor declined from an average of 53.5 per week in 1914 to 50.4 per week in 1920. As a result of high wages and overtime payments, moreover, most workers actually were in a better economic position at the end of the war than at the beginning. By 1918, labor's real income had increased, generally, 20 per cent above the prewar level.

Democracy with a Vengeance

The direct costs of the war to the American people by 1920 were about $33.5 billion. The greatest domestic struggles raged over the question of the amounts to be raised by loans and by taxation. Progressives and socialists demanded that the entire costs of the war be met by taxation, particularly upon the rich. Spokesmen of the wealthy naturally replied that most of the costs should be raised by borrowing. Wilson and his Secretary of the Treasury, McAdoo, supported the advocates of heavy taxation.

It was not possible to raise the entire cost of the war without the disruption of the economy. However, the Revenue Act of October 1917 imposed heavy excess profits taxes, increased maximum income taxes on individuals and corporations to about 65 per cent, and increased estate taxes. The Revenue Act of 1918 increased the excess profits tax and raised maximum income taxes to 77 per cent. As a result, for the first time in American history, those persons most able to pay were saddled with the burdens of the costs of a war, while the real income of most farmers and workers actually increased during the wartime period.

Civil Liberties and Domestic Dissent

"Once lead this people into war," Woodrow Wilson told a newspaper editor just before the United States entered the conflict, "and they'll forget there ever was such a thing as tolerance. To fight you must be brutal and ruthless, and the spirit of ruthless brutality will enter into the very fibre of our national life, infecting Congress, the courts, the policeman on the beat, the man in the street."

To a large degree, Wilson's doleful prophecy came true. Ironically, it came true because the administration helped to contribute to a nationwide hysteria. Only seven days after he signed the war declaration, Wilson created the Committee on Public Information, headed by George Creel, a journalist, to generate public enthusiasm for the war effort. Such an agency was necessary, Wilson believed, because the American people at the outset were still bitterly divided over the wisdom of fighting Germany. Indeed, it is doubtful that a majority of the people really approved the war resolution. To convert what might have been a hostile public, Creel went to work on the biggest and most successful advertising campaign in American history.

The IWW and the Socialist party openly opposed participation in the war, and the IWW fomented strikes in the western copper mines and the lumber camps of the Northwest. No government engaged in fighting a modern total war has ever been willing to tolerate open opposition to the war effort. During the Civil War, Lincoln suppressed opposition ruthlessly, mainly through military courts. Congress responded during the First World War with the Espionage Act of June 1917. It provided heavy punishment for any persons who willfully helped the enemy, engaged in espionage, and obstructed the draft. This measure also empowered the Postmaster General to deny the use of the mails to any newspapers or magazines which, in his opinion and then in the opinion of the courts, advocated treason or forcible resistance to the war effort.

Hysteria, egged on by volunteer organizations which often acted like vigilante groups, mounted as prosecutions were announced, particularly when the government arrested and tried most of the leaders (including Eugene V. Debs) of the IWW and the Socialist party. Fear of internal subversion reached such a height that Congress, in the spring of 1918, adopted a Sedition Act which empowered the federal government to punish persons guilty of disloyal, profane, or abusive language about the American flag, form of government, or uniform.

Postmaster General Albert S. Burleson used his power over the mails severely and, at times, capriciously. On the whole, however, the federal government enforced the Espionage and Sedition acts with considerable restraint and due process. Only 2,000 persons were indicted under these measures; of these, 1,000 were convicted. All of the European belligerents established military courts which shot alleged spies and opponents of the war. There was a tremendous demand in the United States in late 1917 and early 1918, led by Theodore Roosevelt, to establish military courts. Wilson headed it off definitively by a public statement which compared military courts with Prussian militarism and clearly implied that he would veto a measure for military courts then pending in the Senate. Consequently, no person was executed in the United States for alleged treason or sabotage.

Most of the public fury was turned against antiwar radicals and German Americans who did not satisfy the public demand for all-out support of the war effort. Many states forbade the teaching of the German language, while local citizens resorted to such absurdities as renaming sauerkraut "liberty cabbage" and German measles "liberty measles."

The Supreme Court had no alternative but to support the Espionage and Sedition acts since they were based upon the government's inherent wartime powers and numerous judicial precedents. Justice Oliver Wendell Holmes, in Schenck v. the United States (1919), upheld the Espionage Act on the ground that the government had a right to protect itself against internal threats to its security. Moreover, the Court, in Abrams v. the United States (1919), gave the government carte blanche to move against seditionists.

5. TOWARD A NEW WORLD ORDER

Wilson and the Liberal Peace

Woodrow Wilson never deluded himself into thinking that intervention would be a blessing for the American people. However, once he made his decision for war, he tried to make the best of it. He attempted to rally all the peoples of the western world in an irresistible movement for a peace settlement which would remove the causes of future conflicts and establish machinery to preserve peace. As we have seen, Wilson had, in fact, begun his crusade before the United States entered the conflict. His posture and policies inevitably changed after American entry, but his long-range objectives—a peace of reconciliation and the reconstruction of the world community—did not change. He carefully dissociated himself from Allied war aims (he insisted on speaking of the United States as an "associate" of the Allies), and he waited for some move from Germany and Austria-Hungary to open peace negotiations.

Wilson, on August 27, 1917, responded warmly to a peace appeal which Pope Benedict XV had issued earlier in the month. The United States sought no "punitive indemnities" or "dismemberment of empires." But it had to know what the German terms were. The German government replied to the Pope evasively, and the Allies were strongly opposed to any discussions of peace.

Wilson's eagerness to begin a public campaign for peace mounted all during the autumn of 1917. He did not miss the opportunity to speak out once the Bolsheviks had seized power in Russia. The Communists published some of the Allied secret treaties for division of the spoils of war and called upon workers and soldiers in the West to convert the war into a proletarian revolution.

Wilson announced his program to the world in his Fourteen Points Address to Congress on January 8, 1918. It was high time, he said, for peace-loving nations to avow their ideals and objectives. These Wilson summarized in a series of general points, which included "open covenants, openly arrived at" freedom of the seas, reduction of armaments, removal of artificial barriers to international trade, an impartial settlement of colonial claims, and the establishment of a league of nations. Three points—a league of nations, restoration of Belgium, and self-determination for Russia—were, Wilson said, indispensable to a just settlement. Other points, including the return of Alsace-Lorraine to France, an independent Poland with access to the sea, and autonomy for the subject peoples of the Austro-Hungarian Empire, were desirable but presumably negotiable. As Wilson said, they "should," rather than "must," be achieved. There was, finally, an implied fifteenth point—that the United States had no quarrel with the German people and no desire to continue the war for selfish ends.

The Fourteen Points Address was much more than an avowal of peace aims. It was western democracy's statement in its first official debate with international communism. The Bolshevik leaders, Lenin and Trotsky, had appealed to a peace-hungry world for a universal class war to destroy western capitalism. Wilson appealed for peace in order to give modern western civilization a second chance.

The second Marne offensive cut short Wilson's hopes for immediate peace discussions. Moreover, the Germans rebuilt their strength by gaining control of large parts of eastern Europe through the harsh Treaty of Brest-Litovsk which they imposed upon Russia in March 1918. The war, Wilson now realized, had to be fought to the bitter end. But even while the ever growing Allied armies fought with increasing ferocity, Wilson refused to yield to the passion of hatred and a desire for revenge. On the contrary, in the Four Additional Points of July 4 and in the Five Additional Points of September 27, 1918, he set forth his liberal war aims more clearly and eloquently than ever before.

The War Ends

A series of events in the summer and autumn of 1918 gravely impaired Wilson's ability to establish a new world order. The first of these was the Allied decision to intervene in the civil war then raging in Russia between the Bolsheviks and various more conservative groups called Whites. Wilson strongly believed that military intervention in Russia was futile and wrong, because the Russian people had the right to determine their own institutions and form of government. But, under heavy pressure from the Allies, he reluctantly consented to a limited American cooperation with Allied plans. With the approval of the Bolshevik government, he sent a force of some 4,000 to 5,000 men to northern Russia in order to prevent the Germans from seizing military supplies at the ports of Murmansk and Archangel. Wilson dispatched another force of 7,000 men to Siberia to guarantee a safe exit for a Czech army formed from Austro-Hungarian prisoners of war in Russia. More important, Wilson also wanted to keep a close watch on a large Japanese army which had moved into Siberia. Both American expeditions went with strict presidential orders not to intervene in the Russian civil war.

The second blow to Wilson's hopes was the sudden collapse of the Imperial German government in late October. Wilson wanted German participation in the coming peace conference, and he hoped that German military power would, to some degree, offset Allied military might at the conference table. The Germans appealed to Wilson in October for an armistice based upon the Fourteen Points, and Wilson forced the Allies to agree to peace on these terms, with two exceptions. But William II abdicated and fled to Holland, and German morale had collapsed by the time that the Armistice was signed on November 11. Germany was completely at the mercy of the Allies, and Wilson had lost one of his crucial bargaining weapons.

The third event was a very considerable diminution of Wilson's position as spokesman of the American people. On October 25, at the end of a hotly contested congressional campaign, Wilson appealed for the election of a Democratic Congress. His great mistake was to declare that world opinion would interpret a Republican victory as the repudiation of his leadership by the American people. For reasons entirely unrelated to the coming peace settlement, voters elected Republican majorities in both houses of Congress on November 5, and, as Wilson had predicted, the defeat seriously undermined his leadership.

Wilson, nevertheless, proceeded with preparations for the peace conference scheduled to meet in Paris in January 1919. Because he believed that only he could provide the leadership necessary for a permanent settlement, he went to Paris as head of the American Peace Commission. He ignored the results of the recent election and failed to name any prominent Republican to accompany him to the peace conference. This—the fourth event—would have serious repercussions in the near future, when a Republican-dominated Senate would review Wilson's handiwork at Paris.

The Paris Peace Conference

In spite of these handicaps, Wilson went to Europe in late December 1918 with the determination to fight for a just peace. Wilson visited Paris, London, Rome, and other places before the conference opened; everywhere, he was hailed as a new messiah who came from the new world to redeem the old.

It was a different story when the conference opened in Paris on January 18, 1919. No representatives from the defeated powers or Russia were present. Wilson stood alone against the Allied leaders—Prime Minister David Lloyd George of Great Britain, Premier Georges Clemenceau of France, and Prime Minister Vittorio Orlando of Italy. These statesmen, under pressure from nationalistic majorities within their own countries, were determined to divide the territories of the vanquished and to make Germany pay the costs of the war. The American President held certain advantages in the uneven contest. Acknowledged as the one disinterested statesman at Paris, Wilson spoke for liberal opinion throughout the world. He also had one weapon as a last resort—the threat to withdraw and abandon Europe to its own devices.

Wilson declared to his advisers on their voyage to Europe, "Tell me what's right, and I'll fight for it." He did indeed fight throughout the conference, heroically and doggedly, for achievement of the Fourteen Points. He made a number of significant compromises in the peace treaty. Under its provisions, the Allies acquired all former German colonies—Japan, for example, received former German rights in the Chinese province of Shantung—and a potentially huge bill for war damages was imposed on Germany. But Wilson won many more of his Fourteen Points than he lost. Belgium was restored, Alsace-Lorraine returned to France. The former subject peoples of the Austro-Hungarian Empire won independence and self-determination. An independent Poland with access to the sea was established. By dramatically threatening to leave the conference, Wilson also prevented the French from annexing German territory west of the Rhine and establishing a Rhenish republic under French control.

Wilson's greatest victory, however, was the establishment of the League of Nations. He had come to Paris for the chief purpose of writing into the peace treaty the covenant, or constitution, of such an organization. He warned the delegates a month in advance of the conference that, unless they heeded the "mandate of mankind," they would make themselves "the most conspicuous and deserved failures in the history of the world." A few delegates, such as Lord Robert Cecil of Great Britain, Jan Smuts of South Africa, and Léon Bourgeois of France, were enthusiastic supporters of the League. But many leaders, particularly Clemenceau, regarded it with indifference.

Wilson, however, was determined that the League should come first. At his insistence, a commission of ten members was named on January 25, 1919, to draft the covenant of the League. The most important of the provisions of the covenant concerned the reduction of armaments, guarantees of security for all member nations, arbitration of disputes, and measures to be taken against nations that went to war in violation of the covenant. Article X, which Wilson called the heart of the agreement, read in part: "The members of the League undertake to respect and preserve as against external aggression the territorial integrity and existing political independence of all the members of the League."

The treaty was completed and presented to German envoys in early May. Although the Germans protested strongly against the violations of the Fourteen Points, they were in no position to renew hostilities, and, after minor changes were made by the conference, the treaty was signed in the Hall of Mirrors in the Versailles Palace outside Paris on June 28, 1919.

6. THE FAILURE OF THE VERSAILLES TREATY

The Treaty Fight Begins

There were several signs before the conference ended that Wilson would encounter strong opposition in the United States Senate if he insisted upon incorporating the covenant of the League of Nations into the Versailles Treaty. Wilson returned to the United States in late February 1919 to sign bills during the closing days of Congress. On this occasion, he conferred with the House and Senate foreign relations committees and heard criticism of the covenant. Critics noted that it contained no recognition of

Europe after the Versailles Treaty

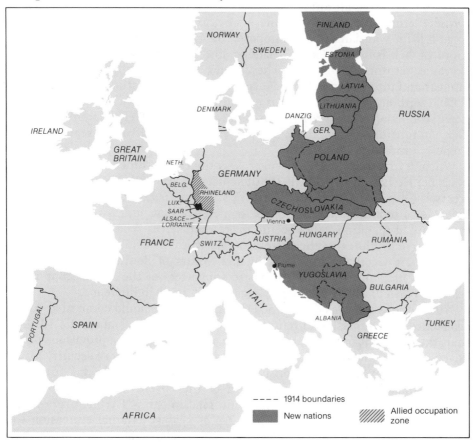

the Monroe Doctrine, did not exclude internal affairs from the jurisdiction of the League, and made no provision for the withdrawal of member nations.

Wilson defied his critics in a speech in New York just before he returned to France. He warned that senators would find the covenant so deeply embedded in the treaty that they could not cut it out. Henry Cabot Lodge of Massachusetts, the Republican leader in the Senate, responded with a statement signed by more than one third of the senators. The signers declared in effect that the upper house would never approve the treaty with the covenant in its present form. Consequently, Wilson set to work and obtained all of the changes which his critics demanded, even though the effort required him to make new compromises with the Allied leaders.

Immediately after his return to the United States in July 1919, Wilson presented the Versailles Treaty to the Senate in an eloquent and confident address. All superficial signs seemed to indicate that his confidence was well-founded. To be sure, a few newspapers were already raising cries of alarm against what they called an entangling alliance. A small group of isolationist senators, called "bitter enders," had announced that they would fight to the bitter end to prevent ratification of the treaty. But Wilson moved serenely in the confidence that the overwhelming majority of Americans was on his side.

Wilson did not know it, but Lodge, new chairman of the Foreign Relations Committee, had decided to kill the treaty if he possibly could do so. Lodge despised Wilson for many of the same reasons that had led his good friend Theodore Roosevelt to abhor the President. Lodge was, moreover, a bitter partisan, who did not intend to help the Democratic party earn credit for a successful peace settlement. Most important, Lodge was himself an extreme nationalist. As such, he disapproved of American participation in the League of Nations and preferred an alliance with Great Britain and France.

Lodge also was a wily strategist. He did not dare at first to oppose the treaty openly; hence, he used delaying tactics in order to give its opponents time to mobilize and get their message to the country. This the Massachusetts senator did by reading aloud every word of the treaty to his committee, and by holding long hearings.

Wilson did what he could to win the support of Republican senators. His conferences revealed that the treaty was in danger, and he decided to go to the country in order, as he put it, to purify the wells of public opinion poisoned by the opponents of the League. He set out from Washington on September 3, traveled more than 8,000 miles, and delivered some thirty-seven major addresses to large and enthusiastic audiences all the way to the Pacific Coast and back to Colorado. Altogether, the speeches were one of the great forensic efforts in American history, but they took a heavy toll of Wilson's limited physical reserves. He collapsed after an eloquent address at Pueblo, Colorado, on September 25. His doctor canceled the rest of Wilson's speeches and sped the presidential train back to Washington. A few days later, on October 2, Wilson suffered a massive stroke which paralyzed his left side.

Meanwhile, on September 10, Lodge had reported the treaty to the Senate with a number of reservations and amendments. The amendments were voted down, whereupon Lodge offered fourteen reservations. Most of them were unimportant. However, the Senator's second reservation stated that the United States, upon ratifying the treaty, assumed no obligations under Article

X of the covenant to preserve the independence and territorial integrity of member nations, and would not commit its armed forces to uphold the covenant unless Congress, by joint resolution in every instance, so provided. Wilson had announced his willingness to accept what he called "interpretive" reservations, but he absolutely refused to accept the second Lodge reservation on the ground that it nullified rather than ratified the treaty. Hence when the treaty came up for a vote in the Senate on November 19, 1919, most Democrats joined the "bitter enders" to defeat approval with the Lodge reservations. On a second vote, the Republicans and "bitter enders" combined to defeat approval without the Lodge reservations.

Debacle and Defeat

Most Americans were shocked and angered; they demanded that Lodge and Wilson reconcile their differences. Lodge wavered under the pressure, then stood firm. Wilson replied that there could be no compromise on Article X, the "heart of the covenant." He also announced that the presidential election of 1920 should be a "great and solemn referendum" on the League of Nations. Wilson's stubborn stand caused public opinion to turn sharply against him, but he would not budge. When the treaty came up for a vote for a second time on March 19, 1920, Wilson again instructed Democratic senators to oppose approval with the Lodge reservations. Enough of them heeded Wilson's command to defeat approval.

Wilson has been accused of infanticide, of killing his own child—the League of Nations. It is certainly true that he prevented Senate approval on the final vote. As is true of all important decisions, the reasons for Wilson's decision not to permit approval of the Versailles Treaty with the Lodge reservations were mixed and various. First, he believed deeply that the question of the character of American participation in the League was so fundamental that it could not be compromised. As he had said repeatedly during his western tour, the United States should either enter the League without crippling reservations and provide leadership in building a new world order, or else the country should stay out of the League. Second, although Wilson's illness had not weakened his ordinary mental processes, it had gravely affected his temperament and ability to make decisions. In normal health, he, himself, would probably have worked out a compromise acceptable to a large majority of senators. Finally, Wilson was so isolated in the White House that he was out of touch both with the situation on Capitol Hill and with public opinion. Perhaps he refused to accept the Lodge reservations because he believed that the Senate would not dare to reject the entire treaty merely because it did not approve of every provision of the League Covenant.

Whatever the reasons, the treaty was doomed. It was returned to the White House with the formal announcement that the Senate had been unable to obtain the constitutional two-thirds majority necessary for consent to ratification. Shortly afterward, Congress adopted a resolution which declared the war with Germany at an end. This Wilson vetoed on May 27 as "an ineffaceable stain on the gallantry and honor of the United States." The House failed to pass the resolution over the veto. Thus the United States remained technically at war with Germany until July 2, 1921, when Wilson's successor approved a resolution for a separate peace.

7. THE LEGACY OF WAR: DOMESTIC CONSEQUENCES, 1919–1920

Demobilization

The signing of the Armistice occurred so unexpectedly that the American government had no plans for a smooth transition from a wartime to a peacetime economy. Demobilization occurred almost overnight. As Wilson put it, "the moment we knew the armistice to have been signed we took the harness off." War agencies were quickly dismantled. More than two thirds of the American Expeditionary Force were back at home before the Versailles Treaty was signed. After January 1920, the only part of Pershing's forces which remained in Europe was a little American army of occupation at Coblenz.

There were urgent domestic problems which the administration and Congress had to face in spite of the overwhelming popular desire for a return to normal life. One problem was what to do with the railroads. The AFL and railroad brotherhoods urged the government to purchase the railroads and give workers a share in their management and profits. Wilson laid the problem before Congress on December 24, 1919, and warned that he would return the railroads to their owners on March 1, 1920, unless Congress decided otherwise. Congress responded with the Esch-Cummins Transportation Act of 1920, which rejected governmental ownership but vastly enlarged the powers of the Interstate Commerce Commission. The ICC was even empowered to supervise the sale of railroad securities and to consolidate competing lines into great regional systems.

Congress met another problem—disposal of the Shipping Board's fleet which now totaled 15,000,000 tons—with the Merchant Marine Act of 1920. It directed the Shipping Board to sell as many vessels as possible to private owners; however, it authorized the Emergency Fleet Corporation to operate vessels which could not be sold. Congress also approved three measures long advocated by the Wilson administration—the General Leasing Act, the Water Power Act, and the Nineteenth Amendment (see pp. 32–33, 42).

Meanwhile, the nation had embarked upon one of the most ambitious efforts at social reform in its history. This was the institution of nationwide prohibition of the manufacture and sale of intoxicating beverages. A prohibition amendment—the Eighteenth—was submitted to the states in 1917 and ratified in January 1919. In the following autumn, Congress adopted (over Wilson's veto) the Volstead Act, which defined alcoholic beverages as any which contained more than one half of 1 per cent of alcohol.

Economic and Labor Problems

The administration was powerless to cope with perhaps the most urgent postwar domestic problem—a spiraling inflation in prices caused by a wild scramble of businessmen and industrialists for scarce goods and raw materials. Wilson tried to stem the tide by establishing an Industrial Board to take the place of the War Industries Board, but the new board lacked any statutory authority whatsoever over prices and soon confessed its inability to halt rising prices. Consequently, the cost of living rose to 77 per cent above the prewar level in 1919 and to 105 per cent above the prewar level in 1920.

The most dramatic repercussion of inflation was an epidemic of strikes in 1919. All told, they involved 4,000,000 workers and cost $2 billion of loss in sales and wages. The strikes of 1919 began on November 1, when 435,000 bituminous coal miners laid down their tools. Winter was approaching, and coal supplies were short. Attorney General A. Mitchell Palmer broke this strike by obtaining an injunction from a federal judge which ordered the miners back to work on the ground that the strike violated the Lever Act, which was still technically in effect. It is doubtful that Wilson, who was extremely sick at the time, knew about Palmer's action. A federal arbitral commission eventually awarded large pay increases to the miners, who had not received a wage hike since August 1917. At about the same time, some 350,000 steelworkers walked out after the steel companies refused to grant union recognition, wage increases, and the eight-hour day. The steel strike was accompanied by widespread violence and accusations of communism against strikers; it ended in January 1920 in the complete surrender of the workers. Another strike—in Boston—seemed to lend credence to the wide-spread popular fear that the country was in the midst of a dangerous social upheaval. The police commissioner of Boston suspended nineteen policemen for organizing a union affiliated with the AFL. Thereupon, in September 1919, 90 per cent of the police force walked out. For two or three days, lawlessness threatened to engulf the city. Volunteers and guards from the Charlestown Navy Yard preserved order. Then Governor Calvin Coolidge mobilized the National Guard and backed the police commissioner's refusal to reinstate the striking policemen. When he received a telegram from Samuel Gompers urging him to show leniency to the discharged strikers, Coolidge wired: "There is no right to strike against the public safety by anybody, anywhere, anytime."

The First Red Scare and Racial Conflict

The churning events of 1919 induced an outbreak of hysteria against Communists that verged on a national madness. The hysteria began in earnest during February 1919, when workers in Seattle staged a general strike. The mayor of that city charged that the strike was the first step in a Bolshevik and IWW plot to paralyze the nation. A crude scheme to assassinate a number of prominent Americans was uncovered in April; then a bomb blew off the front of Attorney General Palmer's home in June, and other bombs exploded before public buildings. The culprits never were found; probably, they were members of a tiny anarchist group. May Day riots in major cities required thousands of policemen and soldiers, and even tanks in one city, before they could be controlled. Americans, disconcerted by the wartime excitement, rocketing prices, gigantic strikes, revolutions abroad, and, now, bombs, riots, and talk of revolt at home, feared that they lived on the brink of catastrophe. When radical Socialists formed the American Communist and Communist Labor parties in August 1919, with the an-nounced intention of promoting a proletarian revolution, otherwise sane Americans believed that these tiny, unarmed, disorganized parties threatened the national government.

Public alarm and demands from Congress for action were so great that the Labor Department rounded up 249 Russian Communists in November, loaded them on the army transport *Buford*—called the "Red Ark"—and shipped them to Russia. The popular excitement also affected Attorney General Palmer, who was a former leader of the most progressive wing of the Democratic party and was now eager for the Democratic presidential nomination. Palmer first set the Justice Department's Bureau of Investigation—predecessor of the Federal Bureau of Investigation (FBI)—to work to infiltrate and investigate Communist groups. To the radical division of the bureau, led by J. Edgar Hoover, was given the task of evaluating the extent of the Communist threat. When Hoover reported that revolution was imminent, Palmer urged Congress to approve a measure to punish persons guilty even of inciting sedition. Congress was more than willing to comply; representatives vied with each other for the privilege of attaching their name to this popular legislation. While the contest continued, however, no bill passed.

Palmer, hounded by critics who demanded action, organized a great federal dragnet to ferret out all alien Communists. On January 2, 1920, federal agents swooped down upon Communist headquarters all over the country and arrested well over 6,000 persons—American citizens as well as aliens—most without proper warrants. They were hustled off to jails and detention centers, where many were held for weeks and even months without the rights of bond or counsel. Eventually only 556 of them were deported as Communist aliens.

Further evidence of hysteria was the expulsion by the New York Assembly in April 1920 of five members for no other offense than their election on the Socialist ticket. From this point on, however, public fear subsided rapidly. Prices fell sharply beginning in early spring of 1920, strikes virtually ceased, the Communist tide in Europe receded, and the bombing and riots in the United States ended completely, except for one later explosion in Wall Street. Palmer, on the advice of his Bureau of Investigation, warned of a great Red uprising on May Day, 1920. When it did not occur, the Attorney General became the laughingstock of the country.

American blacks were among the chief victims of the turbulence which followed the Armistice. The sudden decline in immigration in 1914 had created such a scarcity of unskilled labor in northern and midwestern cities that several hundred thousand blacks left the South to take advantage of employment opportunities opened to them for the first time. They had to crowd into slum areas and at once aroused the suspicion and hatred of white unskilled workers. Race relations deteriorated further during the war—ironically, because some 400,000 blacks served in the armed services, many of them overseas. A terrible assault against blacks took place in East St. Louis, Illinois, in 1917. Southerners, particularly, feared that Negro veterans would return home to demand some measure of equality. Lynchings increased from thirty-four in 1917 to more than seventy in 1919, and ten of the victims in 1919 were black veterans.

Greater agony was in store for black Americans. The worst race riot in American history up to this time broke out in the national capital in July 1919, and an even more bloody conflict between black and white citizens erupted soon afterward in Chicago. Other race riots followed in Omaha and

Knoxville, and a veritable race war raged around Elaine, Arkansas. All told, twenty-five riots left hundreds dead and caused property damage running into the millions. The most significant fact about all these riots was that blacks, determined to protect their families, fought back bravely and gave nearly as much as they took.

The Election of 1920

The country had regained a large measure of sanity by the early months of 1920, when the presidential campaign began. The leading contenders for the Democratic nomination were Wilson's son-in-law, William G. McAdoo, Attorney General Palmer, and Governor James M. Cox of Ohio. Wilson acted as if he wanted a third nomination, but he may have been striking this posture in order to prevent the nomination of McAdoo, who he did not think would make a good President. Palmer had incurred the everlasting wrath of labor leaders, and Governor Cox won the nomination at the Democratic national convention in San Francisco on July 5. He chose for his running mate Franklin D. Roosevelt of New York, a prominent Wilsonian and supporter of the League of Nations.

Republican hopes ran high in the spring of 1920. Senator Hiram W. Johnson tried but failed to rally isolationists and former Progressives. Senator Warren G. Harding of Ohio was also "available," but he ran so poorly in the presidential primaries that he withdrew. The struggle then narrowed to a fierce and evenly matched contest between General Leonard Wood, Theodore Roosevelt's old friend, and Governor Frank O. Lowden of Illinois. Deadlock between the Wood and Lowden delegates ensued as soon as the balloting began at the Republican national convention in Chicago. A group of Republican leaders settled upon Harding, who was the most popular office-holder in the crucial state of Ohio. Harding won the nomination as a compromise candidate on June 12. Governor Coolidge, hero of the Boston police strike, was nominated for the vice-presidency.

Cox and Roosevelt visited Wilson at the White House immediately after their nomination and promised that they would continue the ailing President's fight for the League of Nations. They fulfilled their promise in a strenuous campaign. But they never had a chance because the coalition which had put Wilson back in office in 1916 was in shambles. The Wilson administration had alienated German Americans, Irish Americans, and radicals by entering the war. The administration had alienated businessmen by high taxes, western farmers by putting a ceiling on wheat prices, and labor by breaking the coal strike and a railroad strike early in 1920.

Harding, who read the political signs wisely, conducted a low-keyed campaign full of soothing but meaningless generalities. The main task of the Republican campaign managers was to neutralize the League of Nations as an issue. This they did by persuading thirty-one prominent Republicans to sign a statement which declared that Harding's election would be the best guarantee of American membership in the League of Nations. Not until the end of the campaign did Harding make it clear that he opposed American membership, and by then it was too late for the Democrats to capitalize upon the issue.

The victory of Harding was the most smashing electoral triumph since the election of James Monroe in 1820. The Ohio Senator carried every state in the

North, Middle West, and West, every border state except Kentucky, and broke the Solid South by carrying Tennessee. His 16,152,000 popular and 404 electoral votes dwarfed Cox's 9,147,000 popular and 127 electoral votes. The landslide also carried large Republican majorities into both houses of the next Congress.

The outcome, as one Democrat sadly described it, was a political earthquake, but the vote probably signified even less than Monroe's triumph 100 years before. The election was not a mandate on the League of Nations; nor had the campaign seen a squaring off of Progressives and conservatives. Harding won by a huge majority simply because he was able to add a large number of discontented voters to the ordinary Republican majority.

SUGGESTED READINGS

Link et al., *The Papers of Woodrow Wilson,* and Link, *Wilson,* vols. 3–5, both already cited, cover the period of neutrality and American entrance into the war in most detail. Link covers the same period in brief form in *Woodrow Wilson and the Progressive Era,* already cited, and all of Wilson's foreign policies in *Woodrow Wilson: Revolution, War, and Peace* (1979). Among the general studies, the best are Charles Seymour, *American Neutrality, 1914–1917* (1935) and *American Diplomacy during the World War* (1934); Ernest R. May, *The World War and American Isolation* (1959); and Patrick Devlin, *Too Proud to Fight: Woodrow Wilson's Neutrality* (1974). Robert E. Osgood, *Ideals and Self-Interest in America's Foreign Relations* (1953), and John Milton Cooper, Jr., *The Vanity of Power: American Isolationism and the First World War* (1969), present good analyses of the reactions of the American people to the war in Europe.

For the American home front, 1917–1918, see especially David M. Kennedy, *Over Here: The First World War and American Society* (1980); Robert D. Cuff, *The War Industries Board . . .* (1973); Jordan A. Schwarz, *The Speculator, Bernard Baruch . . .* (1981); David Burner, *Herbert Hoover* (1978); Seward W. Livermore, *Politics Is Adjourned: Woodrow Wilson and the War Congress* (1966); Daniel R. Beaver, *Newton D. Baker and the American War Effort, 1917–1919* (1966); and Stephen Vaughn, *Holding Fast the Inner Lines: Democracy, Nationalism, and the Committee on Public Information* (1980). H. C. Peterson and Gilbert C. Fite, *Opponents of War, 1917–1918* (1957), and Zechariah Chaffee, Jr., *Free Speech in the United States* (1941), relate the suppression of civil liberties during the war period.

The best account of American military participation is in Frank E. Vandiver, *Black Jack: The Life and Times of John J. Pershing,* 2 vols. (1977), but see also David F. Trask, *The United States in the Supreme War Council* (1961). On the American naval effort, see Elting E. Morison, *Admiral Sims and the Modern American Navy* (1942).

We now have an impressive literature on American diplomacy, 1917–1918: W. B. Fowler, *British-American Relations, 1917–1918* (1969); Arno J. Mayer, *Political Origins of the New Diplomacy, 1917–1918* (1959); George F. Kennan, *Russia Leaves the War* (1956), *The Decision to Intervene* (1958), and *Russia and the West under Lenin and Stalin* (1961); Betty Miller Unterberger, *America's Siberian Expedition* (1956); and Carl P. Parrini, *Heir to Empire: United States Economic Diplomacy, 1916–1923* (1969).

For the early American movement for a league of nations, see Ruhl J. Bartlett, *The League to Enforce Peace* (1944). Lawrence E. Gelfand, *The Inquiry: American Preparations for Peace 1917–1919* (1963), is excellent. The best one-volume book on the Paris Peace Conference is Inga Floto, *Colonel House in Paris* (1980). Ray S. Baker, *Woodrow Wilson and World Settlement,* 3 vols. (1922), is especially important because Wilson was a secret coauthor. Also important are N. Gordon Levin, Jr., *Woodrow Wilson and World Politics: America's Response to War and Revolution* (1968); Paul Birdsall, *Versailles Twenty Years After* (1941); and Herbert Hoover, *The Ordeal of Woodrow Wilson* (1958). Arno J. Mayer, *The Politics and Diplomacy of Peacemaking: Containment and Counterrevolution at Versailles, 1918–1919* (1967), and John M. Thompson, *Russia, Bolshevism, and the Versailles Peace* (1966), highlight the Russian problem.

The best accounts of the fight over the Versailles Treaty are Denna F. Fleming, *The United States and the League of Nations* (1932), and Ralph Stone, *The Irreconcilables: The Fight Against the League of Nations* (1970), but see also the discussion in Link, *Woodrow Wilson: Revolution, War, and Peace,* already cited.

There is a growing literature on demobilization and the immediate postwar period. Mark Sullivan, *Our Times: The United States, 1900–1925,* 6 vols. (1926–1935), vols. 5 and 6; the third volume in the Paxson series, already cited; William E. Leuchtenburg, *The Perils of Prosperity, 1914–1932* (1958); and Preston W. Slosson, *The Great Crusade and After* (1930), are all good introductions. Elliott M. Rudwick, *Race Riot at East St. Louis* (1964), and William M. Tuttle, Jr., *Race Riot: Chicago in the Red Summer of 1919* (1970), are both classics. For the Red Scare, see Chaffee, *Free Speech in the United States,* already cited; Robert K. Murray, *Red Scare: A Study in National Hysteria* (1955); Stanley Coben, *A. Mitchell Palmer: Politician* (1963); and Theodore Draper, *The Roots of American Communism* (1957).

The standard work on the presidential campaign of 1920 is Wesley M. Bagby, Jr., *The Road to Normalcy: The Presidential Campaign and Election of 1920* (1962).

CHAPTER 6
SOCIAL AND CULTURAL
CHANGE IN THE 1920s

1. A DECADE OF ABUNDANCE

Population Mobility

Between the end of the First World War and the crash of the stock market in 1929, the shape of modern America emerged. During these eleven years, the American people experienced a fundamental transition because many of the socioeconomic trends which had had their inception during the nineteenth and early twentieth centuries came to full fruition. The United States became an urban nation connected by telephone lines and highway systems. The country also had, for the first time, an economy which depended on the consumer rather than the producer.

The most remarkable development of the 1920s was the rapid pace of economic and social change. Throughout the nineteenth century, Americans had moved from the countryside to urban areas—cities, suburbs, and towns—at an increasing rate. Yet, the massive shift in human resources which began during the 1920s represented a distinctive development. It was distinctive most strikingly because, for the first time since 1790, census enumerators discovered that more Americans lived in urban than in rural areas. By 1930, for example, about 69,000,000 Americans lived in cities, as against almost 54,000,000 who lived in the countryside. While population growth of the United States as a whole slowed to its smallest rate since the seventeenth century, the *rate* of rural migration to urban areas during the 1920s increased exponentially.

For the first time in American history, farm population suffered a net decline during the decade, as more than 13,000,000 rural Americans left their homes and moved, especially to the large metropolitan centers. The five cities which had over 1,000,000 people expanded by more than 50 per cent from 1920 to 1930; the construction of highway systems and the growing availability of the automobile stimulated an even greater growth in suburbs. The population transfer of the 1920s also occurred between regions. In spite of the formal closing of the frontier, Americans continued to move west, with California the prime beneficiary.

The Dynamics of Expansion

The decade of the 1920s, however, did not open optimistically, as the postwar economic boom and price inflation ended abruptly in mid-1920. The speculative boom, after the Armistice, ended in part as a result of the Federal Reserve's restrictive monetary policy; a financial crisis, sharp recession, and declining prices followed. By 1923, the economy had recovered, and during the subsequent six years the most important economic vital signs—total manufacturing, consumer goods, corporate profits, and stock market prices— revealed a vigorously expanding economy. By 1927, businessmen, journalists, politicians, and economists were prophesying a "new economic era" of permanent prosperity and an increasingly higher standard of living for everyone.

Although their prophecies sounded hollow once the depression struck, during the 1920s the American people experienced an impressive improvement in economic status. Between 1914 and 1929, total national wealth almost doubled, while per capita income, adjusted for the cost of living, increased from $480 in 1900 to $620 in 1919 and to $681 in 1929. Manufacturing industries increased their output by 64 per cent during the postwar decade; workers enjoyed an overall increase of 25 per cent in real income during the same period. The construction industry participated in, and was part of, the new prosperity as cities grew, suburbs spread, and roads were built. For example, the value of materials used in construction increased from $12 billion in 1919 to $17.5 billion in 1928.

With the increase in output of goods and services, financial resources grew apace. Despite turmoil in banking—the number of banks actually declined because of mergers and failures—total banking resources nearly doubled between 1919 and 1929, while the resources of life insurance companies and building and loan associations more than trebled. At the same time, the center of international banking shifted from Europe to the United States. One of the important results of the First World War was the transformation of the United States from a debtor to a creditor nation in international trade. In 1914, American citizens had invested some $3.5 billion abroad but still owed Europeans a net debt of nearly $4 billion. After five years of war, Europeans owed Americans a net private debt of nearly $3 billion, and European governments owed the United States Government an additional $10 billion. During the 1920s, the extension each year of about $1 billion in credits and loans by Americans consolidated New York's position as the financial center of the world. Simultaneously, by the end of the decade, the dollar had displaced the pound as the chief medium of international exchange.

Like the other major social and economic transformations in American history, change during the 1920s did not bring unmitigated benefits for all Americans. Although the American economy produced more wealth, it was not distributed equally. A disproportionate share of the substantial increase in income went to the wealthy—perhaps 5 or 10 per cent of the population—while many of those Americans who had been poor and malnourished remained at a precarious level of subsistence. Many of the benefits of the expansion of the 1920s went to new capital-intensive industries, such as automobiles, chemicals, and electronics. Older industries, primarily those which had spearheaded the industrial revolution in the nineteenth century —textiles in New England and soft-coal mining in Appalachia—collapsed during the decade. The most conspicuous "have-nots" of the 1920s, however, were the farmers, who, after a period of prosperity from 1900 to 1920, suffered a precipitate drop in income and financial resources (see pp. 127–28).

New Technologies and New Industries

The American economic advance of the 1920s was largely a product of a technological revolution. Innovation spawned—and, in some cases, even created—new industries, and these industries, in turn, greatly stimulated the entire economy.

The technological revolution largely manifested itself in a dramatic increase in productivity. Working in concert, scientists and industrialists developed new products, invented machinery, and devised methods of production which increased output per man hour. As a result of the growth of large corporations in the American economy, more firms in the 1920s financed and organized research divisions as part of their corporate structure. American universities, which also grew during the 1920s, served as research centers and pioneered industrial innovation by training a new generation of scientists and engineers who manned industrial research laboratories of a size, quality, and number which no other nation could rival.

Apart from technological breakthroughs, the increase in productivity was also a product of an organizational revolution in American industry. The disciples of Frederick Winslow Taylor, who advocated greater worker productivity through a strict regimentation and discipline of time, continued to push for a more efficient—that is, a more productive—work force. Even more important than "Taylorism" in industry was innovation in the organization of the productive process itself. In automobile production, Henry Ford's introduction of the moving assembly line—which separated each part of the process of production into distinct units—increased productivity and established a model of industrial organization.

The best measurement of the increase in industrial output is productivity. Between 1899 and 1909, productivity had increased by only 7 per cent in industry and by 6 per cent in agriculture. In contrast, between 1919 and 1929, productivity increased by 40 per cent in industry and by 26 per cent in agriculture. The productive revolution occurred most strikingly in several infant industries, most of which had come into existence prior to World War I. They not only stimulated the economy but also caused profound alterations in American life.

The Emergence of Consumerism

One of the most fundamental changes in American life during the 1920s was the transformation from a producer to a consumer economy. The health of the American economy, that is, increasingly depended on the differentiated—and to a certain extent cultivated—tastes of the American consumer. Before 1920, manufacturers tended to differentiate their goods from those of their competitors through lower prices and methods of distribution; after 1920, there was an increasing emphasis on marketing, packaging, and, above all, advertising. An underdeveloped industry before World War I, by 1929, advertising, concentrated in New York, had become one of the largest industries in the United States.

Automobiles and Americans

Although Europeans had developed the first gasoline-powered automobile in the 1880s, Charles and Frank Duryea of Springfield, Massachusetts, and Henry Ford of Detroit did not produce the first workable American "horseless carriage" until 1892–1893. Thereafter, progress was slow; only 4,000 automobiles were produced in the United States in 1900, and large-scale production awaited Ford's institution of the moving assembly line in 1914, which enabled him to manufacture the ugly but rugged Model T at cheap prices. Except for a brief cutback during the war, automobile production grew by leaps and bounds to nearly 5,000,000 units in 1929.

Automobile manufacturers were avid users of advertising, and, by the end of the 1920s, they were selling much more than simple transportation. The automobile, they discovered, embodied many of the features of American culture. To own a car made possible independence, autonomy, and heretofore unimagined freedom of movement. With the enthusiastic support of American consumers, automobile manufacturers also appealed to power, luxury, status, and sex appeal. The most popular American cars were large and had lush interiors and appealed to the increasingly differentiated tastes of the American consumer. Appropriately enough, in 1927, Ford abandoned the simple but efficient Model T and replaced it with the more stylish Model A.

Automobile production also had a "multiplier" effect on the economy. Drivers needed paved roads, gasoline, service stations, garages for maintenance, spare tires and parts, and a hundred other products and services. According to one estimate, in 1929 the automobile industry directly or indirectly employed nearly 4,000,000 persons.

The Electric Power and Radio Industries

Other technologically intensive industries grew apace in the 1920s. Electric power expanded from relative insignificance in 1900 into America's second most important economic interest by 1929, with a capital investment of $12 billion and an annual income of nearly $2 billion. By 1929, 68 per cent of American homes were electrified, an increase which had a "ripple" effect on the sale and manufacture of electric turbines, motors, and home appliances. The value of the output of electrical machinery and appliances exceeded $2 billion in 1929.

Radio transmitters and receivers had been invented before the First World

War, but their large-scale production and the consequent development of a nationwide broadcasting industry took place during the 1920s. Before that time, the government had maintained a monopoly on the operation of radio transmitters. In 1929, the industry was turning out nearly 4,500,000 radios a year, and more than 10,000,000 families owned sets.

The Movie Era

The expansion of the motion-picture industry paralleled that of the automobile. Thomas A. Edison invented the first motion-picture camera in 1896, and thereafter both technological innovation and technique in motion-picture production occurred steadily, culminating in the first "spectacular," *The Birth of a Nation*, in 1915. By 1930, motion pictures were highly integrated and well organized as an industry. More than 23,000 motion-picture theaters, many of them owned or controlled by large firms, were operating throughout the country, while the motion-picture production industry itself had a capital investment of $2 billion and employed 325,000 persons.

By 1930, most of the motion-picture industry was located in Los Angeles, because its weather allowed continuous production. Southern California's diverse topography was the scene not only of the popular westerns but also a variety of other sets. Filmmaking acquired a new preeminence in American culture as great directors, actors, and actresses—Charlie Chaplin, Rudolph Valentino, Clara Bow, John Gilbert, and Laurel and Hardy—became the object of intense popular interest. Along with westerns, situation comedies and crime thrillers were popular; some films included sexual themes or even nudity and near nudity. Although some movies violated conventional mores about sex, a self-imposed censorship at the end of the 1920s sharply restricted the discussion of sexual themes until the 1960s.

Growth of Aviation

The most spectacular technological development in the United States during the 1920s was the growth of air transportation. Although Wilbur and Orville Wright made the first successful flight in a heavier-than-air machine at Kitty Hawk, North Carolina, in December 1903, American aviation had advanced slowly before the First World War. But when the Armistice was signed, the United States possessed an air service which had become a permanent and growing branch of both the army and the navy; in 1919, over 800 planes were at the battlefront, and twenty-four plants were capable of producing 21,000 planes a year. In the postwar decade, air routes for mail, passengers, and cargo developed rapidly, especially after the introduction of the all-metal Ford trimotor plane in the late twenties. By 1930, 122 airlines flew routes which covered nearly 50,000 miles.

In the 1920s, aviation heroes tremendously stimulated public interest in flying. On May 21, 1927, the solo flight of a young American pilot, Charles A. Lindbergh, thrilled the entire world. The "Lone Eagle" landed his monoplane, *The Spirit of St. Louis,* at Le Bourget Airport near Paris after a nonstop flight of over thirty-three and a half hours from New York. Another hero of the air was Commander Richard E. Byrd of the United States Navy, who crossed the North Pole by air on May 9, 1926, and, with three companions, flew the next year from New York to the French coast. Byrd's greatest achievement was his exploration of the region of the South Pole in 1928–1929.

Corporate Expansion

Despite antitrust legislation and prosecutions, one of the inexorable trends in American industry was the movement toward consolidation and bigness during the first three decades of the twentieth century. By 1929, the 200 largest corporations controlled 49 per cent of all corporate wealth and received 43 per cent of all corporate income. Nonetheless, competition was livelier in 1929 than it had been in 1900, for in most major American industries an oligopoly, or a few large producers, controlled the major share of production. These few producers, however, often vigorously competed among themselves in pricing and marketing.

Probably the most important change in American industry during the 1920s was the full flowering of the managerial revolution. Before 1900, the control of American industry was largely in the hands of owners such as John D. Rockefeller and Andrew Carnegie. By the end of the 1920s, however, the corporate hierarchical structure and methods dominated American industry. Especially in large firms, professionally trained managers controlled and operated industries which they did not own. The almost complete separation of ownership from control occurred in most large American corporations as a growing class of executives and managers operated corporations in trust for owners interested only in increased dividends.

The Nadir of the Labor Movement

Organized labor suffered heavy losses in spite of a wholesale increase in employment and a shortage of skilled labor. Powerful railroad brotherhoods held their own during the decade, but membership in AFL unions declined from slightly more than 4,000,000 in 1919 to 2,770,000 in 1929. This striking anomaly—a decline in union power during a period of high prosperity—was the result of several factors. Frightened by the labor troubles of 1919, many employers addressed labor discontent by instituting welfare programs of their own, including profit sharing and group health and life insurance programs. Employers supplemented these efforts and precluded labor organization under the AFL by encouraging the formation of unions under the company's sponsorship. These company unions, usually less militant and less aggressive than independent unions, had more than 1,500,000 members in 1929, and they drained much strength away from the main-line trade-union movement. Many employers also engaged, often successfully, in "open shop" drives to root out unions which already existed.

At the same time, the AFL became moribund. Increasingly under the control of conservative trade unionists, the AFL, including its president, William Green, did not adjust well to the technological transformation of the economy. In some industries, such as steel, innovation helped to undermine the position of artisanal workers who were among the AFL's strongest supporters. In new industries, such as automobiles, the AFL expended little effort in labor organization. They also had little interest in risking the welfare of their skilled members by mounting costly campaigns to organize workers in mass-production industries.

The combination of management's "welfare capitalism" and hostility to unions and the AFL's loss of militancy produced the most peaceful period in labor-management relations since the 1870s. In proportion to the number of American workers, strikes declined sharply from 1920 to 1929.

2. CULTURAL CONFLICT DURING THE 1920s

A New Morality?

Many Americans were convinced during the 1920s that the country was in the throes of a sudden and pervasive rebellion against morality, religion, and traditional patterns of family authority. Although social life did change, the real revolution—a revolt against Victorian society and culture—had actually begun before the First World War.

To contemporaries, the most important long-run changes were the appearance and status of women. Most noticeable was that middle-class women cut their hair short and wore revealing clothing; many also broke other taboos against tobacco and alcohol. In themselves, these changes were not particularly consequential and were probably more stereotypical than typical. The spread of central heating, for example, made possible changes in style such as lighter women's clothing. The new assertiveness of women into areas which men had traditionally dominated—politics, professional careers, and sex— were part of a long-term rebellion, which had begun and gathered force at the end of the nineteenth century, against the Victorian standard of the absolute authority of fathers and husbands. Beginning in 1920, many women not only voted but also ran for and won political offices. In increasing numbers, women composed a large portion of the rapidly expanding services and professions and, by 1930, they constituted nearly one fourth of the nonfarm work force. Although increasing economic opportunities also brought increasing independence within the family, fragmentation of the Victorian family was not the immediate result. To begin with, the divorce rate actually declined slightly between 1920 and 1930. Moreover, contemporaries perhaps made too much of the transformation of the status of and opportunities for women during the 1920s. Most of it was confined to upper middle-class women—those most affected by the Victorian definition of sexual roles. Among poor, black, and recent-immigrant women, who constituted the vast majority, the nature of the "sexual revolution" was very different indeed.

Another example to contemporaries of the "revolution" in morality took place in the rebellion of American youth. Many young Americans, to be sure, were in the vanguard of the larger revolt against Victorian culture. For the first time in American history, there was a distinct self-consciousness of youth—indeed, to a large extent, American culture, after 1920, celebrated and even became oriented toward the magical term "youth." This first "generation gap" took several overt forms. In dance, young people rejected older and slower forms in favor of the fast fox-trot and the Charleston, and some older Americans cried out in horror at what they called the "syncopated embrace." Other young Americans, largely those who attended college, also drank to excess and lived what was considered a Bohemian life. Such descriptions of college life as those given by F. Scott Fitzgerald in his famous novel, *This Side of Paradise* (1920), sent chills down the spines of parents.

Yet, on balance, the evidence does not clearly show that the moral standards of young people underwent significant change during the 1920s. Much of the visible rebellion took place on college campuses, as the number of students increased rapidly during the decade. But only a minority of young people attended college, and, of those who did, most were probably rather staid. Most of them were not rebellious; like their parents, they still cherished sobriety, self-control, and the traditional marriage.

Nativism and the Klan

One of the most significant cultural phenomena of the 1920s was an outburst of xenophobia, or nativism—a fear and dislike of elements in the population perceived to be foreign. In part a legacy of the Red Scare of 1919–1920, nativism was also an expression of the resentment of rural Protestants against the cultural hegemony of urban centers. The appearance of nativism in the 1920s manifested itself as an open hostility to anything "un-American"—that is, anything outside the norm of white Protestant America. Nativists thus were often anti-Semitic and anti-Catholic. During the decade, moreover, racism continued to be a pervasive force, and antagonism toward blacks, Hispanics, and Orientals probably did not decrease appreciably.

The most prominent nativist group was the Ku Klux Klan. The Knights of the Ku Klux Klan, the organization which had terrorized black people during the Reconstruction era, was revived in name by a Georgia mystic, William J. Simmons, in Atlanta in 1915. Over the next five years, the organization spread very slowly through the Deep South. After 1920, however, it made rapid progress in the Southwest, Middle West, and the Pacific Coast. At its peak in 1925, it probably had 5,000,000 members and was a powerful force in the politics of Texas, Oklahoma, Illinois, Ohio, Wisconsin, Indiana, Oregon, and a dozen other states.

Americans have always been a nation of joiners, and many joined the Klan simply because it was a popular fraternal organization, and they were attracted by the Klan's regalia and high-flown ritual. But the Klan was something more than just another secret fraternity, or even merely a racist or religious organization. The national leadership was openly anti-Negro, anti-Catholic, and anti-Jewish. Klan leaders were sworn to keep blacks "in their place," to boycott Jewish merchants and not to hire Jewish workers, and to diminish Catholic influence in politics. The Klan expressed a complex range of passions, most of which originated in the uncertainty of rapid social and economic change. The Klan also united nativism with the suspicion of rural and small-town America against the "alien" cities that supposedly were corrupting American life. In some areas, Klansmen were stronger upholders of civic virtue against sexual permissiveness and drinking than they were defenders of racial and religious ideals. In other areas, the Klan was a movement against other Protestants who, they perceived, favored business expansion over traditional moral certainties. Especially in the Southwest and Middle West, the organization also appealed to lower middle-class urban Protestants, who feared competition and intrusion from black, Catholic, and Jewish newcomers.

The majority of Americans eventually came to despise the Klan, and editors, clergymen, and other leaders fought to destroy the organization. Internal conflicts also plagued the order, and it was deprived of its chief leaders and thoroughly discredited when they were imprisoned for theft and immorality. After 1926, the Klan declined rapidly in membership. By 1930, it was reduced to a small but still active organization.

Fundamentalism and Antimodernism

The crusade to forbid the teaching of evolution in public schools, colleges, and universities was yet another manifestation of the reaction to rapid change. To a certain extent, the antievolution movement provides a striking example of what sociologists call cultural lag. Darwin's theory of evolution had caused considerable conflict between its advocates and opponents in science and religion in the late nineteenth century, but, by 1900, theologians and urban churchmen had almost uniformly accepted the evolutionary hypothesis and had long since ceased to regard it as any threat to Christian faith. Yet, this was not true of most rural evangelical Protestants, particularly in the South and Southwest, who deeply abhorred not only the evolutionary concept but also saw it as an intrusion of secular forces on the sanctity of the Bible. Particularly after 1920, the new phenomenon of "fundamentalism" came to represent opposition to Darwinism and to any other secularization of the role of the Protestant church. The struggle between "fundamentalists" and "modernists" occurred in every Protestant denomination, and, in most cases, "modernists" won.

If it had not been for William Jennings Bryan, "fundamentalist" fears would probably only have simmered. The "Great Commoner" was alarmed because he believed that the teaching of evolution undermined the religious faith of schoolchildren and college students, and in 1921 he opened a crusade for the adoption of antievolution laws. Numerous evangelists and ministers answered his call to battle. Florida, North Carolina, and Texas took indirect action to prevent the teaching of evolution in public schools. Tennessee, Mississippi, and Arkansas adopted statutes which forbade the teaching of evolution in public institutions.

In 1925, John Thomas Scopes, a young biology teacher in Dayton, Tennessee, decided to test the validity of the act just passed by his state's legislature. He was arrested and tried. Bryan rushed to Dayton to join the prosecuting authorities, while the American Civil Liberties Union sent the famed trial lawyer, Clarence Darrow of Chicago, to defend Scopes. The conflict became national in scope as reporters from across the country descended on the small Tennessee town. The "monkey trial" soon became a fierce verbal battle between Darrow and Bryan over the literal truth of the Bible. Scopes, who admitted that he had violated the antievolution law, received a light fine which was later revoked.

The antievolution forces had earlier founded the Supreme Kingdom to press for an amendment to the Constitution which forbade the teaching of evolution anywhere in the United States. But Bryan's death shortly after the Scopes trial deprived "fundamentalists" of their only leader of national prominence, and the antievolution crusade fizzled and sputtered almost to an end about 1928. Nonetheless, antievolution—whether in law or by custom—remained a powerful force.

The Prohibition Experiment

Perhaps nothing in recent American history excited higher hopes or began with greater fanfare than prohibition. At a victory celebration in New York in 1920, Bryan, a leader in the movement for the Eighteenth Amendment, announced that the liquor issue finally rested as dead as slavery, and he strongly believed that the United States was better off without both. In many respects, prohibitionists like Bryan were accurate in their assessment. During the nineteenth and early twentieth centuries, consumption of alcohol and alcoholism were at alarming heights—even after almost a century of temperance and state-level prohibition. Prohibition, set in this context, illustrates not only that prohibitionists were reformers—who were addressing what they considered a social problem—but also that the Eighteenth Amendment did have a substantial impact on drinking patterns among Americans. One of its most significant results was an immediate decline in the consumption of alcohol from about 2.60 gallons per capita annually in the period 1906–1910 to 0.97 gallons in 1934. The incidence of alcoholism, alcohol-related disease, and arrests for drunkenness decreased significantly during the 1920s.

While accurate in their assessment, Bryan and like-minded reformers were ultimately wrong about the prohibition experiment. Passage of the prohibition amendment did not stop Americans from consuming alcoholic beverages. Alcohol, as a result of prohibition, became available if bought at extortionate prices. In 1928, for example, Americans thirsty for drink paid on the average 600 per cent more for beer than they had paid in 1916. Illegal distillers, smugglers, and brewers encountered little difficulty in selling alcohol. Speakeasies (illegal saloons) flourished in the cities; and bootleggers, who sold liquor illegally, did a booming business. Prohibition coincided with and even encouraged the emergence of professional criminal gangs in large cities. In the most infamous of these gangs, Al Capone commanded what amounted to a private army in Chicago, and, by 1927, it did a $60 million business in liquor alone. Profits from the liquor trade in turn enabled Capone and others to control additional lucrative and illegal enterprises, such as gambling and prostitution. Bootleggers were the most powerful supporters of prohibition, for it protected their monopoly.

Out of thirst or disgust with the results of the Eighteenth Amendment, many urban Americans favored its repeal and also opposed state laws which forbade gambling and sporting events on Sundays. Prohibition, which became one of the leading political issues of the 1920s, further reinforced the dominant cleavage of the 1920s—the conflict between traditional and modern cultures.

Beginnings of Black Nationalism

Blacks responded to the triumph of the Jim Crow system and the general increase in racial tension across the nation in various ways. Most blacks were both southern and rural, and they rarely possessed the economic or political independence to challenge racial oppression directly. Some, therefore, accommodated themselves within the system. Other blacks made a more visible protest with their feet, which took them in growing numbers to urban centers in the North and the South.

Many of these urban blacks—particularly those in New York and Chicago—possessed a kind of cultural independence which they had heretofore lacked. One of the most visible manifestations of this new urban cultural autonomy was the popularity of Marcus Garvey, by 1920 already the most prominent black nationalist in the Caribbean and Central American areas. Part of Garvey's popularity was the product of his appeal to a rich tradition in the history of black Americans, a tradition which—from Alexander Crummell in the nineteenth century to Booker T. Washington in the twentieth—stressed economic independence and racial pride. Yet, Garvey's distinctiveness lies in the fact that he combined these elements into a new brand of militant nationalism which emphasized separation for blacks in an Africa free from white domination.

Garvey arrived in the United States in 1916, and he at first intended to convert American blacks to his Universal Negro Improvement Association (UNIA), which was based in Jamaica. But Garvey found blacks in the United States so receptive—particularly after the race riots in 1919—that he transferred the headquarters of the UNIA to Harlem. Although Garvey claimed millions of converts, at least 100,000 American blacks formally joined the UNIA. An equal number probably attended meetings, subscribed to Garvey's newspaper, the *Negro World,* and invested in UNIA enterprises. Garvey had a wide appeal from New York to California. But we will never know the extent of Garvey's popularity, for he was prosecuted for mail fraud soon after his rise to leadership. The government charged that Garvey, through the UNIA, had falsely advertised that the UNIA Black Star Shipping Line would be profitable. Garvey was convicted, imprisoned, and then deported.

3. CULTURAL CURRENTS

Growth and Change

American cultural history in the 1920s has long been written in terms of the invectives of its severest critics. These contemporaries were self-consciously part of what Gertrude Stein described as the "lost generation," who revolted against the pervasive Victorian notions of politics, society, and culture. Perhaps the leading critic of the 1920s was H. L. Mencken, editor of *The American Mercury,* who railed at the "boobery" of the lower middle-classes, which, he claimed, had pervaded almost every dimension of American life. Other intellectuals, such as Walter Lippmann, who was a progressive before the war, became disenchanted with democracy in general and with its incapacity to solve social problems, while others saw nativism, antievolution, and prohibition as examples of the failure of popular politics. For many intellectuals, "debunking" of American myths became their objective. In novels, Sinclair Lewis and Sherwood Anderson portrayed the alleged prudery and hypocrisy of the Victorian small town. Historians, such as James Truslow Adams, "debunked" the historical image of Puritanism, in which they found the intellectual origins of the Victorians' repressive attitudes toward sex. Although the indictment of the intellectuals was reasonably accurate, this view has obscured the substantial growth and development which occurred in American culture during the 1920s.

Educational and Religious Development

The American people made greater educational advances during the 1920s than in any earlier decade in their history. Throughout the nation, public schools became—for the first time in American history—the pervasive force that they are today. Overall, expenditures on schools increased from a little more than $1 billion to $2.3 billion, and illiteracy declined from 6 per cent to 4.3 per cent. Several specific accomplishments of the 1920s stand out.

In rural areas, where a significant number of children still attended small (often one-room) schools, the degree of change was perhaps greatest. Central, bureaucratic state agencies acquired greater control over school finances, administration, and curriculum. Moreover, largely aided by the construction of state and federal highways, the consolidated, modern rural school came to replace the isolated rural schoolhouse.

While they expanded and standardized elementary schools, state education-al officials in every state also constructed public high-school systems which made available some secondary education to almost every American child. Poor children still tended to leave school at an early age in order to work, but many of them benefited from new vocational instruction in technical skills or agriculture. High-school enrollment doubled from 2,200,000 in 1920 to 4,400,000 in 1930.

Another noteworthy accomplishment was a tremendous expansion of American colleges and universities and an enrichment of their curricula. Students enrolled in institutions of higher learning increased in number from 598,000 in 1920 to more than 1,000,000 in 1930. At the same time, graduate and professional schools reached such a level of excellence that Americans, for the first time, were freed from dependence upon European universities for advanced training, except for training in advanced theoretical physics. American universities during the 1920s achieved preeminence in research science—biology, astronomy, mathematics, chemistry, and engineering. In 1917, astronomers erected a great telescope on Mt. Wilson in California, and in 1933, the physicist, Ernest O. Lawrence, conceived and built the first cyclotron, or atom smasher, at the University of California at Berkeley.

The explosion of research and graduate training—not only in science, but also in the humanities—was greatly aided by American philanthropic founda-tions. Indeed, the organization and shape of aid to scholarly research took firm shape first during the 1920s. All of the following began programs of assistance during the postwar decade: the National Research Council, the International Education Board, the General Education Board, the Guggenheim Foundation, and, for the humanities and social sciences, the American Council of Learned Societies and the Social Science Research Council. Spurred on by philanthropic resources, American universities became centers and pioneers of research.

At the same time that American universities became research centers, the character of undergraduate education changed. As the high schools produced increasing numbers of graduates, higher education became more and more the preserve of the middle class. Overall academic standards in college and

universities were low for undergraduates; indeed, they probably even deteriorated as the inundation of middle-class youth shifted the attention of
students to nonacademic matters. European visitors frequently commented
that sports stadiums and fraternities were the vital centers of the American
college.

Meanwhile, American churches grew in membership faster than the
population as a whole. There is no measurable evidence that the alleged
revolution in morals undermined the religious faith of most Americans
during the 1920s. On the contrary, some evidence suggests that religious faith
may have increased. A poll taken in 1927 of 250,000 newspaper readers and
36,000 college students reported that young people were even more certain
about their faith than were their parents. Churches not only increased their
membership but also continued to expand their ministries in urban areas as
the Social Gospel experienced a full flowering during the decade.

The "Lost Generation"

Although Mencken and others deplored the banality of cultural life during
the 1920s, the decade was perhaps the most productive one for literature in
American history. All literary forms took part in the renaissance, but the
writing of fiction enjoyed a special upsurge. Not only did the very existence
of these authors belie their description of the United States as a cultural
desert; for at least some of them, their work was a response to the
deficiencies which unquestionably did exist. For example, the southern
literary renaissance, which began in the 1920s and came to full fruition in the
1930s, was largely a response to Mencken's description of the South as the
"Sahara of the Bozarts."

Across the nation, American novelists continued to write in the modes of
social realism and naturalism. F. Scott Fitzgerald wrote elegantly about the
hollow lives of the eastern and midwestern upper classes. William Faulkner
began a series of penetrating novels about the decadent society and apparently
cursed people of his native Mississippi. Thomas Wolfe, who would be one of
the most prolific novelists of the 1930s, published his first and greatest novel
in 1929, *Look Homeward, Angel.* The most important literary trend of the
1920s was the full development of the naturalistic school in the novels of
Ernest Hemingway, John Dos Passos, Theodore Dreiser, and Sherwood
Anderson. It is a commentary on the American literary achievement of the
1920s that three novelists—Lewis, Faulkner, and Hemingway—and one
dramatist, Eugene O'Neill, all began their significant work in the decade and
later won Nobel prizes for literature.

The 1920s were also notable for remarkable advances in American poetry
and drama. The old and great American tradition in poetry was carried
forward in new forms by T. S. Eliot, e. e. cummings, Wallace Stevens,
Robinson Jeffers, Edwin Arlington Robinson, Carl Sandburg, Robert Frost, and
Ezra Pound, while a new school of southern poets—known as the Agrarians—
developed at Vanderbilt University in the late 1920s. The most significant
American literary event of the 1920s, however, was the burgeoning of a
school of first-rate dramatists. Eugene O'Neill was the towering figure among
this group, but a number of lesser playwrights, such as Maxwell Anderson,
also enlivened the American stage.

Meanwhile, black writers, mostly based in Harlem, began a self-consciously distinctive black literature. These writers, partly in response to Du Bois' plea for a black cultural "renaissance," hoped to establish cultural and intellectual vehicles for blacks. Along with Du Bois, the most prominent of these writers were the poets Langston Hughes, Countee Cullen, and Claude McKay (who was also a successful novelist). James Weldon Johnson worked with both forms and was also an essayist, songwriter, and historian. Jean Toomer's mystical celebration of blackness and black culture in his novel-poem, *Cane,* was perhaps the greatest single literary contribution from this group. E. Franklin Frazier joined Du Bois in the front ranks of American sociologists, as did other black scholars of high accomplishment such as Charles S. Johnson and Luther Porter Jackson. Yet, these black intellectuals were mainly urban and middle class in orientation, and they consequently did not have extensive influence among most blacks. The most devoted audience of the Harlem renaissance, for example, was white, and by the 1930s, even it had lost interest in black culture.

Music in the Industrial Age

Before the First World War, America's contributions to the world's store of music had been confined largely to war songs, hymns, cowboy ballads, Negro spirituals, and other kinds of folk music. The American tradition in popular music grew apace during and after the war with the work of many composers such as Cole Porter, Jerome Kern, George Gershwin, and Irving Berlin. The most important development in this field was the beginning of a native American musical form, jazz, a highly sophisticated form based largely on African and Creole traditions. Jazz originated in the bars and brothels of black New Orleans during the early years of the twentieth century, moved up the Mississippi Valley, and reached Chicago about 1916. It rapidly became popular throughout the country and the world in the 1920s, especially after Paul Whiteman, a popular band leader, and the composer George Gershwin demonstrated that jazz could be expressed in a semisymphonic form.

Although jazz became diluted for popular (and largely white) audiences, its driving rhythms and the spirit of improvisation were popular among black audiences. Also popular were "the blues," a form generally less complicated than jazz, which thrived in the black ghettos of St. Louis and Chicago. Louis Armstrong and Bessie Smith, both recognized today as having a significant impact on American music, came out of thriving musical centers in New Orleans and Chicago.

Classical music also developed in the 1920s. By 1930, almost every high school in the country included musical training in its curriculum, and work done in conservatories and colleges and universities was of course even more advanced. By 1930, there were also in the United States seventy-three permanent symphony orchestras, fifty-five chamber music groups, and 576 choral societies. American symphony orchestras had hired great European conductors such as Arturo Toscanini, Bruno Walter, and Serge Koussevitsky, who brought with them or attracted from Europe many fine musicians. Composers such as Aaron Copland and Samuel Barber were self-consciously creating an American style. If the United States was not already the center of the musical world in 1930, it soon would attain that position.

SUGGESTED READINGS

A lively romp through the period covered in this and the following two chapters is available in Frederick Lewis Allen, *Only Yesterday* (1931). Leuchtenburg, *The Perils of Prosperity*, already cited, is equally readable and a much more careful attempt to make the period comprehensible. For an outline of a new emphasis among events and a different interpretive framework, see Stanley Coben, "The First Years of Modern America," in W. E. Leuchtenburg, ed., *The Unfinished Century* (1973).

George Soule, *Prosperity Decade: From War to Depression, 1917–1929* (1947), is a superior economic history. Business attitudes and practices are studied in James W. Prothro, *The Dollar Decade: Business Ideas in the 1920's* (1954). Useful information on the institutions of business will be found in Thomas C. Cochran, *The American Business System: A Historical Perspective, 1900–1955* (1957). Sigfried Giedion, *Mechanization Takes Command: A Contribution to Anonymous History* (1948), is a stimulating interpretation of the growth of industrial technology, but see also Elting E. Morison, *From Know-How to Nowhere: The Development of American Technology* (1974). For a detailed account of the decade's most famous industrialist, see Allan Nevins and F. E. Hill, *Ford: The Times, the Man and the Company* (1954) and *Ford: Expansion and Challenge* (1957). Adolph A. Berle, Jr., and G. C. Means, *The Modern Corporation and Private Property* (1932); Thomas Wilson, *Fluctuations in Income and Employment* (1948); and Emanuel A. Goldenweiser, *American Monetary Policy* (1951), are important specialized studies. Labor and widespread poverty in the twenties are examined in Irving Bernstein, *The Lean Years* (1960).

On intellectual currents, Edmund Wilson, *The Shores of Light* (1952) and *The American Earthquake* (1958), and the appropriate chapters in Alfred Kazin's *On Native Grounds* (1942) provide a good introduction. Among many fine literary portraits are Mark Schorer, *Sinclair Lewis* (1961); Cleanth Brooks, *William Faulkner: The Yoknapatawpha Country* (1963); Joseph L. Blotner, *Faulkner*, 2 vols. (1974); H. D. Piper, *F. Scott Fitzgerald: A Critical Portrait* (1965); and Carlos Baker, *Hemingway: The Writer as Artist* (1956) and *Ernest Hemingway: A Life Story* (1969). Max Eastman, *Enjoyment of Living* (1948), is a lively and perceptive autobiography.

George E. Mowry, ed., *The Twenties: Fords, Flappers and Fanatics* (1963), is an illuminating anthology of contemporary comment. Several excellent and even amusing retrospective essays on the period appear in Isabel Leighton, ed., *The Aspirin Age, 1919–1941* (1949). On college youth in the 1920s, see Paula S. Fass, *The Damned and the Beautiful* (1977).

Norman F. Furniss, *The Fundamentalist Controversy, 1918–1931* (1954), is the standard account of a movement that divided American Protestantism during the twenties. Ray Ginger, *Six Days or Forever?* (1958), is the best description of the Scopes trial. On that subject, see also Lawrence Levine, *Defender of the Faith, William Jennings Bryan: The Last Decade, 1915–1925* (1965).

David M. Chalmers, *Hooded Americanism: The First Century of the Ku Klux Klan* (1965), is especially good on the twenties, but it should be supplemented by Kenneth T. Jackson, *The Ku Klux Klan in the City, 1915–1930* (1967), and Charles C. Alexander, *The Ku Klux Klan in the Southwest* (1965); and Robert A. Goldberg, *Hooded Empire: The Ku Klux Klan in Colorado* (1981). On prohibition, Andrew Sinclair, *The Era of Excess* (1962), is readable and enjoyable, but the older accounts, Herbert Asbury, *The Great Illusion* (1950), and Charles Merz, *Dry Decade* (1931), offer valid viewpoints and additional information. More theoretical works about the meaning of prohibition are Joseph Gusfeld, *Symbolic Crusade: Status Politics and the American Temperance Movement* (1963), and Norman H. Clark, *Deliver Us from Evil: An Interpretation of American Prohibition* (1976). Clark presents what amounts to a modern defense of prohibition, and, to some extent, of the values it represented. Prominent figures associated with prohibition are the subject of a number of books, the best of which are F. D. Pasley, *Al Capone* (1930), and Virginius Dabney, *Dry Messiah: The Life of Bishop Cannon* (1949).

On the Harlem Renaissance, see Nathan I. Huggins, *Harlem Renaissance* (1971); Huggins, ed., *Voices from the Harlem Renaissance* (1976); and the chapters on that subject in Gunther Schuller, *Early Jazz* (1968). The only good biography of Garvey is E. David Cronon, *Black Moses: The Story of Marcus Garvey* (1955), but see also Amy Jacque Garvey, *Garvey and Garveyism* (1963).

CHAPTER 7
REPUBLICAN
ASCENDANCY

1. THE RENEWAL OF THE GOP

The Decline of Reform

It is easy to get a distorted view of American national politics during the 1920s. All superficial signs point to easy generalizations: Harding's landslide victory in the presidential election of 1920, according to the conventional versions, represented a repudiation of progressivism and a return to McKinley-like policies of support for big business. Securely in the hands of financiers, manufacturers, and businessmen, the dominant Republican party enacted tariff, tax, and other legislation to benefit business and neglected labor and agriculture. In addition, probusiness Presidents and a property-minded Supreme Court worked to prevent the adoption, or to achieve the nullification, of progressive legislation.

There is some truth in these generalizations. Two of Woodrow Wilson's successors, Warren G. Harding and Calvin Coolidge, were conservative Republicans who believed that encouragement of business enterprise was the national government's first duty. They also packed federal regulatory agencies with men friendly to the industries which they were supposed to regulate. The most powerful voices in the Republican party were the spokesmen of financial and business interests. Moreover, the Supreme Court wrecked two of progressivism's most notable achievements. In Hammer v. Dagenhart (1918) and Bailey v. Drexel Furniture Company (1922), the court nullified the Child Labor acts of 1916 and 1919 on the ground that they violated the rights of the states to regulate wages and working conditions. The Supreme Court went a step further in Adkins v. Children's Hospital (1923) and outlawed all state attempts to set minimum wages for women workers.

In reality, the shape of politics during the 1920s was considerably more complex than the foregoing description implies. Although progressivism as a force in national politics was at ebb tide, the progressive movement not only survived but also expanded its objectives in the 1920s. The explanation of this contradiction—and an understanding of the nature of politics in the 1920s—lies in a discussion of the history of the progressive movement between the Armistice and the Great Depression.

The desertion of some intellectuals and writers who were disenchanted with democracy because of such popular movements as the prohibition and antievolution crusades gravely weakened progressivism. The urban middle classes, who had composed a large part of the progressive constituency and had provided much of its leadership, also abandoned the reform cause after 1920. They were, perhaps, tired of successive calls to them to reform the nation and then the world; but that is not the full explanation of their change in mood. The middle classes were caught up in one of the greatest technological and economic revolutions in modern history, and they thought that they were building a new business civilization. It was to be a civilization based upon a whole new set of business values—mass production and consumption, short hours and high wages, full employment, and welfare capitalism. With such bright prospects, it was no wonder that the groups who constituted the urban middle classes, whether in New York, Atlanta, or Chicago, lost interest in rebellion or even in mild proposals for reform.

Progressivism, always a nonpartisan movement, had succeeded only when its forces captured a great national party. The movement was most seriously weakened in the 1920s because it was unable to find an acceptable political vehicle. The Republican party passed largely outside the control of its insurgent faction. During the presidential primaries of 1920, the Republican progressives, Hiram W. Johnson, Frank Lowden, and Leonard Wood, won almost all the contested states. Because these three strong-minded progressives refused to compromise, however, the deadlocked convention nominated Warren G. Harding, whom they all had easily defeated in Republican primaries. After Johnson refused Harding's offer of the vice-presidential nomination, the tired convention offhandedly nominated Calvin Coolidge, who, like Harding, had previously shown little ability to win votes outside his home state of Massachusetts. But the wide margin of Harding's victory in 1920 meant that Republican leaders saw no reason to appease progressive voters, and conservative party leaders—representing eastern and midwestern industrial, financial, and oil interests—were able to consolidate and extend their power.

There was always the hope of a third party. Numerous progressive groups came together under Senator Robert M. La Follette's leadership in 1924. Their ranks included insurgent midwestern Republicans, the railroad brotherhoods, the AFL, several state farmer-labor parties, and most of the country's politically active intellectuals. But these progressives soon discovered that third-party movements in the United States are doomed to failure, except in extraordinary circumstances such as those of 1856–1860.

By default, the Democratic party remained the only vehicle through which progressives might work. Yet, that party was not capable of such service in the 1920s. It had not only lost Wilson's magnetic leadership, but the peace in 1918–1919 left the party—particularly its progressive wing—in shambles. Indeed, it lacked national, unifying leadership of any kind. Worse still, the Democrats were so torn by conflicts between their urban constituencies (largely from the East and Middle West) and their southern and western rural voters that they literally ceased to be a national political force. On the local and state level, the party remained strong; but, on the national level, it was so divided over issues such as prohibition, the restriction of immigration, and the Ku Klux Klan that it barely succeeded in nominating a presidential candidate at all in 1924. In 1928, it nominated a candidate from the urban wing, but at the cost of temporary disruption.

Nevertheless, progressive groups—both Republican and Democratic—were still strong enough to dominate Congress during most of the 1920s. However, they were so divided among themselves as partisans that they could not unite to capture the national government, as they had done so dramatically in 1912 and 1916. As a consequence, the conservative groups which controlled the Republican party had little difficulty in winning the presidency and therefore in appointing the other executive and judicial officers of the federal government. This complex situation and series of accidents have given a misleading portrait of politics during the 1920s, and to some extent of the era as a whole.

The Travesty of Warren G. Harding

The history of the presidency has proved that a man of average education and adequate mental equipment can do well in the office if he has the desire to be a strong leader. Above all, he must possess integrity, reasonably good judgment, and the determination to rule wisely. Unfortunately, Warren Gamaliel Harding had barely average intelligence, no desire to be a strong President, and a flawed character. As President, he speculated on the stock market and spent much of his time drinking and playing poker and bridge with his cronies. He was lazy, morally undisciplined, and had a positive dislike of strenuous mental effort. As former editor and proprietor of the Marion, Ohio, *Star,* he had the world view of provincial, small-town America. As an undistinguished member of the Ohio legislature and the United States Senate, he had no training for national leadership. Consequently, Harding as President simply refused to give leadership to his administration, to Congress, to the country, or even to his own friends and subordinates. Fortunately, Harding's abdication of leadership permitted several of his capable cabinet members, particularly Secretary of State Charles Evans Hughes, Secretary of Agriculture Henry C. Wallace, and Secretary of Commerce Herbert Hoover, to carry on vigorous and constructive policies. Able Republicans in Congress also passed an impressive legislative program between 1921 and 1923. But in both cases, neither initiative nor leadership came from the White House.

The "Ohio Gang"

It is difficult to imagine a more striking contrast than the one between the outgoing and incoming Presidents on March 4, 1921. On the one side stood

Wilson, gravely weakened by his stroke and hobbling on a cane, but stronger than ever in his confidence that future events and the American people would vindicate his fight for the League of Nations. On the other side was his handsome and vigorous successor, accompanied by a host of friends who crowded around the new Chief Executive. So many of them came from Ohio that they have been called the "Ohio Gang." They were Harding's own appointees and his personal cronies.

Their leader was Harding's old intimate friend from Ohio and the new Attorney General of the United States, Harry M. Daugherty, who had already earned a nationwide reputation as a corrupt politician and lobbyist. Numerous other members of this group of buccaneers, incompetents, and ne'er-do-wells gathered regularly in a residence known as the Little Green House on K Street in Washington to trade favors, drink, and play poker. Harding's easygoing temperament and dogged devotion to these friends led to tragedy for both himself and the nation. With the possible exception of the Grant and Nixon administrations, the American government has never been so disgraced as it was during the two short years of Harding's tenure.

Colonel Thomas W. Miller, Alien Property Custodian, accepted a bribe for supporting false claims to the property of the American Metal Company, for which he was later sentenced to eighteen months in a federal penitentiary. Colonel Charles R. Forbes, formerly a member of the executive committee of the American Legion in the state of Washington, stole an uncounted amount of money as head of the Veterans' Bureau before he was caught and sent to Leavenworth Prison. "Jess" Smith, an intimate of Daugherty, acted as collector and distributor of graft taken from persons who broke the prohibition and tax laws and who wished to buy immunity from prosecution or presidential pardons (which were recommended by the Attorney General). When Harding ordered him to return to Ohio, Smith committed suicide in the apartment which he shared with Daugherty. (Smith also shared a large bank account with the Attorney General.) Forbes' chief counsel, Charles F. Cramer, also killed himself rather than face investigation. Daugherty was tried in 1927 on charges of sharing bribes with "Jess" Smith and his brother, Mal S. Daugherty, but the indictment was dismissed after the jury twice failed to agree on a verdict, although in both cases a majority of the jurors voted to convict. Harry M. Daugherty perhaps saved himself from conviction because he refused to testify and implied that, if he did so, he might have to implicate the still popular, though deceased, Harding in criminal activity.

Teapot Dome and Beyond

The most sensational scandal of the Harding administration was an attempted theft of some of the federal government's oil reserves. A group of wealthy oil producers, which included Jake Hamon, Republican national committeeman from Oklahoma, Harry F. Sinclair of New York, and Edward L. Doheny of Los Angeles, exercised an influence in the Republican convention of 1920 that rivaled that of the senatorial clique which represented big-business interests.

Oil was a prime necessity for national defense. The oil-burning ships of the navy used 137,500 barrels in 1911 and 7,000,000 barrels in 1919. In 1912, the government had set aside, for the use of the navy, oil reserve No. 1 at Elk

Hills, California; in 1915, it also set aside reserve No. 3 at Teapot Dome, Wyoming. When wells in the neighborhood threatened to draw the oil from these reserves, the government considered pumping out its own oil and storing it in tanks for the use of the navy. Instead, it decided to lease the lands to private operators who would build storage tanks and supply the navy with fuel oil.

Heretofore, the Interior Department had leased public lands. Secretary of the Interior Albert B. Fall, with the consent of Secretary of the Navy Edwin Denby, secured an executive order which transferred jurisdiction over the reserves from the Navy Department to the Interior Department. Fall then proceeded secretly, without competitive bids, to lease Teapot Dome to Sinclair, who had made a large contribution to the Republican campaign fund in 1920, and Elk Hills to Doheny. Not long afterward, Fall's private fortunes, which had been in a bad way, began to show spectacular improvement. He paid up his back taxes, restocked his cattle ranch in New Mexico, and bought additional land.

News of Fall's actions leaked at once, and a special Senate committee headed by Thomas J. Walsh of Montana began a searching investigation in the autumn of 1923. Fall, Sinclair, and Doheny all denied that there had been any wrongdoing, but Walsh stayed on the trail, and the truth of the sordid business was fully revealed in 1924. Fall had accepted a "loan" of $100,000 from Doheny at the time that the lease of Elk Hills was under negotiation. Sinclair had given Fall $223,000 in government bonds, $85,000 in cash, and a herd of cattle while the lease for Teapot Dome was being concluded. Sinclair and the presidents of four other oil companies had organized the Continental Trading Company to drill wells on Teapot Dome. This company had contracted to buy 35,000,000 barrels of oil from Sinclair's Mammoth Oil Company, which owned the lease on Teapot Dome, at $1.50 a barrel. And the presidents of the same oil companies had agreed to sell the same oil to their own companies at $1.75 a barrel. Thus they would realize for themselves a tidy profit of $8 or $9 million.

Sinclair and Doheny were brought to trial for conspiracy and bribery in 1926. They were acquitted, although Sinclair had to spend a term in the District of Columbia jail for attempted bribery of jurors in his case. In the following year, the government easily won its suit for cancellation of the leases. Fall, who had fled to Europe, was brought home and tried for conspiracy to defraud the government in 1929. He was convicted, fined $100,000, and sentenced to a year in jail. Fall, sent to the federal jail in Santa Fe, New Mexico, became the first corrupt cabinet member in American history to that date who received something like his just reward.

The Death of Harding

Harding, his wife, and a large entourage set out upon a transcontinental tour in late June 1923. Far from well when he left Washington, Harding was deeply depressed. He feared disgrace and political doom because he already knew about Forbes' corruption and suspected that Fall was also guilty of fraud. "I have no trouble with my enemies," Harding confided to a friend just before he left Washington. "I can take care of my enemies all right. But my damn friends. . . . They're the ones that keep me walking the floor nights!"

The trip through the Middle West brought no relief because that section was in the midst of a searing heat wave. Harding and his party went on to Alaska from the Northwest. Secretary of Commerce Herbert Hoover joined the voyage at Tacoma, Washington, and found Harding extremely nervous and lonely. "As soon as we were aboard ship," Hoover recalled almost thirty years later, Harding "insisted on playing bridge, beginning every day immediately after breakfast and continuing except for mealtime often until after midnight."

On the return trip, Harding barely completed a speech in Vancouver before he collapsed. When he reached San Francisco, his condition became worse, although it was not considered critical. The country was, therefore, shocked when news came that he had died suddenly of pneumonia in the early evening of August 2, 1923.

Death came none too soon to release Harding from his troubles. Americans mourned for the distinguished President that they thought Harding had been. Friends began to raise money for a Harding Memorial Association to preserve his memory. However, it was not long before most of the truth about the scandals emerged, and Harding's own personal misbehavior was exposed to full view. So quickly was his reputation deflated that some people began to believe such wild rumors as one to the effect that Mrs. Harding had poisoned her husband because of his affairs with other women.

Calvin Coolidge and the Prosperity Decade

The news of Harding's death arrived at the Coolidge farmhouse in Plymouth, Vermont, where Vice-President Calvin Coolidge was spending his vacation, early in the morning of August 3, 1923. The family was immediately aroused from bed and came down to the parlor. There, by the light of a kerosene lamp, John Coolidge, justice of the peace, administered to his son the oath of office as thirtieth President of the United States.

Unlike his predecessor, the new President was no handsome, genial fellow, who was surrounded by cronies and exuded good spirits. Coolidge was a Puritan Yankee—plain and austere. He placed personal honesty, thrift, and individualism at the top of his list of virtues; and he was as rigid as the granite of his Vermont hills, although not nearly as silent as his reputation led people to believe. Coolidge, born in Plymouth, Vermont, on July 4, 1872, made his home in Northampton, Massachusetts, after he was graduated from Amherst College in 1895. He studied law in the old-fashioned way in the office of a successful firm. He entered local politics in 1899 and advanced steadily to election as governor of Massachusetts in 1918. The Boston police strike of 1919 had made him a national hero and provided a reason for the tired delegates at the Republican convention of 1920 to nominate him for Vice-President.

Coolidge had never been to Washington before he went there to take up his new duties in 1921. Indeed, he had scarcely been beyond the boundaries of Massachusetts and Vermont. Reared in the political traditions of the New England countryside, he had the world view of those Americans who lived in rural isolation. Scrupulously honest himself, he systematically cleaned up the mess left by the Harding scandals. He discharged Daugherty and appointed Harlan F. Stone, Dean of the Columbia University Law School, as Attorney

General. Coolidge gave Stone and the Justice Department full support in further investigations and prosecutions.

Coolidge was, moreover, heir to the eastern Hamiltonian, Whig, and Republican tradition of close relations between government, business, and finance. "The business of America is business," he said in his Annual Message to Congress in December 1923. Coolidge did not share Wilson's concern for the downtrodden. Nor did Coolidge have Theodore Roosevelt's and Wilson's faith in governmental regulation and participation in economic and social affairs. Coolidge believed simply in low taxes, encouragement of business enterprise, and as little governmental interference as possible. Hence he followed a policy of massive inaction—both legislative and administrative. When progressive groups in Congress combined to adopt legislation in the reform tradition, Coolidge relentlessly vetoed their bills. Indeed, he is unique among Presidents for having vetoed more important legislation than he signed.

2. DISSENT AND REFORM DURING THE 1920s

Political Patterns, 1921–1928

The presence of do-nothing Presidents in the White House between 1921 and 1929 implies incorrectly that the American national political scene was untroubled during the 1920s. A severe decline in agricultural prices began before Harding's inauguration, and recession spread from the countryside to the cities in the spring of 1921. The dominant group in the Sixty-seventh Congress, which met in April 1921, was the midwestern and western insurgent Republicans. When the insurgents combined with the Democrats, they, rather than the administration, controlled Congress and determined legislative policies on many critical issues. Discontent was so strong that the Democrats narrowly missed winning both houses of Congress in the off-year election of 1922.

A new progressive revolt seemed to impend. The Republican national convention met at Cleveland on June 10, 1924, and ignored the danger signals; it nominated Coolidge for the presidency on a conservative platform.

A rare opportunity thus existed for the Democrats to offer the country a strong candidate and to shape a new agrarian and labor coalition. When they assembled to nominate a presidential candidate on June 24, however, the Democrats seemed more intent on fighting each other rather than conservative Republicans. Northern big-city Democrats, who represented foreign-born and Jewish and Catholic constituencies, demanded an explicit condemnation of the Ku Klux Klan. Southern and rural Democrats, and state delegations controlled by the Klan, fought this resolution either out of sympathy for, or fear of, the secret order. Northern Democrats demanded repeal of the Eighteenth Amendment or modification of the Volstead Act. Southern and rural Democrats, dominated by Protestant dry leaders, fought back bitterly and successfully.

All the tensions within the Democratic party came to a head in the struggle over the presidential nomination. The chief contenders were Governor Alfred E. Smith of New York and former Secretary of the Treasury William G.

McAdoo. Smith was a Roman Catholic, a "wet" on prohibition, and a chieftain of the Tammany organization; McAdoo had the support of southern and western farmers, drys, and most Protestant Democrats. These included members of the Klan. Smith and McAdoo fought it out for 103 ballots, until the convention in desperation turned to John W. Davis. It was a sign of the paralysis of the party, for Davis, although a distinguished lawyer, was allied with great New York banking and industrial interests and was utterly incapable of leading any kind of revolt.

Convinced that both major parties were hopelessly reactionary, some midwestern insurgents, politically inclined intellectuals, most Rooseveltian Progressive leaders who remained in politics, and some leaders of the railroad brotherhoods and AFL met at Cleveland on July 4. They formed a new Progressive party and nominated Senator Robert M. La Follette and Senator Burton K. Wheeler of Montana on their ticket. Their platform demanded nationalization of railroads, public development of hydroelectric facilities, and the right of Congress to override decisions of the Supreme Court. The model of most of the leaders of the new Progressive party was the British Labour party. The comparison went no further, however, mainly because of the strenuous opposition of Samuel Gompers, who had long fought both Socialists and Social Democrats in the labor movement. Without Gompers' support, the Progressive party of 1924 was not able to congeal as a new Social-Democratic party, which had a well-defined and well-publicized program, stable finances, and a strong organization. The AFL could have provided all of these elements of sound party structure in much the same way as the British trade unions did for the Labour party. Without the AFL's support, the senator had insufficient funds for travel or to pay campaign aides and other expenses during the campaign. To make matters more difficult for La Follette, he was barred from the ballot in most southern states.

The campaign that followed was enlivened only by La Follette's strenuous if ill-fated attempt to win that part of the country which he could reach with his message in a new crusade. On election day of 1924, Coolidge ran up a popular vote far larger than the combined vote of Davis and La Follette and apparently enjoyed a clear mandate for the continuation of his policy of inaction. Actually, the election returns more strongly suggested Democratic impotency and public apathy. Only 52 per cent of the voters bothered to go to the polls; and, outside the South, La Follette garnered almost as many popular votes as did Davis.

The Budget Fight

It is impossible to relate the legislative history of the 1920s in sheerly partisan terms, because alignments in Congress were more often sectional and economic than political. There were four major groups in Congress during the decade: midwestern insurgent Republicans, who organized themselves into the so-called Farm Bloc in 1921; southern Democrats, most of whom represented agrarian constituencies and often cooperated with the Farm Bloc; and conservative Republicans and Democrats, mainly from urban areas. Since none of these three groups controlled a reliable majority at any time during the Harding-Coolidge administrations, legislation could be achieved only by coalitions. The fourth group, which by 1930 had emerged as a powerful force, were urban liberals, such as Senator Robert F. Wagner and Representative Fiorello La Guardia, both of New York. They represented northern urban constituencies, including recent immigrants and black migrants from the South, and, by the 1930s—some historians say by 1928—constituted the pivotal group in American politics.

For the most part, these congressional groups were floating entities. In 1921, the Farm Bloc and administration Republicans combined to reenact a measure which increased tariff duties on meat and farm staples, a bill which Wilson had vetoed a year earlier. These two groups cooperated again in 1922 to push through the Fordney-McCumber Tariff Act. It greatly increased duties on farm products and helped new industries such as chemicals but provided only moderate increases for the great mass of industrial products. Actually, the framers of the Fordney-McCumber bill claimed that they tried to follow the Wilsonian policy of equalizing differences in costs of production in the United States and abroad.

Tax legislation was a very different story. All through the 1920s, the chief objective of the business interests and of Secretary of the Treasury Andrew W. Mellon was drastic reduction of the high wartime taxes. A midwestern-southern Democratic coalition wrecked Mellon's plan in 1921 by pushing through a tax bill that only slightly relieved the tax burden on the wealthy. Mellon renewed the struggle again in 1923. Again the midwestern-southern Democratic coalition rebuffed him by reducing income taxes significantly only for middle-income groups and by increasing the estate tax. Mellon finally had his way in the Revenue acts of 1926 and 1928, which cut the maximum surtax on incomes from 40 to 20 per cent and slashed the estate tax in half. But the Secretary won adoption of his program only because surpluses were piling up in the Treasury. The country was prosperous, and the insurgents and southern Democrats could no longer justify punitive taxes on wealth. Meanwhile, Congress also defied the administration by adopting bonus, or adjusted compensation, measures for veterans. These bonuses were to recompense the men who had served in the armed forces at low pay during the First World War, while their neighbors were enjoying full employment and high wages. Harding vetoed a bonus bill in 1922, but Congress reenacted the measure in 1924 and passed it over Coolidge's veto.

Agricultural Problems

The most important domestic problem of the 1920s was the agricultural depression which began in 1920 and continued off and on until about 1935. The recession early in the decade sent agriculture into a tailspin, as total farm income declined from more than $10 billion in 1919 to a little more than $4 billion in 1921. After some recovery, farm income ran between $6 and $7 billion a year between 1923 and 1929. Moreover, the decline of agriculture was relative as well as absolute, for farmers received only 8.8 per cent of the national income in 1929, as compared with 16 per cent in 1919.

The causes for distress in rural areas are not hard to find. Wartime demand had pushed up farm prices, and farmers were thus encouraged to increase their output by expanding the cultivation of marginal farmlands and investing in machinery, both at high prices. With the return of peace in 1919, however, this house of cards quickly collapsed. World output increased significantly in nations such as France, Argentina, and Canada. Canadian wheat output, for example, increased nearly 1,000 per cent in the postwar decade. The result was rapid decline in agricultural prices in the immediate postwar years and generally low prices afterward.

The American farmer's woes did not end there. While prices for the products which he sold were declining, the prices which he paid for such items as tools, machinery, and clothing increased about 30 per cent between 1919 and 1929. Worse still, constantly mounting local taxes and interest charges on mortgages increased the farmer's burden of debt. Taxes on farm property, taking 100 as the index figure for 1914, were 130 in 1919, when farmers were prosperous, and 258 in 1927, when they were in semidepression. Mortgage indebtedness—largely the result of farmers' investment in marginal lands—more than doubled during the same period; foreclosures by country banks also rose, as did the incidence of bank failures in rural areas. Finally, technological advances added to surpluses which were already smothering farmers. Improvements in farm machines, such as drillers, huskers, reapers, combines, and tractors, had made it possible to produce increasing quantities of staples with fewer workers. Furthermore, the number of gasoline tractors in use, which mostly replaced horses and mules, rose from 80,000 in 1919 to more than 800,000 a decade later. The effect on the market for hay and oats was of course disastrous.

Farm Protest

Agrarian distress in the 1920s set off the same kind of demands for governmental relief that it had produced in the late nineteenth century. The big difference between the first agrarian crusade and the second was that, by the 1920s, farmers had learned how to wield political power effectively. Senators and representatives from the midwestern and western states met in Washington in 1921 and formed the Farm Bloc to fight for the relief of agriculture. They won all their demands during the Harding administration. Farmers won high tariff protection for their products. Moreover, the Farm Bloc pushed through bills which prohibited certain kinds of speculation in grains. Other laws provided for stringent control of stockyards and packers by the Secretary of Agriculture, and the establishment of a new federal intermediate system of rural credit. Taken altogether, the farm bills of 1921–1923 were an impressive achievement. They completed the program begun by the Wilson administration and provided farmers with generous credit at low interest rates.

The main problem after 1923, then, was not lack of credit. Rather, it was how to prevent farm surpluses from depressing prices at home. George N. Peek and Hugh S. Johnson, farm-machinery manufacturers of Moline, Illinois, offered an answer in 1922 in a pamphlet entitled *Equality for Agriculture*. Peek and Johnson wrote that the federal government should segregate the surplus and, in effect, guarantee minimum prices for agricultural products sold at home. Under their plan, federal agencies would purchase all major staples produced for the market at stipulated prices and would thus set a floor under them. These agencies would also sell the surplus on the world market at world prices, and would then recoup their losses on products sold abroad by levying so-called equalization fees against farmers at home.

The Peek-Johnson plan was embodied in a bill first introduced in 1924 by Charles L. McNary of Oregon and Gilbert N. Haugen of Iowa, chairmen of the agricultural committees of the Senate and of the House, respectively. The original McNary-Haugen bill applied only to midwestern and western farm products and failed in the House on June 3, 1924. However, the Midwesterners and Westerners won southern allies in 1926 by including cotton, tobacco, and rice in the proposed system. This coalition pushed a new McNary-Haugen bill through Congress in early 1927, only to draw a sharp veto from Coolidge. The southern-western coalition failed to override the veto but pushed the measure through again in 1928 and evoked a second veto from Coolidge. This time the Farm Bloc and its allies came closer to the two-thirds vote needed to override Coolidge's veto.

The complete victory of the Farm Bloc awaited the inauguration of a President less hesitant than either Coolidge or his successor to extend governmental participation in the economy. In reality, the McNary-Haugen approach probably would not have alleviated farm distress, for it diagnosed as the root problem the system of distribution rather than of production. Yet, the extensive support for the bill's main features had momentous significance for the American progressive movement. The espousal by farmers of this measure demonstrated that the best organized and most powerful special-interest groups had accepted the proposition that it was the federal government's duty to protect the economic security of all classes—and particularly of depressed groups.

Beginnings of Public Power

One of the longest battles of the 1920s revolved around the disposition of two nitrate plants and the huge Wilson Dam and hydroelectric facility at Muscle Shoals on the Tennessee River in northern Alabama. The federal government had constructed them during the war in order to free the country from its dependence on imported nitrates. Before this struggle ended, it had become the focus of a larger, nationwide controversy over public development, ownership, or regulation of the entire electric-power industry. More important still, the controversy gave additional evidence that the progressive movement not only survived in the 1920s but was also expanding its horizons and objectives.

The end of the war found the nitrate plants at Muscle Shoals ready to go into full production, while Wilson Dam was not quite completed. One of the first acts of the Harding administration was to announce that it would lease the entire facility to any responsible private company which would complete the dam and guarantee a fair return to the government. Henry Ford excited the greatest enthusiasm by his offer. He promised to produce nitrates for cheap fertilizers and, moreover, to build an industrial complex seventy-five miles long in the Tennessee Valley.

Congress, in 1924, would have approved a bill which authorized the lease of the Muscle Shoals facilities to Ford if it had not been for the obstructionist tactics of Senator George W. Norris of Nebraska. Norris believed that Ford and other power and industrial interests were holding out the lure of cheap fertilizers for farmers in order to steal one of the nation's greatest natural assets—the hydroelectric resources of the Tennessee Valley. As early as 1922, the Nebraska senator had begun to dream of a federal agency which would build and operate a network of dams throughout the valley for flood control and the production of inexpensive electric power.

In 1924, after he blocked the bill which authorized the lease to Ford, Norris opened his own campaign for federal operation of the Muscle Shoals facilities. With strong southern support, he pushed a bill through Congress in 1928 to create a corporation to operate Wilson Dam and the nitrate plants. The lines between the champions of public power and the defenders of the private utilities were now clearly drawn, and it was well understood that federal development of the Tennessee Valley might well be only the first of such regional projects. Coolidge naturally took the side of the private interests and gave the Muscle Shoals bill a pocket veto.* But Norris refused to give up and pushed another Muscle Shoals measure through Congress in 1931. Coolidge's successor, Herbert Hoover, vetoed this bill in a ringing message which denounced governmental operation of power facilities as socialistic. However, Norris had lost only two battles, not the war. He saved the waterpower resources of the Tennessee Valley from private exploitation until a President with a different political philosophy had entered the White House.

A New Immigration Policy

Congress, in several measures in the 1920s, effected a revolution in American public policies by decreeing an end to the longstanding tradition of virtually free and unlimited immigration to the United States. Equally significant was the fact that this change was effected virtually without any partisan controversy or struggle between conservatives and progressives. Obviously, the country had come—temporarily, at least—to a fairly solid consensus on the subject, although different motivations contributed to this consensus.

Organized labor had long believed that a steady infusion of unskilled labor kept wages low and impeded the progress of unionization. The AFL and other unions had been working for restrictive measures since the 1890s. From about 1910 on, many American sociologists and social workers were convinced that unlimited immigration created widespread social disorganization and insuperable problems of assimilation. Most progressives believed in the restriction of immigration. They also thought that the government should use immigration policies to create a homogeneous population. Finally, by 1914, most Anglo-Saxon residents of the West Coast, who feared Oriental influences, were also restrictionists. In short, a majority of Americans changed from restrictionists into virtually outright exclusionists between about 1910 and the early 1920s.

The catalyst of this change was the fear in 1919 and 1920 that millions of poor and homeless Europeans, particularly in war-ravaged central and eastern Europe, were preparing to move to the United States. The postwar Red Scare severely intensified this fear of an uncontrollable inundation. Even employers of unskilled labor, who had earlier been the leading defenders of unlimited immigration, began to associate foreigners with communism and moved into the exclusionist camp.

---

*"An indirect veto of a legislative bill by an executive through retention of the bill unsigned until after adjournment of the legislature." *Webster's New Collegiate Dictionary.*

When some 1,250,000 immigrants poured into American ports in 1920 – 1921, it was no longer a question of whether Congress would act, but of what form the new legislation would take. Congress attempted to stem the flow in 1920 with a temporary measure which limited immigration to 3 per cent of the foreign-born elements in the United States in 1910. Wilson vetoed this measure, but Congress reenacted it in 1921, and Harding signed it. Congress then turned to the task of devising a permanent policy. It was embodied in the National Origins Act of 1924 and was severe enough to please all but the most extreme exclusionists. The measure abrogated the Gentlemen's Agreement with Japan by prohibiting the immigration of "persons ineligible to citizenship"—that is, all Orientals. The act also limited the number of European immigrants to 2 per cent of the foreign-born, according to the Census of 1890. The use of the date of 1890 reduced the quotas from eastern and southern Europe to about one eighth of what they had been under the Emergency Act of 1921. It also boosted the quotas for the British Isles, Germany, and the Scandinavian countries. However, the National Origins Act of 1924 also stipulated that, after July 1, 1927, only 150,000 immigrants should be admitted annually. They were to be divided among the several countries in proportion to the numbers of their nationals in the United States according to the Census of 1920.

It took longer than had been anticipated to determine the national origins of the American people; indeed, no reasonable person familiar with the problem even pretended that the result was anything more than a rough guess. But the experts had completed their work by 1929, and the new system was put into effect on July 1 of that year. President Hoover drastically reduced the quotas in 1931, largely in response to high unemployment, and the total net immigration for the decade of the 1930s was only 69,000. In part, this decline was a result of the Great Depression, which prompted immigrants to return home. Nonetheless, the quota system was undeniably rigid, and it discriminated most against eastern and southern Europeans and especially Jews.

3. REPUBLICAN FOREIGN POLICY, 1921 – 1933

The Legacy of Versailles

Most Americans in the 1920s desired only to be left alone by the rest of the world, although a minority still carried the Wilsonian torch of internationalism. Virtually all Americans were determined to defend the Monroe Doctrine and to brook no threat to the supremacy of the United States in the areas close to the Panama Canal. Moreover, the great majority of Americans were disillusioned by the results of their intervention in the First World War and by more recent events in Europe and were determined to avoid entangling obligations that might draw them into some future war.

Yet, a powerful and wealthy nation cannot remain isolated merely by wanting to be left alone, unless, perhaps, it is both willing and able to ignore its interests abroad. The United States, however, was a great power in the 1920s with economic and political interests around the world; it was also the hub of world trade and the generator of much of the world's new capital for investment. It was therefore impossible for the Harding and Coolidge administrations either to withdraw completely from world affairs or to ignore events beyond American borders.

In fact, the United States played a more active and important role in international councils during the 1920s than it usually had during the century between the Monroe and Wilson administrations. However, there were clear limits to American foreign policy during the decade: the United States would cooperate in various endeavors for peace and international economic stabilization, but only upon its own terms. The most important of these terms was the understanding that the American government would assume no obligations to maintain peace outside the Western Hemisphere.

The Washington Conference

Harding started rather blithely on his way in foreign policy by announcing in his inaugural: "We do not mean to be entangled." His Secretary of State, Charles Evans Hughes, the former Supreme Court justice and Republican presidential candidate in 1916, dutifully followed his chief's lead. For several months, Hughes refused to answer communications from the League of Nations out of fear that he would anger the extreme isolationists in the Senate. In addition, once Harding had signed a new congressional resolution which declared the war with the Central Powers at an end, Hughes proceeded to negotiate separate peace treaties with Germany, Austria, and Hungary.

Harding and Hughes clearly realized, however, that the United States in 1921 was on the brink of an intense naval race with Great Britain and Japan. Moreover, controversies at the Paris Peace Conference and the stationing, for the first time, of a large American fleet in the Pacific in 1919 had embittered relations with Japan, and chauvinistic newspapers in both countries began to talk of war. Another problem was the Anglo-Japanese Alliance of 1902, still in effect, which, in certain circumstances, might bind the British to come to Japan's aid in the event of a Japanese-American war.

Few Americans wanted a naval race, and fewer still wanted war with Japan. Senator William E. Borah of Idaho, therefore, came forward on May 15, 1921, with an amendment to the nearly half-billion-dollar naval appropriations bill. Borah's amendment requested the President to invite Great Britain and Japan to a conference in Washington to discuss reduction in naval armaments. Both houses of Congress approved the Borah resolution by overwhelming majorities. The British government, burdened by debt, was also eager for negotiations. In fact, the British Foreign Office informed the State Department that it would move for a conference if the United States did not act soon. Under this pressure, Harding sent invitations, not only to Great Britain and Japan, but also to France and Italy as important naval powers. He also invited China, the Netherlands, Belgium, and Portugal, as nations with important interests in the Far East.

Delegates from these eight countries and the United States met in Washington on November 12, 1921. In his address of welcome, Hughes startled his listeners by proposing a ten-year "holiday" in the construction of battleships. A number of capital ships (warships of over 10,000 tons or carrying guns of over eight inches bore) either already built or under construction should be scrapped. The United States, Hughes went on, was willing to scrap thirty ships totaling 845,700 tons. Great Britain should scrap nineteen ships of 583,375 tons; Japan, seventeen ships of 448,928 tons. This would amount to a total reduction in the navies of the three major naval powers of about 2,000,000 tons and leave the ratio in capital ships at five for Great Britain, five for the United States, and three for Japan. For the first time in over 200 years, Great Britain would relinquish its naval supremacy and accept the United States as a naval equal. The two great naval powers would also, for the first time, formally recognize Japan as a "great power" in the Pacific.

The Washington Treaties

Negotiations proceeded very smoothly, in spite of some difficulties in persuading France and Italy to accept definite and inferior tonnages. In fact, Hughes seized the opportunity offered by the cooperation of Great Britain and Japan to conclude a comprehensive series of treaties relating, not only to naval construction and tonnage, but to the Far East as well:

1. In the *Five-Power Treaty,* Great Britain, Japan, France, Italy, and the United States accepted Hughes' proposals relating to capital ships. France and Italy agreed to a tonnage allotment a little more than half that of Japan. In addition, the United States, Great Britain, and Japan promised not to fortify further their outlying possessions in the western Pacific.

2. *The Four-Power Treaty,* among the United States, Great Britain, Japan, and France, nullified an Anglo-Japanese Alliance of 1902. More important, it bound its signatories to respect one another's possessions in the Pacific area and to submit to joint conference any issue that seemed likely to disturb the peace of the Far East.

3. *The Nine-Power Treaty,* signed by all the delegates at the conference, guaranteed the integrity of China and the preservation of the commercial Open Door in that country. It thus gave official sanction for the first time to the policy inaugurated by Secretary of State John Hay in 1899–1900.

4. Under Hughes' auspices, delegates from China and Japan signed a treaty which provided for the return to China of Shantung Province, which the Japanese had seized from Germany during the war.

5. A final treaty by the signatories of the Five-Power Treaty prohibited the use of submarines as commerce destroyers during wartime and outlawed the use of poisonous gases.

Harding presented all these treaties to the Senate and asked speedy approval to prove that American talk about peace was not so much hollow mockery. The Senate, without much ado, gave its consent to ratification, but with an important reservation appended to the Four-Power Treaty. It said that the United States, by the terms of that treaty, had assumed "no commitment to armed force, no alliance, no obligation to join in any defense." It was one of the clearest statements on record of American determination to cooperate whenever possible to promote world peace—but to assume no obligations whatever to defend that peace. Even so, through mutual concessions, the conference stopped the naval race in capital ships and provided a political understanding which helped to preserve peace in the Orient for a decade. It was the chief accomplishment of the Harding administration.

It would have been well if congressmen and senators had remembered that international understanding is a two-way street. On one side, Japanese friendship for the United States was heightened in 1923, when a great earthquake devastated the island empire and Americans poured out millions of dollars in relief. On the other side, Congress, in the National Origins bill of 1924, abrogated the Gentlemen's Agreement which had governed immigration from Japan to the United States since 1907. Worse still, Congress prohibited immigration from Asia in language which the Japanese found humiliating. Although both Coolidge and Hughes pleaded for the deletion of these provisions, Coolidge reluctantly signed the measure on the ground that his signature was necessary if there was to be any immigration legislation at all. It was a terrible mistake. Reaction in Japan was so violent that it is no exaggeration to say that the National Origins Act of 1924 destroyed all the progress that Hughes and the liberal Japanese leaders had made since 1921 in restoring cordial relations between their two countries.

German Reparations and Allied War Debts

The necessity to work out some solution for the most vexing economic legacy of the war—the huge burden of war debts and reparations—gave additional proof that it was impossible for the American government to withdraw into blissful isolation.

The burden of intergovernmental debts was a cancer on the body of the international economy. The British government had lent some $4 billion to seventeen nations during the war; the French had borrowed from the British and also lent to many countries. The Allied governments, principally Great Britain, France, and Italy, had borrowed more than $7 billion from the United States during the war, and another $3.25 billion immediately after the Armistice. These nations, especially Great Britain, had also sold most of the assets which their citizens had owned in the United States before 1914—such as stocks in American corporations and United States government bonds—before they turned to borrowing. From 1918 to 1920, the Allied governments had stripped Germany of about $5 billion in gold, goods, railroad equipment, ships, and so on and had then imposed a reparations bill of $33 billion on that vanquished nation in 1921. Throughout the 1920s, as a result, the international system of finance was stretched taut and easily susceptible to any new shock.

The Allies, from the Paris Peace Conference onward, proposed a mutual cancellation of intergovernmental debts on the ground that they had been incurred in a common struggle against Germany. At the same time, however, they were less eager to reduce their reparations against Germany. Later in the 1920s, the former Allied governments tried over and over to tie German reparation payments directly to their own debt payments to the United States.

The Harding and Coolidge administrations followed the policy set by the Wilson administration (largely because of the adamant Allied stand on reparations) and insisted that the former Allies pay their debts to the United States in full. Congress established a World War Foreign Debt Commission in 1922, which eventually negotiated long-term funding agreements with Great Britain, France and Italy. But developments soon demonstrated that Allied debt payments depended unofficially upon German reparation payments; the latter, in turn, depended on American capital, which, after 1920, entered Germany in large amounts for industrial redevelopment.

The entire precarious structure of intergovernmental payments broke down temporarily when the German government—under the stress of making these unpopular heavy payments—defaulted on reparations payments in 1922. The French occupied the Ruhr Valley in retaliation, and the government in Berlin embarked upon a course of wild inflation. Since all of Europe was heading toward economic chaos, Secretary Hughes intervened. A special committee headed by two American bankers, Charles G. Dawes and Owen D. Young, worked out a settlement which provided for an American gold loan to Germany and a scaling down of that nation's reparations burden. In 1929, a new committee, headed by Young, further reduced the German reparations debt to $2 billion, but the structure of intergovernmental payments remained still somewhat shaky. Indeed, it collapsed entirely when depression struck the world economy after 1929. The former Allies then abandoned the effort to collect reparations payments from Germany, defaulted on their own debts to the United States, and embarked upon policies of economic nationalism which aggravated the worldwide depression by disrupting almost all trade and financial exchange.

A Peaceful International Order?

Americans were in the vanguard of the pursuit of world peace—but without accepting any obligations for its maintenance beyond some reductions in armaments. Events abroad, particularly after the settlement of the Franco-German dispute over reparations, greatly encouraged hopes that the world had entered a new era. The League of Nations seemed to be functioning well, even without American participation. The democratic German Republic entered the League in 1926. Russia, renamed the Union of Soviet Socialist Republics (USSR, or Soviet Union) was controlled by a Bolshevik government hostile to the West, but that nation was so torn by internal convulsions that it offered no threat to its neighbors, much less to the world. A liberal government in Japan sought understanding with China and cooperation with the United States and European governments.

American political leaders, for the most part, were not inclined to stand idly by when international relations seemed to be moving in new channels. The United States Government slowly established cordial relations with the League of Nations, sent unofficial "observers" to that organization, and participated in numerous League conferences. In 1923, Hughes, with Harding's approval, began a campaign for American membership in the League's judicial agency—the Permanent Court of International Justice, commonly called the World Court. Senate isolationists, led by Borah, blocked this campaign, which was carried on by every President from Harding to Franklin D. Roosevelt.

Perhaps the American people and their government would have come to maturity in international relations had it not been for the Great Depression and the collapse of the League of Nations in the early 1930s, events which caused the United States and all other nations to turn inward in their concern for domestic problems. In any case, the American thrust into world affairs in the 1920s was both extremely cautious and naive because it was based on the assumption that the United States could play a leading role in the pursuit of peace without carrying commensurate responsibility.

Leadership without responsibility was also the assumption of the most spectacular peace movement of the 1920s. This was a campaign to outlaw war, which American peace groups and isolationists such as Borah avidly supported. It culminated in the Pact of Paris, or Kellogg-Briand Treaty (so named because Secretary of State Frank B. Kellogg and the French foreign minister, Aristide Briand, were its chief negotiators and sponsors). The treaty was signed in the French capital on August 27, 1928, by representatives of all the great powers except the Soviet Union, which later signed it. "The High Contracting Parties," the pact said, "solemnly declare in the names of their respective people that they condemn recourse to war for the solution of international controversies, and renounce it as an instrument of national policy in their relations with one another." The Pact of Paris was certainly a pious affirmation of good intentions, but it provided no penalties against nations which resorted to force. It also contained enough holes and other weaknesses to satisfy any major nation. For example, it excluded wars fought in "self-defense," a term which allowed broad definition.

Coolidge continued to fight for reduction in naval armaments by calling a conference of naval powers at Geneva, Switzerland, in 1927, to limit submarines and cruisers not covered by the Five-Power Treaty of 1922. The Geneva Conference was a complete fiasco, mainly because the British and American governments had failed to settle technical details beforehand. But a new conference in London in 1930 produced a complete understanding among Great Britain, the United States, and Japan. The Treaty of London extended the "holiday" on construction of capital ships for five years and provided for the scrapping of nine battleships. It also established definite limitations on submarines, destroyers, and cruisers.

The United States and Latin America

Fear of European intervention in the Caribbean and Central America had chiefly motivated the administrations of Roosevelt, Taft, and Wilson to establish and preserve the supremacy of the United States in those areas for the protection of the Panama Canal. Various American efforts included customs receiverships, "dollar diplomacy," and outright military occupations. The removal of any threat to American supremacy in the 1920s permitted leaders in Washington to view developments in the Caribbean and Central American regions with less concern than at any time since the Venezuelan blockade crisis of 1902–1903.

First evidence that a new and more relaxed policy might be in the making came when Hughes permitted the people of the Dominican Republic, which had been administered by an American military government since 1916, to form a constitutional regime from 1922 to 1924. Hughes withdrew American troops in the latter year. He was also eager to call home the marines whom Wilson had sent into Haiti in 1915, but, because an investigating commission warned that anarchy would follow an American withdrawal, he postponed his plan.

In 1925, Hughes also withdrew a force of marines which had been stationed in Nicaragua since 1909. When civil war broke out in that country soon afterward, however, Coolidge sent back the marines to maintain an unpopular, pro-American regime. Such violent criticism among antiimperialists in the United States ensued that Coolidge hastily sent Henry L. Stimson, former Secretary of War, to mediate between the warring factions. Stimson's stern but honest mediation brought to power the antigovernment faction, which the United States not only supported but also helped to suppress a bandit faction. As peace returned to Nicaragua from 1931 to 1933, American troops were withdrawn. But American intervention insured that a family dynasty, the Somozas, would control Nicaragua and rule it corruptly and violently, with the aid of American arms and military training for its troops, for over forty-five years.

Dealing with small Caribbean and Central American republics was easy compared to the difficulties of following wise policies toward the larger and more sensitive population of Mexico—a country with a long history of antagonistic relations with the United States. Americans had invested about $1 billion in Mexican mines, oil fields, railroads, and other enterprises. Leaders of of the Mexican Revolution had adopted a constitution in 1917, Article XXVII of which vested ownership of all oil and mineral resources in the Mexican people. All went reasonably well between the United States and Mexico so long as the Mexican government did not try to implement Article XXVII.

Dangerous friction developed when a strong nationalist, Plutarco Elías Calles, came to power in 1924. Two years later, the Mexican Congress adopted laws to enforce Article XXVII. Calles also embarked upon a bloody persecution of the Roman Catholic Church which inflamed sentiment in the United States.

Coolidge and Kellogg, who had succeeded Hughes in 1925, reacted violently. They accused Calles of violating international law—a dubious interpretation of his actions—and also of establishing a Bolshevik-controlled regime in Mexico. However, tempers cooled on both sides of the border once the new American ambassador, the New York banker Dwight W. Morrow, arrived in Mexico City in 1927. Through tact, understanding of Mexican pride and nationalism, and demonstrations of sympathy for Mexican ambitions, Morrow won the confidence of the Mexican government and people. He also won a new agreement on American-owned oil fields and persuaded Calles to halt his campaign against the Roman Catholic Church. Mexican-American friendship was further strengthened when Charles A. Lindbergh landed at Mexico City on December 14, 1927, after a nonstop goodwill flight of 2,200 miles from Washington. This mood in Mexico lasted until 1938, when the Mexican government practically confiscated the remaining American oil properties.

Meanwhile, the State Department had also undertaken a retreat from the Roosevelt Corollary to the Monroe Doctrine. Although the United States was not yet ready to abandon the alleged right to intervene when it thought that its vital interests were at stake—a position which former Secretary of State Hughes made clear at the sixth Pan American Congress in Havana in 1928—the State Department, in a memorandum prepared by Counselor J. Reuben Clark, admitted that intervention in the affairs of other countries could not be justified by appealing to the Monroe Doctrine. Coolidge's successor, Herbert Hoover, refused to intervene in Latin America during his tenure from 1929 to 1933, in spite of widespread repudiations and revolutions. Thus the way was well prepared for what would be called the Good Neighbor Policy of nonintervention and cooperation by Hoover's successor, Franklin D. Roosevelt.

SUGGESTED READINGS

In addition to the general works by Allen, Leuchtenburg, and Soule, mentioned in the Suggested Readings for the preceding chapter, Arthur M. Schlesinger, Jr., *The Crisis of the Old Order* (1957), is a lucid interpretation of the decade. For a rather conventional political history, see John D. Hicks, *Republican Ascendancy* (1960). Two major problems of the period are discussed in the relevant chapters of Theodore Saloutos and John D. Hicks, *Agricultural Discontent in the Middle West, 1900—1939* (1951), and Randolph E. Paul, *Taxation in the United States* (1954). For a classic history of the South during this period, see Tindall, *The Emergence of the New South,* already cited.

The Harding scandals receive a thorough airing in Samuel H. Adams, *Incredible Era* (1939), and Karl Schriftgiesser, *This Was Normalcy* (1948). Andrew Sinclair attempts, with little success, to redeem some part of Harding's reputation in *The Available Man* (1965). Robert K. Murray's *The Harding Era* (1968), although based on more original research than Sinclair's book, is an even less persuasive defense of its subject. Francis Russell arouses sympathy for and understanding of Harding somewhat more successfully in *The Shadow of Blooming Grove* (1968). J. Chalmers Vinson, *The Parchment Peace* (1950), is a good study of the Washington Conference. Dexter Perkins, *Charles Evans Hughes and American Democratic Statesmanship* (1953), is an exceptional study of the Republican Secretary of State. Calvin Coolidge is the subject of William A. White's entertaining, *A Puritan in Babylon* (1938). A more sympathetic, fuller, and somewhat more penetrating biography is Donald R. McCoy, *Calvin Coolidge: The Quiet President* (1967).

Adequate, brief accounts of the election of 1924 can be found in Nye, *Midwestern Progressive Politics,* already cited. A more detailed analysis is provided in Kenneth C. MacKay, *The Progressive Movement of 1924* (1947). For a revisionist analysis of the thesis that the La Follette candidacy possessed a potentiality which most "consensus" historians have ignored, see James Weinstein, *The Decline of Socialism in America, 1912–1925* (1967). The fragmentation and reorientation of the Democratic party is analyzed in David Burner, *The Politics of Provincialism: The Democratic Party in Transition, 1918–1932* (1968).

Several good biographies illuminate this period. Among them are Frank Freidel, *Franklin Roosevelt: The Ordeal* (1954); Matthew and Hannah Josephson, *Al Smith: Hero of the Cities* (1969); Oscar Handlin, *Al Smith and His America* (1958); Arthur Mann, *La Guardia: A Fighter against His Times* (1959); Elting E. Morison, *Tradition and Turmoil: A Study of the Life and Times of Henry L. Stimson* (1960); William H. Harbaugh, *Lawyer's Lawyer: The Life of John W. Davis* (1973); and Richard Lowitt, *George W. Norris: The Persistence of a Progressive* (1971). Two autobiographical accounts of exceptional importance are Henry L. Stimson and McGeorge Bundy, *On Active Service in Peace and War* (1948), and George W. Norris, *Fighting Liberal* (1945).

CHAPTER 8
HERBERT HOOVER AND
THE GREAT DEPRESSION

1. THE POLITICS OF PROSPERITY

The Election of 1928

While on vacation in the Black Hills of South Dakota, President Coolidge handed the following cryptic statement to reporters on August 2, 1927: "I do not choose to run for President in 1928." We now know that Coolidge would have welcomed a draft, although he did not relish the effort required to arrange his own renomination. Nonetheless, rank-and-file Republicans were delighted to release him from the burdens of office. Tired of a do-nothing President, they demanded the nomination of Herbert Hoover, Secretary of Commerce since 1921, who enjoyed a reputation for vigor and moderate progressivism. The Republican national convention gracefully yielded to this popular desire by nominating Hoover on the first ballot. The Republican platform endorsed prohibition and tariff protection. It also promised farm relief, but declared that the government should not engage in price fixing.

The Democratic party remained deeply split among its southern and eastern and its Protestant and Catholic wings. Although Southerners warned that the nomination of Governor Alfred E. Smith of New York would wreck the party, he was the only Democrat of national stature available in 1928. With the support of northern and western delegates (especially those from urban areas, or rural areas settled by Irish-American or recent immigrants), the New Yorker won the nomination easily at the Democratic national convention in Houston. Southerners were mollified somewhat by the

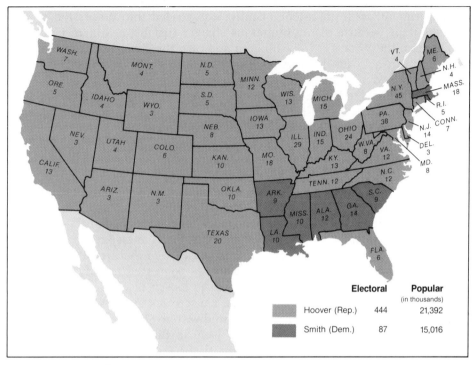

The Election of 1928

defeat of a Smith-sponsored platform plank which demanded the repeal of the Eighteenth Amendment.

Never had the nation as a whole been more content with its present situation or more confident of its future than in the summer and autumn of 1928. Not since James Monroe had a presidential candidate faced so easy a campaign as Hoover. He made only half a dozen speeches and emphasized the general prosperity under Republican rule and promised its continuance. As he put it in his acceptance speech: "We in America today are nearer to the final triumph over poverty than ever before in the history of any land. The poorhouse is vanishing from among us. We have not yet reached the goal, but, given a chance to go forward with the policies of the last eight years, we shall soon, with the help of God, be in sight of the day when poverty will be banished from this nation." Moreover, Hoover made it plain that he stood foursquare against such proposals as the McNary-Haugen bill, federal operation of power projects, and legislation that singled out organized labor for special benefits.

Smith had a long record as a defender of civil rights and as a champion of progressive legislation in New York. Yet, he demurred from trying to shape a new reform coalition based on farmers and urban Americans and chose instead to make his campaign on the two issues of prohibition and religious toleration. Immediately after his nomination, Smith notified the Houston convention that he would feel free to advocate repeal of the Volstead Act, and perhaps also of the Eighteenth Amendment. Throughout his campaign, he attacked prohibition, which Hoover had defended in his acceptance speech as an "experiment noble in intent." Smith was goaded into discussion of the religious issue because of the numerous charges that he, a Roman Catholic, would move the Vatican to Washington and turn the government over to his church. Smith hit back hard at bigotry, but by so doing he helped to make religion the leading issue of the campaign.

It was evident long before election day, November 6, 1928, that Smith was struggling hopelessly against an overwhelming Republican tide. Few observers were surprised when Hoover won. He carried forty out of the forty-eight states; broke the Solid South by capturing Virginia, North Carolina, Tennessee, Florida, and Texas; and won 21,392,190 popular votes to 15,016,443 for Smith. Yet, there were signs of profound changes in American national politics. The Solid South was gone forever, at least in presidential elections; Democrats could no longer wage a campaign absolutely assured of solid southern support. Of even greater significance for the future, Smith—the hero of the urban democracy—made the Democratic party indisputably the party of the non-Protestant masses in the great cities. Smith carried the twelve largest cities and ran very well in all counties populated heavily by Roman Catholics and recent immigrants. He began to loosen black ties to the party of Lincoln by attracting about half of the black votes in the northern cities. Finally, Smith ran far better in the midwestern farm states than any Democratic candidate since Woodrow Wilson. In these respects, Smith, and the Democratic party, inherited elements of La Follette's coalition.

Hoover and American Individualism

Herbert Hoover delivered his inaugural address on March 4, 1929, in a cold, drizzling rain. By contrast, his speech radiated bright hope for the future.

The man whom the American people had chosen to lead the way to permanent prosperity was a perfect symbol of old hopes of economic abundance and living proof of the vitality of the American tradition of success through character and hard work. Herbert Clark Hoover was born on a small farm at West Branch, Iowa, on August 10, 1874. He was orphaned at the age of ten and later worked his way through Stanford University. He gradually accumulated a large fortune as a mining engineer and investor in mining properties in many parts of the world. Hoover was director of the Belgian Relief Commission and devoted his superb administrative talents to the task of feeding the people of Belgium and northeastern France. When his own country entered the war in 1917, he returned home to become Food Administrator. He probably could have had the Democratic presidential nomination in 1920, but he decided that he was a Republican and refused all Democratic overtures.

As President, Hoover brought with him experience in administration and a well-defined philosophy about the role of government in society. As Secretary of Commerce under Harding and Coolidge, Hoover drew on the pattern of successful cooperation between government and industry during the First World War. He fervently believed that the security of democratic freedoms depended on the federal government's ability to strike a balance between excessive bureaucratic regulation and the chaotic tendencies of unlimited competition in industry. Thus he advocated the creation of business and industrial trade associations as vehicles of self-regulation, elimination of wasteful competition, and promotion of increased standardization. In certain "sick" industries, such as oil and textiles, Hoover advocated the relaxation of antitrust legislation.

The American people had elected generals, lawyers, and politicians to lead their government, but Hoover was the first and so far the only business executive of stature to occupy the White House. Hoover had never run for elective office or engaged in mere politics. He was accustomed to directing great enterprises and to giving orders which would be obeyed without question. Such experience might be an advantage so long as the new President had comfortable majorities in Congress and the strong support of public opinion. But his lack of political experience, particularly the lack of experience in getting on with persons of opposing views, would place a heavy burden on Hoover's abilities as a leader once the political tide turned against him.

The Political Economy of Prosperity

In the prosperous early months of 1929, it seemed to political leaders, especially Republicans, that the only serious national problem was relief for agriculture. Soon after his inauguration, Hoover called the Seventy-first Congress into special session. Farm leaders still insisted that only something like the McNary-Haugen plan would afford a lasting solution, but the new President made it plain that he would not accept any far-reaching governmental intervention to maintain agricultural prices. Hoover's alternative—the Agricultural Marketing bill—was, at least in its original draft, perfectly tailored to fit Hoover's philosophy. It created a Federal Farm Board and gave it a revolving fund of $500 million to be lent to agricultural cooperatives to enable them to build warehouses and sell crops in an orderly way. However, midwestern Republicans and southern Democrats in the Senate changed the measure significantly. They added a provision which authorized the Federal Farm Board to establish corporations to purchase farm products in order to stabilize prices. Hoover reluctantly accepted the amendment in order to obtain his bill.

Hoover also urged Congress to give farmers additional tariff protection. But manufacturers, with their powerful lobbies, were in control when the House Ways and Means Committee, headed by W. C. Hawley of Oregon, began to draft a new tariff bill. Joseph Grundy, president of the Pennsylvania Manufacturers' Association, confessed that he was spending $2,000 a month to boost tariff rates. Hence the Hawley bill, presented to the House of Representatives in May 1929, not only increased duties on agricultural products but also included some 925 increases in the rates on manufactured goods. Senator Reed Smoot of Utah, chairman of the Finance Committee, pushed the measure through the upper house in May 1930 in spite of growing public opposition. One thousand members of the American Economic Association signed a petition which begged President Hoover to veto the Hawley-Smoot bill. What the world needed, they asserted, was freer trade, not economic nationalism, since a reversion to McKinley-like tariff policies would start a cycle of similar actions by other nations.

Hoover not only signed the Hawley-Smoot bill, but also, long afterward, argued that it had had no significant effect on world trade. From a purely statistical point of view, Hoover was probably correct. The measure's increases in duties on agricultural products were meaningless except for meat and dairy products, since American farmers exported their surplus staples to the world market in any event. Moreover, the Hawley-Smoot Act's increased rates on manufactured products applied, aside from textiles and chemicals, largely to specialties traded in comparatively small quantities. The tariff increases barely affected most American industrial products; most other foreign producers could hardly compete with them in the world market, much less in the United States. But the Hawley-Smoot Act was unfortunate in that it gave European countries an excuse for sharply increasing their own tariff rates. The British, for example, adopted protection and a system of imperial preference in 1932, in retaliation, they asserted, against American tariff policies.

Hoover believed that all problems could be solved by action based on careful investigation and study. Therefore, before he recommended action to strengthen the prohibition laws, Hoover appointed eleven distinguished citizens to a Commission on Law Observance and Enforcement, headed by former Attorney General George W. Wickersham. "No nation," Hoover said to the commission, "can long survive the failure of its citizens to respect and obey the laws which they themselves make."

The Wickersham Commission, after nearly two years of investigation, reported in January 1931 what everyone already knew: enforcement of the Eighteenth Amendment had simply collapsed because of widespread public opposition, especially in urban areas. The commission as a whole did not recommend repeal of the amendment, but seven members attached individual opinions which favored either modification or repeal. Hoover, when he submitted the report to Congress, could only say lamely that he did not favor abandoning the "noble experiment." Ironically, the report of the Wickersham Commission was the death knell of the Eighteenth Amendment because it gave convincing proof that effective enforcement was impossible. Both parties came out in 1932 in favor of a return of the liquor problem to the states. Congress, with an almost audible sigh of relief, approved the Twenty-first Amendment in February 1933. It repealed the Eighteenth Amendment and forbade the shipment of alcoholic beverages into dry states. Repeal went into effect in December 1933 and thus ended America's foremost growth industry during the 1920s—the production, smuggling, shipment, and sale of illegal liquor. The underworld empires which it had fostered, in turn shifted their accumulated profits into other industries, such as gambling casinos, and, finally, drugs.

2. THE CRISIS BEGINS

Origins

In retrospect, it is easy for historians to see that the worst depression in American history, the Great Depression of the 1930s, was the result of several long-term causes or structural problems in the American economy. It is also clear, given the advantage of hindsight, that public economic policies did little to avert the coming of the depression, and also, in some respects worsened its impact when it occurred.

In spite of the enormous expansion of state and federal powers during the first quarter of the twentieth century, most Americans felt a strong abhorrence for the growing involvement of government. Classical economic theory, after all, held that, in periods of recession, the best policy was for government to withdraw from the economy—by cutting expenditures—and to allow it, through free-market mechanisms, to regain a state of equilibrium. Although decisive governmental intervention was conceivable, during the early stages of the depression most Americans, especially Herbert Hoover, were loath to use the federal government to reinvigorate the economy.

Despite its apparent vigor in 1929, the American economy suffered from some significant weaknesses. By the late 1920s, the expansion in the automobile industry had largely run its course, and it appeared that the market had approached a saturation level. Rising construction and land costs, combined with a decline in the growth of families, had an adverse effect on the residential construction industry. The markets for new housing and cars was so easily saturated partly because consumption had not fully expanded during the 1920s. Put another way, the American economy suffered from "underconsumption" because of maldistribution of resources and income. As a result of the agricultural depression, for example, the potential market for consumer goods never matured in farm areas; underconsumption also weakened banks and other financial institutions with loans outstanding to farmers. Much of the nation's wealth was concentrated in a few hands; a significant portion of the tremendous increases in productivity did not go into wages. Between 1919 and 1929, for example, wages for industrial workers increased by 26 per cent, while productivity rose by about 40 per cent. At the same time, over 70 per cent of the American people lived at or below subsistence. These people were without savings, unemployment insurance, or other cushions; their ability to consume—which had been aided by the vast expansion of credit—depended on the overall health of the economy.

The domestic economy was also endangered by a rickety system of international trade. During the 1920s, it depended upon an annual outpouring of American dollars for payment; it also operated on the inflexible gold standard. Some other alleged causes of the depression, such as the poor structure of the banking system, abuse of credit, and high incidence of dishonesty within the business community, were conditions which probably were no worse in 1929 than in most earlier periods of American history.

The Stock-Market Crash

The most dramatic and immediate cause of the depression was the collapse of the stock market in the autumn of 1929. Between 1925 and 1929, stock market prices rose about 300 per cent. By 1929, the cycle of rising corporate sales, profits, dividends, and the prices of common stock had become so regular and pleasant that more than 1,000,000 American stock buyers were bidding up the prices of shares much faster than corporate profits increased. The process could not continue indefinitely.

In one terrible month, which started on October 23, 1929, prices on the New York Stock Exchange alone fell in value about $26 billion, and prices proceeded irregularly downward for two and a half more years. This catastrophe might have served as no more than an interesting example of the extremes to which Americans sometimes carry their affairs, except for its clear relationship to the nationwide disaster that followed. The loss of $26 billion in less than a month and of more than $35 billion in a year on the New York Stock Exchange alone, takes on added meaning when compared to the American gross national product (GNP = the total of all goods and services produced), which was slightly over $100 billion in 1929, and $95 billion in 1930. The enormous loss of wealth by individuals and institutions holding common stocks played a major role in the subsequent failure of the American economy.

From Recession to Depression

There were two distinct stages in the depression in the United States. The first, which lasted from the autumn of 1929 to the summer of 1931, might be called a severe recession. By the last quarter of 1930, for example, industrial production was only 26 per cent below its peak level of 1929, and unemployment ran only between 3,000,000 and 4,000,000 in 1930. The second stage was the severe depression which set in during the summer of 1931 and lasted, in the United States, until 1935 and 1936. This second stage was related, not only to domestic events, but also to serious financial stringencies in Germany, Austria, and Great Britain, which were induced primarily by a sharp decline in American investment, purchasing, and lending abroad. The German and Austrian governments were nearly bankrupt, and the British were forced off the gold standard in September 1931. These developments, in turn, not only wrecked the system of international exchange but also drove international commodity prices to absurd depths. Repercussions were severe in the United States, especially on agricultural prices and on banks with extensive foreign holdings. Some 2,300 banks, with deposits of nearly $1.7 billion, failed in the United States during 1931.

Some of the dimensions of the economic catastrophe which befell the American people can be seen when we examine the statistical progress of the depression from 1929 to 1933. During these four years, national income declined from $87.8 billion to $40.2 billion. Per capita income, adjusted for the cost of living, shrank from $681 to $495. More than 100,000 businesses failed, with losses of nearly $3 billion. The number of unemployed, already at 7,000,000 in the autumn of 1931, swelled to about 14,000,000 in the early months of 1933. Gross farm income plummeted from nearly $12 billion in 1929 to $5.3 billion in 1932. Between 1929 and 1933, salaries decreased 40 per cent; dividends, nearly 57 per cent; and manufacturing wages, 60 per cent.

The Trauma of the Depression

The trauma of the Great Depression was in many respects more devastating in its effects than the experience of fighting a great war. Two to three million persons moved from cities back to the country in the hope of being able to scratch a living from the soil. Family tensions multiplied as mothers lost their jobs, fathers gave up hope and remained at home all day, and relatives doubled up in houses and apartments. The number of marriages declined sharply, as did the birthrate. The worst result was the grinding poverty which millions had to endure with all its dire consequences. People suffered and some died from malnutrition, lack of clothing, fuel, and proper medical care. Despair came to millions who wanted work, could not find it, and had to accept charity or relief. Hardest hit were blacks ("the last to be hired, the first to be fired"), women workers, and recent immigrants in the large cities.

The foundations of America's two great social institutions—churches and educational facilities—were seriously eroded. Church membership and attendance decreased, and donations to church causes plummeted sharply. Localities and states struggled heroically to save their schools and universities. In general they succeeded until about 1933, when the retreat on the educational front turned into a full-scale rout. Hardest hit were schools in the rural states, and in Michigan, where staggering unemployment in the automobile industry caused tax revenues to drop steeply.

One of the most significant long-term impacts of the depression was the change which it produced in attitudes toward business and government. Loss of popular confidence in the nation's business and financial leadership was almost complete by 1933. Mistrust increased particularly after several congressional investigations revealed the extent to which bankers had misused depositors' funds and manipulated the stock market during the 1920s. Indeed, the major investment bankers, along with President Hoover, became the chief scapegoats of the debacle.

The trauma of the depression prompted many Americans to look to the federal government for protection. The stage was set first in 1930, when private charitable organizations ran out of money, and further private efforts at alleviation failed. Persons in distress then turned to city and state relief agencies. Local governments assumed this burden during 1931 and 1932, but local governmental relief efforts collapsed for lack of funds. The unemployed, and the cities and states as well, turned to the federal government in Washington. The third stage occurred in the mid-1930s, when a majority of Americans finally concluded that the federal government should provide jobs for the unemployed whenever private business proved unable to do so.

Given the dimensions of the economic distress, remarkably few Americans lost faith in capitalism as a system of production and distribution. The Communist party made an intensive effort to take advantage of the discontent, but it had only 12,000 members in 1932, as compared with 8,000 in 1928. On the other hand, the conviction about the necessity for change spread among religious leaders, organized labor, agriculture, and even in the business community itself. The old system of relatively unregulated free enterprise, they argued, had to give way to a new system of governmental planning which assured the successful functioning of the economy. Even the United States Chamber of Commerce approved a plan, early in 1933, for business and governmental partnership in planning for full production and employment.

Surprisingly few eruptions of disorder occurred. Unemployed persons rioted in Dearborn, Michigan, in the spring of 1932, and a number of hunger marches took place. Throughout the Middle West, farmers banded together. They threatened to shoot bank and insurance agents who attempted to foreclose farm mortgages, and they went armed to auction sales to buy back their own foreclosed farms at low prices. In Le Mars, Iowa, a large crowd of enraged farmers dragged a foreclosing judge from the bench and beat him into unconsciousness.

Some officials in the Hoover administration feared that serious disorder would result from the descent of the so-called Bonus Expeditionary Force upon Washington in the spring of 1932. About 12,000 to 15,000 veterans and other unemployed persons built a shantytown on Anacostia Flats, just outside Washington. They demanded immediate payment of the soldiers' bonus by the issuance of $2.4 billion in paper money. About half the Bonus Army went home when the Senate refused to approve the bonus bill, but 6,000 to 7,000 remained. On July 28, 1932, a riot occurred, and two persons were killed when bonus marchers invaded a construction area in Washington. The District government, which apparently had been waiting for just such an opportunity, promptly declared that it could not control the situation, and Hoover just as promptly called upon the army to maintain order. General Douglas MacArthur, then Chief of Staff, led an armored force which burned down the shantytown and dispersed its residents with tear gas. Hoover blamed Communists and persons with criminal records for causing the trouble.

3. HOOVER FACES THE CRISIS

Hoover and Classical Economic Theory

The old partisan myth about President Hoover fiddling while the country burned has long since been discredited. He did not exaggerate when he claimed, during the campaign of 1932, that he had labored night and day to turn back the forces of economic disintegration and to restore national confidence. Moreover, he operated not blindly, but in harmony with a consistent philosophy based upon belief in the fundamental goodness of his fellow men and in the power of democracy to correct social and economic injustices. No man ever came to the presidency with broader experience in international and domestic affairs than Hoover. Yet, he failed to meet the challenge posed by the greatest crisis in the history of American capitalism.

Hoover was a prisoner of his own political and economic ideology; he was unable to consider seriously, much less to devise, new remedies to meet an unforeseen catastrophe. While the United States suffered from severe deflation, Hoover followed deflationary policies which only aggravated the condition. The nation might have been set on the road to prosperity by well-coordinated policies: a large increase of the money supply, substantial relief and public-works programs, and encouragement of private investment. By 1932, concerted moves such as these were being recommended by Republican businessmen as well as by Democratic critics of the President. The trouble, in Hoover's mind, was that such a program flagrantly violated sound economic theory. To the embattled Hoover, it seemed to be nothing less than economic heresy.

The questions of a balanced budget and preservation of the gold standard stood as the two most controversial political issues before the country during the last two years of the Hoover administration. An increasing number of leaders in Congress and the country pressed hard for monetary inflation and a huge relief and public-works program. To all such appeals, Hoover replied with stubborn determination. The only thing which could bring real recovery, he insisted, was popular confidence in the soundness of the dollar and business confidence in the integrity of the government. Both would be destroyed by inflation and wasteful expenditures for public works.

Shaping a Policy

Hoover's antidepression policies went through two distinct stages. During the first stage of the crisis—the recession of 1929–1931—Hoover tried to mobilize a national voluntary effort. He recognized the danger signals after the market crash and called business executives and labor leaders to the White House in the autumn of 1929. Hoover won their promise to maintain normal operations without severe wage reductions or strikes. At the same time, he called upon mayors and governors to increase expenditures for public works, and the Federal Farm Board went actively into the market to maintain farm prices.

For a time it seemed that the nation would weather the slump without major difficulties. When employers began to cut production (the industrial index fell from 96.3 in April 1930, to 84.6 in October of the same year), Hoover appointed a Committee for Unemployment Relief and requested local and private agencies to increase their relief assistance. The economy seemed, briefly, to be recovering. Indices of production, payrolls, and employment showed faint signs of recovery between February and June of 1931, although most had slowed down again by June, even before international events aggravated the situation.

Hoover responded to the breakdown of the world economy, occasioned by the financial crisis in central Europe and the British abandonment of the gold standard, by moving quickly to obtain a moratorium on war debts and reparations. The most immediate consequence of the international breakdown of 1931 was the withdrawal of about $1.5 billion of foreign-owned gold from American banks. This shock, which was followed by the dumping of securities on the New York Stock Exchange and large losses abroad by American banks, exaggerated further the dire crisis in the United States.

Hoover still hoped for miracles through voluntary efforts and called upon bankers to meet the crisis by cooperation. But the strain on private resources was too great, and the President reluctantly set to work to devise a recovery program. The chief antidepression weapon in Hoover's arsenal was the Reconstruction Finance Corporation (RFC), chartered by Congress on January 16, 1932, with a capital of $500 million and authority to borrow up to an additional $1.5 billion. It went to work at once to save banks, railroads, and other financial institutions. The RFC earmarked no funds for small businesses or for consumers, but it did prevent the collapse of the nation's large banks. The Glass-Steagall Act of February 27, 1932, permitted Federal Reserve Banks to expand the currency and released about $1 billion in gold to meet continuing foreign withdrawals. A Federal Home Loan Bank Act made new capital available to building and loan associations, while the capital of Federal Land Banks was also increased. These measures brought new confidence and helped to save the financial structure from total collapse in 1932.

Meanwhile, the administration's efforts on the agricultural front were less successful. The Federal Farm Board was simply powerless to maintain prices after they dropped sharply on world markets in the summer of 1931. Wheat fell in price from sixty-seven cents a bushel in 1929 to thirty-nine cents in 1932; cotton, from seventeen to seven cents a pound; corn, from eighty to thirty-two cents a bushel. The Federal Farm Board tried to support prices through open market purchases and voluntary reductions in farm production. Both efforts failed miserably because of the dimensions of the agricultural surplus. Agricultural production actually increased in 1931, and the Board had lost some $354 million in futile purchasing operations by 1932. The Board confessed its impotence in December 1932 and urged Congress to institute an effective system to limit acreage and production as the only solution to the farm problem.

Fierce struggles took place in Washington during 1932 over relief and monetary policies. Progressives and inflationists in Congress combined in a nonpartisan bloc to demand immediate payment of the veterans' bonus by the issuance of paper money. They also urged adoption of a federal direct relief program. Hoover retained sufficient support in Congress to block these proposals. On relief, however, he did compromise by authorizing the RFC to lend $300 million to the states for self-liquidating public works such as airports, bridges, and tunnels. But these measures were mere palliatives.

4. THE DEPRESSION: POLITICAL CONSEQUENCES

The Depression and Party Politics

The Great Depression was one of those profound internal upheavals which have fundamentally changed political alignments on several occasions in American history. From the early nineteenth century, American politics have been dominated by a two-party system: from the late 1830s to the late 1850s, the Whig-Democratic system; from the late 1850s to the 1890s, the Republican-Democratic system; and, from the 1890s to the 1930s, the so-called progressive party system. In several systems, there were periods of close party competition—as was the case during the first two systems—or of party hegemony—as was the case during the early twentieth century. In each case, these party systems collapsed as a result of a great shock which realigned the basis of politics by dramatic changes in the preferences and loyalties of voters.

By the election of 1936, a similarly dramatic realignment had taken place, a political revolution which insured Democratic control—with several exceptions—of both the presidency and Congress for most of the next thirty years. A large part of the realignment was a direct result of the depression. During the mid-term elections of 1930, Americans elected the first Democratic Congress since 1916, but the results constituted no landslide. The Democrats controlled the Seventy-second Congress, which met in December 1931, by a bare majority in both houses, and some members of that majority held economic views as conservative as Hoover's. Extensive loss of confidence in the Hoover administration and in the Republican party did not begin until the autumn of 1931. The conviction grew that Hoover was more interested in saving banks, railroads, and corporations than he was in saving people. Hoover became the object not merely of popular dislike, but also of contempt.

Shantytowns, erected by the poor on the edges of great cities, were named "Hoovervilles," while horse-drawn broken down automobiles were called "Hoovercarts."

Forging a Democratic Majority

Democratic presidential fever rose rapidly between 1930 and 1932 because it became obvious that almost any breathing Democrat probably would win in 1932. Favorite sons abounded in number, but the decisive struggle for party leadership was between former Governor Alfred E. Smith and Franklin Delano Roosevelt, governor of New York.

Smith, desperately eager for a second nomination and popular vindication, had the support of the Tammany organization in New York and of Democratic organizations in New Jersey, Massachusetts, and other eastern states. However, the odds were heavily against Smith. Many Democrats resented his stand against prohibition and his emphasis upon the religious issue in the campaign of 1928. A greater liability for the former Democratic standard-bearer was the fact that he had never developed any strong support in rural areas. Furthermore, the Democratic party was not yet quite free of religious bigotry, and politicians could point out accurately, if not sincerely, that they had given Smith a chance in 1928 and that he had failed to win.

Smith's possibilities for a second nomination were imperiled most of all because the Democratic party now had another leader, Franklin D. Roosevelt. He had suffered a severe attack of polio in 1921 but had gradually fought his way back to partial recovery by 1928. Meanwhile, he had maintained his political connections and friendships, without, however, engaging in any of the controversies which disrupted the Democratic party during the 1920s.

Roosevelt ran for governor of New York in 1928 at Smith's urgent request in order to strengthen the national Democratic ticket in the state. Roosevelt was elected by a narrow margin in the face of the Hoover landslide and won reelection in 1930 by the largest majority ever given a gubernatorial candidate in the history of New York. The magic of that majority at once made Roosevelt the leading contender for the Democratic presidential nomination in 1932. So successful were his managers, led by James A. Farley and Louis M. Howe, who garnered support in the South, Middle West, and West, that, by the early months of 1932, the Democratic preconvention contest had become a struggle of Roosevelt against the field.

A riotous, confident Democratic national convention opened in Chicago on June 27, 1932. Roosevelt had a majority of the delegates, but not the two-thirds majority then necessary for a Democratic presidential nomination. For the first three ballots, it seemed as if Smith's managers had succeeded in creating a solid anti-Roosevelt bloc which could prevent the New York governor's nomination. The deadlock was broken on the fourth ballot, when John Nance Garner of Texas, conservative Speaker of the House of Representatives and a strong favorite son, threw his support to Roosevelt in return for the vice-presidential nomination.

Roosevelt electrified the country by flying to Chicago to accept the nomination in person. He promised a "new deal" for the American people if they sent him to the White House, but neither his speech nor the Democratic platform, which he endorsed item by item, gave any promise of fundamental changes in federal policies. The platform demanded repeal of the Eighteenth Amendment. It promised to cut federal expenditures by 25 per cent and to balance the budget. It demanded the removal of government from all fields of private enterprise, "except where necessary to develop public works and natural resources." The Democratic platform also promised that the party would reform the banking system and maintain a "sound" currency "at all hazards." It proposed to lend money to the states to provide relief for the unemployed, and it approved social-security legislation by the states. Finally, the platform promised tariff reduction and effective crop controls to restore agricultural purchasing power.

Meanwhile, the Republicans had assembled in a gloomy national convention. They could not repudiate a President in office, so they duly renominated Hoover on the first ballot. The Republican platform, after it commended the President for his fight against the depression, approved federal loans to the states for relief, repeal of the Eighteenth Amendment, and cooperative efforts by farmers to limit production. On fiscal policy, the platform promised economy, defense of the gold standard, and reform of the banking system.

The Election of 1932

Both Hoover and Roosevelt campaigned strenuously, but the contest was an unequal one. Actually, the two men said much the same things. Their main differences were over agricultural and public-power policies. Hoover made it plain that he would not budge from his earlier opposition to federal crop controls and the development of regional hydroelectric projects, which Roosevelt strongly supported.

The two candidates, however, *sounded* very different. While Hoover talked mournfully about his battles on a thousand fronts to stem the tide of the depression, Roosevelt exuded confidence in his ability to make things come out right, quickly. Moreover, Roosevelt hit hard at Hoover's alleged callousness about the suffering of the poor and promised that he would do anything to keep people from starving. Hoover's chances, and his public image, were also severely damaged by his use of military force to disperse the Bonus Army.

Roosevelt could hardly have failed to win in this unhappy year of depression. His active, nationwide campaign also convinced voters that he was physically fit for the burdens of the presidency and undoubtedly swelled the Democratic vote on election day. Hoover retained extensive business and upper-class support and did well in industrial centers which depended on tariff protection. He carried Maine, New Hampshire, Vermont, Connecticut, Delaware, and Pennsylvania, and won nearly 16,000,000 popular and fifty-nine electoral votes. Roosevelt swept the large cities and the rural areas outside New England, carried the rest of the states, and won nearly 23,000,000 popular and 472 electoral votes. Democrats also elected majorities of 191 and twenty-two in the House of Representatives and Senate, respectively, in the Seventy-third Congress, which would sit from 1933 through 1934. The Socialists made their strongest effort since 1920, but their candidate, Norman Thomas, polled only 885,000 votes. The Communist candidate, William Z. Foster, trailed far behind with only 103,000 votes.

The final session of the Seventy-second Congress from December 1932 to

March 1933, proved to be the last for "lame ducks." These were members of the House and Senate who had been defeated for reelection in November but continued to make laws in the three months still left before their successors took office. The Twentieth Amendment, sponsored by Senator George W. Norris of Nebraska, was ratified in January 1933. It provided that henceforth the Congress elected in November should begin its session on the third of the following January, and that the President should be inaugurated on January 20 instead of on March 4.

SUGGESTED READINGS

The surveys of the period cited in the previous two chapters end with accounts of the Hoover administration. The best accounts of that subject are Harris G. Warren, *Herbert Hoover and the Great Depression* (1959), and Albert U. Romasco, *The Poverty of Abundance* (1965). The administration is defended in Ray L. Wilbur and A. M. Hyde, *The Hoover Policies* (1937), Burner, *Hoover,* already cited, and, Herbert Hoover, *Memoirs: The Great Depression, 1929–1941* (1952). See also Elliot A. Rosen, *Hoover, Roosevelt, and the Brains Trust* (1977), and Jordan A. Schwarz, *The Interregnum of Despair: Hoover, Congress, and the Depression* (1970).

John K. Galbraith, *The Great Crash* (1955), is a superb account of that tragedy. Thomas Wilson, *Fluctuations in Income and Employment* (1948), written from a business-cycle approach, and Milton Friedman and Anna J. Schwartz, *The Great Contraction, 1929–1933* (1965), a monetary history, are superior books, although many economists disagree with Friedman's "monetarist" interpretation. The impact of the depression on American society is vividly portrayed in Bernstein, *The Lean Years,* already cited; David A. Shannon, ed., *The Great Depression* (1960), a book of poignant documents; Caroline Bird, *The Invisible Scar* (1967); Dixon Wecter, *The Age of the Great Depression* (1948); Frederick Lewis Allen, *Since Yesterday* (1940); and Studs Terkel, *Hard Times: An Oral History of the Great Depression* (1970).

For the election of 1928, see Edmund A. Moore, *A Catholic Runs for President* (1956), and Allan J. Lichtman, *Prejudice and the Old Politics: The Presidential Election of 1928* (1979), which argues convincingly that religion was *the* issue. For the election of 1932, in addition to the surveys already mentioned, see Frank Freidel, *Franklin D. Roosevelt: The Triumph* (1956); James McGregor Burns, *Roosevelt: The Lion and the Fox* (1956); Rexford G. Tugwell, *The Democratic Roosevelt* (1957); and William E. Leuchtenburg, *Franklin D. Roosevelt and the New Deal* (1963).

CHAPTER 9
THE AGE OF
FRANKLIN D. ROOSEVELT

1. BEGINNING THE NEW DEAL

FDR and the Reform Tradition

A new era in American history began when Franklin D. Roosevelt took the oath of office shortly after noon on March 4, 1933. It commenced with a history-making special session of Congress, which in 100 days laid the framework of a New Deal aimed to combat the depression. It ended in the victory of the United States and its allies over dictatorships which had all but enslaved the peoples of Europe and Asia.

The man who led the American people from depression into prosperity and from near defeat in war to global victory was born at Hyde Park, New York, on January 30, 1882. He received a proper patrician education at Groton and Harvard without revealing special promise or ambition. After a half-hearted study and practice of law, Roosevelt entered politics as an anti-Tammany Democrat. He won election to the New York State Senate in 1910 and fought Tammany and supported Woodrow Wilson for the Democratic presidential nomination. Wilson rewarded Roosevelt (and took advantage of the Roosevelt name) by appointing him Assistant Secretary of the Navy in 1913.

The young Roosevelt showed talent as an able administrator, but he was extremely ambitious and somewhat disloyal both to President Wilson and to his genial chief, Secretary of the Navy Josephus Daniels. The rising young politician made his peace with the Tammany organization, and he received the Democratic vice-presidential nomination in 1920 largely because he was the leading New York Wilsonian acceptable to Tammany.

Roosevelt can best be described politically as an old-fashioned democrat. A reporter once asked him to describe his political philosophy. "What do you mean?" Roosevelt replied. "Well, are you a Socialist?" the reporter asked. "No," Roosevelt said. "Are you a Communist?" the reporter went on. "Of course not," Roosevelt replied. "Are you a capitalist?" the reporter persisted. "No," Roosevelt answered. "Well, Mr. President, then what are you?" the reporter asked in puzzlement. "Why, I'm a Christian and a democrat," Roosevelt replied.

Hoover also was a Christian and a democrat. What distinguished Roosevelt from his predecessor was that, while Hoover was the prisoner of his political and economic ideology, Roosevelt possessed virtually no ideology. Hoover was an eloquent advocate of voluntary cooperation, limited government, and the efficacy of classical economic doctrine, but he was unable, largely because of intellectual rigidity, to address the human problems which the Great Depression created. Roosevelt, on the other hand, felt no strong commitment to any particular method; his open-mindedness—some have called it lack of principle—made him willing and even eager to experiment. For example, although Roosevelt held an old-fashioned belief in sound money and a balanced budget, he tried new paths of economic policy without hesitation when conventional methods failed. Furthermore, Roosevelt, like his fifth cousin and uncle-in-law, Theodore, believed that government should play the leading role in organizing and guiding the American economy and society.

Roosevelt was the most effective political campaigner in American history. In eleven campaigns for office or nomination to office, he succeeded nine times and never suffered defeat in a general election when he ran on his own. Roosevelt was, moreover, one of the strongest and most effective Presidents in American history, for, like his two great teachers—Theodore Roosevelt and Woodrow Wilson—he believed in strong and responsible leadership as the most indispensable force in democracy. Roosevelt believed in a strong President who alone spoke for all people, coordinated various departments of the government, and directed foreign affairs. He mastered the techniques of leadership by developing a keen understanding of public opinion and a canny sense of timing. He also established direct communication with the rank and file of the people through addresses, press conferences, and the radio talks to the American people which he called "fireside chats." A dogged partisan, he commanded the support of his party in Congress, precisely because he succeeded so well in interpreting the contradictions, nuances, and trends in public opinion.

Roosevelt possessed faults, of course. He was deficient as an administrator because he could not bear to dismiss a loyal but incompetent friend, and also because he carefully never permitted his subordinates to acquire much power. Some of his most important programs may have failed because he deliberately divided authority. He used his charm so successfully that he gave the impression—not altogether mistaken—of enjoying the game of manipulating people. His lack of any consistent guide to policies and methods was a source of weakness as well as of strength because it led him to place unmerited faith in experimentation for its own sake. Roosevelt's diffuse and occasionally shallow intellectual training compounded this fault and sometimes made it difficult for him to evaluate various explanations of complex economic problems. Whether these defects proved so marring as to overbalance Roosevelt's positive personal qualities will, of course, remain forever a matter of personal opinion.

Nonetheless, Roosevelt revitalized the progressive movement. He not only revived progressive faith in democracy; he also restructured the entire political economy of the United States so that the government could achieve the main goals of the progressive movement. These goals were protection for the underprivileged and economic security for all people. Roosevelt carried these policies much closer to their inevitable conclusion in a welfare state than Wilson or Theodore Roosevelt could possibly have done, given the political attitudes of Americans during their presidencies.

Prelude to the New Deal

The severity of the economic crisis crucially influenced the policies of the Roosevelt administration during its first year in office. The United States, indeed, might have followed an entirely different path during the next eight years had the worst single economic catastrophe in its history—the banking panic of the early months of 1933—not made emergency action of a drastic kind appear to be absolutely necessary.

The panic which occurred was the product of a chain reaction of irrational fear. One contributing factor was the widespread suspicion that Roosevelt, in spite of his campaign assurances, planned to abolish the gold standard and inflate the currency. The result of this suspicion became particularly visible during the week of January 18, 1933. Thousands of Americans hastened to withdraw bank deposits, purchase gold or tangible property, and send their money abroad. Withdrawals of currency totaled $1.7 billion between February 8 and March 3, while the excess gold reserves of the Federal Reserve System declined from $1.5 billion in January to $400 million in March. Bank after bank was forced to close its doors, either permanently or temporarily. In response, governors in various states began to declare bank holidays; that is, they closed the banks in their states for various periods in order to stop the withdrawals. By March 3, 1933, general closings had occurred in twenty-three states. During the early morning hours of March 4, the remainder of the governors followed suit under pressure from Treasury officials.

While Roosevelt rode to take the presidential oath, the economic life of the country was literally grinding to a halt, and the United States faced an economic paralysis such as no other civilized nation—except perhaps Germany—had ever confronted during peacetime. In accepting the nomination for President, Roosevelt had declared, "I pledge myself to a New Deal for the American people." Now, on March 4, 1933, in words of confidence, he pledged himself to a dynamic program of action for the general welfare. Then Roosevelt asked the people to join him in a "national consecration" to the work of restoring prosperity through united and unselfish effort. Calling for faith and courage, he exclaimed:

This great nation will endure as it has endured, will revive and prosper. So, first of all, let me assert my firm belief that the only thing we have to fear is fear itself. . . . We face the arduous days that lie before us in the warm courage of national unity. . . . We do not distrust the future of essential democracy.

The President's Men

No previous President could call upon so many competent advisers as could Franklin Roosevelt when he took office. No President ever needed so many, so immense and complex were the problems which Roosevelt faced. In planning his early program, Roosevelt turned especially to Professors Raymond Moley, Adolf A. Berle, Jr., and Rexford G. Tugwell of Columbia University—the original "Brain Trust." Later, important advisers included Harry L. Hopkins, a former social worker, and Felix Frankfurter of the Harvard Law School, whom Roosevelt appointed to the Supreme Court. Judge Samuel I. Rosenman served as Roosevelt's chief speech writer and also wrote one of the best memoirs of the New Deal period. No previous administration drew so heavily upon the resources of American universities. Professorial experts, appointed to dozens of commissions, did much of the work involved in preparing the hundreds of laws which Congress enacted between 1933 and 1940.

Several members of the Roosevelt cabinet also helped to shape the President's policies. Secretary of State Cordell Hull of Tennessee, a strong believer in inter-American cooperation and unshackled world trade, obtained substantial freedom to make economic foreign policy, especially before the Second World War erupted. Secretary of the Interior Harold L. Ickes, a follower of Theodore Roosevelt in 1912, revived the old crusade for conservation of natural resources. Secretary of Agriculture Henry A. Wallace of Iowa, a former Republican, carried on the work which his father had done as Secretary of Agriculture under Harding and Coolidge. Postmaster General James A. Farley skillfully dispensed the patronage, managed campaigns, and gave sound political advice. Secretary of Labor Frances Perkins, the first woman to hold a cabinet seat, was perhaps the most important person in the administration, aside from Roosevelt, in shaping labor policies and planning for economic security. Secretary of the Treasury Henry Morgenthau, Jr., Roosevelt's neighbor in upstate New York, exercised influence far beyond his own department. The budget director, Lewis Douglas, an advocate of balanced budgets, also enjoyed access to the new President's ear. The most striking characteristics of the group around Roosevelt were creativity and diversity—within a certain range. Roosevelt's advisers included Republicans and Democrats, conservatives and progressives, but very few who could, by any stretch of a reasonable person's imagination, be called "radical." Among those persons who influenced Roosevelt, only Tugwell, who favored some permanent type of centralized governmental planning, could perhaps be placed in that category.

2. THE FIRST NEW DEAL

Two New Deals?

One of the oldest and most useful concepts for interpreting the New Deal era is the suggestion that there were in fact two New Deals—that is, two separate stages in legislative and administrative policies. The first New Deal, according to this interpretation, operated during 1933 and 1934 and represented the spectrum of the classes and interests which had united behind Roosevelt's leadership to fight the depression. During this period, the administration worked on the assumption that recovery could be achieved quickly and easily, mainly by the continuation and expansion of the Hoover policies.

Legislation and administrative action would strengthen the banking structure and clean up the securities markets, but all such activities would be aimed at securing private ownership and making financial institutions more secure in the future. The dollar would be devalued in order to bring prices up to a normal level; however, devaluation would not be accompanied by any massive countercyclical moves, such as large-scale deficit spending. Business and industry would be given a relatively free hand to work out their own salvation under federal supervision. Labor would be given new protections, but mainly through federal action for minimum wages and maximum hours, not through governmental support of collective bargaining. As for relief, all that was needed was to extend further assistance to the states and to stimulate the construction industry with a federal public-works program. Once recovery had set in, the federal government would get out of the relief business altogether. Finally, agriculture would be put on its feet by restriction of output through production controls.

Parts of this program worked well. However, according to the "two New Deals" interpretation, the first New Deal was in deep trouble by the middle of 1934. Recovery did not occur as planned. Various mass movements gave evidence that the first New Deal had failed to improve the lot or to assuage the discontent of workers, old people, small farmers, tenant farmers, and the unemployed. The first New Deal coalition thus fell apart in the spring of 1934, when the business classes deserted Roosevelt.

The first New Deal came to an end in the off-year election of 1934, according to the "two New Deals" scenario, when the voters repudiated conservative policies and sent a huge Democratic majority to Congress. The new members were very responsive to such groups as organized labor, the unemployed, and impoverished farmers. Roosevelt, who read the auguries shrewdly, veered sharply leftward and set about to launch a second New Deal to satisfy the demands of the new left-of-center coalition.

The "two New Deals" interpretation contains some major deficiencies. By magnifying the changes which did occur between 1933 and 1935, the interpretation gives the impression that the two New Deals were largely separated. Actually, the legislation of 1935–1938 was to a considerable extent a natural outgrowth of earlier programs. For example, the Banking and Holding Company acts of 1935 belong chronologically to the second New Deal but were, in fact, culminations of reforms originated early in the Roosevelt administration. Planning for social-security legislation began soon after Roosevelt took office, but the complicated bills took time to prepare. The "two New Deals" interpretation also implies too strongly that Roosevelt, the master politician, deliberately tailored the entire second New Deal program in order to retain the support of segments of his new coalition. In many cases, the coalition pushed him, rather than the other way around. For example, Roosevelt and Perkins did not support the most important labor legislation of the period—the Wagner Act—until the bill was about to be passed by Congress. Finally, the "two New Deals" interpretation incorrectly implies that the first New Deal was conservative, the second New Deal, progressive. Actually, no such sharp delineation existed. Yet, the interpretation which assumes the existence of two New Deals is correct in its major outlines and provides a helpful guideline through the complexities of the Roosevelt era.

Reforming the Financial System

Roosevelt's first important move as President was popular, effective, and dramatic. On March 6, he issued an order which closed all banks in the country for a four-day period and then, three days later, summoned Congress to meet in extra session. On that same day, March 9, after four hours of debate, both houses passed the administration's Emergency Banking bill by overwhelming majorities. This measure approved Roosevelt's actions and authorized the Secretary of the Treasury to investigate the condition of all banks and to reopen them at his discretion.

Treasury officials immediately went to work. By midsummer, three fourths of the banks, holding 94 per cent of all deposits, were again in business with additional help from the RFC. Confidence returned immediately, and, during the first month alone of the new administration, more than $1 billion flowed back to the banks.

Congress followed by adopting the Glass-Steagall Act. It increased the Federal Reserve Board's control over the credit system; required commercial banks to divorce themselves from their investment affiliates, which in some cases had been speculating with their depositors' money; and, at the insistence of southern and western Democrats, established the Federal Deposit Insurance Corporation (FDIC). The FDIC insured deposits in member banks up to $5,000 (later increased to $100,000). All member banks of the Federal Reserve System were required to belong to the FDIC, and others could join if they met certain requirements. The American Bankers' Association denounced the FDIC as "unsound, unjust, and dangerous"; but the epidemic of bank failures ceased as soon as it was established.

To save embattled homeowners, Congress established the Home Owners Loan Corporation (HOLC) on June 13, 1933. During the next three years, the HOLC lent more than $3 billion to some 1,000,000 homeowners. It turned back the tide of foreclosures for the first time since the onset of the depression.

There was some sentiment in Congress and the country for governmental ownership of banks and other financial institutions. Roosevelt spurned all such suggestions and restored and actually strengthened private ownership in the financial field. As Raymond Moley observed in 1939: "The policies which vanquished the bank crisis were thoroughly conservative policies. The sole departure from convention lay in the swiftness and boldness with which they were carried out."

Experimenting with Devaluation

Swiftness and boldness were also required to meet the problem of deflation. To use a somewhat homely metaphor, the American economic automobile had four flat tires. First, purchasing power had declined tremendously, and, for millions of the unemployed, it had disappeared altogether. Second, prices had fallen because of a huge surplus of all kinds of goods and services compared to available money and buyers. Third, exports had plummeted for the same reason, plus the erection of the nationalistic barriers mentioned earlier. Fourth, debtors were finding it increasingly difficult to meet their obligations.

If the administration devalued the currency, inflationists argued, wages, prices, purchasing power, and exports would all rise, and it would be easier to pay debts. Trade of all kinds could then proceed at a more normal pace. Yet, the difficult question was how much inflation the tires required. Inflationists in Congress—probably a majority of that body—demanded the printing of billions in paper money. Other economists argued that the answer lay in taking the country off the domestic gold standard and in sufficiently reducing the gold value of the dollar in international exchange to bring the domestic price level back to that of 1926.

Roosevelt turned a deaf ear to the pleas of paper-money inflationists and again adopted the more cautious course. On March 6, 1933, he took the country off the domestic gold standard, in the expectation that the dollar would fall precipitately in value on international exchanges. By October 1933, the dollar had declined in value by about 30 per cent, and domestic prices had risen by 19 per cent. This was not enough inflation to restore the price level of 1926, and Roosevelt instructed the RFC to purchase gold at increased prices, which resulted in further devaluation of the dollar. Finally, on January 31, 1934, Roosevelt used authority granted earlier by Congress to set the price of gold at thirty-five dollars an ounce and the gold content of the dollar at 59.06 per cent of its pre-1933 value. According to the calculations of the commodity-dollar theorists, this action should have restored prices to their 1926 level.

The whole experiment in devaluation failed almost completely from beginning to end. Prices rose slightly as a result of Roosevelt's first steps in 1933 and because of anticipation of such policies; but during the following year they did not rise significantly because a significant increase in the domestic money supply and bank credits did not accompany devaluation. Roosevelt put so much trust in the simple device of dollar devaluation that he intentionally wrecked all hopes of achieving international monetary cooperation toward stabilization at the World Economic Conference, which met in London in June 1933. Roosevelt, in 1936, recognized his mistake and approved conclusion of an agreement with Great Britain and France for international currency stabilization.

Protecting Investors

Meanwhile, Congress moved to protect the public from fraud in the purchase and sale of stocks and other securities. The Truth-in-Securities Act of 1933 compelled underwriters and brokers to furnish complete information about the true value of securities being offered for sale. The Securities Exchange Act of 1934 created the Securities and Exchange Commission (SEC). It was empowered to license and regulate stock exchanges, to require basic data on securities listed, to oversee investment counselors, and to initiate litigation against persons engaged in fraud. Similar regulations were later applied to the commodity exchanges.

Extending Financial Reform

Two important measures brought the New Deal's efforts at financial reorganization and reform to fruition. The first was the Banking Act of 1935—the only fundamental revision of the Federal Reserve Act since its adoption in 1913. The Banking Act of 1935 was the kind of measure which Bryanites and agrarians had urged the Wilson administration to adopt. It concentrated immense power in a reorganized central board called the Board of Governors of the Federal Reserve System, which now had direct and complete control over interest rates, reserve requirements, and the open-market operations of the Federal Reserve Banks. In addition, the measure created new classes of securities and commercial paper against which Federal Reserve notes might be issued. Populist demands for tight public control over the banking system and the money supply were finally satisfied.

The second measure was the Holding Company Act of 1935, the outcome of a long fight by Roosevelt to break up electric power holding companies which had pyramided company upon company in often irrational and uneconomical systems. Roosevelt wanted to destroy holding companies altogether in the field of electric power. The Holding Company Act, adopted over the bitter resistance and frenzied propaganda of the utilities companies, gave Roosevelt virtually everything that he wanted. It compelled the dissolution of large holding companies within five years, but permitted small holding companies, which controlled integrated operating systems, to survive. The measure also subjected the financial operations of holding companies to the control of the SEC.

The New Deal and American Agriculture

By the early months of 1933, the condition of American farmers had fallen to such a desperate state that hardly anyone questioned whether the federal government should move swiftly to relieve agrarian distress; they disagreed only about how to proceed. The administration first acted by consolidating all farm credit agencies into a Farm Credit Administration. Large quantities of new credit became available to farmers through an Emergency Farm Mortgage Act. In addition, Congress, in 1934, adopted the Frazier-Lemke Farm Bankruptcy Act, which enabled farmers to recover foreclosed property on easy terms.

Such measures, of course, did nothing to stop the decline of agricultural prices—the result of production in excess of consumption. Roosevelt entered office in an atmosphere of crisis, for, by 1933, the income of farmers had fallen 60 per cent below that of 1929. The new President supported any reasonable crop-control measure which had the approval of farm leaders. That bill was the Agricultural Adjustment Act, written by Secretary Wallace in conference with farm leaders, and approved by Roosevelt on May 12, 1933. The act's objective was to raise the real income of farmers to the level which they had enjoyed in the five-year period, 1909–1914, when farm prices were supposed to have been at parity, or equality, with prices of manufactured goods. The measure assumed that the chief cause of low prices was overproduction, and it therefore proposed to reduce surpluses by limiting production of major staples, milk, and meat by various devices. The Department of Agriculture thus persuaded cotton growers to plow under about 30 per cent of their growing crop, or the equivalent of 4,000,000 bales of cotton. The Agricultural Adjustment Administration (AAA), established by the act of May 12, 1933, bought 220,000 sows and 6,000,000 pigs and slaughtered them. For a reduction in output, farmers received cash payments from the Treasury which were financed by a processing tax on industries which prepared raw agricultural products for market.

A severe drought in the Middle West and Southwest cooperated with the AAA in reducing farm production in those sections. When cotton and tobacco farmers poured fertilizer on reduced acres and produced large crops in 1933, Congress imposed direct production controls on both staples in 1934. Altogether, the administration's credit assistance, the AAA, bad weather, and international economic recovery worked a quick miracle. Net farm income rose 250 per cent between 1932 and 1935, and the farm mortgage loan decreased some $1.5 billion during the same period. Moreover, the principle of equality for agriculture was not only written into American law, but also was nearly achieved. The ratio of prices which the farmer paid for manufactured products to the prices which he received for his products rose from 58 per cent in 1932 to 88 per cent in 1935. To be sure, the AAA program contained major deficiencies. Its main benefits went to large farmers and planters, and it largely ignored small farmers, tenant farmers, and sharecroppers. However, the AAA saved the great bulk of American farm owners from bankruptcy through purposeful planning.

The NRA Experiment

Industry was in about as desperate a situation as were agriculture and banking when Roosevelt assumed office. Millions of men and women, who with their families made up fully a third of the population, were out of work. How to bring about business recovery and to employ this army of jobless workers posed a problem for which no one was prepared when the New Deal was launched.

Indeed, Roosevelt and his advisers had no specific plan at all for industrial recovery in early March 1933. Spokesmen of organized labor in Congress, led by Senator Hugo L. Black of Alabama, pressed for a measure to impose a thirty-hour work week in industry. Convinced that the Black bill would impede recovery, Roosevelt and his advisers hastily sought an alternative. They worked it out in conference with the United States Chamber of Commerce in the form of the National Industrial Recovery Act (NIRA), approved on June 16, 1933.

This measure created the National Recovery Administration (NRA), headed by Hugh S. Johnson, to establish so-called code authorities for various branches of industry. These groups, composed of representatives of industry, the government, unions, and consumers, were empowered to prepare codes to establish production goals and determine fair prices for their particular industries. In addition, the code authorities were directed to eliminate child labor and to establish minimum wages and maximum hours for workers. The codes were to be exempt from the antitrust laws and were to have the force of law once approved by the President. At Secretary Perkins' insistence, Section 7a, which affirmed labor's right to organize and to bargain collectively, was inserted into the bill at the last minute. Also incorporated at the end was

Title II, which appropriated $3.3 billion for a Public Works Administration (PWA) under Harold L. Ickes to stimulate the construction industry and, ultimately, consumer buying power.

Johnson went about his job with tremendous enthusiasm. He prepared a blanket code for all industry until specific codes could be worked out, held NRA parades, and devised an emblem—the Blue Eagle—which cooperating employers could display. From the autumn of 1933 through 1934, the code authorities then prepared 557 basic and 208 supplementary codes which covered every phase of trade and industry in the United States. Partly because of the administration's haste, larger firms—which exerted a commanding influence within the code authorities—established standards, wages, and prices to their liking. Other codes mandated lower wages for females, a disparity which code makers justified by claiming that the wages of most women workers represented a second family income.

Bitter opposition to the NRA soon developed. Small businessmen and manufacturers were in revolt by the spring of 1934 because, they claimed, big business dominated the code authorities. Although these allegations contained a good deal of truth, many of the small employers also resented the fact that the NRA had deprived them of their traditional competitive weapons of low wages, long hours, and cutthroat prices. Section 7a was widely ignored, except in a few major industries, as an unnecessary concession to labor. The NRA also found it difficult to police large corporations, who also objected to governmental intervention in their labor relations. When the NRA attempted to discipline violators of the codes, the courts became jammed with cases, and enforcement broke down completely. Johnson, worn out from arguments, grew increasingly erratic and authoritarian and resigned under heavy fire. Roosevelt then abolished the office of administrator and substituted a National Recovery Board in September 1934. Meanwhile, in 1933, the cautious Ickes, fearful of wasting governmental funds, spent virtually none of the PWA's $3.3 billion to fuel consumption under the NRA. Therefore, the country suffered from increased prices when few consumers received new jobs at sufficiently high incomes to buy the higher priced goods. Eventually, when sites for major construction had been carefully selected, and architects had completed their tasks, the PWA spent heavily. However, that occurred much too late to save the NRA.

As the only peacetime effort at national industrial planning, the NRA was a significant experiment. It wiped out child labor in industry and went a long way toward eliminating sweat shops and substandard wages and working conditions. But the NRA not only failed to encourage but also probably impeded recovery. The NRA and the entire series of early New Deal policies assumed that the country was suffering from industrial overproduction and that the government, therefore, should limit production to actual need. It was an absurd assumption. The United States was suffering from severe underconsumption in 1933 because of unemployment and the decline in wages and in farm and business income. The country needed most of all a vast injection of purchasing power.

Unemployment Relief

Roosevelt was personally responsible for the Civilian Conservation Corps

(CCC), which enrolled some 300,000 young men in camps throughout the country and engaged in reforestation and other work in national parks. Aside from this successful exception, all the relief policies of the first New Deal continued policies begun by the Hoover administration. The Federal Housing Authority was established in 1934 to provide long-term credit at moderate rates for home repairs and new housing. Between 1934 and 1940, this agency insured 554,000 loans which totaled $2.3 billion for new housing. The Federal Emergency Relief Act of May 12, 1933, appropriated $500 million for assistance to the unemployed, to be disbursed by the states.

A sharp increase in industrial production and employment took place during the summer of 1933, because employers raced to produce as much as they could before the NRA codes became effective. But the indices of production and employment slumped again in the autumn. As a harsh winter seemed to be fast approaching, Roosevelt created the Civil Works Administration (CWA), with Harry L. Hopkins as administrator, and took $400 million from the dilatory PWA to enable the CWA to provide temporary jobs for some 4,000,000 unemployed. Roosevelt liquidated the CWA in the spring of 1934 and then returned to the policy of providing relief assistance to the states through the Federal Emergency Relief Act.

The Development of Public Power

Roosevelt, always an ardent conservationist, gave personal leadership to a broad movement in the 1930s for federal development of regional multipurpose projects. These promoted flood control, river navigation, irrigation, and production of hydroelectric power. Roosevelt would have readily signed bills for regional projects in every section of the country, but he obtained congressional approval for development only of the Tennessee Valley. He also secured completion of Boulder (later called Hoover) Dam on the Colorado River in Arizona; construction of Fort Peck Dam on the Missouri River in Montana; and of Bonneville and Grand Coulee dams on the Columbia River. The latter dam, completed in 1942, was the largest masonry structure in the world.

The New Deal's work in the Tennessee Valley fired the imagination of the world. Congress, at Roosevelt's suggestion, created the Tennessee Valley Authority (TVA) in the spring of 1933. Congress directed the new agency to improve the navigation of the Tennessee River, to provide for flood control, and, generally, to improve the agricultural and industrial development of the Tennessee Valley. The TVA built twenty new dams and improved five old ones and achieved a nearly perfect system of flood control and an inland waterway stretching from the Ohio River into the heart of the Appalachians. The authority also operated the electric power facilities at Wilson Dam in Alabama and installed turbines at its other dams. The TVA gradually purchased private power distribution facilities and established a monopoly on the production and sale of electric power in the entire Tennessee Valley. It erected over 5,000 miles of transmission lines and provided cheap power to industrial concerns as well as to farmers and urban households.

Balanced against these impressive accomplishments were the costs which almost always accompany economic development. The construction of a vast system of flood control and hydroelectric power occurred only with the destruction of rivers and streams, along with innumerable forms of plant and animal life.

3. THE SECOND NEW DEAL

Origins

Powerful forces of discontent destroyed the first New Deal coalition of all classes and divided the country, roughly speaking, into a right and a left during the months just before the mid-term election of 1934.

With some exceptions, the manufacturing, business, and financial classes turned against the administration. They charged that Roosevelt was destroying constitutional government, coddling labor, and spending the Treasury into bankruptcy. The American Liberty League, formed by conservative Democrats in August 1934 and allied with big business and Wall Street, took the lead in the conservative revolt; its avowed purpose was to capture the Democratic party.

Roosevelt, thus battered by conservatives, also felt the wrath of demagogues and radicals who accused him of being a tool of Wall Street. Among these critics were the Communists and Senator Huey P. Long of Louisiana, a twentieth-century-style populist who had a passionate concern for the poor and a ruthless desire for power. He proposed to divide the national wealth and give every American family a $2,500 guaranteed annual wage. Also prominent were Father Charles E. Coughlin, a priest from Detroit with fascist tendencies, a hatred of eastern bankers, and a large radio audience; and Dr. Francis E. Townsend of southern California, who organized a national movement among old people for federal pensions of $200 a month to every person over sixty. These demagogues and numerous others worked hard to stir the discontent of workers, small farmers, the unemployed, and the aged. Signs that they were succeeding disturbed Roosevelt more than the revolt of the conservatives. Long seemed to pose the most serious threat to Roosevelt's reelection. A poll conducted by the Democratic National Committee revealed that, if Long ran as an independent candidate in 1936, he could take three to four million votes from Roosevelt.

The revolt of the conservatives actually worked to Roosevelt's advantage by coalescing the lower classes and a large portion of the middle class into a solid New Deal front. In the congressional election on November 6, 1934, the Democrats increased their already large majorities in both houses of Congress. Yet, many among this new majority saw Roosevelt's early New Deal measures as insufficient, and they applied pressure for a more extensive program of reform.

Launching the Second New Deal

"Boys," said Harry Hopkins, a leader of the welfare-state advocates in the Roosevelt circle, to his friends after the election, "this is our hour. We've got to get everything we want." It was not difficult to persuade Roosevelt to take a new tack, for he well understood the meaning of the election returns. He aggressively assumed leadership of the new left-of-center majority coalition and virtually jettisoned much of the first New Deal in his Annual Message to Congress of January 4, 1935. At the same time, he demanded that the federal government assume direct responsibility for the economic security of the masses of people.

The spearhead of the second New Deal was the $5 billion work-relief program authorized by the Emergency Relief Appropriation Act of April 8, 1935. Under its provisions, Roosevelt created the Works Progress Administration (WPA) and appointed Hopkins as its director. Hopkins immediately began to provide jobs for unemployed and needy workers, professional people, musicians, writers, actors, college students, and even historians, among others. Between 1935 and 1941, the WPA spent a total of $11.4 billion and gave work to a monthly average of 2,112,000 persons.

Signs that the Supreme Court might call a halt to social-welfare legislation had appeared even before the launching of the second New Deal. In January 1935, the court nullified a section of the NIRA which gave the President power to prohibit interstate transportation of oil produced in excess of quotas imposed by the NRA code. The vote was eight to one, and the decision seemed to imperil the entire NRA itself. On May 6, the court, in a five-to-four decision, nullified the Railroad Retirement Act of 1934 in language that appeared to doom any general social-security legislation. The court delivered its heaviest blow on May 27, 1935, in a decision in A.L.A. Schechter Corporation *v.* United States, which tested the constitutionality of the NIRA. The justices unanimously nullified that measure and the NRA as well, some on the ground that the NIRA delegated too much legislative authority to the executive branch, others because the measure permitted the federal government to regulate commerce which was purely intrastate in character.

New Laws for Old

The Schechter decision shocked both the nation and the President. In a press conference a few days later, Roosevelt spoke of the members of the Supreme Court as living in the "horse and buggy" days. The decision also plunged the administration into considerable confusion about its future course. Roosevelt had just urged Congress to extend the life of the NRA for an additional two years, even though that agency had been far from successful in most respects. After the Schechter decision, Roosevelt obviously had to abandon the enterprise, and for a short time it seemed that he was uncertain where to go.

Roosevelt quickly recovered his balance and sense of direction and decided to proceed at full steam with his program, in spite of threatened new reversals by the Supreme Court. Senator Robert F. Wagner had been working almost single-handedly on a National Labor Relations bill. Roosevelt had opposed the Wagner bill on the ground that it was better to provide protection for labor through the NRA. But, in practice, Section 7a of the NIRA provided little protection for organized labor, because both Roosevelt and Secretary Perkins permitted company-created and managed unions—even units of one or two individuals in an industrial plant—to fulfill the collective-bargaining requirement. The twin pressures of the election of 1934 and the Schechter decision, however, prompted Roosevelt to support the Wagner bill and to help give it a decisive push through Congress in July.

The National Labor Relations Act (NLRA) was by far the most significant piece of labor legislation in American history. It strengthened and broadened Section 7a of the NIRA by affirming the right of workers to bargain collectively through representatives of their own choosing and by outlawing a number of so-called unfair practices by employers. The act established the National Labor Relations Board (NLRB), which was empowered to prevent unfair employer practices by issuing "cease and desist" orders, which courts were ordered by law to enforce. Most important, on the petition of workers, the NLRB was empowered to administer and supervise collective-bargaining elections and to compel employers to bargain with unions if a majority of the workers voted to join one. This provision represented an enormous victory for organized labor; it gave collective bargaining the force of law and effectively destroyed company unions.

The first sessions of the Seventy-fourth Congress passed a number of other history-making laws before it adjourned in the autumn of 1935. The Guffey-Snyder Coal Conservation Act reenacted the bituminous coal code of the old NRA in language carefully tailored to meet the Supreme Court's objections. Another measure revived the liquor code. New railroad-retirement and mortgage-moratorium acts replaced those declared unconstitutional by the court in May. The Revenue Act, or wealth-tax bill, increased the surtax on incomes to the highest level in American history, and the federal estate tax to a maximum of 70 per cent.

Beginnings of the Welfare State: The Social Security Act

The most far-reaching law adopted in the summer of 1935 was the Social Security Act, which Roosevelt signed on August 14, 1935. It was significant, not only for what it did, but for what it symbolized. It marked the end of old American traditions of individual self-help, and, at the same time, it marked the beginning, on a national scale, of the kind of system to protect economic security which virtually every European nation had possessed for half a century. The Social Security Act was divided into three main parts:

1. It provided a federal system of insurance against poverty in old age. A compulsory old-age insurance fund, to which both employers and employees contributed, provided retirement pensions for workers after the age of sixty-five.

2. The act established a system of unemployment insurance and levied a 3 per cent tax on payrolls to provide unemployment payments through the states.

3. The Social Security Act provided financial assistance to the states for a variety of welfare programs. The federal government, for example, offered to match state appropriations dollar for dollar up to a certain amount to provide old-age assistance to needy persons already over sixty-five. The act provided similar assistance for needy children, blind persons, the physically handicapped, widows with dependent children, and for various public-health purposes.

The Social Security Act was weak in that it provided no coverage for agricultural workers, domestic servants, public servants, and professional people. Roosevelt and the authors of the measure were the first to admit that it was experimental and inadequate, but they knew that the Social Security system would be enlarged and strengthened in the future. That process began in 1937 and has continued to our own time.

4. POLITICAL DEVELOPMENTS AND THE COURT CONTROVERSY

The Election of 1936

Republicans turned their backs on former President Hoover in 1936 and nominated the progressive governor of Kansas, Alfred M. Landon. They named Colonel Frank Knox, newspaper publisher of Chicago and former follower of Theodore Roosevelt, as Landon's running mate. The Democrats renominated Roosevelt and Garner by acclamation. They also repealed the rule which required a two-thirds vote for the nomination of a presidential candidate. Roosevelt's acceptance speech amounted to a declaration of war against "economic royalists" and was an eloquent call for national dedication: "This generation of Americans has a rendezvous with destiny. . . . We are fighting to save a great and precious form of government for ourselves and for the world."

The Socialists again nominated Norman Thomas, while their bitter enemies, the Communists, named Earl Browder. A new party appeared in the field under the banner of the Union for Social Justice. It consisted of the

---

The Election of 1936

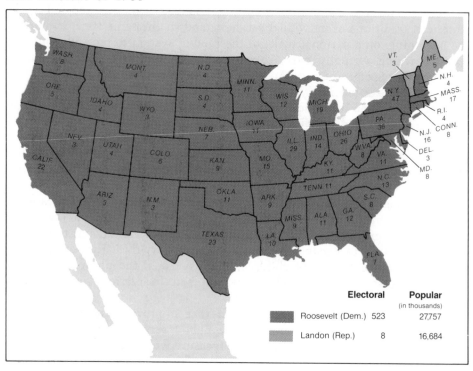

	Electoral	Popular (in thousands)
Roosevelt (Dem.)	523	27,757
Landon (Rep.)	8	16,684

followers of Dr. Townsend and Father Coughlin and the heirs of Senator Long, who had been assassinated in 1935. The party nominated Representative William Lemke of North Dakota for the presidency, but, without the charismatic and clever Long, the Union party mounted no real threat to Roosevelt.

The campaign was one of the most unequal presidential contests in American history. Landon made a game fight, but he was an inept campaigner and failed utterly to arouse the voters. He suffered from two other crippling handicaps. Because he ran on his own progressive background and a platform which endorsed all the basic legislation of the New Deal, Landon could promise little more than a better administration of New Deal programs. During the summer of 1936, moreover, substantial recovery was in progress after agonizingly slow improvement in economic conditions between 1933 and 1936. Production, employment, and real per capita income were all nearing their 1929 levels by the middle of 1936, and the upswing obviously did not help Landon's ailing campaign.

To make the situation almost hopeless for the Republicans, Roosevelt conducted his best campaign ever in 1936. He stumped the country as if the contest was close and appealed frankly for the support of the common people. On the basis of a much publicized poll of its readers, the weekly magazine, *Literary Digest,* predicted a Republican victory. But when the votes were counted, Roosevelt had carried every state except Maine and Vermont, with nearly 28,000,000 popular and 523 electoral votes, as compared to nearly 17,000,000 popular and eight electoral votes for Landon. The landslide also reduced the Republicans to a corporal's guard of eighty-nine in the House of Representatives and twenty-one in the Senate. The Socialist, Communist, and Union parties combined received a little over 1,000,000 votes. The *Literary Digest* became the laughingstock of the nation and soon went out of business.

A great majority of the American people had obviously given a strong mandate for the continuation of the New Deal. Analysts discovered three other developments in the returns: organized labor had played a significant part in the Democratic victory; an overwhelming majority of blacks had voted for a Democratic presidential candidate for the first time in American history; and the white ethnic groups, who still formed a majority of the urban poor, voted almost completely for Roosevelt.

Conflict with the Supreme Court

At the end of 1936, it appeared doubtful whether Roosevelt could execute his mandate, because a bare majority of the Supreme Court had almost paralyzed the ability of Congress and the President to deal with national economic problems.

The central issue in 1936 was whether Congress could use its taxing power and its power over interstate commerce to control economic activities which had traditionally been defined as intrastate or local in character. The conservative majority of the Supreme Court gave its answer in two key decisions in 1936: United States *v.* Butler nullified the Agricultural Adjustment Act on the ground that the production of foodstuffs was local and not interstate in nature; and Carter *v.* Carter Coal Company nullified the Coal

Conservation Act on the ground that the mining of coal was a local activity.

The court, once it had deprived Congress of basic control over manufacturing, mining, agricultural production, and, by implication, labor relations, struck at social legislation again. In Morehead *v.* New York *ex rel.* Tipaldo, the justices denied that the state could regulate the hours, wages, and conditions of labor, because such regulation was a violation of the freedom of contract guaranteed by the Fourteenth Amendment.

Reformers of both parties were outraged and demanded a limitation in the power of the Supreme Court. Some suggested that such an extraordinary majority as six to three be required before the court could declare an act of Congress unconstitutional. Others proposed to permit Congress to override court decisions by a two-thirds vote. Still others wanted Congress to deprive the court of the right of judicial review altogether.

The Court-Packing Crisis

Neither the Democratic platform of 1936, nor Roosevelt during the campaign of that year, had given any intimation of an impending assault against the supreme tribunal. But, soon after his triumphant reelection, Roosevelt virtually declared war on the Supreme Court's conservative majority. On February 5, 1937, he sent to Congress the draft of a bill for the reorganization of the federal judiciary. It provided for a number of procedural reforms and a retirement system for federal judges. It also authorized the appointment of up to fifty new judges if incumbents failed to retire at age seventy. Six of these judges might be added to the Supreme Court. In an accompanying message Roosevelt justified his proposal mainly on the ground that insufficient and infirm judicial personnel had caused crowded dockets and intolerable delays.

For the first time in his career, Roosevelt committed major errors in both strategy and timing. Partly because he had failed to inform his leaders in Congress of his plan, he grossly underestimated the degree of popular and congressional support for traditional separation of powers and the independence of the judiciary in the federal system. Worse still, Roosevelt had also failed to be frank with Congress and the people. Once the battle began, Roosevelt came out in the open and asserted that his plan was necessary to save the country. But he could not repair the damage already done. Democrats joined Republicans in Congress in attacking the judicial reorganization bill as an attempt to pack the Supreme Court and to destroy the independence of the entire judicial branch.

We will never know who would have won the battle because the constitutional crisis was resolved in an unexpected way. Roosevelt might well have won a modified version of his judicial reorganization bill. However, the Supreme Court itself ended the quarrel, and, with it, Roosevelt's court plan. While the controversy raged at its height, the case of West Coast Hotel *v.* Parrish, which involved the constitutionality of a minimum wage law of the state of Washington, came before the court. The court not only reversed the Tipaldo decision of the year before; it also approved the Washington statute in language which left room for any reasonable state regulation of wages, hours, and working conditions. Two weeks later, an even more important case—National Labor Relations Board *v.* Jones and Laughlin Steel

Corporation, which involved the constitutionality of the National Labor Relations Act—came before the court. The justices now said that the Wagner Act was constitutional because Congress' power over interstate commerce was absolute and extended to every economic activity which affected the manufacture of goods.

Roosevelt obviously had lost the battle and won the war. As has so often been the case in its history, the Supreme Court realized the dangers of flouting popular and congressional opinion, and several of the justices swung in favor of the New Deal measures. The retirement after 1937 of a number of Supreme Court justices who were among the staunchest opponents of the New Deal enabled Roosevelt to pack the court with men closer to his political and economic philosophy. This new "Roosevelt Court" in turn upheld the constitutionality of every subsequent New Deal measure.

5. STRENGTHENING THE SECOND NEW DEAL

The Rise of the CIO

In retrospect, it is clear that the New Deal effected a near revolution in American life by stimulating the growth of a politically self-conscious labor movement which could bargain on more or less equal terms with management in most major industries.

These profound changes were not, of course, all of Roosevelt's making. In 1934 and 1935, a group within the AFL, led by John L. Lewis, president of the United Mine Workers, and Sidney Hillman and David Dubinsky, presidents of the garment workers' unions, made some changes of their own. They demanded that the AFL organize industrial unions (that is, unions which combined all workers in a single industry, regardless of their craft) in such still unorganized industries as steel, automobiles, and rubber. A majority of the leaders of the AFL were old, conservative, and still hostile to the very concept of industrial unionism. Lewis and his colleagues, rebuffed by the national convention of the AFL in 1935, formed the Committee for Industrial Organization; three years later it became the separate, independent Congress of Industrial Organizations (CIO).

In 1936, the CIO launched a campaign to organize the steel industry, the citadel of antiunionism since about 1900. It won this crucial struggle in early 1937 and turned next to the automobile industry. The union organizers won the right to bargain for workers in General Motors and Chrysler in 1937, and in Ford in 1940. One of the most prominent techniques of the CIO unions were sit-down strikes, that is, the refusal to leave factories until managers agreed to negotiate with their representatives.

The CIO organized virtually every mass-production industry in the United States and had grown in membership to about 5,000,000 by 1941. A revived AFL had reached a membership of 4,569,000 by this time. To be sure, labor won these gains mainly by its own efforts and sacrifices, but the support of the administration, particularly of the NLRB in drives for recognition, played a crucial role in labor's success. In turn, this powerful new labor movement became an indispensable source of political power for the second New Deal.

Reform Continues

Roosevelt's Annual Message and second inaugural of January 1937 were clarion calls for new legislation to benefit the "one-third of a nation ill-housed, ill-clad, ill-nourished." The fight over the judicial reorganization bill diverted congressional energies and temporarily disrupted Democratic unity. But Roosevelt drew his forces together again in 1937 and 1938 and won most of the measures which he said were necessary for completion of his program. Assistance came to Roosevelt from an unexpected source. Largely because the administration slashed expenditures in 1937 to balance the budget while new taxes for Social Security were imposed, a sharp recession occurred in early 1938. Industrial output fell 33 per cent, unemployment rose rapidly, and, once more, stock market prices collapsed. Congressmen and senators, with nervous eyes on the impending mid-term election, suddenly became very ardent New Dealers, eager to renew the spending program.

1. The Farm Tenancy Act of 1937 established the Farm Security Administration. It provided various kinds of assistance, particularly credit for the purchase of land, to tenants, sharecroppers, and migratory farm laborers who had benefited hardly at all from the AAA.

2. The National Housing Act of 1937 created the United States Housing Authority and furnished it with large sums to begin the first serious war on urban slums.

3. The Agricultural Adjustment Act of 1938 replaced the temporary and ineffective Soil Conservation Act, which Congress had adopted in 1936 when the Supreme Court invalidated the first AAA. The second Agricultural Adjustment Act continued soil conservation payments to farmers and permitted producers of the major staples to limit production by a two-thirds vote. The act provided for an "ever-normal granary" by keeping farm surpluses off the market in fat years and releasing them in lean years.

4. The Fair Labor Standards, or Wages and Hours, Act of 1938 rounded out the second New Deal's comprehensive structure of labor legislation. The measure established a minimum wage of twenty-five cents an hour, to be increased to forty cents, and limited hours of labor to forty a week.

5. A frightened Congress made some $3 billion available to the WPA, launched a huge public-works program in cooperation with the states, and greatly expanded the lending power of federal credit agencies.

6. Congress, in response to a special request from the President, established the Temporary National Economic Committee to study the American economy with a view to increasing price competition with new antitrust legislation. Roosevelt, influenced by Louis D. Brandeis and his disciples, much as Wilson had been in 1912, returned to the idea that large business combinations kept prices artificially high and restricted consumption.

Blacks and the New Deal

The record of the New Deal's impact on the status of blacks is ambiguous. On the one hand, blacks were not—as they were during the progressive era—excluded from Roosevelt's program of relief and reform. Yet, at the same time, Roosevelt and his advisers resisted taking any steps to further the civil and political status of blacks during the 1930s.

Like most men of his day, Franklin D. Roosevelt did not question the propriety or justice of the Jim Crow system as it operated either in the South or in northern cities. In fact, on a personal level, Roosevelt rarely came into contact with blacks, except domestic servants at the White House or at his retreat in Warm Springs, Georgia. Whatever Roosevelt's views on race—and he never expressed them clearly—his overwhelming concern was to avoid alienating the support of southern Democratic politicians, particularly at the end of the 1930s, when their support for his international policies was critical. He therefore adopted an ambiguous policy of public silence on the race issue. As the Brain Truster Rexford G. Tugwell put it, Roosevelt was interested in the issue of race but did not consider it "important politically, never as far as I knew."

This ambiguity was reflected in the extent to which blacks were affected by the New Deal. Early in 1933, Secretary Perkins assured blacks that they would not "be overlooked" in the New Deal. In many respects, the administration kept its promise. Ickes banned racial discrimination in the PWA in the autumn of 1933; in the CCC, blacks composed 10 per cent of the workers by 1936. Yet, the Roosevelt administration fell short of pressing for an effective end to discrimination; indeed, such a policy would not only have been political suicide but also practically impossible in many areas of the South. In the administration of the AAA, the New Deal did little for black tenants and sharecroppers, although programs such as the Resettlement Administration and the Farm Security Administration did help to improve the condition of blacks who lived in rural poverty.

In other respects, blacks were very much involved in the Roosevelt administration. Early in the New Deal, the administration appointed "racial advisers" to each department and agency. Their duties were to supervise each agency and to insure that discrimination did not occur in the administration of relief. Although the racial advisers evoked much criticism and lacked any real power, their appointment marked an important beginning in ending discrimination in the federal government. By 1936, these advisers constituted an informal group known as the "Black Cabinet." Moreover, the President's wife, Eleanor Roosevelt, was an active and influential supporter of blacks.

Nothing better illustrates the limitations of Roosevelt's approach than the issue of lynching. After the incidence of lynching increased during the early 1930s, considerable support developed in the South and in Washington for a federal antilynching law, and, in January 1934, Senator Wagner introduced such a bill. Although Roosevelt publicly condemned lynching in November 1933, he scrupulously refused to support antilynching legislation because he feared its repercussions for his supporters among southern Democrats.

Despite the limitations of Roosevelt's support for even a modicum of civil rights, he was undeniably popular among blacks. In 1936, indeed, a major shift occurred in northern cities where blacks had the franchise. The shift in voting patterns between the presidential elections of 1932 and 1936 was startling. In Harlem, where blacks had voted 51 per cent Democratic in 1932, 79 per cent of the voters supported Roosevelt in 1936. In other areas, the shift was even more substantial: in Philadelphia, black support for Democrats rose from 27 per cent in 1932 to 69 per cent four years later; in Cincinnati, from 29 per cent to 65 per cent; in Detroit, from 37 per cent to 64 per cent; and in Pittsburgh, from 53 per cent to 77 per cent.

In all, the New Deal marked several important changes in the status of black Americans. Unfortunately, little evidence exists about how blacks fared on account of New Deal policies in terms of income or jobs. Nonetheless, the long-term implications are clear. The creation of the "Black Cabinet" meant that blacks now had some oversight of federal relief and employment policies. In response, Roosevelt made a beginning—strictly limited by political considerations, to be sure—to include blacks in federal recovery programs. Moveover, with the election of 1936, northern urban blacks became an important constituency in the New Deal coalition.

6. THE END OF THE NEW DEAL

The Passing of Reform

The forward motion of the New Deal slowed down perceptibly between 1938 and 1939 as the result of developments both at home and abroad. The most important of these was the completion of Roosevelt's program for reform and reconstruction. Moreover, by 1938 – 1939, many signs indicated that the majority of Americans were eager for a breathing spell and believed that the time had come to digest and perfect the reform gains of the past six years. This feeling had important political manifestations. During the summer of 1938, Roosevelt set out to prevent the renomination of several Democratic congressmen and senators whom had opposed some of the administration's measures. With a single exception (a congressman from New York), Democratic voters defeated Roosevelt's candidates in primary elections and renominated the men whom he had attempted to purge. What is more, the Republicans gained eighty-one seats in the House of Representatives and eight seats in the Senate in the mid-term election on November 8, 1938. They also elected thirteen additional governors; one of them was Thomas E. Dewey in Roosevelt's home state of New York. By joining with Democratic conservatives, Republicans now had the power to prevent further enactment of New Deal legislation.

Finally, Roosevelt was trying to build congressional support for a stronger policy of resistance to Nazi Germany's aggressions. In order to accomplish this end, Roosevelt had to avoid alienating conservative southern Democrats, who were the most consistent internationalists in Congress.

The New Deal in Retrospect

The New Deal tried to achieve economic recovery as well as extensive economic and social reform. Even now it is difficult to say whether the Roosevelt administration achieved its first objective. A certain measure of recovery did undoubtedly occur, for per capita real income exceeded the 1929 level in 1940, before the full effect of the Second World War had stimulated the economy. Yet, substantial unemployment remained until 1941. Some economists believe that New Deal measures actually slowed down the return of normal economic activity by raising the prices of construction materials disproportionately, and, in general, by causing dislocations and discouraging corporate investment. In any event, it is difficult for a nation to engage in thoroughgoing reform and recovery at the same time, for the reform of basic institutions frightens the business and investing classes.

The New Deal and Twentieth-Century America

1. The New Deal effected sweeping administrative and regulatory reforms. For the first time since the industrial revolution, the American people and their leaders faced most of the challenges raised by industrialization and urbanization. The New Deal's answer was a vast increase in the power of the federal government to guide and promote general social and economic welfare. Theodore Roosevelt and Woodrow Wilson had laid the foundations for a modern regulatory and welfare state, but Franklin D. Roosevelt completed the superstructure of that state.

2. The New Deal greatly strengthened the system of free-enterprise capitalism. To be sure, New Deal legislation put many restraints upon business and finance in order to guarantee that they would be socially responsible. But, while it subjected private economic institutions to new regulation, the New Deal left most important economic decisions to individuals and groups of individuals. The New Deal also gave to hitherto submerged groups, such as farmers and workers, a large share in decision making, and hence a profound stake in the successful operation of the new economy. Some Americans in the 1930s—and not only the wealthy—thought that the New Deal was radical. However, most historians now agree with Roosevelt's claim, made in 1937, that he was in fact a conservative. As he put it: "To preserve we had to reform. Wise and prudent men—intelligent conservatives—have long known that in a changing world worthy institutions can be conserved only by adjusting them to the changing time. In the words of the great essayist, 'The voice of great events is proclaiming to us, "Reform if you would preserve.' " I am that kind of a conservative."

3. The New Deal restored faith in democracy at a time when democracy seemed on the verge of extinction almost everywhere else in the world. It proved that men of good will could deal with serious national problems without revolution, violence, dictatorship, or a slave state.

4. Finally, Roosevelt helped to revive confidence in the human spirit itself by his own example in overcoming a catastrophic illness and continuing to fight for the principles in which he believed. No doubt he was thinking about himself when he uttered the following words during the presidential campaign of 1936:

It is not the critic who counts, not the man who points out how the strong man stumbled, or where the doer of deeds could have done them better. The credit belongs to the man who is actually in the arena; whose face is marred by dust and sweat and blood; who strives valiantly; who errs and comes short again and again; who knows the great enthusiasms, the great devotions, and spends himself in a worthy cause; who at the best knows in the end the triumphs of high achievement; and who at the worst, if he fails, at least fails while daring greatly; so that his place shall never be with those cold and timid souls who know neither defeat nor victory.

SUGGESTED READINGS

Arthur M. Schlesinger, Jr., *The Coming of the New Deal* (1959), and *The Politics of Up-* *heaval* (1960), offer the most comprehensive treatment of the period covered in this chapter. An excellent one-volume account is Leuchtenburg, *Franklin D. Roosevelt and the New Deal,* already cited. Other good political commentaries are Basil Rauch, *History of the New Deal* (1944); Dennis W. Brogan, *The Era of Franklin D. Roosevelt* (1951); Dexter Perkins, *The New Age of Franklin Roosevelt* (1957); and Burns, *Roosevelt: The Lion and the Fox,* already cited. Wecter, *The Age of the Great Depression,* and Allen, *Since Yesterday,* already cited, are good social histories. The biographies cited in the preceding chapter should also be consulted. All the books mentioned above regard the New Deal favorably and often uncritically. For more negative views from the Right, see Edgar E. Robinson, *The Roosevelt Leadership, 1932–1945* (1955); for another thoughtful criticism, see Paul Conkin, *The New Deal* (1975).

Biographies and memoirs constitute a significant part of the literature on the New Deal. Robert E. Sherwood, *Roosevelt and Hopkins* (rev. ed., 1950); J. Joseph Huthmacher, *Senator Robert F. Wagner and the Rise of Urban Liberalism* (1968); T. Harry Williams, *Huey Long* (1969); and John M. Blum, *From the Morgenthau Diaries* (1959, 1960), are illuminating. A "collective biography" of the old progressives in this period is provided in Otis L. Graham, Jr., *Encore for Reform* (1967). Most opposed the New Deal. Some of the memoirs and personal accounts which ought to be consulted are Frances Perkins, *The Roosevelt I Knew* (1946); *The Secret Diary of Harold L. Ickes,* 3 vols. (1953–1954); James A. Farley, *Behind the Ballots* (1938); Hugh S. Johnson, *The Blue Eagle* (1935); Samuel I. Rosenman, *Working with Roosevelt* (1952); and Eleanor Roosevelt's indispensable *This I Remember* (1949). Less sympathetic accounts are Raymond Moley, *After Seven Years* (1939) and *The First New Deal* (1966). S.I. Rosenman, ed., *The Public Papers of Franklin D. Roosevelt,* 13 vols. (1938–1950), contain fascinating material.

There are many specialized studies of the New Deal. On the divergence of New Deal from Hoover's policies, and what might be called the ideology of the New Deal, see Rosen, *Hoover, Roosevelt, and the Brains Trust,* already cited, and Rexford G. Tugwell, *The Brains Trust* (1968). For economic policies and their effects, see Broadus Mitchell, *Depression Decade* (1947); Kenneth D. Roose, *Economics of Recession and Revival* (1954); and Otis L. Graham, *Toward a Planned Society: From Roosevelt to Nixon* (1976). A keen analysis is Thurman Arnold, *The Folklore of Capitalism* (1937). Ellis W.

Hawley, *The New Deal and the Problem of Monopoly* (1966), is an adequate treatment. David E. Lilienthal, *The T.V.A.* (rev. ed., 1953), contains useful information on that regional development. New Deal agricultural policy is discussed in Christiana M. Campbell, *The Farm Bureaus: A Study of the Making of National Farm Policy, 1933–1940* (1962); Richard S. Kirkendall, *Social Scientists and Farm Politics in the Age of Roosevelt* (1966); Gilbert C. Fite, *George M. Peek and the Fight for Farm Parity* (1954); Sidney Baldwin, *Poverty and Politics* (1968); and Anthony Badger, *Prosperity Road: The New Deal, Tobacco, and North Carolina* (1980). Leonard Baker, *Back to Back: The Duel between FDR and the Supreme Court* (1967), is the most comprehensive account of that subject, but Edward S. Corwin, *Twilight of the Supreme Court* (1934), *Court over Constitution* (1938), and *Constitutional Revolution* (rev. ed., 1946), and Alpheus T. Mason, *Harlan Fiske Stone: Pillar of the Law* (1956), are valuable.

Incisive essays on social history can be found in Isabel Leighton, *The Aspirin Age,* already cited. Good studies of the Left are David A. Shannon, *The Socialist Party of America,* already cited; Daniel Bell, *Marxian Socialism in the United States* (1967); Earl Latham, *The Communist Controversy in Washington* (1966); Robert W. Iverson, *The Communists and the Schools* (1959); Murray Kempton, *Part of Our Time* (1955); and Daniel Aaron, *Writers on the Left* (1961); a contemporary account of the Right is Raymond Gram Swing, *Forerunners of American Fascism* (1935). Huey P. Long, *Every Man a King* (1933), is a fascinating introduction to southern radicalism, and to Long; but also see T. Harry Williams' excellent biography of Long, already cited; David H. Bennett, *Demagogues in the Depression: American Radicals and the Union Party, 1932–1936* (1969); and Charles J. Tull, *Father Coughlin and the New Deal* (1965).

The conservative reaction to the New Deal is discussed in George Wolfskill, *The Revolt of Conservatives* (1962), and Wolfskill and John A. Hudson, *All but the People* (1969), and in James T. Patterson, *Congressional Conservatism and the New Deal* (1967). Samuel Lubell, *The Future of American Politics* (1952), is a pathbreaking analysis of political changes during the period.

The New Deal and black Americans are examined in Raymond Wolters, *Negroes and the Great Depression* (1970), and in the essays in Bernard Sternsher, ed., *The Negro in Depression and War* (1969).

CHAPTER 10
THE UNITED STATES AND
WORLD CRISIS, 1933 – 1941

1. JAPANESE IMPERIALISM

A Decade of Turmoil

Depression, hunger, and domestic violence assaulted the populations of the nations of Europe and the Far East at the same time and with almost the same ferocity as they did in the United States. The American people met these challenges without significant harm to their democratic institutions. Other nations throughout the world, which lacked a democratic heritage, followed political or military leaders who promised economic security in exchange for liberties. Half the governments in Latin America, for example, toppled during the early 1930s without elections. During this worldwide chaos, several major industrial powers fell into the hands of groups which envisioned economic salvation and national aggrandizement through conquest.

The Japanese, utterly dependent upon international trade, had suffered an economic crisis because of the tariffs and trade boycotts of the 1930s. They therefore permitted an oligarchy of militarists and imperialists to subvert weak democratic institutions and to turn their island empire upon an expansionist course. The Germans, in their anger against the Versailles Treaty, despair about economic conditions, and fear of communism, turned to Adolf Hitler and watched the Nazis destroy the remnants of German democracy. Hitler and his followers, with their messianic plans for a "Greater Germany" and their fanatical anti-Semitism, plunged their nation into an abyss of terror.

Some of the legitimate aspirations and claims of the dictatorships might well have been satisfied through ordinary diplomacy. Unhappily for the world, the men and parties who led the expansionist nations eventually became impatient with the slow course and unsatisfactory results of normal negotiations. Many of their aims conflicted with those of other major powers. In their efforts to achieve their objectives through violence, the leaders of Germany and Japan, especially, plunged the world into a decade of turmoil, crisis, and war. As the 1930s ended, whole continents were involved in a death struggle.

Conflict with China

The first critical challenge to the postwar peace structure occurred in 1931, when Japan wrested Manchuria from China in open violation of the covenant of the League of Nations. Manchuria had been Japan's most important area for investment and development since the 1890s. Fear that China under its new leader, Chiang Kai-shek, would succeed in reasserting control over Manchuria prompted the leaders of the Japanese Kwantung Army in Manchuria to attempt to settle the question before Chiang had an opportunity to do so. The Kwantung generals manufactured an incident to serve as a pretext, defied their home government, and attacked Chinese forces throughout Manchuria on September 18, 1931. Civilians in the Japanese cabinet were unable to regain control over the army, and, in a campaign of about eight weeks, the Japanese troops occupied all of Manchuria.

The blow fell at the very moment that leaders in Washington and London floundered in the depths of the international financial crisis, which had just forced Great Britain to abandon the gold standard. Western leaders reacted slowly and cautiously. While they debated about an appropriate response, the liberal government in Tokyo gave way in December to a coalition of military officers and imperialistic politicians. Clearly, Japanese aggression in Manchuria had established a precedent for further military adventures.

The League of Nations could have responded forcefully, but only if the two great naval powers, the United States and Great Britain, had been willing to enforce the covenant. The British were unwilling to take the initiative, and Hoover and Secretary of State Stimson refused any steps, such as an economic boycott, which carried the risk of war with Japan. Domestic opinion supported their policy, for China seemed far away, and most Americans invoked the apparent lesson of the First World War. A combination of domestic creditors of warring countries, munitions makers, and foreign propaganda, many Americans believed, had tricked the nation into war in 1917. Unless the United States was attacked directly, most Americans told poll takers, they preferred to avoid involvement in overseas conflicts. A strong verbal and moral condemnation of the Japanese, they believed, would suffice. A Quaker and a true pacifist, Hoover agreed with them.

In these circumstances, Stimson used his only available weapon—moral suasion. On January 7, 1932, he warned both the Chinese and Japanese governments that the United States would not recognize any territorial or political changes brought about in the Far East by force. Stimson enunciated this policy of nonrecognition more plainly in a public letter to Senator Borah on February 23. The League of Nations endorsed the Stimson policy, but it did not act when Japan created the puppet state of Manchukuo in Manchuria and withdrew from the League of Nations.

2. THE UNITED STATES AND THE RISE OF EUROPEAN FASCISM

The Versailles System

After the international economic collapse of 1931, leaders in western Europe and the United States tried last-ditch efforts to save the Versailles Treaty system. It soon became evident that one part of the Paris settlement—war debts and reparations—could not be salvaged. It would have been wise for Hoover to have agreed to mutual cancellation of all intergovernmental obligations which stemmed from the First World War. However, fear of reactions at home again paralyzed the President, and hence the European nations took matters into their own hands. Representatives of the western European governments met at Lausanne, Switzerland, in 1932 and agreed in effect to cancel Germany's reparations debt. The following year, all governments which owed war debts to the United States, except Finland, defaulted on their payments. In the same year, 1933, leaders of western Europe tried to build the foundations for a revival of world trade at the London Economic Conference. On this occasion, however, Roosevelt prevented agreement on the first step, monetary stabilization, because he was intent upon further devaluation of the dollar.

It cannot be said, therefore, that the United States, either under Hoover or under Roosevelt during his first year in office, gave any leadership in the reconstruction of the world economy. The American government did, however, do all that it could to save the peace system through a reduction in land armaments. A World Disarmament Conference finally opened in Geneva in 1932 after years of discussion and preparation. Hoover proposed the destruction of all offensive weapons and the reduction by one third of all naval and ordinary military forces. When Roosevelt took office, he not only supported Hoover's proposal, but also promised American participation in a new collective security system. In addition, France and Great Britain agreed that the Versailles Treaty should be revised to give Germany equality in land armaments.

Unfortunately, this concession came too late, for Adolf Hitler became Chancellor of Germany on January 30, 1933. He wanted, not equality in armaments, but military superiority in order to carry out his plans to dominate Europe. He therefore withdrew German delegates from the World Disarmament Conference and the League of Nations in October 1933.

Hitler and Mussolini

Europe careened from one crisis to another during the next six years while Hitler and the Italian dictator, Benito Mussolini, destroyed both the Versailles Treaty system and the League of Nations. Hitler made the first move on March 16, 1935. He renounced the provisions of the Versailles Treaty for

German disarmament and began a military buildup, and, when Great Britain and France took no action to halt German rearmament—which they could easily have done—Mussolini launched an attack on Ethiopia. The League of Nations condemned this aggression, and the United States would have been willing to support an embargo against the shipment of oil to Italy. However, Great Britain and France prevented any effective retaliation by the League out of fear that it would drive Mussolini into an alliance with Hitler.

Encouraged and actively supported by Hitler and Mussolini, in 1936, Spanish army leaders headed by General Francisco Franco launched a civil war to destroy the liberal government in Madrid. Powerful industrialists, landowners, and Roman Catholics, who felt unsafe under a democratic regime, supported Franco. France and Great Britain stood by while Franco's armies destroyed the Spanish Republic between 1936 and 1939.

In the same year that the Spanish Civil War began, Hitler sent his armies into the demilitarized German Rhineland. Again the French and British did nothing. Hitler then encouraged the Nazi movement in Austria and occupied that country in March 1938. Earlier, in 1936, he had concluded sympathetic alliances with Italy and Japan.

Europe approached the brink of war in the autumn of 1938. Hitler threatened to invade Czechoslovakia when that country refused to hand over to Germany its Sudetenland, which contained more than 3,000,000 ethnic Germans. The Czechs, who relied on help from Great Britain, France, and Russia, mobilized, but neither of the western democracies was willing to go to war to save the Czech Republic, and Russia would not act alone. Instead, Prime Minister Neville Chamberlain of Great Britain and Premier Edouard Daladier of France met Hitler and Mussolini at Munich on September 28, 1938. There, in a classic act of appeasement, Chamberlain and Daladier agreed to the dismemberment of the one surviving democracy east of the Rhine River. The British Prime Minister reported this agreement to the House of Commons as a guarantee of "peace in our time." Meanwhile, Hitler occupied the Sudetenland and soon destroyed the remnant of the Czech Republic.

Isolationism

Concerted and only slightly bold action by Great Britain and France could have stopped Mussolini and Hitler in their tracks at any time before 1938. However, these democracies were unwilling to run even a slight risk of war. Great Britain and France had been bled white by the First World War. The British and French leaders were, moreover, so afraid of communism that they did not look altogether with disfavor upon the rise of the militantly anti-Communist Nazi regime.

Americans viewed events in Europe from 1935 to 1938 with mixed emotions. Most Americans abhorred Hitler, especially for his systematic persecution of German Jews (although the dimensions of his brutality were not yet realized). Many sympathized with beleaguered Ethiopia in 1935–1936 and with the Loyalists' fight to preserve the liberal Spanish Popular Front government. But almost all Americans assumed that, if it came to war, the British navy and the supposedly great French army would make short work of

Hitler and Mussolini. This assumption affected all American thinking about developments in Europe at this time and led directly to one conclusion and one policy: the bridling of Hitler and Mussolini was primarily Great Britain's and France's job, and the United States could safely avoid the responsibility of entanglement in another European war.

Other developments in the mid-thirties made this choice by Americans virtually a unanimous one. Obsession with recovery and reconstruction of their own institutions caused Americans to turn inward in the belief that their most important tasks were domestic and not foreign. Many thoughtful Americans also believed that, in Hitler and Mussolini, the former Allies had reaped the fruits of their vindictiveness and imperialism at the Paris Peace Conference. The repudiation of war debts only confirmed the American suspicion that the European democracies were selfish, faithless, and dishonest. Moreover, an investigation of the armaments industry led by Senator Gerald P. Nye of North Dakota reinforced the popular belief that bankers and munitions makers had manipulated the country into the First World War. Although Nye reached his well-publicized conclusions with little evidence, so-called revisionist historians echoed the charges of the Nye Committee. Finally, an organized peace movement in the United States gathered strength during the 1930s as a wave of pacifism swept through the churches and college campuses. Movies and plays embellished the theme that war was a grand illusion—the delight only of idiots.

While war clouds gathered in Europe and Asia, American sentiment for noninvolvement grew. In 1935 and 1936, Congress enacted a series of laws which prohibited the shipment of arms to Italy or Ethiopia, or to either side in the Spanish Civil War, and refused to distinguish between military aggressors and established governments acting in self-defense. In practice, neutrality worked to the benefit of Mussolini's and Franco's armies, for they did not need American arms and the Ethiopian government and the Spanish Republic did. A third and more comprehensive Neutrality Act of May 1, 1937, banned the sale of arms and munitions, or the extension of loans, to *any* belligerents. This act also included a cash-and-carry provision which stipulated that *all* belligerents had to pay cash for nonmilitary goods purchased in the United States and had to carry them away in non-American ships. In addition, the law warned Americans that they would travel on belligerent ships at their own risk. Finally, the act empowered the President to determine when a state of war existed and to place an embargo on other exports besides munitions at his own discretion. The history of the First World War, the advocates of neutrality legislation believed, would not be repeated.

Isolationism was so strong that Roosevelt and Hull were virtual prisoners of public opinion in working out policies toward Europe and the Far East. The President and his Secretary of State thought that the neutrality legislation was ill-timed and unwise; they realized that strict American neutrality usually favored aggressors, such as Japan and Italy, which possessed war supplies which their victims lacked.

Although Roosevelt and Hull worked to modify neutrality legislation so as to give the President more discretion in the application of the laws, Roosevelt signed the bills even though they made no concessions to the administration's wishes. Moreover, the State Department, under pressure from conservatives and pro-Franco Roman Catholic groups, took the initiative in applying the neutrality laws to the Spanish Civil War. On one occasion, Roosevelt sent up a trial balloon to see whether the winds of public opinion were changing. In a speech in Chicago on October 5, 1937, he said that the time had come for peace-loving nations to quarantine aggressors. The violent public negative reaction made it clear that Americans were, if anything, more strongly isolationist than before.

British and French reluctance to stand firm would have made a strong American foreign policy difficult to execute, even if American public opinion had encouraged Roosevelt and Hull to follow one. For example, they eagerly wanted to cooperate with the League of Nations in applying an oil embargo against Italy during the Ethiopian crisis, but the French government prevented effective action on this occasion. In late 1937 and early 1938, Roosevelt sought British and French cooperation in convoking a conference to find a basis for international cooperation. His efforts were frustrated by Prime Minister Chamberlain, who had decided to try to appease Italy, and also by a cabinet crisis in Great Britain. In such circumstances, Roosevelt and Hull could only follow Britain's and France's lead and hope for the best. Roosevelt, therefore, reluctantly supported Chamberlain's policy in Munich. Again, on April 14, 1939, Roosevelt asked both Hitler and Mussolini to promise to refrain, for at least ten years, from attacking any one of the thirty-one nations, which the President listed. In return, he would ask these nations to promise not to attack Italy or Germany. Hitler replied with a sarcastic, abusive, two-hour speech before the German Reichstag in which he tried to justify his recent aggressions.

The United States and Japanese Expansionism

On July 7, 1937, the Japanese army began full-scale war to wrench the five northern provinces of China from the control of Chiang Kai-shek's government at Nanking. In response to this clear-cut aggression, the League of Nations suggested that the signatories of the Nine-Power Treaty meet to consider what should be done. The United States Government endorsed the proposal, and a conference was scheduled for Brussels in early November 1937.

The Brussels Conference was doomed even before it could assemble. The British government was not eager to take strong action against Japan, but it informed the State Department that it would support any program which the United States put into effect. However, American public reaction in the wake of Roosevelt's quarantine speech paralyzed the Washington government. In these circumstances, the Brussels Conference issued only a harmless statement, and the Japanese air force replied on December 12, 1937, by bombing U.S.S. *Panay*, a gunboat, and three American oil tankers in the Yangtze River. The reaction of most Americans was to demand that their government withdraw its small military and naval forces from China. The State Department accepted Tokyo's probably sincere apologies for the attack and payment of damages. The Japanese government still could not control its military forces—an ominous sign for the future.

3. A NEW LATIN AMERICAN POLICY

The Good Neighbor in Economic Policy

Secretary Hull was an old-fashioned internationalist who believed profoundly that the United States should take leadership in reconstructing the world economy through currency stabilization and liberal trade policies. Economic nationalists overshadowed Hull during the first months of the Roosevelt administration, but Hull patiently bided his time. He was able to take the initiative once the President, late in 1933, had decided on stabilization. With Roosevelt's blessing, Hull persuaded Congress to adopt the Reciprocal Trade Agreements Act in June 1934. It authorized the President to negotiate trade agreements, which would go into effect without congressional approval, and in these agreements to lower or raise the existing Hawley-Smoot rates by as much as 50 per cent. Moreover, American tariff reductions would apply to all nations which accorded the United States the status of a "most favored nation," that is, those which gave the United States the benefits of their own lowest tariff rates.

By 1936, Hull had negotiated trade agreements with thirteen nations, including Holland, France, and Canada. Congress renewed the Trade Agreements Act the following year. Hull then worked hard to persuade the British to lower their tariff barriers. He achieved some success in the Canadian-American and British-American trade agreements of 1938. By 1940, when the Trade Agreements Act was again renewed, Hull had concluded agreements with twenty-one nations. Partly as a result (general worldwide recovery also helped), the volume of the foreign trade of the United States increased from $2.5 billion in 1932 to $5.4 billion in 1940.

Hopes of stimulating a lively trade with Russia played an important part in the administration's decision to extend diplomatic recognition to the Soviet Union. Many Americans, including most representatives of large business corporations, had long asserted that it was foolish not to recognize a great power simply because one did not like its form of government. The Soviet economy had grown rapidly during the late 1920s and early 1930s. Russia, it seemed to American businessmen, offered an enormous opportunity as a market, especially for machinery of various kinds. In exchange for recognition by the United States, the Soviet foreign minister, Maxim Litvinov, promised that the USSR would negotiate a settlement of the old czarist debt to the United States and refrain from propaganda activity in the United States. Roosevelt extended recognition on November 16, 1933, and a short time later established the Export-Import Bank to facilitate Russian-American trade. Yet, until Germany attacked Russia in 1941, hopes both for friendly relations and for a flourishing Russian-American trade did not materialize. Soviet leaders soon made it plain that they did not intend either to pay past Russian debts or to cease propaganda in the United States through the Communist Party of America.

Economic motivation also prompted the United States to end its experiment in colonialism in the Philippine Islands. American sugar and tobacco producers, represented by powerful southern Democratic congressmen, disliked the low tariffs on Philippine sugar and tobacco. If the Filipinos obtained independence, the tariffs could be raised. In 1933, Congress, under the pressure of these and other American business interests, adopted a bill which forced independence upon the Philippine Islands after ten years. The Filipinos, who feared the Japanese and wanted to remain within the American customs union, rejected the measure and asked for dominion status instead. Nonetheless, Congress had its way with passage of the Philippine Independence Act in 1934, and under its provisions Filipinos adopted a new constitution and elected Manuel Quezon President of the Philippine Commonwealth in 1935. July 4, 1946, was set as the date for the full-fledged independence of the Philippine Republic.

The Good Neighbor and Latin America

In his inaugural address, Roosevelt announced that the United States would try to play the role of a good neighbor in foreign affairs in general. A few weeks later, in an address on Pan-American Day, he used the phrase "good neighbor" again, and this time applied it specifically to the Latin American policy of the United States. Roosevelt completed the retreat from intervention and occupation which preceding Republican administrations had already begun. Roosevelt and his advisers put a policy of genuine Pan-Americanism into effect. They sincerely believed that all the republics of the western hemisphere should stand on a basis of equality, and that mutual respect and cooperation should replace the unilateral domination of the United States. The Good Neighbor policy, Roosevelt and Hull maintained, worked in the interest of the United States; should the old world succumb to German domination, they believed that the United States would desperately need good friends in the western hemisphere.

As evidence of these neighborly intentions, Roosevelt withdrew American marines from Haiti. He also surrendered treaty rights to interfere in the internal affairs of the Dominican Republic, Haiti, and Panama. Although a revolution broke out in Cuba in 1933, Roosevelt refused to interfere. When a conservative regime took over the Cuban government in 1934, Roosevelt negotiated a treaty with it which abrogated the right of the United States to intervene in Cuban affairs under the Cuban-American treaty of 1903 (see pg. 43).

At the same time, the soft-spoken Hull took leadership at Pan-American conferences in building a new hemispheric system of mutual understanding and collective security. The Montevideo Conference of 1933 adopted a "Convention on the Rights and Duties of States." It sweepingly affirmed earlier Latin American claims, proclaimed the equality of states, and firmly embodied the principles of mutual nonintervention. A special inter-American conference, in Buenos Aires in 1936, adopted a "Convention to Coordinate, Extend and Assure the Fulfillment of Existing Treaties"—treaties which pledged the signatories to consult with one another if war should threaten the peace of the western hemisphere. Another convention, approved at Buenos Aires, pledged the American republics to settle all disputes peacefully. It also outlawed territorial conquests, the collection of debts by force, and interference by one state in the affairs of another state. The Declaration of Lima, adopted by the eighth Pan-American Conference in 1938, affirmed the determination of the American republics to resist jointly any Fascist or Nazi threat to the peace of the new world.

The Good Neighbor policy reaped large dividends in Latin American cooperation when war broke out in Europe in 1939. At a special conference in Havana in 1940, Hull won unanimous approval of a warning that an attack on any single American state would be considered an attack on all of them. The Havana Conference also established an Inter-American Commission for Territorial Administration to take control of any European colonies in the new world which seemed about to fall into Nazi hands. Once the United States had entered the war, all Latin American states, except Argentina and Chile, at once broke relations with, or declared war upon, the Axis nations. Chile and Argentina later broke relations with them also, although not until Nazi defeat seemed certain. Brazil not only provided airfields for the use of the United States, but also sent a division to fight alongside the Allies in Italy.

The climax of Roosevelt's and Hull's long efforts to build a new inter-American system was the Act of Chapultepec, adopted by a special conference at Mexico City on March 3, 1945. This treaty completed the transformation of the Monroe Doctrine from a policy supported in self-defense by the United States alone into one supported by all American republics. The Act of Chapultepec declared that any attack upon the territory or sovereignty of one American state would be met by the combined forces of all of them. Succeeding inter-American conferences created and used the Organization of American States to defend the peace and security of the western hemisphere. This unity deteriorated during the 1950s and 1960s, when, as will be described later, the United States Government again began to intervene in Latin American affairs.

A New Relationship with Mexico

Certain policies by the Mexican government put the Good Neighbor policy to the acid test. Beginning in 1934, the new administration of President Lázaro Cárdenas began to expropriate American-owned estates in order to provide land for the Mexican peons. Repeated inquiries from the State Department brought repeated answers from the Mexican Foreign Ministry that payment would be made in the future.

One act brought matters to a crisis. On March 18, 1938, Cárdenas announced that the Mexican government would expropriate all foreign oil properties. These holdings of seventeen British and American companies were valued by the companies at $459 million. Although compensation was promised, it was clear that Mexico could not pay even a small fraction of what the oil companies demanded. The British government protested in such a manner as to cause the Mexican government to break diplomatic relations with Great Britain. But Roosevelt, Hull, and the United States ambassador in Mexico City, Josephus Daniels, knew that the Mexicans were a proud people. Bluster and force would only provoke bitter resistance and resentment throughout Latin America.

Friendly but firm negotiations led to the conclusion on November 19, 1941, of a full settlement of land and oil claims by the United States, which had meanwhile been greatly reduced. Moreover, the United States also promised to help to stabilize the Mexican peso and to provide funds to promote Mexican-American trade. Thus the Roosevelt administration won some degree of friendship from the Mexican people, gained a valuable ally during

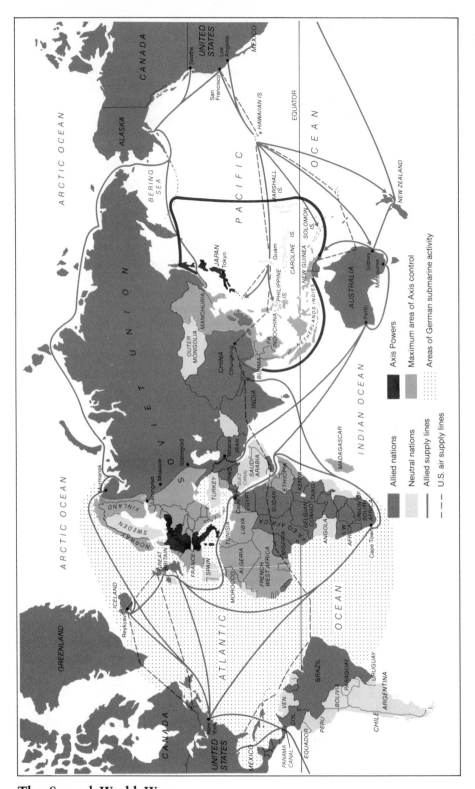

The Second World War

the Second World War, and demonstrated to doubting Latin Americans that the Good Neighbor meant what it said.

4. THE OUTBREAK OF WAR, 1939–1941

The "Phony War"

Adolf Hitler set out upon a collision course in March 1939 by invading Prague and taking over the remnants of the Czech Republic. Mussolini invaded Albania in the following month. By this time, the British and French were aroused to the enormity of the Nazi peril, and they hastened to conclude treaties with Poland which guaranteed the security of that nation, next on Hitler's list of victims.

The British and French also turned to the Soviet Union for help in stopping Hitler, but the Soviets instead concluded a nonaggression pact with the German government on August 23, 1939. The pact's secret provisions gave western Poland to Germany, while Russian occupied Estonia, Latvia, eastern Poland, Bessarabia in Rumania, and later, Lithuania. Hitler thus protected Germany against a two-front war, while the Russian dictator, Josef Stalin, gained almost two years in which to prepare his country against possible German attack. And if attack should come, Russia had gained territories to absorb the first shock.

Hitler sent his armies into Poland on September 1, 1939, and Britain and France declared war on Germany two days later. Stalin's armies invaded Poland on September 17, and that helpless nation was partitioned between Germany and Russia on September 29. Europeans had turned upon each other again, almost exactly twenty-five years after the outbreak of the "war to end all wars."

Roosevelt foresaw the events of the late spring and early summer of 1939. He begged Congress either to repeal the arms embargo, or else to permit the European democracies to purchase war supplies under the cash-and-carry provision of the Neutrality Act of 1937. In spite of the President's plea that such action would help to prevent war, both houses of Congress refused to act.

Once war had broken out in Europe, Roosevelt called Congress into extra session for September 21. Again, he asked the lawmakers to amend the Neutrality Act so as to permit Allied purchases of arms and munitions in the United States. The many voices raised in protest included those of Senator Borah and Colonel Charles A. Lindbergh, but Roosevelt now had the support of southern and eastern Democrats. He also had behind him a number of Republicans, including Henry L. Stimson and Frank Knox, and also an organization called the Non-Partisan Committee for Peace through Revision of the Neutrality Law. William Allen White, a respected journalist of Emporia, Kansas, headed this group. After a sharp debate, the Senate voted to repeal the arms embargo and also to impose new restrictions on American shipping. The House quickly concurred, and Roosevelt signed the repeal measure on November 4, 1939.

Americans reacted angrily when Russia invaded Finland in November. To the west, quiet reigned as the German and French armies faced each other in their fortified Siegfried and Maginot lines. During this period of what press and radio commentators misleadingly called the "phony war," Americans continued to view events in Europe with calm detachment. They felt secure in the belief that the Royal Navy would strangle the German economy and that the French army would crush its foe, once large-scale fighting broke out.

The *Blitzkrieg* and the American Response

Under cover of the "phony war," Hitler spent the winter of 1939–1940 in frantic preparation for a spring offensive. He launched a *blitzkrieg,* or lightning war, on April 10, 1940, and invaded and overran Denmark, Norway, Holland, Belgium, Luxembourg, and France. In all these attacks, Hitler used an overwhelming combination of tanks, dive bombers, airborne troops, and motorized infantry. To these were added the advantages of surprise and treachery by Nazi sympathizers, or fifth columnists, in the attacked nations. Paris fell on June 16, and the Germans soon occupied all of northern and western France. Southern France—one third of the nation—was left to the rump government of the aged Marshal Henri-Philippe Pétain, who agreed to act as the symbol of partial French independence. A fervent anti-Communist, Pétain evidently wished for true cooperation with Germany in its war against the Soviet Union, an attitude which, later popular myths to the contrary, enjoyed wide popularity in France.

Chamberlain resigned as Prime Minister of Great Britain on the day that the Germans hurtled into the Low Countries and was succeeded by Winston Spencer Churchill. After the rout of the Allies in Europe, the British army of over 335,000 men escaped destruction and was miraculously evacuated from Dunkirk, France. Virtually every seaworthy English vessel—including small fishing boats and barges—participated in this rescue effort, despite continuous fire from German planes, artillery, and infantry machine guns and rifles. Although the British abandoned their armor and heavy equipment at Dunkirk, they still possessed a great navy and a well-equipped Royal Air Force, and, as their new Prime Minister demonstrated, plenty of raw courage. Churchill promised his people nothing but "blood, toil, tears, and sweat" —and ultimate victory. He hurled defiance at the Nazi hordes which massed across the English Channel.

In reply, Hitler sent a vast fleet of bombers to rain devastation and death upon London and other British cities night after night, month after month. Fortunately for the British, the Germans did not have enough vessels available to carry their vastly superior army across the English Channel. Hitler had been unprepared for the rapidity of the German triumph in France, and he had neglected to consider sufficiently what the needs of the German armies would be for an amphibious assault. Furthermore, he expected the British to come to terms without a necessary bloody invasion. Mussolini entered the war as France was collapsing; he thus extended the hostilities to the Mediterranean and Africa. Hitler then unexpectedly turned to the Balkans, made satellites out of Rumania and Bulgaria, and conquered Yugoslavia and Greece. But he did not attempt an invasion of England.

As these events unfolded, alarm, even terror, gripped the American people. Only a tiny minority wanted the Nazis to win, but the great majority of Americans who loathed Hitler remained deeply divided over the wise course for the United States. The noninterventionists united in a nationwide organization called America First. Its supporters included Senators Nye, Wheeler, Bennett Champ Clark of Missouri, and Hiram W. Johnson of California. Charles A. Lindbergh was also a leading member. The America First group favored arming for defense, but it declared that the United States could not save western Europe and should not waste its resources in an attempt to do so.

In opposition stood the so-called internationalists, united in William Allen White's reorganized and expanded organization, now called the Committee to Defend America by Aiding the Allies. Internationalists believed that a Europe dominated by Hitler would be a dangerous threat to the security of the United States. They refused to agree that totalitarianism was "the wave of the future," as Lindbergh's wife, Anne Morrow Lindbergh, put it.

All through the spring and summer of 1940—indeed, throughout the period of American nonbelligerency—noninterventionists and internationalists conducted a bitter debate. Americans listened and then changed their minds as the arguments of the internationalists and the lessons of events struck home. By July 1940, 69 per cent of the persons queried in a public opinion poll replied that they thought that a German victory would imperil American security.

The prime mover in this change in American public opinion was Roosevelt himself. He cast all political caution aside and put himself at the head of the movement to rally Americans to the peril of a Nazi victory. A month before the fall of France, he called for the production of 50,000 planes a year and a vast expansion of defense expenditures. In the belief that the British would not go under, he used his authority as commander in chief to rush every available rifle, cartridge, and artillery piece to the British Isles. In September, Roosevelt transferred fifty old but useful destroyers to Great Britain to enable the Royal Navy to convoy merchantmen and hunt down German submarines. In return, the United States received the use of eight naval bases ranging from Newfoundland to British Guiana, and the assurance that Great Britain would not surrender her fleet even if invaded and conquered. The most important —and controversial—part of Roosevelt's defense program was a Selective Service bill. It was introduced on June 20, 1940, and passed both houses of Congress in September by large majorities.

The Election of 1940

Politics continued also, because 1940 was a presidential election year, but not politics of the usual sort. Early in 1940, it seemed certain that one of the three leading Republican noninterventionists—Senator Robert A. Taft of Ohio, Senator Arthur H. Vandenberg of Michigan, or Thomas E. Dewey of New York—would win the presidential nomination. But the Republican national convention met in Philadelphia in the middle of the panic set off by the fall of France, and the delegates took control out of the hands of the party managers. They nominated Wendell L. Willkie, president of the Commonwealth & Southern (utilities) Company, a former Democrat, and, most important, an ardent proponent of all-out aid to Great Britain. In a bid for the farm vote, the Republicans nominated Senator Charles L. McNary of Oregon for Vice-President.

Roosevelt almost certainly had decided to run for a third term long before the preconvention campaign began. In a message to the Democratic national convention in Chicago on July 16, he said that he would accept a third nomination if the delegates insisted. Although party leaders would have preferred another candidate, they had to go along with the majority of delegates in renominating Roosevelt on the first ballot. Roosevelt then forced the nomination of the sometimes erratic but eloquent Secretary of Agriculture, Henry A. Wallace, as his running mate.

It was soon apparent that the rugged and forceful Willkie was the first dynamic Republican candidate since Theodore Roosevelt. Willkie tried to capitalize upon the strong tradition against a third term, but he was severely handicapped by his substantial agreement with Roosevelt's domestic and foreign policies. Indeed, Willkie had generously supported the Selective Service bill and endorsed the transfer of the destroyers to Great Britain. Faced with defeat, Willkie suddenly shifted gears in early October and began to attack Roosevelt for allegedly leading the country into the war. Roosevelt replied that he would not send American boys into any "foreign" wars.

In the election on November 5, 1940, Willkie polled 45 per cent of the popular vote, but he carried only ten states with eighty-two electoral votes, to Roosevelt's 449 electoral votes. The election made little change in the relative strength of the two parties in the Seventy-seventh Congress, which would sit during 1941 and 1942.

An Arsenal of Democracy

Roosevelt left for a Caribbean cruise aboard U.S.S. *Tuscaloosa* soon after the election. On December 9, 1940, a seaplane delivered a long letter from Churchill to the President. Great Britain was rapidly approaching a crisis, Churchill explained, because she had spent almost all her available dollars for supplies in the United States. Britain would be unable to conduct any offensive operations if she could no longer obtain airplanes, munitions, and other supplies from the United States. Moreover, Churchill continued, the Royal Navy desperately needed American help in keeping the North Atlantic supply lanes open in the face of a mounting German submarine threat.

Roosevelt devised a solution during the next few days, which he announced at a press conference on December 17 and in a fireside chat twelve days later. Because Great Britain was fighting America's fight, Roosevelt declared, the United States would lend or lease to her the equipment and supplies necessary for victory over the common foe: "We must be the great arsenal of democracy," Roosevelt concluded in his fireside chat. "I call upon our people with absolute confidence that our common cause will greatly succeed."

The Lend-Lease bill, introduced into Congress on January 9, 1941, received full and frank debate, for Congress and the entire country well understood its momentous significance. Passage of the measure would mean nothing less than full-scale American commitment to the defeat of Germany, by aid to Great Britain if possible, and, if necessary, by American military participation. The Senate approved the Lend-Lease bill by a vote of sixty to thirty-one on March 8; the House, by a vote of 317 to seventy-one three days later. Roosevelt signed the Lend-Lease Act at once and recommended an appropriation of $7 billion for the production of lend-lease materials. Congress voted the money two weeks later.

Growing Belligerency

Roosevelt was still eager to avoid full-scale military participation, but, like a growing majority of the American people, he intended to do everything necessary to assure Germany's defeat, no matter what the risks. Above all, he was determined that crucial lend-lease supplies should get through to Great Britain. Consequently, during the spring and early summer, Roosevelt seized ninety-two ships in American ports which belonged to German, Italian, French, Dutch, and Norwegian owners; froze German and Italian assets in the United States; occupied the Danish islands of Greenland and Iceland; and extended the American "neutrality" patrol to the mid-Atlantic. When German armies invaded Russia on June 21, 1941, the President sent Harry Hopkins, by now his closest personal adviser, to Moscow to assure Russian leaders that they would receive lend-lease assistance as soon as possible.

In August 1941, Roosevelt met Churchill aboard U.S.S. *Augusta* off the coast of Newfoundland. They agreed to eight principles upon which they based their hopes for mankind. This declaration, known as the Atlantic Charter, called for the restoration of self-government to peoples oppressed by dictators. It also demanded equal access to raw materials for all nations, freedom of the seas, a peace with justice, and relief from the crushing burden of armaments.

Now that American naval vessels in fact convoyed British ships to Iceland, clashes between American warships and German submarines were inevitable. A submarine, after having been chased for several miles by the destroyer *Grier*, attacked it on September 4, but the torpedo missed its mark. On October 17, the destroyer *Kearny* was hit and badly damaged, with the loss of eleven lives. Then, on October 31, a German submarine sank the destroyer *Reuben James* with the loss of half her crew.

Roosevelt did not ask Congress to declare war, but he publicly denounced the "piratical" acts of Nazi submarines. Moreover, he instituted an undeclared naval war with Germany by ordering American naval vessels to "shoot on sight" at any submarine which appeared in waters west of Iceland. In November 1941, Congress authorized American merchantmen to arm and to sail through war zones to British ports. Congress renewed the Selective Service Act in August and eliminated the prohibition in that measure against sending draftees outside the western hemisphere. The United States thus became a full member of a new alliance in every respect except for a formal declaration of war against the common enemy. Admiral Harold R. Stark, Chief of Naval Operations, confided to his diary that Hitler had been given "every excuse in the world to declare war on us now," but, with his armies already fully occupied, Hitler refrained from official war with the United States.

SUGGESTED READINGS

The best survey of Roosevelt's foreign policy is Robert Dallek, *Franklin D. Roosevelt and American Foreign Policy, 1932–1945* (1979). Allan Nevins, *The New Deal and World Affairs* (1951), is brief. Charles A. Beard, *American Foreign Policy in the Making, 1932–1940* (1946), is an isolationist account which is refuted by Basil Rauch, *Roosevelt: From Munich to Pearl Harbor* (1950). William L. Langer and S. E. Gleason, *The Challenge to Isolation* (1952) and *The Undeclared War* (1953) are excellent, comprehensive studies. For an interesting account of the debate over neutrality, see Robert Divine, *The Illusion of Neutrality* (1962). On Roosevelt's problem with isolationists, see also Wayne S. Cole, *America First* (1953) and *Gerald P. Nye and American Foreign Relations* (1962); John K. Nelson, *The Peace Prophets: American Pacifist Thought 1919–1941*; and Manfred Jonas, *Isolationism in America, 1935–1941* (1966). James M. Burns, *Roosevelt: The Soldier of Freedom* (1970), is a worthy sequel to his study of Roosevelt as a domestic leader.

On more specialized problems, see Bryce Wood, *The Making of the Good Neighbor Policy* (1961); Howard C. Cline, *The United-States and Mexico* (1953); and E. David Cronon, *Josephus Daniels in Mexico* (1960).

Robert P. Browder, *The Origins of Soviet-American Diplomacy* (1953), is the best work on American recognition of the USSR. Dorothy Borg, *The United States and the Far Eastern Crisis of 1933–1938* (1964), is the fullest treatment of that subject. Warren Moscow, *Roosevelt and Willkie* (1968), covers adequately their presidential campaigns and later cooperation during the war. Early sections of John Costello, *The Battle of the Atlantic* (1977), deal with the "undeclared war." Winston S. Churchill's *The Gathering Storm* (1948) and *Their Finest Hour* (1949), and Hans L. Trefousse, *Germany and American Neutrality* (1951), are helpful in placing American policy in a global context.

CHAPTER 11
THE UNITED STATES IN
THE SECOND WORLD WAR

1. AMERICAN INTERVENTION

Rising Japanese-American Tensions

In view of America's growing commitment to Great Britain by late 1941, it probably remained only a question of *when,* not of *whether,* full-scale fighting would break out with Germany. As events turned out, the United States was plunged into active belligerency, not by any incident in the North Atlantic, but by the action of Japan.

Even though the Japanese continued their aggression against China and occupied northern Indochina after the fall of France in 1940, the United States Government followed a cautious policy toward Tokyo out of fear that too much pressure might cause the Japanese to attack Siberia or the Dutch East Indies. Roosevelt, however, issued a sharp warning on July 26, 1939, by renouncing the Japanese-American Commercial Treaty of 1911. According to the terms of that treaty, the United States Government could now limit or halt entirely trade between the two countries within six months and thus block Japan's access to American scrap iron, oil, and other war materials.

The attitude of leaders in Washington hardened rapidly during the autumn of 1940 in the wake of what seemed to be new signs of hostility from Tokyo. In September, the Japanese, German, and Italian governments concluded the Triple, or Axis, Alliance, which was apparently directed at the United States. The Japanese government also made it clear that it intended to establish what it called a Greater East

Asia Co-Prosperity Sphere, or, in essence, Japanese dominance over the entire Far East. Certain powerful Japanese leaders specified that they would pursue their plans in spite of the risk of war with the United States. As Foreign Minister Yosuke Matsuoka told the Japanese parliament on January 26, 1941: "There is nothing left but to face America. . . . Japan must demand America's reconsideration of her attitude, and if she does not listen, there is slim hope for friendly relations between Japan and the United States."

Japanese military leaders and the more militaristic of the Japanese political leaders hoped to take advantage of German victories in Europe and seize the relatively unprotected French, British, and Dutch possessions in Asia. Yet, they also wanted a successful end to their war with China, which had caused a terrible drain on their manpower and resources, and peace with the United States.

The Japanese first occupied bases in southern French Indochina to seal off supply lines to China and provide bases for possible future expansion southward. Roosevelt and Hull, who interpreted this action as the opening move in a campaign of conquest, responded by freezing Japanese assets in the United States in July 1941; they also clamped an embargo on the export to Japan of oil, steel, aviation gasoline, and other materials. The British and Dutch followed suit immediately.

Authorities in Tokyo were now in a desperate dilemma. Half their supplies of oil, iron, and steel came from the United States. Without these supplies, it would be impossible to maintain the Japanese economy—or war machine. Some way had to be found to resume normal trade with the United States or else to find vital raw materials elsewhere. Since all but the most extreme military leaders in Tokyo continued to oppose war with the giant of the West, Japanese diplomats turned to Washington in the hope of finding some compromise arrangement.

Japanese-American negotiations had started in the early months of 1941. After an interruption caused by the embargo, they were resumed in the summer and dragged on into the autumn. The Japanese offered many concessions. They promised to make no move southward and not to attack the Soviet Union. They declared also that they would not feel bound by the Triple Alliance to go to war against the United States if the latter became involved in hostilities with Germany. The more the Japanese conceded, the harder Secretary Hull turned the vise in the mistaken belief that the Japanese had to cave in and ultimately would do so. In the final analysis, the one sticking point was China. The Japanese demanded that the United States stop all aid to Chiang Kai-shek. Hull not only refused to abandon the Chinese or to make any compromising concessions which would have postponed if not avoided war; he also insisted that the Japanese withdraw from China at once. The Japanese were faced with the alternative of either enormous blows to their pride and their new empire, on the one hand, or war, on the other hand. They reluctantly chose the latter course. The Nazi attack on the Soviet Union, which removed a potential threat to the Japanese northern flank, made their choice easier.

The Attack on Pearl Harbor

On the morning of Sunday, December 7, 1941, three waves of bombers from

Japanese aircraft carriers suddenly struck the great American naval and air bases at Pearl Harbor and elsewhere in the Hawaiian Islands. Their rain of destruction completely surprised all American leaders, despite warnings that a Japanese attack somewhere might be imminent. An American code analyst had broken the Japanese top-priority diplomatic code, and Americans had also deciphered the Japanese intelligence code. United States agents had furthermore monitored the movements of a huge Japanese fleet moving through the South China Sea; other evidence from intelligence sources suggested the location of the attack and its date. Nonetheless, American leaders, who simply refused to believe that a Japanese carrier flotilla could reach Pearl Harbor, neglected to send full intelligence information, or to suggest its urgency, to naval and army commanders in Hawaii.

Altogether, the Japanese sank or disabled nineteen ships, including eight battleships; in addition, they destroyed 120 planes on the ground and killed more than 2,300 men. Their success exceeded the most optimistic Japanese hopes. Their task force even escaped without detection by American planes or ships. The Japanese also blasted naval and air bases in Guam, Midway, British Hong Kong, and the Malay Peninsula. The Japanese also almost completely annihilated the American air force in the Philippines when it was caught on the ground near Manila, even though military leaders in that area knew of the earlier attack on Pearl Harbor.

This negligence on the part of American leadership appears to defy rational explanation. Some historians have assigned the blame of the Pearl Harbor fiasco to Roosevelt, who, they claim, had prior knowledge of the Japanese attack and yet allowed it to occur as a way to galvanize public opinion in support of entering the war. This Machiavellian view of Roosevelt, however, questions not only his concern for human life but also his intelligence. A more plausible explanation is simply that American political and military leaders grossly underestimated the military capabilities of the Japanese. Whatever its cause, Pearl Harbor was the most devastating military disaster that the United States had ever suffered.

Roosevelt appeared before Congress on December 8, 1941, to ask for a declaration of war against Japan. It was voted with but one dissenting voice (Jeannette Rankin of Montana, who had also voted against the war resolution in 1917) in the House and unanimously in the Senate. Three days later, Germany and Italy somewhat reluctantly honored their agreement with Japan and declared war on the United States on December 11. The American government replied in kind on the same day.

General George C. Marshall served as Army Chief of Staff from 1939 to the end of the war. Admiral Ernest J. King was named commander in chief of the fleet in December 1941 and, a few months later, was also appointed Chief of Naval Operations. Later these leaders received the new five-star ranks of General of the Army and Admiral of the Fleet.

2. THE AMERICAN PEOPLE AND THE SECOND WORLD WAR

First Phases

Not since the Civil War had the American people faced such stupendous military tasks as in 1941. In the Second World War, they were called upon to fight two major wars on two far-flung fronts at the same time. The government rounded up the small number of open Nazi sympathizers and later tried them, unsuccessfully, for sedition. At Roosevelt's instructions, the army apprehended all inhabitants of Japanese ancestry, some 100,000 persons, citizens and noncitizens alike, on the West Coast, although no evidence existed (or does now) to show that they were anything but loyal to the United States. Nevertheless, the army transferred them to makeshift camps in the interior. The evidence is unmistakable that Caucasian Californians took advantage of the panic after Pearl Harbor to persuade federal authorities to "settle" the Japanese-American "problem" once and for all. Thus California authorities, including Attorney General Earl Warren, were primarily responsible for one of the single greatest violations of civil liberty in American history. Thousands of Californians of Japanese ancestry lost their homes, farms, and other businesses, and most of their possessions. In what can best be described as "concentration camps," many persons lost their health and some their lives. Yet, thousands of young men in the camps volunteered to fight for the United States in the war against Japan as well as against Germany.

Domestic Mobilization

Young men rushed to recruiting stations after Pearl Harbor, but the main task of raising an army and navy fell on the Selective Service authorities. In all, they registered some 31,000,000 men, of whom 10,000,000 were inducted into service. A total of more than 15,000,000 men and women (including volunteers) served before the end of the war. There were more than 10,000,000 men and women in the army, 3,884,000 in the navy, nearly 600,000 in the marines, and 242,000 in the Coast Guard. It was by far the largest mobilization of manpower in American history, but it was not exceptional compared to the mobilization of 22,000,000 in the Soviet Union, 17,000,000 in Germany, and 12,000,000 in Great Britain, the dominions, and the British Empire.

American casualties numbered 253,573 dead and 65,834 missing, 651,042 wounded, and 114,205 prisoners. However, these figures were remarkably low considering the numbers involved and the length and ferocity of the fighting. These low casualties were largely the result of recent medical advances such as penicillin and the use of blood for transfusions. Technology also provided new and superior medical equipment.

Industrial mobilization went through several stages, just as it had done during the First World War. In January 1942, with the creation of the War Production Board, Roosevelt first tried to institute effective controls. The failure of the War Production Board to gain control of raw materials led Roosevelt, in October 1942, to establish the Office of Economic Stabilization, with former Supreme Court Justice James F. Byrnes at its head. He successfully imposed priorities that assured an uninterrupted flow of raw materials to war industries. In May 1943, Roosevelt made Byrnes head of the new Office of

War Mobilization, with near dictatorial authority over the entire economy.

Next in importance was the task of preventing runaway inflation, which could have seriously impeded the entire war effort. Roosevelt established an Office of Price Administration (OPA) in April 1941, but it lacked authority to prevent price increases, and during the next year the cost of living rose at the rate of 2 per cent a month. But the OPA received statutory authority from the Emergency Price Control and Anti-Inflation acts of 1942, and the OPA and Office of Economic Stabilization thereafter fought successfully to hold the line in the face of pressures for increases in wages and farm prices. The cost of living increased less than 1.5 per cent between the spring of 1943 and the summer of 1945, despite the severe scarcity of consumer goods (no cars were made during the period, for example) and the huge increase in the number of Americans employed and in their incomes. The government's success in stabilizing prices was a remarkable achievement, which could have been accomplished only with wide cooperation from the American civilian population.

The lifting of production controls was all that was necessary to achieve an abundant supply of food, in spite of a decline in the number of agricultural workers during the war. The index of farm production rose from 108 in 1940 to 123 in 1945, and the increases in food crops were even more striking. There was never any threat of food shortages, and the rationing of scarce items such as sugar and meat to the public assured a plentiful supply of these items to the armed forces.

The growing demands of war industries pushed domestic civilian employment up from 46,500,000 in 1940 to 53,000,000 in 1945, despite the induction of millions of men into the fighting services. The government had no such difficulty manning new shipyards and assembly lines during the Second World War as it had experienced during the First, because the United States went to war in 1941 with about 7,000,000 unemployed workers. They were quickly trained and absorbed into the labor force and provided the core of the new labor required. Women who might otherwise have remained at home constituted another huge pool of workers which was tapped to fill wartime needs. In April 1942, Roosevelt created a War Manpower Commission, which helped to direct the flow of labor into war industries. The United States never suffered a serious shortage of workers; thus the country was spared the necessity of having to institute severe manpower controls, such as the conscription of labor.

The main task in the mobilization of labor was to see that strikes did not slow down the war economy. The War Labor Board, created by Roosevelt in January 1942, went to work at once to establish guidelines for wages, hours, and collective bargaining. Employers, workers, and unions cooperated with an unprecedented show of unity. Under the protection of the War Labor Board, union membership grew to nearly 15,000,000 by 1945. The weekly earnings of persons engaged in manufacturing increased by 70 per cent from 1941 to 1945, while the cost of living rose by 23 per cent (mostly before the Anti-Inflation Act of 1942). There were numerous irritating work stoppages, but most were short-lived and caused a loss of only one ninth of 1 per cent of total working time. Even the British, with much more rigorous controls, did not exceed this record.

Blacks and the War

The Second World War was a dividing line in the history of race relations in the United States. Open segregation still prevailed throughout the South, to be sure, but blacks acquired a new sense of participation in national affairs from the knowledge that 1,000,000 of their number were serving in the armed forces.

American blacks also benefited more than any other single group in the country from the expanded opportunities which came with wartime full employment. More than 1,000,000 black men and women left the South and found jobs in war industries in the North, Middle West, and the Pacific Coast area.

But participation in the war effort also demonstrated the problems facing blacks. Although many blacks served their country, they were forced to fight in Jim Crow armed services. Other blacks remembered that the reward for patriotism in the First World War was lynchings and mob beatings and a series of terrible race riots (see pp. 99–100).

The demands for employment opportunities for blacks and the dire need for labor combined to cause Roosevelt, on June 25, 1941, to issue Executive Order 8802 which forbade discrimination in defense hiring on account of color. Roosevelt's order was a response to the threat of a gigantic march by blacks on Washington, to be led by A. Philip Randolph, head of the sleeping-car porters' union, to press for equal opportunity in federal hiring. At the same time, Roosevelt established the Fair Employment Practices Committee (FEPC) to investigate charges of racial discrimination in industry. This first federal agency dedicated to the protection of the rights of blacks since the Freedmen's Bureau worked ineffectively until 1943; then, Roosevelt gave the FEPC real authority to enforce Executive Order 8802. By the beginning of 1945, nearly 2,000,000 blacks were at work in war plants throughout the country. In some areas, the influx of black workers led to mob violence, as in Detroit, where a "riot" in June 1943 left twenty-three blacks and nine whites dead, and many more injured.

The War Economy

Most American businessmen and economists thought that Roosevelt was dreaming when he talked in 1940 and 1941 about producing 100,000 planes and 50,000 tanks a year. As it turned out, Roosevelt overestimated only moderately the productive potential of the American economy once it received stimulus from unlimited governmental credit, wartime demand, and effective organization. American factories turned out a total of 275,000 military aircraft, 75,000 tanks, and 650,000 pieces of artillery. American shipyards built 55,239,000 tons of merchant shipping. A brand new synthetic rubber industry, built during 1942 and 1943, produced 762,000 tons in 1944 and 820,000 tons in 1945. The total value of all goods and services in the United States increased about 75 per cent between 1939 and 1945—a tremendous achievement—while war-related goods never exceeded one third of America's industrial production.

Furthermore, American scientists at least kept pace with Germany's research and development—despite the latter's head start—of decisive military weapons. In cooperation with the British, American scientists made available effective radar which detected enemy ships, submarines, and planes, and accurately directed shells against them; proximity fuses, which detonate explosives just before impact; and rockets, which enormously increased the firepower of planes, ships, and tanks (although Americans lagged behind German research in this area). Fortunately, the Germans did not develop an atomic bomb, or the war might have had an entirely different conclusion.

The War: Costs and Consequences

Federal expenditures, virtually all of which went for the war effort, totaled a little more than $321 billion from 1941 to 1945. This sum was twice as large as all federal expenditures between 1789 and 1941, and ten times as large as expenditures during the First World War.

The government met 59 per cent of these costs by borrowing. As a result, the gross national debt increased from $49 billion in 1941 to $259 billion at the end of hostilities. The American people, already faced with greatly increased taxes in a bill passed in September 1941, accepted with little grumbling a new Revenue Act in October 1942 which more than doubled the tax burden. Tax receipts between 1941 and 1945 totaled about $131 billion and paid for 41 per cent of the costs of the war. It was the highest percentage of expenditures raised by taxes during any major war in American history. Moreover, this draining off of private income helped significantly to combat price inflation and to prevent handing to future generations a larger burden of debt.

3. A WAR ON TWO FRONTS

North Africa

The first massive operation in which American forces played a leading role was the campaign to drive the Italians and Germans from North Africa and to break their stranglehold on the Mediterranean supply line. The Italians had bogged down in their drive for the Suez Canal and the oil fields of Arabia. Hitler's Afrika Korps, commanded by the dashing "Desert Fox," General (later Field Marshal) Erwin Rommel, poured into North Africa and fought the British for possession of Egypt. American ships, forced to take the long route around southern Africa, arrived with tanks at Alexandria just in time to help stop the Nazis. Then, on October 23, 1942, General Sir Bernard Montgomery and his British Eighth Army launched a counteroffensive. Montgomery defeated Rommel at El Alamein and then drove the Italians and Germans 2,000 miles westward to the borders of Tunisia. At this point, the Americans struck at the enemy's rear through Morocco and Algeria.

On November 8, 1942, a huge Anglo-American force, in 500 transports convoyed by 350 warships, landed on the northwestern coast of Africa. The campaign was directed by General Dwight D. Eisenhower, new American commander in the European theater of operations. It had been planned by Roosevelt and Churchill to aid the Russians by diverting German troops and equipment from their crucial campaign against Stalingrad.

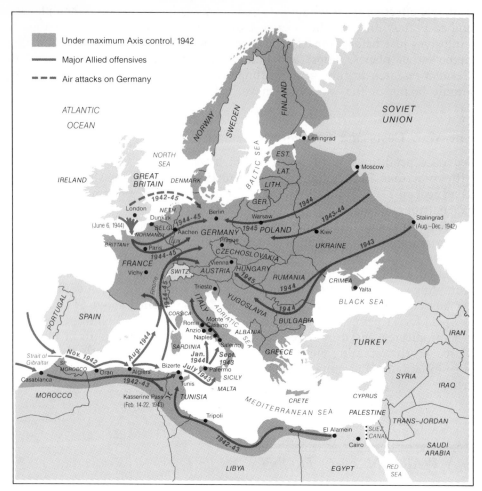

World War II in Europe and North Africa

The German and Vichy French forces were caught napping. Within three days, the Anglo-American armies had gained the whole of French North Africa up to the border of Tunisia. They succeeded in bottling up the Germans in the narrow Tunisian salient while Montgomery's Eighth Army moved in from the east. The Germans continued the fight all through the winter, but their losses were heavy because the Allies controlled both the sea and the air. Tunis was captured on May 7, 1943, after a bitter struggle, and the Axis army surrendered five days later. The entire campaign had cost the Axis more than 349,000 men killed or captured, in comparison to only 70,000 casualties for the Allies.

The victory at Tunis ended the Axis threat to the Mediterranean. This strategically important sea was now safe for Allied ships from Gibraltar to the Suez Canal. In the meantime, Soviet armies had captured an entire German army at Stalingrad and raised the siege of Leningrad.

The Italian Invasion

From Africa, the Anglo-American forces launched an attack on Italy. General George S. Patton's American Seventh Army and General Montgomery's Eighth Army invaded Sicily on July 10, 1943, and captured the island on August 17 after bitter fighting. While the battle for Sicily raged, momentous events were transpiring in Rome. The Italians were thoroughly sick of war, of the Nazis, and of Mussolini. The Fascist Grand Council deposed the Dictator on July 25, and King Victor Emmanuel appointed Marshal Pietro Badoglio as head of a new non-Fascist government. Mussolini was arrested but was rescued by German paratroopers, who took him to Lake Como in northern Italy. There he established a rump Fascist government.

Meanwhile, Allied armies prepared for the conquest of Italy. They landed on the toe of the peninsula on September 3, 1943, and made their way slowly northward against mud, rain, mountainous terrain, and desperate resistance by the Germans. The same day that the Allies landed, the Italian government signed an armistice which permitted it to become a cobelligerent of the Allies. Nevertheless, the American and British armies in Italy endured a grueling test against the heavily reinforced Germans. Americans suffered heavy losses at the Gulf of Salerno, south of Naples, and at the Anzio beachhead near Rome. Then the Americans ran into one clever ambush after another as they attempted to move inland. The Americans paid dearly when they stormed the towering monastery of Monte Cassino, south of Rome, which the Germans had heavily fortified. However, the Allied armies finally entered the Italian capital on June 4, 1944. The Germans hung on doggedly to the northern part of Italy and still held that area when the Nazi armies surrendered in May 1945. Meanwhile, the Americans had lost more than 70,000 men during their generally unproductive campaign in Italy.

Reversing the Tide in the Pacific

During the six months after the attack on Pearl Harbor, the Japanese engulfed more than 1,000,000 square miles of the area of the Pacific Ocean. They captured the Philippines, Thailand, Burma, the Malay Peninsula, and the great British naval base at Singapore, as well as New Guinea and the Dutch East Indies. In addition, the Japanese occupied hundreds of islands from which they hoped to cut the Allied supply lines to the South Pacific and to capture Australia and New Zealand as well. The United States, crippled by the losses at Pearl Harbor and in the Philippines, required several months before it could bring sufficient military and naval strength to the Pacific to try even to stop the onrushing Japanese.

Two huge naval-air battles turned the tide. In the Battle of the Coral Sea, southeast of New Guinea, fought on May 7−8, 1942, both sides suffered heavy losses, but planes from the American carriers *Lexington* and *Yorktown* repulsed a large Japanese armada on its way to attack Australia. Soon afterward, the Japanese made a bold bid to cut American communications in the Pacific by sending a large invasion force against Midway, an outpost of the Hawaiian Islands. American experts had broken the Japanese secret military code, and the fleet under Admiral Chester Nimitz was ready and waiting when the Japanese warships neared Midway on June 3. In a furious battle which lasted until June 6, American carrier planes sank four of the

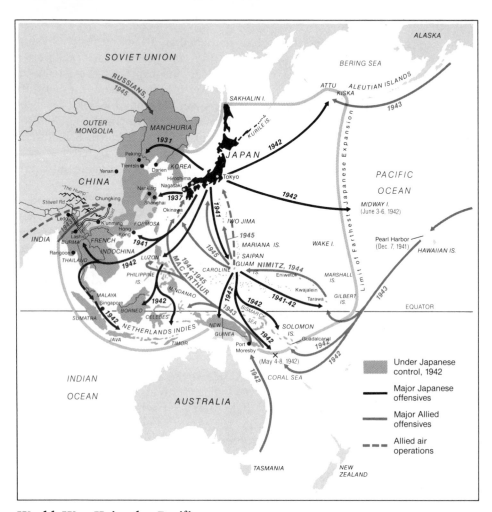

World War II in the Pacific

enemy's finest carriers, a heavy cruiser, and three destroyers. The battle dealt a death blow to Japanese naval aviation. The balance of naval power thereafter rested in American hands, although the Japanese navy and army remained strong.

American land operations began on August 7, 1942, when the 1st Marine Division went ashore on the steaming island of Guadalcanal in the Solomon Islands. Then began a two-year struggle to regain other islands, which the Japanese had heavily fortified and defended with extraordinary courage. American losses were, therefore, high in the capture of Tarawa in the Gilberts in November 1943. Kwajalein and other islands in the Marshalls, and Guam and Saipan in the Marianas, fell in 1944. It took a month of desperate fighting—from February 19 to March 16, 1945—at the frightful cost of 24,000 men, before marines planted the American flag on Mount Suribachi on Iwo Jima and rooted out the last defenders. An even more furious battle followed when marine and army forces attacked the island of Okinawa, only 350 miles south of Japan itself, in April 1945. The battle for Okinawa ended on June 21, and American naval and air forces were now within easy striking distance of the Japanese homeland.

By this time, 1945, the Pacific Fleet, under Admirals Nimitz and William F. Halsey, had grown to twenty-four battleships, twenty-six heavy cruisers, sixty-four escort carriers, fifty-two light cruisers, and 323 destroyers. In addition, twenty army divisions and some 15,000 combat aircraft were in the Pacific area. The Japanese fleet had been almost totally destroyed. Japanese merchant ships were being sunk by airplanes and submarines at so fast a pace that Japan faced starvation in the near future.

The Philippines

After the Japanese invaded the Philippine Islands in early 1942, the American commander, General Douglas MacArthur, was ordered to Australia to take supreme command of Allied forces in the South Pacific. He left with the dramatic parting prophecy "I shall return." General Jonathan Wainwright commanded American and Filipino troops on Luzon in a heroic defense of Bataan and the rock of Corregidor. Japanese troops forced them to surrender on May 6, 1942.

It took two and a half years before MacArthur could redeem his promise. In a brilliant strategy, he first fought his way up the eastern and northern coast of New Guinea; he then assembled huge land, air, and sea forces for the invasion of the Philippines in October 1944. It began on October 20, as Americans swarmed ashore at Leyte Island in the southeastern part of the archipelago. The Japanese navy made one last suicidal bid for victory in the Battle of Leyte Gulf and then withdrew. Again and again, the Japanese tried to land reinforcements on the islands, but the American navy frustrated every such attempt. American troops landed on the main island of Luzon on January 9, 1945, and fought their way southward to Manila. They took the city on February 4; organized Japanese resistance in the islands ended in March 1945. All told, the Japanese lost more than 400,000 men and 9,000 planes in the battle for the Philippines.

MacArthur turned the government of the Philippines over to President Sergio Osmeña in March 1945. The independence of the Philippine Republic was proclaimed on July 4, 1946, in accordance with the Philippine Independence Act of 1934. In March 1947, the United States and the new republic signed a treaty which gave the United States military and naval bases in the islands.

The Normandy Invasion and Its Aftermath

The crucial operation on the western front was termed OVERLORD—the long-awaited invasion of France and Hitler's *Festung* (Fortress) *Europa.* Early in the morning of June 6, 1944, some 11,000 American and British planes began to pound German coastal defenses in northern France. Then three airborne divisions landed in the fields of Normandy. Soon afterward, at 7:30 A.M., Anglo-American forces under the command of General Eisenhower, now Supreme Allied Commander in Europe, poured out of more than 4,000 transports and war vessels to assault five beaches on the Cotentin Peninsula. Altogether, it was the greatest amphibious landing ever undertaken.

For weeks the Allied armies battled against the stiff resistance of German forces under Field Marshals Rommel and Karl von Rundstedt. But the Allies enjoyed complete control of the air, and the Germans had to divide their forces in expectation of attacks elsewhere. A huge hole was opened in the German lines at Saint-Lô on about July 25. Soon General Patton's tanks were pouring through by the thousands. French underground forces rose openly to aid their liberators, and the American Seventh Army under General Alexander M. Patch came up from the Mediterranean to join the eastward-moving troops. Paris was freed on August 25, Brussels and Antwerp a few days later. Units of General Courtney Hodges' American First Army entered the "sacred soil" of Hitler's Third Reich on September 12, 1944. Soon six Allied armies, which totaled more than 2,000,000 men, faced the great Siegfried Line which extended the whole length of Germany's western border from the Netherlands to Switzerland.

The Election of 1944

By constitutional stipulation, the United States held its quadrennial presidential campaign, even though the time was hardly propitious for ordinary political debate. The Republicans had done so well in the mid-term election of 1942 that a spirited contest took place among their leaders for the presidential nomination. Wendell Willkie at first seemed the favorite for the Republican nomination, but he was soon vanquished in state conventions and primary elections by the young and energetic Governor Dewey of New York. Dewey won the nomination handily on the first ballot. The Republicans adopted a platform which endorsed the basic New Deal programs and promised Republican cooperation in the movement then under way for the creation of an international agency to preserve peace in the postwar era.

Even though Roosevelt was in ailing health (he suffered a heart attack in June 1944), and it was doubtful whether he could survive the rigors of a fourth term, he was determined to direct the war effort through to victory and to take the lead in establishing a lasting peace. Although the Democratic national convention, which met at Chicago on July 19, had no alternative but to name Roosevelt as its standard-bearer for a fourth time, a bitter fight ensued over the vice-presidential nomination. Democratic leaders were determined to unseat Vice-President Wallace because of his alleged temperamental defects. Some feared Wallace's egalitarian social and economic ideals; others worried about the political unorthodoxy of the man who might succeed the ailing President. Roosevelt did not insist upon Wallace's renomination and indicated that he would accept a number of other running mates. After much skirmishing, Roosevelt and the party managers settled upon Senator Harry S Truman of Missouri. Truman, an ardent New Dealer, was acceptable to labor, Southerners, farmers, and workers.

Dewey put up a good fight, but the voters were more interested in the smashing Allied victories in Europe and the Pacific than in the New York governor's speeches. Moreover, Roosevelt's health and spirits improved visibly as the campaign progressed. He won a decisive victory on November 7, 1944; Roosevelt garnered 25,600,000 popular votes and 432 electoral votes, against 22,000,000 popular votes and ninety-nine electoral votes for Dewey.

In addition, the Democrats gained twenty seats in the next House of Representatives and elected governors in such key states as Ohio and Massachusetts.

The Battle of the Bulge

Von Rundstedt took advantage of bad weather, which grounded Allied planes, and of the rough terrain of the Ardennes Forest to launch a powerful counterattack on December 16, 1944. It was a final, desperate attempt to split the Allied lines and reach the Channel ports. The attack caught the Americans, who bore the brunt of the assault, by surprise. Generals Eisenhower and Omar N. Bradley had taken a calculated risk; they had left the Ardennes Forest area lightly guarded and concentrated heavy forces north and south of it. The German reserves, spearheaded by armored divisions, penetrated sixty miles, almost to the Meuse River near the Belgian-French border. They were finally stopped near Dinant by Patton's and Montgomery's armies. In this battle, the American 101st Airborne Division under General Anthony C. McAuliffe made a heroic stand at the vital rail junction and road center of Bastogne. McAuliffe and his men, although completely surrounded, disrupted the German timetables and transportation until relieved by the American Third Army.

Counterattacking Allied forces pinched off the Bulge on about January 21, 1945. Allied losses had been high—there were 77,000 American casualties alone—but the battle had cost the Germans 120,000 of their best reserves and untold quantities of war supplies.

Germany Surrenders

The Allies now closed in for the kill. On March 7, 1945, the American First Army crossed the Rhine River over the bridge at Remagen just before it was to be blown up by the retreating Germans. All Allied armies were across the Rhine by April 1.

At this point, the Allied high command faced a difficult choice. One alternative, fervently urged by Churchill, was a direct drive to seize Berlin before the Russians could enter the city. The other was to let the Russians enter Berlin first.

Eisenhower chose the second alternative, largely because of military considerations. He divided his army and sent Patton into Bavaria in order to prevent the escape of the German army to mountain strongholds in that state. Eisenhower knew that the American, Russian, and British governments had agreed earlier on postwar occupation zones in Germany, and he did not consider the capture of Berlin worth the loss of American and British lives.

At this point, Churchill pleaded that Patton be sent into Prague to save Czechoslovakia from Russian domination. Eisenhower ordered Patton to take Prague but then reversed his decision after receipt of a strong protest from Stalin. In all these critical decisions, Eisenhower had the full support of General Marshall and of Roosevelt.

Meanwhile, the Russian armies steadily advanced from the east on a march of 2,300 miles from the Volga River. American First Army units met Soviet troops at Torgau, on the Elbe River, on April 25, 1945. Soviet troops then

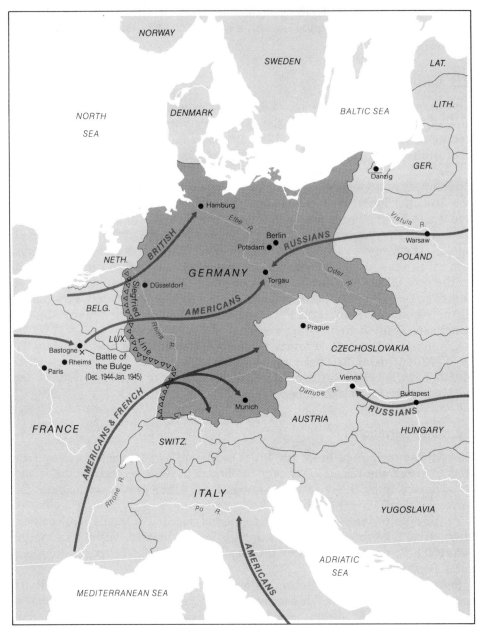

Allied Victory in Europe

entered Berlin and fought their way from house to house through the heaps of rubble to which Allied planes and Soviet cannon had reduced the city. The German capital surrendered on May 2.

Instead of dying in defense of his country, as he had pledged that he would, Hitler committed suicide in his bunker beneath the chancellery in Berlin. Other leading Nazis who had not killed themselves or disappeared in the postwar confusion later were brought to trial before a four-power tribunal at Nuremberg. Robert H. Jackson, a justice of the United States Supreme Court, presided over the trial. Ten German leaders were hanged, and others received life or long-term prison sentences for crimes against humanity.

Hitler's successor, Grand Admiral Karl Doenitz, ordered all German sea, air, and land forces to surrender on May 7. On the following day, German delegates signed terms of unconditional surrender at Eisenhower's headquarters in the French city of Rheims.

Preparing for Peace

During the Second World War, Roosevelt, Churchill, and other Allied heads of state met from time to time to coordinate their war efforts and to plan final peace settlements. As we have seen, Roosevelt and Churchill had met to draft the Atlantic Charter in 1941, even before the United States entered the war. The Anglo-American leaders later met at Washington, Quebec, and Hyde Park to plan common strategy. Early in January 1943, they came together again at Casablanca, Morocco, to plan the invasion of Italy.

In November 1943, Roosevelt and Churchill met with the Chinese leader, Chiang Kai-shek, at Cairo. They agreed to drive Japan from the Asiatic mainland and from the islands which she had seized since the beginning of her expansion in the Pacific. From Cairo, Roosevelt and Churchill flew to Teheran to meet Stalin and his advisers. There they discussed plans for an Anglo-American second front in Europe.

Throughout the first two and a half years of their association, Roosevelt and Churchill worked together in remarkable friendship and accord. To be sure, personal difficulties existed, and they did not always agree on policy. Roosevelt seems to have been jealous of Churchill's commanding position as the chief spokesman of the free world. While Roosevelt and his advisers were more eager to open a second front in France, Churchill was obsessed with postwar Soviet domination of the Balkans and eastern Europe, and he consistently pressed for an Allied invasion from the Mediterranean. But discord did not seriously mar the warm relationship between Roosevelt and Churchill until about the time of the Teheran Conference, when differences over specific problems occasionally strained relations.

Both agreed, however, that one of their prime tasks was to win Russian friendship and postwar cooperation. Attainment of this objective had become imperative by early 1945, for the war obviously was coming to a close. The Russians had already indicated their intention to control the countries of eastern Europe which their armies were overrunning. Consequently, Roosevelt, Churchill, and Stalin met with their respective entourages in the Crimean city of Yalta from February 4 through February 11, 1945. The following is a brief summary of their agreements on crucial issues:

1. *Germany.* Roosevelt, Churchill, and Stalin approved the boundaries of the postwar zones of occupation in Germany already drawn by an Allied commission in London. Germany was to be administered by an Inter-Allied Control Commission in Berlin. Russia and Poland were to receive territory in eastern Germany, and Germany was to pay reparations.

2. *Poland and eastern Europe.* The Russians had already installed a pro-Soviet government in Poland. Churchill and Roosevelt accepted a compro-

mise by which Stalin agreed to include democratic leaders in the Polish government and to permit free elections to determine the future of the country. The three leaders also signed a declaration which promised the free election of democratic governments in the other countries of eastern Europe.

3. *The United Nations.* Stalin promised to cooperate with Roosevelt and Churchill in creating a new international security agency along the lines already drawn by the American government.

4. *The Far East.* In a secret agreement between Roosevelt and Stalin, the latter agreed to come into the war against Japan within two or three months after the surrender of Germany. Stalin also promised to support the government of Chiang Kai-shek. In return, Roosevelt agreed that the Russians should acquire the Kurile Islands and all rights and territory lost to Japan at the end of the Russo-Japanese War. This meant the transfer of the southern half of the island of Sakhalin to Russia, Soviet control of the Manchurian ports of Dairen and Port Arthur, and Soviet-Chinese operation of the Chinese Eastern and South Manchurian railroads. Roosevelt's military advisers strongly urged him to make these concessions in order to assure Russian help in subduing Japan.

Churchill believed at the time of the Yalta Conference that Roosevelt was physically and mentally incapacitated, and that he, therefore, made too many concessions to Stalin. Churchill's belief had some justification, but in retrospect it is difficult to see how Roosevelt could have acted differently. As Churchill later put it in his *Triumph and Tragedy:* "Our hopeful assumptions were soon to be falsified. Still they were the only ones possible at the time." The overriding realities of the Yalta Conference were that the Soviets occupied, or were soon to occupy, most of eastern Europe and that they were determined that hostile governments would not surround them. Even if Roosevelt had obtained the "more specific" language about eastern Europe which many critics believe that he should have insisted upon at Yalta, the "loss" of eastern Europe would nonetheless have occurred.

The Death of Roosevelt

Roosevelt sought relief from his labors in a brief vacation early in April 1945 at Warm Springs, Georgia. He was sitting for a portrait in his cottage there on the afternoon of April 12 when he complained of a severe headache. Two hours later he died of a cerebral hemorrhage. Most Americans, regardless of race, creed, social status, or political persuasion, responded with a spontaneous expression of mourning which bespoke the loss of a great man. Roosevelt's body was brought to Washington, and he was soon afterward buried with simple ceremonies at his ancestral home at Hyde Park, New York. On the day before his death, he had been preparing a radio address for Jefferson's birthday, April 13. In it, he had written his last message to the nation which he led so long: "The only limit to our realization of tomorrow will be our doubts of today. Let us move forward with a strong and active faith."

Atomic Warfare

The task of concluding the war in the Pacific and planning for peace now fell to Roosevelt's successor, Harry S Truman. Truman, utterly unprepared to deal with Churchill's proposal for the capture of Prague, supported Eisenhower and Marshall in their decision not to move against the Czech capital. But Truman did not conceal his anger at Russian violation of the Yalta accords when he met with Stalin, Churchill, and Clement Attlee, Churchill's successor as Prime Minister, at Potsdam, Germany, from July 17 through August 2, 1945. The Allied leaders, in spite of differences over eastern Europe, did unite on July 26 in issuing the Potsdam Declaration, which called upon Japan to surrender unconditionally and threatened "prompt and utter destruction" if she did not.

Truman was emboldened to resist Stalin and to join in issuing the Potsdam Declaration because he knew that the United States now possessed a new weapon of incredible destructive power—the atomic bomb. Scientists had long known that immense energy could be produced by splitting the atom. Roosevelt had been persuaded of the vast military potential of atomic power. There were reports that Hitler was trying to develop an atomic bomb, and the American government had spent $2 billion on its development. An Anglo-American scientific team, headed by J. Robert Oppenheimer, a theoretical physicist from the University of California, Berkeley, made the first test on July 16, 1945, in a desert area near Los Alamos, New Mexico. The bomb, on a high steel tower, exploded with a force equal to that of 20,000 tons of TNT. It sent a column of fire and smoke five miles into the air and shattered house windows 100 miles away. The terrible heat fused the desert sand into a substance like glass.

Overwhelmed and threatened from all sides though they were, the Japanese prepared for a suicidal defense of their home islands. Truman decided to use atomic bombs against Japan because he was convinced that, by doing so, he would end the war and save perhaps the million Japanese and American lives which would otherwise be lost in an invasion of the Japanese homeland. Some scientists argued that a demonstration of the bomb's terrible destructiveness in an uninhabited area for the benefit of Japanese observers would end the war without further deaths; other scientists said that the United States should not bear the stigma of being the first nation to use atomic weapons—and against largely civilian targets. These arguments were brushed aside. Only two atomic bombs were immediately available, and military and political leaders were convinced that both might be needed to force Japan to recognize the hopelessness of her position.

A lone B-29 Superfortress, winging its way over the Japanese island of Honshu, dropped an atomic bomb on the city of Hiroshima on the morning of August 6. A blinding explosion, followed by roaring balls of fire, completely demolished four square miles of the city. It killed close to 80,000 persons and wounded at least that many others. When the Japanese still did not respond forthrightly to the Potsdam Declaration, three days later, a second bomb was dropped on Nagasaki and turned it into an inferno in which many thousands died immediately. The atomic bomb also had long-lasting effects, as thousands more in both cities died slowly from radiation poisoning. The survivors at Hiroshima and Nagasaki also suffered from various forms of cancer and from genetic defects in their children. On the same day that the atomic bomb exploded over Nagasaki, Russia declared war on Japan and sent troops into Manchuria.

Japan Surrenders

The Japanese government, faced with the choice of annihilation or surrender, gave up the struggle on August 14. Before the end, however, an extremist military group invaded the imperial palace and tried, unsuccessfully, to prevent the broadcast of Emperor Hirohito's declaration of surrender. Two weeks later, air transports landed the first Americans on the island of Honshu. On September 2, MacArthur received Japanese delegates aboard Halsey's flagship, *Missouri,* in Tokyo Bay, for the formal signing of surrender terms.

Hirohito, although permitted to remain on his throne, was forced to renounce the ancient Japanese legend that he was of divine origin. The Supreme Commander of the Allied Powers in the Far East, MacArthur, was vested with full power over Japan, and the Emperor was made subject to his orders until a treaty of peace had been concluded.

Thus ended the most destructive war in history.

4. PAX AMERICANA AND A NEW WORLD ORDER

The Declaration of the United Nations

American leaders remembered vividly the events of the 1920s and 1930s and were determined that their country should not repeat the error of refusing to take leadership in a postwar international organization to preserve peace. Roosevelt and Hull, both veterans of the Wilson administration, shared this conviction. They were also determined to avoid Wilson's mistake of making a partisan issue out of peace, but they did not want to frighten the public by pushing their plans too fast. So, even though Roosevelt and Hull had a new postwar organization in mind from the outset, they moved very slowly.

Roosevelt's and Hull's first step along the road to international cooperation was the Declaration of the United Nations, signed in Washington on January 1, 1942, by representatives of twenty-six countries, including the United States, Great Britain, the Soviet Union, and China. This declaration was a pledge of partnership "in a common struggle against savage and brutal forces seeking to subjugate the world." The signatories—members of what Churchill would later call the Grand Alliance—agreed to accept the principles of the Atlantic Charter. They also pledged their full resources to the defeat of the common enemy and promised not to make a separate peace. From time to time, other nations joined the alliance, until, by 1945, it represented almost the entire population of the non-Axis world.

Origins of the United Nations

Many signs indicated that Congress was eager for the United States to cooperate with other nations in planning for the postwar world. For example, in September 1943, the House of Representatives overwhelmingly adopted a resolution introduced by J. William Fulbright of Arkansas which endorsed American participation in the creation of international machinery "with power adequate to establish and maintain a just and lasting peace."

In October 1943, Hull flew to Moscow for a conference with the foreign ministers of Great Britain and the Soviet Union. The fourth paragraph of the declaration which emanated from their conference asserted that they recognized "the necessity of establishing at the earliest practical date a general international organization, based on the principle of the sovereign equality of all peace-loving states, and open to membership of all such states, large and small." A few days later, this paragraph was incorporated, verbatim, in a resolution introduced in the Senate by Tom Connally, chairman of the Foreign Relations Committee. The Senate approved the resolution on November 5, 1943, by a vote of eighty-five to five.

The American course was, therefore, well charted by the time that American, British, Soviet, and Chinese delegates met at the colonial mansion of Dumbarton Oaks near Washington on August 21, 1944, to consider a tentative plan for a new international agency. They agreed in principle upon the basic structure of a new organization to be called the United Nations. Certain disagreements over membership and voting procedures were later settled at Yalta, when Stalin accepted the American point of view.

Formation of the United Nations

The Conference on International Organization, approved at Yalta, opened on schedule in San Francisco on April 25, 1945. Roosevelt had appointed the American delegation shortly before his death. It consisted of Cordell Hull, who had resigned as Secretary of State on November 21, 1944, and his successor, Edward R. Stettinius, Jr.; the chairmen and ranking minority members of the Senate Foreign Relations Committee and House Foreign Affairs Committee; and various leaders in education and public life. More than 200 delegates from fifty nations assembled at the city's War Memorial Opera House.

The charter of the United Nations, completed after two months of hard work and controversy, was to go into force when ratified by the United States, Great Britain, Russia, France, and China, and by a majority of the other forty-five member nations. Truman made the closing speech to the conference on June 26 and almost immediately sent the charter to the Senate. He expressed his confidence that "the overwhelming sentiment of the people and of their representatives in the Senate" favored immediate ratification. Truman did not misjudge American sentiment. The Senate gave its consent to ratification of the charter by a vote of eighty-nine to two on July 28, 1945, and the charter went into effect about three months later.

SUGGESTED READINGS

For the background of Pearl Harbor, see Langer and Gleason, *The Challenge to Isolation* and *The Undeclared War,* already cited; Roberta Wohlsetter, *Pearl Harbor: Warning and Decision* (1962); Paul W. Schroeder, *The Axis Alliance and Japanese-American Relations, 1941* (1958); Robert J.C. Butow, *Tojo and the Coming of the War* (1961); and, most particularly, Herbert Feis,

The Road to Pearl Harbor (1950).

The most useful survey of this period is A. Russell Buchanan, *The United States and World War II,* 2 vols. (1964). Interesting but polemical accounts of governmental and business cooperative relations during the war can be found in Bruce Catton, *The War Lords of Washington* (1948), and Eliot Janeway, *The Struggle for Survival* (1951). Robert H.

Connery, *Navy and Industrial Mobilization in World War II* (1951); Lester V. Chandler, *Inflation in the United States, 1940—1948* (1951); and James P. Baxter III, *Scientists against Time* (1946), are good studies of the domestic front. Jack Goodman, ed., *While You Were Gone: A Report on Wartime Life in the United States* (1946); Ruben Hill, *Families Under Stress* (1949); and Richard Polenberg, *War and Society: The United States, 1941 – 1945* (1972), are adequate accounts of American society during the war, but see especially John M. Blum, *V Was for Victory: Politics and American Culture During World War II* (1976). On the status of black Americans, see Neil A. Wynn, *The Afro-American and the Second World War* (1976). The tragic story of Japanese-Americans is told in Roger Daniels, *Concentration Camps U.S.A.: Japanese-Americans and World War II* (1971); Michi Weglyn, *The Untold Story of America's Concentration Camps* (1976); and Dorothy S. Thomas et al., *The Spoilage* (1946). For the politics of the period, see Jonathan Daniels, *Frontier on the Potomac* (1946), and Roland Young, *Congressional Politics in the Second World War* (1956).

Multivolume accounts of military, naval, and air operations have been published by the Department of the Army, Office of the Chief of Military History. A better introduction to the battles and strategy, however, would be Fletcher Pratt, *War for the World* (1951); Martha Byrd Hoyle, *A World in Flames: The History of World War II* (1970); Samuel E. Morison, *Strategy and Compromise* (1958); or Kenneth R. Greenfield, *American Strategy in World War II* (1963). The overriding role of General Marshall in devising American military strategy and Marshall's training for that role are described in Forrest C. Pogue, *George C. Marshall*, 3 vols. (1963 – 73). On the European theater, see Chester Wilmot, *The Struggle for Europe* (1952), and the war memoirs of Dwight D. Ei-

senhower, Omar N. Bradley, W. Bedell Smith, and Henry H. Arnold. For the Pacific theater, see Herbert Feis, *Japan Subdued* (1961); J. K. Eyre, *The Roosevelt-MacArthur Conflict* (1950); and the memoirs of Douglas MacArthur, Robert Eichelberger, and William F. Halsey. D. Clayton James, *The Years of MacArthur*, 2 vols. (1970), and Gavin Long, *MacArthur as Military Commander* (1969), are severely critical of MacArthur's general strategy in the war against Japan; William R. Manchester, *American Caesar: Douglas MacArthur, 1880 – 1964* (1978), in contrast, is almost wholly admiring. The war of the common soldier is described by Ernie Pyle in *Here Is Your War* (1943), *Brave Men* (1944), and *The Story of G.I. Joe* (1945). Important fictional treatments include Norman Mailer, *The Naked and the Dead* (1948), James Jones, *From Here to Eternity* (1951); and Joseph Heller, *Catch-22* (1961).

Herbert Feis has written excellent accounts of the diplomacy of the war: *Churchill, Roosevelt, Stalin* (1947), *Between War and Peace* (1960), *The China Tangle* (1953), and *Japan Subdued*, cited above. William L. Neuman, *After Victory* (1967); Edward R. Stettinius, *Roosevelt and the Russians—The Yalta Conference* (1949); and Milton Viorst, *Hostile Allies: FDR and Charles de Gaulle* (1965), are some of the books that illustrate the complexity of the diplomacy of war and peace. Gabriel Kolko, *The Politics of War* (1968), from a New Left perspective, harshly indicts United States foreign policy during the Second World War for its anti-Soviet bias.

There is a large and growing literature on the atomic bomb project. Among the most valuable books are Robert Jungk, *Brighter than a Thousand Suns* (1958); Nuel Pharr Davis, *Lawrence and Oppenheimer* (1969); and Martin J. Sherwin, *A World Destroyed: The Atomic Bomb and the Grand Alliance* (1975). John Hersey's *Hiroshima* (1946) resembles a novel in its dramatic impact.

CHAPTER 12
HARRY S TRUMAN AND
THE POSTWAR WORLD

1. TRUMAN AND THE SHAPE OF POSTWAR POLITICS

The Rise of Harry Truman

When news of Roosevelt's death reached Washington on April 12, 1945, Vice-President Truman was presiding over a session of the Senate. That same evening, at 7:09 P.M., Chief Justice Stone swore him in as President.

Harry S Truman (1884 – 1972), born and reared in a small Missouri town, worked as a bank clerk and farmer after he finished high school. He never attended college. Truman served in the field artillery during the First World War and rose to the rank of major. The business which he entered when he returned home failed during the recession of 1921. Then Truman went into politics with the help of the notorious Kansas City Democratic organization headed by Tom Pendergast. Truman was elected to the Board of County Commissioners of Jackson County in 1922 and served as head of that board from 1926 to 1934.

With Pendergast's backing, Truman was elected to the United States Senate in 1934, and again in 1940. There he gained a reputation for loyalty to the New Deal and conscientious attention to duty. He won national prominence as the efficient and fair chairman of a special Senate committee which investigated defense contracts and saved the government billions of dollars.

The country knew very little about Truman when he succeeded Roosevelt, but it soon became apparent that his strengths far outweighed his weaknesses.

When he confronted important matters, he possessed uncommon good sense, and his close study of American history gave him a great store of knowledge about the problems which he faced. In times of crisis, he seemed to know almost instinctively what the circumstances demanded. He was determined to provide vigorous leadership both at home and abroad; consequently, he left the presidency as strong an institution as he found it. He had a deep sense of fair play. Hence he defended and tried to expand civil liberties at a time when some of the most ferocious assaults in American history were being made against these cherished rights. As President, Truman was a stronger advocate of civil rights than any of his predecessors, and he supported a program of racial equality far beyond anything which Franklin Roosevelt had ever dared to suggest. Despite his modest beginnings, Truman expressed a well-developed world view, and, once he found his bearings, he provided bold leadership to the West and its allies in Asia. Above all, Truman was courageous. As President, he made a habit of overcoming seemingly insuperable odds—whether in dismissing a popular general or in running for reelection without much visible public support.

Postwar Problems

The day after he assumed office, Truman met reporters for his first news conference. With simple frankness, Truman said to them, "Last night the moon, the stars, and all the planets fell on me."

Truman's first tasks were to conclude the war both in Europe and in the Pacific, to carry through for Roosevelt on the organization of the United Nations, and then to give leadership to the relief and reconstruction of war-torn lands. For these tasks, Roosevelt had done almost nothing to prepare his Vice-President. Furthermore, to be an effective President Truman had to exert control over a cabinet and administration of strangers—Roosevelt loyalists—and, even more difficult, to establish himself as a party leader as well as the leader of the American people. These were not easy tasks, for Americans regarded Roosevelt as indispensable and found it hard to imagine anyone else in the White House. Moreover, Truman came to the presidency without a distinctive style such as the one which had won immediate confidence for Roosevelt. Indeed, Truman gave the impression of being overwhelmed and confused.

Truman and Reform

Military and foreign affairs so engrossed Truman during the spring and summer of 1945 that many Democratic politicians assumed that he would be content to serve as caretaker while a postwar reaction dismantled major portions of the New Deal. In fact, Truman, slowly and quietly, had decided domestic policy on his own, just as he had in the field of international affairs.

On September 6, 1945, he startled Congress by calling for an expansion of the New Deal. He asked for extension of the Social Security system, an increase in the minimum wage, national health insurance, revival of the war against urban slums, and new regional developments similar to the TVA. Truman also called for federal guarantees of full employment and prosperity and maintenance of economic controls through the period of conversion to a peacetime economy. "It was on that day and with this message," Truman later wrote in his memoirs, "that I first spelled out the details of the program of liberalism and progressivism which was to be the foundation of my administration."

2. RECONVERSION TO PEACETIME

Veterans

To get the boys back home without delay was the reigning passion of the American people in 1945, and the demand for immediate demobilization was so powerful that leaders in the executive branch and in Congress did not dare to ignore it. The great army and navy were thus dismantled; by midsummer 1946, the army counted only 1,500,000 men and the navy, 700,000 men.

In most respects, the government prepared well for the homeward rush of former servicemen. Congress had made provision beforehand by passing the Servicemen's Readjustment Act, better known as the "GI Bill of Rights," or simply as the GI bill, in June 1944. When the tide of demobilized veterans poured home from local camps and far-flung battlegrounds, a grateful nation was ready with measures to help them make the transition to civilian life.

The GI Bill of Rights established the most extensive system of benefits for veterans in American history. The Veterans' Administration (VA) rapidly expanded its hospitals to care for the sick and wounded, and, by 1950, some 159 veterans' hospitals served an average of 108,000 patients daily. Vocational rehabilitation centers provided guidance clinics and helped more than 610,000 disabled servicemen to discover their aptitudes and find appropriate jobs. Unemployed veterans received unemployment compensation for a full year, while special privileges were accorded servicemen who entered the civil service. Financial assistance and priority were given for the purchase of homes, farms, and businesses. Finally, veterans who wanted them received free tuition, books, and expenses for job training, college, or other advanced education.

Altogether, it was the largest assistance program undertaken by any government in history. The expenditures of the VA increased from less than $1 billion in 1944 to about $10 billion in 1950. Between 1945 and 1952, the VA spent $13.5 billion for the education and training of nearly 8,000,000 veterans, and $4 billion for unemployment benefits and self-employment help. The VA also insured nearly $16.5 billion of loans to veterans for homes, farms, and businesses.

The Transition to a Peacetime Economy

In the late summer of 1945, the American economy resembled a great overheated steam engine about to explode. Per capita disposable income stood at an all-time high. Individuals and corporations had amassed savings of $48.5 billion, and state and local governments had surpluses totaling more than $10 billion. Demand, which had been pent up for four years, was tremendous, but, because of wartime restrictions, not enough automobiles, appliances, homes, meat, and countless other commodities existed for sale to satisfy the demand.

When Congress reduced taxes some $6 billion in November 1945, it only expanded consumer demands and placed even greater pressure on prices.

Led by Senator Robert A. Taft of Ohio, Republicans and conservative Democrats in Congress advocated increasing consumer goods by lifting the wartime controls. In order to spur production, the administration quickly disposed of most government-owned war plants, which possessed 29 per cent of the industrial capacity of the country. Yet, Truman insisted upon rigorous price controls to dam up inflationary pressures until output could satisfy demand. The OPA, which still operated under wartime authority, held the line against price increases remarkably well in 1945–1946, but after Truman vetoed a price-control bill in June 1946 (on the ground that Congress had weakened it to the point of ineffectiveness), prices rose wildly. Congress adopted another price-control measure in July, but, as Truman predicted, it proved ineffective, and he ended most price controls in November 1946. As a consequence, the Consumer Price Index (CPI) increased by almost 34 per cent between 1945 and 1948.

Labor Strife

The end of the war found leaders of organized labor troubled by fears of inflation, unemployment, and the possibility of a postwar depression. Unions now boasted 14,600,000 members, and their leaders were determined to maintain wartime gains and to seek wage increases sufficient to hold their own against the rising cost of living. But higher wages added to the cost of production, which meant higher prices, which in turn stimulated strikes for higher wages. The spiraling cycle went on until about 1948.

In October 1945, the Office of War Mobilization agreed that a general wage increase of 24 per cent could be granted by industry without endangering either profits or price controls. A month later, Truman called a National Labor-Management Conference to work out a program to preserve industrial peace. It failed, and 180,000 automobile workers, 200,000 electrical workers, and 750,000 steelworkers all went out on strike. A wage compromise followed recommendations made by a presidential fact-finding board, and it set the pattern of wages for most of American industry and gave hope of peaceful industrial relations.

Conflicts in two major industries, however, upset the balance in the spring of 1946. After a nationwide railroad strike threatened to paralyze the economy, Truman seized the railroads on May 17, 1946. Then he offered a compromise settlement which was accepted by eighteen unions. But when the engineers and trainmen walked out, Truman asked Congress for power to declare a state of national emergency whenever a strike in a vital industry under federal control endangered national security. Under Truman's proposal, workers who continued to strike lost all benefits of seniority, were subject to conscription into the army, and their leaders could be fined and imprisoned. The House of Representatives approved the bill, but the Senate buried it because the striking railway workers returned to their jobs.

Meanwhile, John L. Lewis had led his United Mine Workers out on strike for higher wages and a number of fringe benefits. After fruitless negotiations, the government took over the mines to protect the national interest. The government granted most of Lewis' demands, but he made new ones in October 1946. The government, supported by a federal judge's injunction, stood firm. Lewis defied the injunction and called a strike, only to draw fines of $10,000 against himself and $3.5 million against his union. A new contract, which conceded most of Lewis' demands, ended the impasse in June 1947. The Supreme Court then reduced the fine against the union to $700,000.

A second round of nationwide strikes broke out in the autumn of 1946, but from then until 1950 labor and management settled most of their differences over the bargaining table. In the process, however, workers obtained additional wage increases, which contributed to further increases in prices.

Congress and Demobilization

The fierce struggles between Truman and Congress over price controls and labor policies gave the impression of a general political breakdown which in fact did not exist. On the contrary, Truman and the Democratic Seventy-ninth Congress cooperated to enact two epochal pieces of legislation.

One—the Full Employment Act—approved in February 1946, fulfilled a major pledge in the Democratic platform of 1944. Liberal Democrats wanted the government to take major responsibility for new investment and full employment. Conservative Democrats and most Republicans opposed statutory governmental responsibility for these matters. The act of 1946—a compromise between the extreme points of view—established a Council of Economic Advisers to study the economy and advise the President and Congress on measures best calculated to promote prosperity. The act also directed the President to make an annual economic report to Congress and created a congressional Joint Committee on the Economic Report to study and propose appropriate legislation.

The most significant section of the Employment Act was its assertion that the federal government bore chief responsibility for maintaining prosperity. As Edwin G. Nourse, the first chairman of the Council of Economic Advisers, declared, the measure established machinery for "mobilizing all our organizational resources, public and private, within our system of free enterprise, for a sustained high level of national production." Both Truman and his successor used the Council of Economic Advisers only sparingly, but, in the 1960s, the council finally became what the framers of the Employment Act of 1946 had intended it to be. It grew into an expert body, manned by professional economists, which exercised vital influence. It marshaled knowledge in the formulation of public policy; it was largely aided by revolutionary developments in data-gathering techniques, econometric models, and high-speed computers.

Truman and Congress also cooperated in the passage of the epochal Atomic Energy Act. Approved on August 1, 1946, it laid the foundations for postwar development of atomic energy (see pp. 246–47). The measure gave to the President alone power to order the use of the atomic bomb in warfare and prohibited the divulgence of important atomic information to foreign governments. The act also retained a governmental monopoly on fissionable materials and vested complete control of research and production in a new five-man Atomic Energy Commission.

The Election of 1946 and Its Aftermath

Popular discontent rose high in the early autumn of 1946 because of skyrocketing prices and a shortage of essential commodities, particularly meat. Public anger against organized labor grew because of what seemed to be union irresponsibility. Many Americans, already annoyed by the railroad and coal strikes, were irritated further by Communist infiltration of the leadership of a number of key unions, racketeering in certain unions, and the widespread use of what many persons believed were unfair practices. In 1947, more than thirty states outlawed the most important of these practices: featherbedding (demanding the employment of more labor than was necessary); jurisdictional strikes (strikes which resulted from the warfare of rival labor unions); and secondary boycotts (the refusal of members of a union to handle nonunion goods). Moreover, in 1946–1947, Congress outlawed featherbedding and tried to stamp out labor racketeering.

In 1946, most of the benefits of this discontent accrued to the Republicans. With the slogan "Had enough? Vote Republican!" they swept to victory in the mid-term election on November 5, 1946, by winning control of both houses of Congress for the first time since 1928 and capturing governorships in twenty-five of the thirty-two nonsouthern states.

The new Eightieth Congress acted immediately on its mandate by adopting the Labor-Management Relations, or Taft-Hartley, Act, which was passed over Truman's angry veto in June 1947. Taft, the measure's chief sponsor, wanted to strike heavy blows at union power, principally by banning industry-wide bargaining; but, despite the solid Republican majorities in both houses of Congress, he had to accept a compromise measure. The Taft-Hartley Act outlawed the closed shop—an arrangement by which an employer could hire only members of a union. It forbade "unfair" union practices, such as refusal to bargain in good faith, secondary boycotts, jurisdictional strikes, and pay for work not performed. The Taft-Hartley Act also permitted employers to sue unions for breach of contract, to petition the NLRB for elections to determine bargaining agents, and to speak out during union organizational campaigns. In strikes which endangered the national health and safety, the act provided for "cooling off" periods and for use of temporary injunctions by the President. The measure also compelled union officers to sign anti-Communist affidavits in order to bring their cases before the NLRB. Finally, the measure prohibited union contributions to political parties.

Organized labor bitterly attacked the Taft-Hartley Act as "slave legislation" aimed at the destruction of the labor movement. The Taft-Hartley Act did, to be sure, represent the popular conviction that big labor, irresponsible and uncontrolled, was as dangerous to the national interest as big business or big finance. The measure tried to rectify what a majority of Americans in 1946 thought was the prolabor bias of the National Labor Relations Act of 1935. Nonetheless, unions continued to bargain effectively under the provisions of the Taft-Hartley Act; in fact, labor was functioning merely in harness, not in chains. In short, the measure not only did not strip members of the power which they had won during the New Deal, but it also reinforced their dependency upon the Democratic party as the guarantor of their rights.

Bipartisanship

Superficial appearances gave the impression of constant warfare between the White House and Congress during 1947 and 1948. On the contrary, the two branches of government cooperated during these years very much as they had done before. The most important product of this bipartisan collaboration was the National Security Act of July 26, 1947, the result of a long struggle to reorganize the defense structure of the United States. The lack of communication between the various armed services at Pearl Harbor had dramatized the need for unification of the forces. The army favored unification; but the navy, which feared the elimination of the Marine Corps and the eventual domination by a land-based air force, fought unification bitterly. The National Security Act provided for a single cabinet department and a single Secretary of Defense and Joint Chiefs of Staff. It also established an independent air force and three noncabinet departments of the Army, Navy, and Air Force. Finally, the measure created a National Security Council and a National Security Resources Board to advise the President and Congress, and a new Central Intelligence Agency (CIA) to take charge of intelligence work overseas.

Congress also responded when Truman requested a change in the presidential succession. At this time, the next person in line for the presidency after the Vice-President was the Secretary of State, followed by the other cabinet members in the order of the creation of their offices. The Presidential Succession Act of 1947 fixed the succession after the Vice-President, first in the Speaker of the House, and then in the presiding officer of the Senate. Cabinet members were then to follow in the same order as before. On its own volition, Congress passed the Twenty-second Amendment, which limited the tenure of Presidents after Truman to two terms. It was ratified on February 26, 1951.

The second session of the Eightieth Congress sat from January 6 to June 30, 1948. It was an election year, and Truman submitted seventeen major measures, eight of which Congress approved: first, a bill to draft men from nineteen to twenty-five years of age for twenty-one months of service in the armed forces (it supplanted a weak Selective Service Act adopted in 1946); second, the appropriation of $6 billion for foreign aid; third, temporary support of farm prices at 90 per cent of parity; fourth, extension of the Reciprocal Trade Agreements Act for one year; fifth, a bill which increased Social Security benefits for the aged, the blind, and dependent children; sixth, the extension of rent controls; seventh, admission of 205,000 displaced persons into the United States during the next two years; and, eighth, extension of governmental credit for veterans' homes and cooperative housing projects.

3. SOVIET-AMERICAN COMPETITION AND THE COLD WAR

Beginnings of Deadlock

The Potsdam Conference directed the foreign ministers of the United States, Great Britain, France, and Russia to draw up peace treaties with Germany,

Italy, and former Axis satellites in Europe. Repeated meetings only revealed the extent of disagreement, particularly over Germany. Located in the geographical and strategic center of Europe, with a population of 70,000,000, Germany in 1945 was in desperate condition: its cities lay in rubble, and its industries were crippled or destroyed. Its territory was truncated into four zones, each controlled by a military governor appointed by Russia, Great Britain, the United States, and France. The capital city of Berlin also had been divided among the four powers, but it was surrounded by Soviet-controlled territory.

Germany also was in the middle of the new Soviet-American competition and an accelerating cycle of paranoia and mutual recrimination. While the United States and its allies pressed for liberal democratic governments in eastern Europe, Soviet leaders were determined to insure that hostile regimes did not lie along their borders. More than any other Allied nation, the Soviet Union had borne the brunt of the fighting and casualties of the Second World War. Much of the Soviet Union was in ruins because of the second great German invasion of Russia in less than thirty years, and more than 20,000,000 Russians—many of them civilians—had been killed. Soviet officials, and especially Stalin himself, were determined that Germany must not be allowed to grow strong enough for a third invasion of their country.

Secretary of State James F. Byrnes, who had succeeded Stettinius in 1945, made seven trips to London, Paris, and Moscow in vain efforts to find a definitive settlement satisfactory to the Truman administration. The foreign ministers finally agreed on treaties for Italy, Finland, Bulgaria, Rumania, and Hungary. These treaties, signed at Paris on February 10, 1947, confirmed western supremacy over Italy and Soviet supremacy over Hungary, Finland, Rumania, and Bulgaria. By default, the western powers also accepted Soviet control of Poland. But then all progress came to a halt. On the all-important question of a settlement with Germany, the by now antagonistic foreign ministers could make no progress. Consequently, the western powers took steps to unify their three zones, while the Russians began to erect the apparatus of a separate East German government.

Russian-American differences were also acute in 1945–1946 on the overshadowing issue of disarmament and the international control of atomic energy. In June 1946, Bernard M. Baruch, on behalf of the American government, submitted a plan to the Atomic Energy Commission of the United Nations. This proposal, the so-called Baruch Plan, created an International Atomic Development Authority under the United Nations (UN) with a worldwide monopoly on the production of atomic energy and the right to inspect atomic plants anywhere in the world. According to the Baruch Plan, the Authority would not be subject to a veto in the Security Council of the UN.* The Russians accepted all features of the plan except the one which forbade use of the veto. The United States Government then insisted that effective international control would be impossible. Thus the Baruch Plan, like all proposals for the unification of Germany, foundered upon the shoals of Russian-American mutual suspicion.

*The "legislative" branch of the United Nations consisted of an Assembly, in which all members had seats, and a Security Council with permanent representatives from the United States, Russia, Great Britain, France, and China, and four other nations. Any permanent member could exercise an absolute veto over action by the Security Council.

The Truman Doctrine

The Grand Alliance had obviously broken up by 1946, and the Soviet Union and the western powers had come to an uneasy truce for the division of Europe. What destroyed the truce and set off in earnest what is called the Cold War were certain clear signs that the Soviet Union intended to expand its influence into areas which the West deemed vital to its security, while the United States hoped to reduce Soviet influence throughout Europe, indeed, to turn it back in western Europe.

George F. Kennan, Counselor of the American Embassy in Moscow, had warned as early as February 1946 that Stalin and his government were implacably hostile to the West. Then, Churchill, in an address at Fulton, Missouri, on March 5, 1946, reiterated Kennan's warning and also said that Russia had lowered an "iron curtain" between eastern and western Europe. Events of the next twelve months seemed to confirm Kennan's and Churchill's warnings. The Russians attempted to create a puppet regime in northern Iran, and they withdrew their troops from that country only after Truman sent a blunt personal warning to Stalin. Furthermore, the Russians demanded that Turkey cede territory and permit them to build naval bases in the Bosporus. At the same time, it was believed that the Russians supported a Communist-led rebellion against the government of Greece.

The crisis came to a head on February 24, 1947, when the British government informed the State Department that it could no longer maintain military and naval forces in Greece and the eastern Mediterranean. Truman reacted quickly. On March 12, he asked Congress to appropriate $400 million for military and economic aid to Greece and Turkey. Going further, the President announced what soon was called the Truman Doctrine: "I believe that it must be the foreign policy of the United States to support free peoples who are resisting attempted subjugation by armed minorities or by outside pressures."

Many Americans still advocated peaceful collaboration with the Soviet Union. Truman's request, therefore, especially his request for military assistance, met strong opposition in Congress. Some congressmen maintained that the United States should work through the United Nations, not alone. Truman replied that Russia could easily paralyze action by the UN with her veto. Arthur H. Vandenberg of Michigan, Republican spokesman on foreign policy and chairman of the Senate Foreign Relations Committee, then solved the dilemma. He proposed an amendment which stated that the United States would cease its unilateral aid to Greece and Turkey as soon as the Security Council gave evidence of willingness and ability to act. Thus amended, the Greek-Turkish Aid bill was approved by large majorities in both houses of Congress in May 1947.

The Truman Doctrine was in a certain sense a logical extension of American foreign policy of the previous two decades. It drew on the heritage of the Good Neighbor policy by insisting, at least in principle, on the rights of self-determination and nonintervention. And yet the Truman Doctrine was a radical departure which left a dangerous legacy for postwar American foreign policy. Without fully understanding the contradiction, it justified American intervention in the internal affairs of other countries as a way to preserve nonintervention and self-determination. Even more dangerously, the Truman

Doctrine identified the worldwide phenomenon of communism as responsible for all local disturbances or outside pressures. At the same time it committed the United States to a role as the policeman of world communism.

Assistance totaling some $350 million enabled the Turks to withstand Russian pressure. The struggle to rid Greece of domestic Communist rebels was more difficult, but American aid and military cooperation turned the tide, and the Greek civil war ended in 1949.

European Economic Recovery

The crisis in Greece and Turkey paled into insignificance when compared with the crisis which was developing in western Europe. The United States had poured $11 billion into Europe since the end of the war in relief, loans, and assistance of various kinds. Even so, Great Britain, France, Italy, Germany, and other western European nations were literally on the verge of bankruptcy, and the Communist parties were almost strong enough to assume office in Italy and France. It was clear to the Policy Planning Staff of the State Department, headed by Kennan, that only immense American aid could prevent chaos and the extension of Communist influence. The new Secretary of State, George C. Marshall, discussed the matter with Truman, who agreed with his ideas. Then, in a speech at Harvard University on June 5, 1947, Marshall announced that the United States stood ready to help European nations (including Russia) to rebuild their economies, provided only that these nations themselves contribute as much as they could to general European recovery and prosperity.

The Russians condemned Marshall's offer as a cloak for American imperialism. They also forbade their satellites to join in the pan-European effort which Marshall had proposed. Delegates from sixteen non-Communist nations (Fascist-ruled Spain was excluded) met at Paris on July 12, 1947, to prepare estimates of both their needs and their abilities to contribute to European recovery. Their Committee of European Economic Cooperation (CEEC) submitted a master recovery plan two months later. It called for $22.4 billion in assistance from the United States.

Congress debated the European Recovery Program (ERP), as the Marshall Plan was called, for ten months; Vandenberg led the discussion and mustered votes for the administration. The seizure of the government of Czechoslovakia by that country's Communists in February 1948 assured congressional approval of the ERP. The Senate approved the bill by a huge majority on March 13, and the House concurred by an equally overwhelming majority on March 31. Truman signed the measure on April 3, 1948. In its final form, the ERP bill appropriated $5.3 billion for the first twelve months, with the understanding that the total American appropriation would come to about $17 billion.

Between April 1948, when the Marshall Plan began, and December 1951, when its tasks were taken over by the Mutual Security Agency, the United States poured some $12 billion into Europe through an Economic Cooperation Administration. At the same time, the CEEC distributed the money and began numerous projects for European cooperation. As early as 1950, western Europe had not only recovered its prewar levels of production, but it was well along the road to a much more substantial prosperity. Industrial production had risen by almost two thirds, to a total above prewar levels, and Communist parties throughout western Europe had become weaker and quieter.

The Berlin Airlift and the Formation of NATO

All investigations during the long period of discussion over the ERP pointed to one all-important conclusion: West Germany, the industrial heart of Europe, was the key to European recovery. Hence the United States, Great Britain, and France decided, not only to include West Germany in the ERP, but also to create a separate West German state, particularly after the USSR, in 1946, rejected a proposal by Byrnes for the creation of a unified and demilitarized German Republic. First steps toward West German unification, taken in February 1948, culminated the following June in the formation of a West German Federal Republic and its inclusion in the ERP.

The Soviet Union retaliated at once by limiting Allied and German access to Berlin and then, on June 23, by blocking all traffic into Berlin from the western zones. The Soviets made no secret of their intention to force the western powers either to abandon Berlin and accept the permanent division of Germany, or to abandon all plans for a West German state.

Truman might have settled the German issue, once and for all, if he had sent American forces through the Russian zone to Berlin. However, in collaboration with the British and French governments, Truman decided not to challenge the Russians militarily but to supply Berlin by airlift. If the Russians desired war, they had only to shoot down one of the thousands of planes that, day and night, regardless of weather, winged their way through narrow air corridors across the Russian zone to and from Berlin. The Soviet government did not risk conflict with the United States. The cargo carriers flew 2,500,000 tons of fuel, food, and raw materials to Berlin in defiance of the blockade, and the leaders of West Germany met at Bonn on October 20, 1948, to draft a constitution for the new Federal German Republic. Meanwhile, the Soviets looked for a compromise. In February 1949, Stalin offered to lift the Berlin blockade if the western powers would agree to hold a new meeting of the foreign ministers. They agreed, and the blockade ended on May 12, 1949; eleven days later, the foreign ministers met in Paris for another futile discussion of the German problem.

The movement for European economic cooperation and what seemed to be the growing Soviet threat had also spurred a movement for the common defense of western Europe. Representatives of Britain, France, Belgium, the Netherlands, and Luxembourg signed a fifty-year treaty of economic cooperation and military alliance at Brussels on March 17, 1948. The Brussels Union was reconstituted in January 1949 as the Council of Europe and was enlarged to include Italy, West Germany, Ireland, Denmark, Norway, and Sweden.

Leaders of western Europe now turned to the United States to fulfill the Vandenberg Resolution of June 11, 1948, which had promised American cooperation with a western European military alliance. Out of the discussions which ensued came the North Atlantic Treaty, signed in Washington on April 4, 1949, by representatives of the United States, Great Britain, France, Italy, the Netherlands, Belgium, Canada, Iceland, Luxembourg, Denmark,

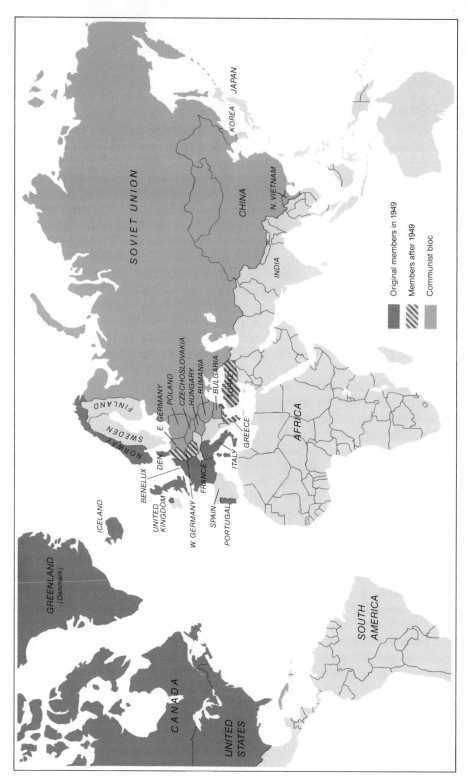

North Atlantic Treaty Organization

Norway, and Portugal. The treaty was later signed by West Germany, Turkey, and Greece. The key article of the treaty declared that an attack upon any one of the signatories would be considered an attack upon all, and would be resisted by all with armed force. Another article looked forward to the creation of joint military forces.

Senate debate on the North Atlantic Treaty was sharp but not prolonged. In the highly charged atmosphere of that time, even those senators who remained doubtful that the United States should involve itself deeply in European affairs were reluctant to join American Communists in opposition to the treaty. The Senate gave its consent to ratification by the bipartisan vote of eighty-two to thirteen on July 21, 1949.

4. THE ELECTION OF 1948 AND THE POLITICS OF REFORM

Republican Gains

Republican hopes of capturing both Congress and the presidency were running higher in early 1948 than at any time since Herbert Hoover's nomination two decades before. Republicans were reasonably well united and believed that they could go to the country with considerable pride in the work of the Eightieth Congress. Even more auspicious auguries of Republican victory appeared in the Democratic camp, where President Truman had come under violent attack on several sides within his own party.

One revolt was brewing in the South. In 1946, Truman had appointed a Committee on Civil Rights, which, the following year, issued an epochal report, *To Secure These Rights*. It called for a systematic campaign—including a permanent FEPC and antipoll tax and antilynching legislation—to root out racial discrimination. Such legislation had no chance of passage at the time, but many Southerners were outraged when Truman urged Congress to implement the committee's recommendations.

Another revolt against Truman brewed in the left wing of the Democratic party. Truman's measures to rally the western world against the Soviet Union and his dismissal in 1946 of Secretary of Commerce Henry A. Wallace, had alienated this faction. Wallace, now the leader of the left-wing faction of the Democratic party, had warned that Truman's policies could lead to another war and had advocated friendship and collaboration with the USSR.

With prospects for victory so alluring, many Republican candidates clamored for the presidential nomination. Senator Robert A. Taft, former Governor Harold E. Stassen of Minnesota, Governor Earl Warren of California, and Governor Dewey were all eager for the honor. Considerable sentiment existed for drafting General Eisenhower, but he refused to be a candidate. The Republican national convention of 1948 nominated Dewey on the third ballot. Its platform endorsed most of the New Deal and the bipartisan foreign policy but promised that the Republicans would run the government more efficiently. Warren was named as Dewey's running mate.

Democratic Infighting

Democrats remained in deep gloom all through the spring of 1948. Party leaders tried, unsuccessfully, to persuade Truman to withdraw and General Eisenhower or Justice William O. Douglas to accept the Democratic nomination. Big-city bosses felt certain that the party would fail with Truman, and public opinion polls gave them grounds for pessimism. But Truman insisted on running. The Democratic convention could find no alternative but to nominate the incumbent and his choice for the vice-presidency, Senator Alben W. Barkley of Kentucky. After a bitter floor fight, a coalition of northern liberals and urban bosses drove through a strong civil rights plank which demanded a permanent FEPC and federal legislation against lynching and poll taxes.

Upon the adoption of the civil rights plank, thirty-five members of the Mississippi and Alabama delegations, waving the battle flag of the Confederacy, marched out of the hall. Delegates from thirteen southern states held their own convention at Birmingham on July 17 and organized the States' Rights Democratic party. The so-called Dixiecrats waved Confederate battle flags, sang "Dixie," and nominated Governor J. Strom Thurmond of South Carolina and Governor Fielding Wright of Mississippi for the presidency and vice-presidency. The Dixiecrats did not, of course, expect to win the presidency, but they did hope to win enough southern states to throw the election into the House of Representatives. They then hoped to strike a bargain with the Republicans.

Only five days after the eruption of the southern revolt in Birmingham, the Democratic left wing met in Philadelphia and organized the Progressive party. The convention nominated Wallace and Senator Glen Taylor of Idaho on a platform which demanded further New Deal social reforms, gradual nationalization of certain basic industries, and a policy of friendship with the Soviet Union. Communists appeared well represented in the new party and may have gained a large measure of control of the organization before the campaign was over. In any event, Wallace permitted Communist party members and fellow travelers* of note, such as the great black singer and actor Paul Robeson, to take a prominent part in his campaign.

The Election of 1948

Public opinion polls all predicted a sweeping Republican victory, and Governor Dewey conducted a leisurely campaign while he made plans for his inauguration and new administration. Truman was undaunted and acted as if he had not heard about his impending defeat. He set out upon a whirlwind, whistle-stop campaign by railroad in which he gave 351 speeches to an estimated 12,000,000 people. Truman appealed to the loyalties of the New Deal coalition. He also acted on the advice of Clark Clifford, a shrewd observer and liberal attorney, and concentrated on the large metropolitan areas. He blamed bad agricultural conditions on Congress which, dominated by Republicans, had rejected his farm program. Overall, he stressed the continuity between his programs and the New Deal, a theme which Clifford insisted would win him the votes of those who had supported Roosevelt. Truman also called Congress into special session and urged it to carry out at

*A person who was not an avowed member of the Communist party but who usually supported its policies and the Soviet Union.

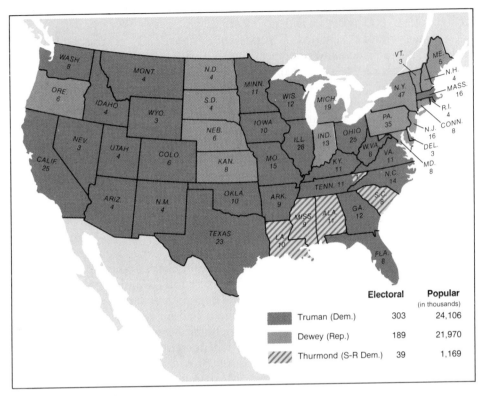

	Electoral	Popular (in thousands)
Truman (Dem.)	303	24,106
Dewey (Rep.)	189	21,970
Thurmond (S-R Dem.)	39	1,169

The Election of 1948

least the Republican platform by adopting civil-rights and other progressive legislation. When it did not, Truman castigated the Republican Eightieth Congress before audiences of workers and farmers as a "do-nothing Congress." Soon these crowds began shouting: "Pour it on, Harry!" and "Give 'em Hell, Harry!"

Election day, November 2, 1948, found Truman still fighting and all pollsters and commentators agreeing that Dewey would win by a landslide. The outcome seemed so certain that the Chicago *Tribune* ran large headlines which hailed Dewey as the next President. In the most surprising upset in American political history, Truman won 24,106,000 popular and 303 electoral votes, to 21,969,000 popular and 189 electoral votes for Dewey. The Democratic tide also carried into office a Congress with substantial Democratic majorities in both houses.

In retrospect, Truman's victory does not seem so surprising as it did in 1948. The revolts of the Dixiecrats and of the left wing actually benefited rather than hurt the Democrats. The southern rebellion convinced blacks that southern segregationists did not dominate the Democratic party. The left insurgency mocked the Republicans' charge that the Truman administration was "soft" on communism. Most important, neither the Dixiecrats nor the Progressive party amounted to much. Thurmond polled only 1,169,000 popular and thirty-nine electoral votes, mostly in areas of the Deep South which had a large (and disfranchised) black population. Wallace meanwhile received 1,156,000 popular and no electoral votes.

Truman's victory revealed a persistence, above all, of the New Deal coalition. By their demand for repeal of the Taft-Hartley Act, the Democrats received the aggressive support of organized labor. They also gained midwestern farm support by coming out for retention of price supports at 90 per cent of parity, while the Republicans talked only about "flexible" price supports. Finally, the country was at peace and prosperous as never before. In such circumstances, the voters do not usually turn out a party in power.

The Fair Deal

Truman interpreted his victory as proof that the American people wanted to intensify the march of domestic reform. He outlined his program, which he called the Fair Deal, in his inaugural address of January 20, 1949, and in later messages to Congress.

During the next two years, before the attention of the country was diverted by a war in the Far East and other problems of foreign policy, Truman won adoption of some Fair Deal measures. They included an increase in the minimum wage from 40 to 75 cents an hour and an extension of the Social Security system to 10,000,000 new beneficiaries, with large increases in benefits to retired workers. In addition, federal rent controls were extended until March 31, 1951, while a Housing Act provided for the construction of 810,000 units for low-income families. Most important was the Agricultural Act of 1949, which set agricultural price supports at 90 per cent of parity through 1950.

Truman could have achieved substantial modification of the Taft-Hartley Act, but he threw away his chances when he refused to accept anything less than outright repeal of the law. Truman's other Fair Deal legislation—in civil rights, national health insurance, the St. Lawrence Seaway, and federal aid to education—fell victim to the opposition of powerful special-interest groups. Thus, most of what Truman obtained constituted an expansion of New Deal programs. Nevertheless, Truman used his independent executive power to promote the cause of civil rights. He strengthened the Civil Rights Division of the Justice Department, began the abolition of segregation in the federal civil service and the armed forces, and appointed a number of blacks to high offices.

5. ASIA AND THE COLD WAR AT HOME

Partisanship Resumes

The nation divided into warring camps from 1949 to 1952, as a second Red Scare spread throughout the United States. Although the division was not altogether a partisan one, leading Republicans, including Senator Taft, attempted to reap political benefit from it by attacking the patriotism and even the loyalty of the Truman administration, and of the Democratic party in general. In the process, the Republicans shattered bipartisanship in foreign policy and almost destroyed the mutual confidence necessary for the successful functioning of the two-party system.

The Fall of Nationalist China

American confidence in the peace of the postwar world was shaken anew by the collapse of Nationalist China in 1949. During the postwar period, the United States increasingly moved closer to Chiang Kai-shek's Nationalist regime. It extended military aid to the Nationalist government immediately after the Japanese surrender, and American airplanes transported Nationalist troops into the provinces surrendered by the Japanese. Chiang faced awesome problems of inflation, political corruption, poverty, and disorganization. His most serious problem, however, was the threat from a large and well-disciplined group of Chinese Communists led by Mao Tse-tung in the northwestern provinces, who enjoyed the support of the mass of peasants and workers. Civil war between the Nationalists and Communists had simmered off and on since 1928. It broke out full-scale in late 1945. Truman sent General Marshall to mediate the civil war and to persuade Chiang and Mao to form a unified government—one in which the Communists would occupy a subordinate position. Marshall tried hard but failed. When he returned to the United States in early 1947, Marshall reported that he could do no more to prevent the renewal of the Chinese civil war. He blamed both the Communists and Chiang's government; both sides believed that they would win control of the whole country.

War broke out again soon after Marshall's departure from China. The Nationalists enjoyed an initial advantage in manpower and supplies, but they soon collapsed under the assault of the better-disciplined and more determined Communist troops. By the summer of 1947, it was obvious that nothing less than full-scale American military participation in a Chinese land war would turn the tide in favor of the Nationalists; given the determination of the Communists, even full-scale American support of Chiang would probably have been futile. The Truman administration concluded that the American people would never approve participation in a Chinese civil war, and that such participation would be extremely foolish in any event. It therefore did not intervene directly while the Chinese Communist armies overran China and drove Chiang and his government to Taiwan in October 1949. Moreover, in January 1950, Truman made it clear that the United States would not fight to prevent a Communist seizure of Taiwan. A week later, the new Secretary of State, Dean Acheson, announced that the United States would defend Japan and the Philippines, but would not attempt to protect Korea, Taiwan, and southeastern Asia from Communist revolution or attacks.

The Second Red Scare

The fall of China occurred at a time when the American people were already in shock over revelations of Communist subversion at home. In 1946, a Canadian Royal Commission had reported the existence of a far-flung Soviet spy ring which had been engaged in stealing and sending atomic secrets to Moscow. The report was so sensational that it set off an intense security drive in the United States. On March 22, 1947, Truman issued an executive order which directed the FBI and the Civil Service Commission to investigate the loyalty of all federal employees. Within the next four years, 3,000,000 employees were cleared, about 2,000 resigned, and 212 were dismissed because they were considered bad security risks. The investigation was not only thoroughgoing, but also completely successful in its objectives. After the Republicans came to power in 1953, numerous investigations by various congressional committees, the Justice Department, and security officials turned up only one Communist in the government, and that one in a subordinate job in the Government Printing Office.

The catalyst of the nationwide alarm was a series of dramatic cases which revealed that, prior to 1947, Communist agents had infiltrated the Anglo-American team that developed the atomic bomb. This led to the trial and conviction of three American Communist couriers, two of whom—Julius and Ethel Rosenberg—were executed in 1953. The FBI and various other branches of government, evidence revealed, had been infiltrated as well. The most publicized of these cases involved Alger Hiss, who had held a position of trust in the State Department and was president of the Carnegie Endowment for International Peace. In 1948, Whittaker Chambers, a former Soviet courier, accused Hiss of having furnished him with valuable classified documents which Communist agents had photographed. Hiss denied the charges under oath, and character witnesses in his defense included some of the highest officers in the government. His indictment and trial, and his conviction on charges of perjury on January 21, 1950, shocked the nation.

Some Republicans charged—many of them for political purposes—that the federal government was honeycombed with Communists. More particularly, the Republicans linked so-called infiltration in the State Department and the Foreign Service with Chiang's defeat. The foremost and most extreme exponent of the Republican strategy was Senator Joseph R. McCarthy of Wisconsin, who took up the anti-Communist cause less than a month after Hiss' conviction. McCarthy made headlines throughout the country by announcing, in a speech on February 9, 1950, that he held in his hand a list with the names of 205 card-carrying Communists in the State Department. When the validity of his charges became dubious, McCarthy attacked a number of American political leaders, among them General Marshall, whom McCarthy called the leading American traitor. As chairman of a Senate investigation committee in 1953–1954, McCarthy hounded and bullied federal employees and a wide variety of other individuals but discovered only one Communist in an insignificant job. The Wisconsin demagogue went too far, however, when he turned his bitter attacks against members of the Eisenhower administration, which had come into power in 1953, and even against Eisenhower himself. For his reckless, abusive actions, and even more for his political error in attacking Republican as well as Democratic officials, the Senate censured McCarthy in 1954 by a vote of sixty-six to twenty-two. Before the senator's death in 1957, the term "McCarthyism" had become firmly established in the American vocabulary as a synonym for demagoguery, intentionally false accusations, and other loathsome political practices.

Meanwhile, the Truman administration (to say nothing of part of the public) had been swept along to some degree in the anti-Communist hysteria. In 1948, eleven Communist leaders were indicted, tried, and sentenced to prison under the Smith Act of 1940 for conspiracy to *teach* the violent overthrow of the government. The Supreme Court, on June 4, 1951, in Dennis et al. *v.* the United States upheld the constitutionality of the Smith Act—and the conviction of the Communist leaders—by invoking the clear-and-present-danger doctrine of the Schenck case of 1919 (see pg. 90). Nearly 100 state and regional Communist leaders were tried, convicted, and imprisoned under the Smith Act for allegedly *advocating* the violent overthrow of the government, not for any criminal acts.

Congress reflected the panic of the Second Red Scare much more sensitively than the executive branch. The chief contribution of the legislative branch to the drive against communism was the McCarran Internal Security Act of 1950. It required Communist organizations to register with the Attorney General and to furnish membership lists and financial statements. Membership in the Communist party was not made a crime, but the employment of Communists in defense plants was forbidden. A provision of the McCarran Act, which forbade former members of totalitarian organizations to enter the country, was opposed by the Department of Justice and the Central Intelligence Agency because it removed incentives for Communist agents to renounce their party and seek refuge in the United States. Truman vetoed the bill on this and other grounds, but Congress adopted it over his veto. Congressional eagerness to be seen by voters as striking at communism was reflected also in the McCarran-Walter Immigration and Nationality bill of 1952, also passed over Truman's veto. It rectified an old injustice by permitting the annual admission of some 2,000 Orientals on a quota basis, but its provisions for the exclusion and deportation of aliens from southern and eastern Europe, and those with "wrong" political views, were very severe.

War in Korea

The explosion of war in Korea in June 1950 drew the United States into the far eastern vortex in spite of the administration's desire to remain uninvolved. Korea had been annexed by Japan in 1910 and surrendered by her to the Allies in 1945. Russian troops penetrated as far as a line drawn across the Korean peninsula at 38° northern latitude, while American troops occupied the area south of that line. It was assumed, of course, that Korea would not only be united but would also be free of foreign domination. In fact, the UN held elections in South Korea in 1947, but a Communist government in the North refused either to participate or to permit UN personnel to enter its territory.

In 1948, the Republic of Korea was established in the south with a dictator, Syngman Rhee, as President. The UN General Assembly, the United States, and thirty other UN members recognized the new regime; the United States then withdrew its troops from Korea. Just a year later, on June 25, 1950, an army from North Korea invaded the Republic of Korea without warning. The move had been approved by the Soviet Union.

News of the invasion reached Truman at Independence, Missouri, on the evening of June 24. Truman rushed back to Washington and instructed Secretary of State Acheson to bring the issue before an emergency meeting of the UN Security Council. The Russians had walked out of the Council six months earlier, after it had refused to seat a delegate from the Communist People's Republic of China. Free of the Russian veto, the Council lost no time

**The Korean War,
1950-1953**

in adopting, by a vote of nine to nothing, a resolution which condemned the invasion as aggression and demanded the immediate withdrawal of North Korean troops from South Korea.

Meanwhile, Truman met with his civilian and military advisers and ordered the Seventh Fleet to protect Taiwan. General MacArthur (still in Japan as Supreme Allied Commander) was to furnish arms and air and naval support to the South Koreans. Truman called Democratic and Republican congressional leaders to the White House and informed them of his determination to stop the North Korean aggression. Not only were they heartily in accord, but members of the House of Representatives stood and cheered when they heard the news of Truman's action. Nonetheless, Truman had established an important precedent of a "police action"—that is, waging war without a formal congressional delcaration of war.

The Security Council, on June 27, called on all members of the UN to assist the Republic of Korea in every way possible. It also established a United Nations Command and invited the United States Government to name a Supreme Commander of UN forces. Truman nominated General MacArthur. Although nineteen nations eventually sent troops to fight under the UN flag, in June 1950, only two divisions of American occupation troops in Japan were ready for combat. These were rushed to Korea, where they fought a brilliant delaying action against overwhelming odds. The troops were hard pressed for a time to defend their last foothold on the peninsula at the port of Pusan, but the tide turned on September 15, 1950, when MacArthur's forces made a daring flank attack by sea at Inchon. MacArthur then captured Seoul, and UN forces reached the thirty-eighth parallel on about October 1.

On October 3, the foreign minister of the Chinese People's Republic told the Indian Ambassador in Peking that, if United States or UN forces crossed the thirty-eighth parallel, China would send troops across the Korean frontier to defend North Korea. Few leaders in the West took the warning seriously. The UN General Assembly, on October 7, called on MacArthur to take all steps necessary to establish the control of the UN over *all* of Korea. MacArthur himself informed Truman on October 15 that his intelligence organization had found little danger of Chinese intervention. If the Chinese did intervene, the general promised, they would be slaughtered. The UN forces soon drove the North Koreans toward the Yalu River—the boundary between Korea and Manchuria; on Thanksgiving Day, MacArthur announced a new offensive to push the enemy beyond the Yalu and to conclude the war before Christmas. The general unknowingly drove his troops into a huge trap set by about 1,000,000 Chinese troops already in North Korea. It required several weeks of desperate fighting and severe casualties before the retreating American forces could extricate themselves and stabilize a defensive line along the thirty-eighth parallel.

As General MacArthur put it, UN forces now found themselves in "an entirely new war." He urged that the United States blockade the Chinese coast, bomb the Chinese mainland, use atomic bombs if necessary, and help Chiang Kai-shek to invade China from Taiwan. The Joint Chiefs of Staff in Washington refused to heed his advice. To General Omar N. Bradley, chairman of the Joint Chiefs, a war with China would be "the wrong war, at the wrong place, at the wrong time, and with the wrong enemy." No one knew what the immediate future would bring, but the dangers appeared clear enough. There was the danger, first, that the Soviet Union would come to the aid of its Chinese ally, for the two nations had signed a mutual defense alliance in early 1950. There was also the danger that the Soviets would turn against western Europe while American forces were preoccupied in the Far East.

Europe or Asia?

Congress was, at this very time, in the midst of a heated debate over whether American troops should be sent to bolster the defenses of Europe. United States forces were asked to participate in a North Atlantic Treaty Organization (NATO) combined army, created in 1950, with General Eisenhower as supreme commander in Paris. The debate over Truman's recommendation of United States participation broke out with considerable rancor in Congress on January 8, 1951. Senator Kenneth Wherry, Republican of Nebraska, offered a resolution to the effect that no ground forces be sent to Europe until Congress had rendered a decision on the matter.

It seemed for a moment that the administration had lost control of foreign policy to its opponents in Congress led by Senator Taft. These men, most of them midwestern and western Republicans, were not isolationists, for they demanded an all-out military effort against communism in the Far East, but they were prepared to choose Asia over Europe if the choice had to be made. General Eisenhower rushed to Washington from Paris to plead against the abandonment of Europe. On April 4, 1951, the Senate adopted a resolution which approved the dispatch of four divisions to support American commitments to NATO, but the Senate warned Truman not to send additional troops without further congressional approval.

Truman and MacArthur

Meanwhile, the Truman administration had decided to limit military operations in the Far East. The Chiefs of Staff, in January 1951, ordered MacArthur and General Matthew B. Ridgway, commander of the American Eighth Army in Korea, to limit their activities to the defense of the Republic of Korea and to avoid a general war with China. MacArthur and Ridgway were to meet Communist attacks against their entrenched positions along the thirty-eighth parallel with a fire so deadly as "to break down not only the morale but the trained fabric of the Chinese armies." This is precisely what the American-UN armies under the successive commands of Generals Ridgway, Mark Clark, and James A. Van Fleet proceeded to do. Communist Korean and Chinese casualties rose to more than 1,000,000.

MacArthur was in fundamental disagreement with this defensive strategy. In a letter to Representative Joseph W. Martin, Republican minority leader in the House of Representatives, MacArthur called for a victory offensive against China. "We must win," the general wrote. "There is no substitute for victory." MacArthur's letter, read to the House by Martin on April 5, 1951, was a direct challenge to the administration's foreign policy, and the Republicans made the most of it. Truman replied at once by relieving MacArthur of his command. "I could do nothing else and still be President of the United States," Truman wrote on April 10. "Even the Chiefs of Staff came to the conclusion that civilian control of the military was at stake, and I didn't let it stay at stake very long."

Truman's act was both courageous and necessary, but it set off wild excitement and demands for his impeachment. MacArthur returned home, greeted by triumphal tours and an equally triumphant welcome before a joint session of Congress. The Senate Armed Services Committee then began a long investigation of recent far eastern policies and MacArthur's recall, in which even MacArthur was obliged to admit that he knew nothing of the government's global strategy beyond the local situation in Korea. Moreover, the Joint Chiefs of Staff had unanimously advised Truman not to begin an offensive war against China and, once civilian control of the military was at stake, it also advocated the dismissal of MacArthur. After considerable testimony, the committee vindicated the administration and discredited MacArthur.

The Militarization of the United States

The most important result of the Korean War was the militarization of the United States and a vast extension of its military and security commitments around the world, while the expenditures of the United States for defense, at home and abroad, increased from $15 billion in 1950 to about $40 billion in 1960.

The basis on which the Truman administration set out upon this arms buildup was a document known as National Security Council Paper No. 68, prepared under the guidance of Paul Nitze, head of the Policy Planning Staff of the State Department in January 1950. The report said that Soviet-led worldwide communism was a dire threat to the United States and to free governments everywhere. Worse still, the Soviet Union, which had detonated its own atomic bomb in 1949, was "developing the military capacity to support its design for world domination." To counter the Soviet threat, the report recommended a quick and massive increase in the military resources of the United States and her allies.

The outbreak of the Korean War convinced Truman that the report's assumptions and recommendations were sound, and he approved the report in September 1950. Four divisions were sent to General Eisenhower, while military supplies in ever-growing volume flowed from the United States to the NATO countries. The United States also constructed a system of air bases in Great Britain, France, Italy, North Africa, and Turkey within easy striking distance of strategic Soviet centers. As we will see, the Truman and Eisenhower administrations extended the military-security commitments of the United States on a global basis. Meanwhile, as Eisenhower noted in 1961, a "military-industrial complex" had created "a permanent armaments industry of vast proportions." By the time that Eisenhower spoke, the government's defense establishment employed 3,500,000 persons.

The Cold War in the Pacific

While it fought a limited war in Korea, the Truman administration also constructed a system of security pacts in the Pacific area comparable, at least in terminology, to those in the North Atlantic. A mutual defense treaty between the United States and the Philippines was concluded on August 30, 1951. Two days later, Australia, New Zealand, and the United States signed the Tripartite Security Treaty known as the ANZUS Pact.

A few days later—on September 8—Japan and forty-eight of her former enemies concluded a peace treaty in San Francisco. It was largely the work of John Foster Dulles, Republican adviser to the State Department, and it seemed a generous settlement. Japan was required to relinquish her overseas empire, but the treaty contained no provisions for punitive reparations or economic restrictions, and it restored full sovereignty to the Japanese people. On the same day, the United States concluded a security treaty with Japan which granted the American government the right to maintain land, sea, and air bases there. Thus the former enemy of the United States became the cornerstone of the security system in the Far East under which Japanese security became part of the American defense system.

6. THE EMERGENCE OF DWIGHT D. EISENHOWER

Republicans and the Struggle for Leadership

Republican hopes for victory in the coming presidential campaign increased in the early months of 1952. McCarthy's unceasing attacks had raised grave doubts in wide quarters about the ability of the Truman administration to protect the country from internal subversion. Vastly exaggerated charges of corruption in Washington aroused further doubts. A jump in wholesale prices of 13 per cent between 1950 and 1952—largely war-induced inflation—hurt many persons who lived on fixed incomes or on Social Security. Finally, although peace talks had been going on since the summer of 1951, many Americans were frustrated by the Korean War, which continued intermittently without any end in sight.

The Republicans, while hopeful, were also bitterly divided. The more conservative and isolationist (or Asia-first) wing, with strong support in the Middle West, was determined to end what Senator Taft called Dewey's "metooism." Taft proposed to give the American people a clear-cut alternative to the New Deal and Fair Deal, although he never made it clear how far he would go in dismantling the reform structure created by the Roosevelt and Truman administrations. Standing in opposition to Taft and his forces were Senator Henry Cabot Lodge, Jr., of Massachusetts (grandson of Woodrow Wilson's foe), Governor Dewey, Governor Warren, and others. They accepted the New Deal and Fair Deal and considered NATO to be the cornerstone of American foreign policy.

Taft swept the Middle West and South so completely during the early stages of the Republican preconvention campaign that he seemed irresistible. Without a strong candidate to head off Taft, the Republican moderates and Europe-firsters felt hopeless. But their despair turned into elation when General Eisenhower agreed to accept the Republican presidential nomination —mainly, he said, to defeat Taft. The battle was fully joined when Eisenhower resigned his NATO command and returned home in June to fight for the nomination.

Eisenhower almost made his decision too late, for the Taft forces seemed to dominate the Republican national convention which opened in Chicago on July 7, 1952. But the overconfident Taft managers made the error—inconceivable from this distance—of permitting the seating of most of the Eisenhower delegates in contested delegations from Texas, Georgia, and Louisiana. These delegates provided a bare majority for Eisenhower on the first ballot. For his running mate, Eisenhower chose young Senator Richard M. Nixon of California, who had established a national reputation as an anti-Communist by leading the congressional fight to expose Hiss and by conducting a vigorous red-baiting senatorial campaign against Helen Gahagan Douglas, a liberal Democrat from California. The Republican platform promised maintenance of basic New Deal-Fair Deal programs at home and a dynamic new foreign policy abroad.

The Campaign of 1952

Assembled in national convention in Chicago on July 21, the Democrats were badly split between southern opponents of civil-rights legislation and the progressive-labor forces from the large cities. Before the convention met, Vice-President Barkley and Senator Estes Kefauver of Tennessee appeared to hold the lead among the major contenders for the presidential nomination. But Barkley withdrew after leaders of the AFL and CIO decided that he was too old to run. Truman and the party leaders then drafted Governor Adlai E. Stevenson of Illinois, who received the nomination on the third ballot. Stevenson chose Senator John J. Sparkman of Alabama as his running mate.

The campaign which followed was more exciting than any presidential contest that the country had seen since Franklin D. Roosevelt began to dominate American national politics. Stevenson easily ranked as one of the most eloquent American politicians of the twentieth century. In a series of addresses, the Illinois governor attempted to educate the people for their responsibilities in the complex mid-twentieth-century world. While Stevenson made few original suggestions, he did promise to extend the New Deal and the Fair Deal. He also spoke of increasingly complicated world problems with which the United States would have to deal. Stevenson promised no easy solutions and warned that the struggles ahead would be dangerous and difficult.

Eisenhower's campaign was very different. It was, to begin with, much more adept. Eisenhower, endowed with immense magnetism, went before the country like a conquering hero. He called on Americans to join him in a crusade and promised to clean up what he referred to as the "mess" in Washington. Eisenhower conciliated conservatives by placating Taft. The general promised to stop "creeping socialism," but he did not specify which of the New Deal-Fair Deal programs he would repeal or curtail. Eisenhower also stood aside while McCarthy carried on a vicious personal campaign against Stevenson. Eisenhower even remained silent while McCarthy attacked the loyalty of General Marshall—the man most responsible for raising Eisenhower to his high command during the Second World War—and actually deleted a passage in one speech which praised Marshall in order to avoid offending McCarthy and his supporters. Eisenhower's most effective stroke was a promise, made in Detroit on October 24, that he would go to Korea in person and bring the Korean War to "an early and honorable end."

More than 61,000,000 Americans went to the polls on election day and swept Eisenhower to victory. He carried thirty-nine states, including four in the South, and amassed a total of 33,824,000 popular and 442 electoral votes. Stevenson polled 26,584,000 popular and eighty-nine electoral votes. Yet, Eisenhower's victory was no sweeping mandate for the Republicans. It was instead an endorsement of America's most popular wartime hero and a vote of impatience with the deadlocked Korean War. Despite Eisenhower's impressive popular majority, the Republicans won control of Congress by the margin of one vote in the Senate and eight in the House of Representatives.

SUGGESTED READINGS

Eric F. Goldman, *The Crucial Decade, and After* (1960), is a casual survey relevant to this and the following two chapters. For the Truman administration, see Cabell Phillips, *The Truman Presidency* (1966); Alonzo L. Hamby, *Beyond the New Deal: Harry S. Truman and American Liberalism* (1973), a sympathetic account; and Robert J. Donovan, *Conflict and Crisis: The Presidency of Harry S. Truman* (1977), *The Presidency of Harry S. Truman, 1949–1953* (1982), and Bert Cochran, *Harry Truman and the Crisis Presidency* (1973), which are more critical. For a radical critique, see Barton J. Bernstein and A. J. Matusow, eds., *The Truman Administration: A Documentary History* (1966). For biographical information on Truman, see Jonathan Daniels, *The Man from Independence* (1950), and *Memoirs by Harry S. Truman*, 2 vols. (1955-1956). Truman's political origins are discussed in Lyle W. Dorsett, *The Pendergast Machine* (1968).

Most of the works cited on diplomacy in the preceding chapter are relevant to the origins of the Cold War. These should be supplemented by John L. Gaddis, *The United States and the Origins of the Cold War, 1941–1947* (1972), and *Russia, the Soviet Union, and the United States* (1978); Walter LaFeber, *America, Russia, and the Cold War, 1945–1966* (1967); Herbert Feis, *Contest over Japan* (1967) and *From Trust to Terror: The Onset of the Cold War* (1970); Daniel Yergin, *Shattered Peace: The Origins of the Cold War and the National Security State* (1977); Lisle A. Rose, *Roots of Tragedy: The United States and the Struggle for Asia, 1945–1953* (1976); Thomas G. Patterson, *Soviet-American Confrontation: Postwar Reconstruction and the Origins of the Cold War* (1974); William H. McNeill, *America, Britain, and Russia: Their Cooperation and Conflict, 1941–1946* (1953); Martin F. Herz, *The Beginnings of the Cold War* (1966); and Paul Seabury, *The Rise and Decline of the Cold War* (1967). Gar Alperowitz, *Atomic Diplomacy: Hiroshima and Potsdam* (1965), a New Left analysis, has been subjected to sharp scrutiny and criticism. On this matter, also see the books by Jungk, Davis, and Sherwin cited in the Suggested Readings for the preceding chapter. An interesting survey is George F. Kennan, *American Diplomacy*, already cited. The Truman Doctrine and the Marshall Plan are discussed in Joseph Jones, *The Fifteen Weeks* (1955). Other important memoirs and personal accounts include Dean Acheson, *The Pattern of Responsibility* (1952) and *Present at the Creation* (1969); Walter Millis, ed., *The Forrestal Diaries* (1951); Arthur H.

Vandenberg, Jr., ed., *The Private Papers of Senator Vandenberg* (1952); and Robert A. Taft, *A Foreign Policy for Americans* (1951).

The American occupations can be studied in Lucius C. Clay, *Decision in Germany* (1950); Jean Smith, *The Defense of Berlin* (1963); Edwin O. Reischauer, *The United States and Japan* (1957); and William J. Sebald, *With MacArthur in Japan* (1965). Further American involvement in Asia is surveyed in John K. Fairbank, *The United States and China* (1958), and Ellen Hammer, *The Struggle for Indochina* (1954).

Trygve Lie, *In the Cause of Peace* (1954), and J. G. Stoessinger, *The United Nations and the Superpowers* (1965), adequately cover the early years of that organization.

T. R. Fehrenbach, *This Kind of War: A Study in Unpreparedness* (1963); Carl Berger, *The Korea Knot: A Military-Political History* (1957); David Rees, *Korea: The Limited War* (1964); and Malcolm W. Cagle and F. A. Manson, *The Sea War in Korea* (1957), are the best general surveys. The best account of the Truman-MacArthur conflict is John W. Spanier, *The Truman-MacArthur Controversy and the Korean War* (1959). Richard H. Rovere and Arthur M. Schlesinger, Jr., *The general and the President* (1951), is another reasonably balanced analysis. Trumbull Higgins, *Korea and the Fall of MacArthur* (1960), is a military history hostile to the general; William Manchester, *American Caesar*, cited earlier, presents a favorable portrait and at times ignores MacArthur's mistakes.

An analysis of general political tendencies can be found in Lubell, *The Future of American Politics*, cited earlier. C. Vann Woodward, *The Strange Career of Jim Crow*, 3rd rev. ed. (1974), and Arnold M. Rose, *The Negro in Postwar America* (1950), are good on the growing concern for black rights. Some of the better special studies of Truman's domestic policies are William C. Berman, *The Politics of Civil Rights in the Truman Administration* (1971); Allen Yarnell, *Democrats and Progressives* (1974); Edward S. Flash, Jr., *Economic Advice and Presidential Leadership* (1965); Richard Davies, *Housing Reform during the Truman Administration* (1966); and R. Alton Lee, *Truman and Taft-Hartley* (1967). Jules Abels, *Out of the Jaws of Victory* (1959), and Irwin Ross, *The Loneliest Campaign: The Truman Victory of 1948* (1968), are good on the election of 1948. There is no satisfactory analysis of the election of 1952, but the interested student will find useful information in Kenneth S. Davis' *The Politics of Honor: A Biography of Adlai E. Stevenson* (1967), and particularly in John Bartlow Martin, *Adlai Stevenson of Illinois* (1976) and

Adlai Stevenson and the World (1977).
James T. Patterson, *Mr. Republican: A Biography of Robert A. Taft* (1972), is indispensable for Republican politics during this period.

Edward A. Shils, *The Torment of Secrecy* (1956), is a good analysis of the growth of wild fears about national security. The danger to civil liberties posed by this attitude is the subject of Francis Biddle, *The Fear of Freedom* (1951), and Sidney Gook, *Heresy, Yes—Conspiracy, No* (1953). On this topic see also Richard M. Freeland, *The Truman Doctrine* and the Origins of McCarthyism (1972); Earl Latham, *The Communist Controversy in Washington: From the New Deal to McCarthy* (1966); Allen P. Harper, *The Politics of Loyalty* (1969); Robert Griffith, *The Politics of Fear* (1970); and Edwin R. Bayley, *Joe McCarthy and the Press* (1981). Allen Weinstein, *Perjury! The Hiss-Chambers Conflict* (1977), makes a persuasive case for Hiss' guilt, as does the earlier Alistair Cooke, *A Generation on Trial* (1950).

CHAPTER 13
THE AFFLUENT SOCIETY, 1945 – 1982

1. SOCIAL CHANGE IN THE POSTWAR ERA

Demographic Changes

The most important demographic change of the postwar period was the rapid growth in the birthrate. During the 1920s and 1930s, demographic patterns in the United States suggested that the nation faced a long-term decline in the birthrate. The national birthrate had earlier declined sharply, from 23.7 births per 1,000 in 1920 to a low of 16.6 per 1,000 thirteen years later. By the mid-1930s, indeed, experts were predicting that the American population would increase at a slow rate until the 1950s and then level off and perhaps even decline during the next two decades. The Census of 1940 appeared to support their projections, for the population increase of 7.2 per cent of the 1930s was by far the smallest proportionate increase in American history.

Yet, by the end of the 1930s, this picture had begun to change radically. The birthrate increased after 1939, and, although it declined slightly at the end of the Second World War, it soared on the return of veterans during 1945 and 1946. Americans began to have large families of three or four children more frequently than they did during the 1930s, for the marriage rate actually declined from 12.2 per 1,000 in 1945 to 9.3 in 1955. Nonetheless, Americans in the postwar generation were having children at a rate which approximated the same high rate of their grandparents. Between 1940 and 1950, the population of the United States registered an increase of 14.5 per cent, and in the fifteen years after 1950, it rose by another 28 per cent. Most of this increase occurred without a deluge of immigrants. Although immigration did increase from 1,035,000 in the 1940s to 2,516,000 in the 1950s, most of the population increase—about 20,000,000 in the 1940s and 28,000,000 in the 1950s—was the result of a "baby boom." By the end of the 1950s, one person was being added to the nation's population every twelve seconds.

This rapid expansion in births began to fall off in the 1960s. By 1965, it had declined to 19.4 births per 1,000 people, a rate equal to that of 1940. The absolute decline continued apace during the late 1960s and 1970s: from a rate of 18.4 in 1970, it dropped to a rate of 15.3 in 1977. Much of this drop was the result of a decline in the average family size of American households. Marriage rates between 1955 and 1977 actually *increased,* from 9.3 per 1,000 in 1955 to 10.1 per 1,000 in 1977. At the same time, the fertility rate of American couples declined substantially—from an increase of 21.1 per cent from 1955 to 1959 to a *decline* of 6.7 per cent in 1976.

The end of the "baby boom" had many causes. The increasing availability of contraceptives, particularly the "pill," and abortions made it possible for Americans to enjoy sex without procreation. In 1976, about 69 per cent of whites and 58 per cent of blacks used contraceptives. In 1974, 19.6 legal abortions per 1,000 women occurred; two years later, it had increased to 24.5 per 1,000. An even more subtle influence in the decline of the birthrate was the transformation in attitudes toward childbearing, marriage, and the family. With the increasing entry of women into the work force and with the increasing cost of child rearing, family size declined precipitately during the 1960s and 1970s.

The Transformation of the Family

The end of the "baby boom" during the late 1960s was part of a larger development—the transformation of the American family. Even while the rate of the marriages actually increased (if slightly), the nature of marriage changed significantly. The number of adults living by themselves increased by seven times between 1970 and 1977. At the same time, between 1970 and 1980, the number of unmarried people living together trebled from 523,000 to 1,500,000.

The most striking evidence of the overall fragmentation of the family was the growing incidence of divorce during the 1960s, and especially during the 1970s. In 1970, there were 47 divorced people per 1,000 married people; that figure had more than doubled to 100 divorced people per 1,000 married people by 1980. The breakup of many marriages was reflected in the growth of single-parent households between 1960 and 1980, many of which were headed by females. In 1960, for example, about 9.4 per cent of white households and about 27.9 per cent of black households were headed by women; in 1980, 11.9 per cent of white families and 41.7 per cent of black families were headed by women.

The transformation of social and sexual mores also accompanied the general fragmentation of the familial structure. There was, to begin with, a large increase in the incidence of premarital sex, a trend which accelerated during the postwar period. Partly as a result of the increasing availability of contraceptives and partly as a result of the loosening of social strictures against sexual involvement outside of marriage, young Americans of the

1950s, 1960s, and 1970s were more often willing to engage in sex. Two side effects of this transformation were an increase in teen-age illegitimate births—which about doubled between 1950 and 1980—and a large increase in the incidence of venereal diseases.

The Mobile Society

The wholesale growth of the American population after 1945 was accompanied by a tremendous increase in the geographical mobility of Americans. On the average, one out of five Americans moved annually. Several factors explain this increase in mobility. During the postwar period, a large shift occurred away from rural areas and toward metropolitan and suburban areas. Because of the mechanization of American agriculture, the number of dwellers on farms dropped from 23.2 per cent of the total population in 1940 to 6.8 per cent in 1964; by the mid-1970s, that figure had declined to below 4 per cent. Rural depopulation, which accelerated during the 1950s and 1960s, had largely abated in intensity by the 1970s.

The growth of urban areas between 1945 and 1965 is largely the story of the growth of the suburbs. Overall, American urban population grew from 56.5 per cent in 1940 to 70 per cent in 1964, but the rate of increase for suburbs during this period was twice what it was for metropolitan cities. The growth of suburbs was the product of the availability of cheap homes; through equally cheap automobiles and gasoline, suburban residents had access to large metropolitan areas where they often worked. State and federal governments also encouraged the growth of suburbs by the construction of an extensive highway system which linked together metropolitan areas and made access to and from the workplace easy. With suburbs, moreover, came "suburbia"—white and middle class in orientation, highly mobile, and ringed with new shopping malls.

During the 1970s and early 1980s, these trends continued apace, but in a different form. In some inner cities, urban decay was somewhat reversed in districts to which the white middle class returned. In these "gentrified" districts, older structures were renovated or restored; yet, their former black or Hispanic occupants were forced into even shabbier areas of the cities. At the same time, there was a considerable movement during the 1970s and 1980s away from cities to rural areas. This migration—popularly know as the "back-to-the-land movement"—was largely one of younger, generally middle-class whites who found suburban and urban living undesirable. Nonetheless, since these areas were located near urban areas and since the migrants almost invariably were oriented toward the city, this process was actually an extension of the overall twentieth-century trend of urbanization.

Americans moved in increasing numbers across regions in the twenty years after the Second World War. Much of this migration after 1940 was from agricultural to industrial areas. The Pacific Coast states, the Southwest, and the urban South were, for various reasons, the chief gainers. The Pacific states, for example, grew by about 140 per cent from 1940 to 1965. The clearest manifestation, both of the movement from region to region and from countryside to the city, was the shift of blacks from the South to cities outside that region. Although 80 per cent of American blacks resided in the South as late as the middle 1930s, many of them left the region after 1940, when jobs in the defense industry lured them northward. The virtual end of sharecropping also encouraged black immigration; especially after the introduction of the mechanical cotton picker during the 1940s, southern rural blacks found that their means of livelihood no longer existed. By the 1960s, over half of the American blacks lived outside the South, most of them in large urban centers. By the 1970s, however, the northward migration—largely because of the bitter experience which many blacks had had in northern cities—had ended, and, indeed, there was considerable evidence that blacks began to return to the South during the decade of the 1970s.

Other population shifts among Americans helped to diffuse population away from northeastern centers. Many Americans were attracted to warmer climates in Florida and California, the two fastest growing states throughout the postwar period. By 1964, California was the most populous state in the Union, and it claimed fully one tenth of the nation's population in 1970. During the 1970s, California's population increased by 19 per cent, while the population of Florida grew by 44 per cent. The shift to the "Sunbelt" portended even more extensive ramifications for politics.

The Aging of America

The makeup of the American people in the postwar era changed in other more dramatic respects. By the latter half of the twentieth century, largely because of better nutrition and significant advances in the practice of medicine, Americans were living longer. During the 1960s and 1970s, medical science made new progress in drugs, surgical techniques, and preventive medicine. In the 1970s, for example, the incidence of strokes declined substantially, largely because of strides in preventive medicine and the development of new antihypertensive medicines. Moreover, between 1900 and 1960, life expectancy increased by twenty-one years for men and twenty-five years for women.

In part, the advance in the average age of Americans resulted from a decline in infant mortality. But, undeniably, especially after 1945, there were more Americans who lived beyond the age of sixty-five. In 1977, almost 11 per cent of the population of the United States was over sixty-five; as the generation born after 1940 ages in the twenty-first century, the long-term prospect is that that proportion will grow even larger. The strains on welfare agencies and the Social Security system will probably grow acute by the end of this century.

2. AFFLUENCE AND THE POSTWAR ECONOMY

The Postwar Boom, 1945–1965

Few Americans who lived in the years of the Great Depression could have had any conception of the economic growth which occurred after 1945. In fact, recovery came quickly. By 1940, per capita income and the GNP had increased to the levels of 1929—before governmental military spending had had much effect. Although it is common wisdom that the American economy came out of the depression only as a result of the Second World War, these data seem to suggest that the economy was actually on the verge of a vigorous expansion at the beginning of the 1940s. Indeed, the war effort—because of the enormous wastage of materials and the dislocation of the entire economy—probably hindered the beginning of the mid-twentieth century economic boom.

Whatever its causes, the boom between 1945 and 1965 was unparalleled in American history. Brief recessions occurred in 1949, 1954, 1957–1958, and 1960–1961. But each of these declines was mild and did not indicate any serious obstacles to economic growth and expansion. Moreover, there was virtually no inflation, and unemployment remained between 4 and 5 per cent during this period. The GNP (measured in 1954 dollars) increased from $314 billion in 1945 to $570 billion in 1965. Similarly, per capita income before taxes rose from $1,224 to $2,700 during the same period, an increase of about 120 per cent.

The causes of the postwar boom were both numerous and complex. Because of wartime rationing, an enormous pent-up demand existed in 1945 for housing and for all sorts of consumer goods. American consumers, both civilian and military, had accumulated huge savings; and even poorer Americans eagerly awaited the goods promised by American manufacturers at the conclusion of the war. The American economy was also boosted by several long-term factors. The "baby boom" stimulated expansion in consumption and demand, not only for goods, but also for a variety of services. Overall, the American economy experienced great increases in productivity—indeed, the greatest increases in productivity in American history took place during the period 1945–1965—both in agriculture and industry. Between 1947 and 1964, for example, productivity in the entire American economy grew by 70 per cent. Finally, the new industries of the 1920s—electrical appliances, chemicals (especially petrochemicals), and automobiles—grew tremendously, largely because of the ready supply and cheap price of oil and other forms of energy.

The role of government in the postwar economic boom was critical. Military expenditures, especially after the Korean War, remained high. After 1945, military spending remained at close to 10 per cent of the GNP, and, in several key industries, such as automobiles and aeronautics, military spending greatly stimulated development. The benefits of military spending went disproportionately to regions such as the South and the West and to certain states such as California and Texas. Moreover, the military establishment stimulated the development of research science both in industry and in the nation's colleges and universities; by the late 1960s, the federal government paid for about two thirds of the research and development in academic institutions and for about a half in industry.

Nonetheless, some economists have questioned the long-term impact which military spending had on American industry. Military spending during the postwar period resulted in the diversion of resources, both human and material, from domestic consumption to the military sector; and it often resulted, particularly in the case of the Vietnam War, in the outbreak of inflation. Military spending also affected only a few industries and protected them from the discipline of the free market; as a result, enormous waste in cost and resources occurred.

The role of the federal government in the economy grew in many other ways. Federal subsidies to farmers, veterans, and homeowners stimulated growth in agriculture and housing and a variety of other industries. Even more important was federal expenditures on public works projects such as water projects—particularly in the arid western states—and for the new interstate highway system. In June 1956, Congress authorized the expenditure of $33 billion for a 40,000-mile network of superhighways. The construction of the interstate highway system stimulated the expansion of the construction industry as well as the trucking and automobile industries. The federal government was also responsible for subsidizing the expansion of the airline industry through the construction of federally supervised airports across the nation. In all, the government played a critical role in stimulating postwar economic expansion. By the 1960s, governmental spending—federal, state, and local—had risen to a level of 20 per cent of the GNP.

The Structure of Modern American Business

The development of the American economy after 1945 followed the patterns established during the early twentieth century. The most successful mode of industrial organization was the corporate form, and corporations in turn became both more diversified and highly integrated. The managerial revolution—which placed the direction of these corporations in the hands of a salaried cadre of managers—continued and even dominated American industry at the end of the postwar period more extensively than it had in 1930.

Postwar corporate growth followed a similar pattern. After the 1930s, many large firms took advantage of their capital resources and began to diversify their products and markets. Before 1920, for instance, General Electric produced only light generators, but during the 1920s and 1930s it diversified into household appliances, elevators, and generating machinery. After 1945, General Electric expanded production in these areas and also moved into new markets in jet engines, computers, industrial automation, and nuclear power. The overwhelming majority of large corporations had diversified by the beginning of the 1960s.

Closely related to corporate diversification was the emergence of the industrial conglomerate. During the early 1950s and late 1960s, a great wave of mergers occurred which was comparable in scale to the wave of industrial consolidation which took place during the 1890s and the 1920s. Unlike the previous merger waves, however, this latter period of consolidation involved the merger of corporations which had very different markets and products. Conglomerates such as International Telephone and Telegraph (ITT) acquired holdings in industries as diverse as baking, hotels, and insurance. Moreover, the postwar conglomerates also tended to expand across international borders to become multinational in character. American in origin, these "multinationals" had by the mid-1970s become a crucial factor in the international economy.

Diversification and consolidation of American industry, in turn, tended to concentrate control in the American economy in the hands of fewer firms. The 200 largest firms in the United States had accounted for 30 per cent of the value added by manufacturing in 1947; that figure had risen to 41 per cent in 1963. In industries such as chemicals, automobiles, steel, and communications, a few firms held control over the pricing and production decisions of an entire industry. The trend of consolidation, nonetheless, defies easy explanation, for, on the retail level, especially in the distribution of products such as automobiles and energy, market forces were still paramount. Moreover, the relaxation of trade barriers after 1945 added considerable competitive pressure from European and Japanese manufacturers. In addition, in certain industries, particularly those in which technology was important (such as computers, transistors, and chemicals), the pricing and marketing of products was extremely competitive.

Technology and Economic Growth

Perhaps the greatest spur to economic expansion after the Second World War was the infusion of technology into all aspects of American industry. For almost all conglomerates and corporations, research and development (R & D) became not only necessary but also indispensable to the firm's survival in the marketplace. Among the new or greatly expanded industries which relied on technological innovation were chemical synthetics, which produced such widely used materials as plastics, rubber, rayon, and polyester, as well as detergents, drugs, insecticides, and liquid fertilizers. Moreover, older industries also employed technology to produce new products. For example, the electrical appliance industry produced new goods, such as air conditioners, dehumidifiers, electric blankets, and home freezers.

The most startling innovations occurred in those industries which used electronic equipment. The use of television sets, for example, grew prodigiously. In 1947, Americans owned 7,000 television sets; in 1960, they owned 54,000,000 sets. The development of television networks—conglomerates themselves—stimulated vast increases in the advertising industry and in the whole nature of the entertainment industry. The beginning of deregulation in television broadcasting during the 1970s, in turn, promoted a revolution in the entire industry during the 1980s—the growth of "cable" television, in which a variety of national programming, movies, and sports entertainment were transmitted through cable or satellite signals.

Similarly, significant advances occurred in the field of computers and electronic circuitry. The first computer was developed during the 1940s, but the real age of the computer began during the 1960s and 1970s. Computers regulated the production line in many industries, performed typesetting in book and newspaper publishing, and controlled the transmission of information in countless other ways. The development of transistors and silicon chips during the 1960s and 1970s, respectively, also made computers increasingly cheaper to produce and more available to a variety of industries and consumers. During the 1970s, in particular, the advantages of these innovations became clear in the increased availability—at increasingly cheaper prices—of calculators, digital watches, video games, electronic word processors, and home computers.

The advent of the space age during the early 1960s brought substantial advances in technology, particularly in the field of telecommunications. Satellites provided a wealth of data and a variety of uses, including military intelligence and the tracking of weather conditions. Most remarkable of all was the application of satellite technology to telecommunications. By the 1980s, television broadcasts by satellite were commonplace, and millions of telephone transmissions occurred daily through satellites.

Developments in the field of genetics were poised to provide the most important technological breakthroughs of the 1980s. In 1953, James Watson and Francis Crick discovered deoxyribonucleic acid (DNA), the chemical substance which composed the genetic "code" of life. Subsequent research by Crick, Watson, and others led in 1980 to the successful "splicing" of a gene—and the possibility of extensive and wide-ranging genetic engineering. Recombinant DNA research offered diverse applications not only for humans but for the artificial production of substances—petroleum, for example—heretofore produced only through natural processes. Nonetheless, significant opposition to the application of genetic research arose from a variety of groups troubled by its moral and ethical implications.

The Postwar American Economy and the Environment

By the mid-1970s, Americans began to discover that the technological revolution after the Second World War often came at a high price. Particularly in those industries which thrived in the golden years of industrial innovation—the chemical and nuclear-power industries, most notably—Americans found that they threatened their livelihood and health.

During the 1970s, the American petrochemical industry faced controversy on several fronts. First, the powerful but extremely toxic pesticide DDT was banned by the United States Government during the early 1970s after it had become clear that it had inflicted serious damage on the environment. After 1976, attention was increasingly focused on the family of herbicides —"plant-killers"—which were derived from the chemical substance dioxin, one of the most toxic substances on earth. In 1978, the Environmental Protection Agency (EPA), therefore, banned the use of the herbicide 2,3,5 – T, otherwise known as "Agent Orange."

Another problem which the petrochemical industry faced during the 1970s was that of the disposal of toxic wastes. In the wide variety of chemical processes employed, toxic wastes were often a by-product, and their disposal posed a staggering problem for petrochemical corporations. Some chose to dump them, often in violation of the law. In Hopewell, Virginia, for example, the Allied Chemical Company illegally dumped tons of kepone, a highly toxic substance, into the James River in 1976; in the process, it severely damaged the fishing and shellfish industries in the lower Chesapeake area. In other instances, chemical companies stored toxic substances in underground silos which were faulty in design and contaminated areas inhabited by humans and poisoned their water supplies. In Love Canal, New York, for example, residents were forced to abandon their homes in 1979 after leaking storage silos were discovered.

To a large degree, the problems which high-technology industry posed for the ecosystem were addressed as early as the 1960s. The publication of Rachel Carson's *Silent Spring* in 1962 warned against the harmful effects of unlimited use of pesticides. Partly in response, environmentalist groups lobbied strenuously in Congress for stricter governmental regulation of air and water pollution. In a series of laws, Congress established the Environmental Protection Agency and set strict emission standards for air pollution by cars and initiated an expensive cleanup campaign for the nation's streams, rivers, and harbors. Automobile manufacturers complained that the installation of costly antipollution devices gave Japanese and German competitors an advantage. Other industries, from coal mining to chemicals, voiced similar complaints. Nonetheless, it is indisputable that, while the antipollution effort was not cheap, it had produced a substantial reduction of the pollution of the postwar era.

The Nuclear-Power Industry

The benefits of technology—and its potential disadvantages—were nowhere more evident than in the development of the nuclear-power industry. For many persons, atomic energy offered an available and renewable form of electrical power; others replied that its costs and dangers were too high to accept.

The history of the nuclear-power industry began soon after the United States dropped the first atomic bombs on Hiroshima and Nagasaki in August 1945. In 1946, Congress passed the Atomic Energy Act, which committed the United States to the development of atomic energy for peaceful purposes. Under the provisions of this act, Congress appointed two agencies to supervise and direct the growth of the nuclear-power industry. The Atomic Energy Commission (AEC) was established and given exclusive control over the production and ownership of all nuclear facilities. At the same time, the Atomic Energy Act created a standing committee in Congress to oversee the activities of the AEC. This committee—the Joint Committee on Atomic Energy—soon became the directive force for the expansion of nuclear power; the AEC usually followed its directives, as did Congress, which, with one exception, passed all legislation recommended by the Joint Committee between 1946 and 1974.

Before the late 1960s, nuclear power was largely in the hands of these governmental agencies. In 1954, the Joint Committee drafted, and Congress passed, the Atomic Energy Act, which allowed the AEC to license private companies to develop nuclear power, but support from the private sector was not immediately forthcoming. A year later, in 1955, the Power Demonstration Reactor was launched. Under this program, the AEC financed research, paid the cost of manufacturing, and supplied nuclear fuel free; the AEC also constructed the first nuclear-power plant in Shippingsport, Pennsylvania, in 1957. The federal government's most important subsidy of nuclear power, however, was provided for in the Price-Anderson Act, passed in 1957, which limited the liability of the utilities in a nuclear accident and provided governmental compensation instead.

Largely because of massive governmental support and growing concern about diminishing supplies of fossil fuels, the nuclear industry began a dramatic growth in the late 1960s. Fifteen plants were in operation at the end of 1970, and expansion continued throughout the 1970s. By 1980, fifty nuclear-power plants were operating in the United States. During 1976, about 8.3 per cent of the nation's electricity was generated by nuclear plants; by the early 1980s, nuclear power produced about 10 per cent of the total.

Just as the nuclear-power industry appeared on the threshold of great success during the late 1970s, grave problems appeared on the horizon. The biggest of them was the growing public uncertainty about the safety of nuclear power. Of the fifty nuclear-power plants operating in 1980, the

Nuclear Regulatory Commission (the successor to the AEC) reported in October 1981 that fifteen were "below average" in maintenance, management, and radiation and fire protection. Only nine plants, or 18 per cent of the total, were rated as "above average" in these same categories.

Antinuclear demonstrations took place at nuclear plants at Seabrook, New Hampshire, in 1977; in Washington, D.C., in 1978; and at Diablo Canyon, California, in September 1981. Several incidents seemed to support the fears of antinuclear groups. In March 1975, one of the most serious accidents in the history of the industry took place at Brown's Ferry, Tennessee, in a plant run by the TVA, when a worker accidentally set off a fire in a cable room and damaged the plant control and safety equipment. According to one engineer present, a dangerous release of radioactivity was avoided only through "sheer luck." Even more serious—and more publicized—was the near-miss at the Three-Mile Island nuclear-power plant, near Harrisburg, Pennsylvania, during the spring of 1979. Equally troubling and persistent was the problem of the disposal of the radioactive waste from nuclear reactors. In 1968, for example, nuclear waste was stored at AEC facilities in Washington, Idaho, and South Carolina; and about 227,000 gallons had leaked in these facilities. By the year 2000, it has been estimated that the requirements for waste storage will be about eighty times greater than they were in 1970.

Despite the problems which accompanied the expansion of the nuclear-power industry after 1945, it was clear by the 1980s that it would continue to expand and would provide a significant portion of the electricity generated in the United States during the late twentieth century. But this expansion will probably take place within the context of at least two limitations. After the well-publicized incident at Three-Mile Island, the Nuclear Regulatory Commission refused to license any new plants until it had promulgated, in the spring of 1980, a new set of strict regulations. The public demand for strong safety measures will undoubtedly remain insistent. Moreover, nuclear power seems likely to remain an increasingly costly alternative as a source of energy throughout the remainder of the twentieth century.

American Workers in the Age of Affluence

The expansion of the American economy transformed the position of the American worker. Largely because of the success and power of organized labor, skilled workers experienced a substantial increase in their standard of living. Even marginal laborers achieved real gains in income. In 1929, for example, about 60 per cent of all Americans earned no more than a subsistence income; almost fifty years later, in 1977, that figure had declined to 11.6 per cent.

Part of the explanation of this stunning increase in the well-being of the American worker is that the opportunities for employment—at every level of the economy—expanded tremendously during the postwar period. Those new industries which matured after 1945 paid higher wages than did older industries. Moreover, "service" industries expanded during this period—particularly between 1960 and 1980—in government, trade, finance, and the preparation of food. A large clerical work force staffed the bureaucracies of government as well as corporations, and, by 1970, clerical workers comprised the largest single category of workers.

The increase in the standard of living of the American worker was also a result of the power of organized labor. As we have seen, during the administration of Franklin D. Roosevelt, organized labor won the right to bargain collectively and also obtained the protection of the federal government. After 1950, organized labor won wage increases, shorter hours, and larger benefits in pensions, holidays, and insurance. Organized labor in the United States was at its pinnacle of strength about 1955, when the AFL and CIO reunited in the AFL-CIO and claimed 15,000,000 members.

Yet, by 1970 organized labor was facing a real decline in its influence among workers. In 1974, organized labor could count only 26.2 per cent of all nonfarm workers as members. The decline of the unions was partly the result of the transformation of the nature of work. Unions fared badly in organizing clerical workers and laborers in the service industries, and they also found numerous obstacles in organizing in the South, where many of the postwar plants were built and strong antiunion traditions prevailed. At the same time, as the union leadership aged, it became more identified with bureaucratic governmental and corporate management and less with the interests of the average worker.

As we will see, although American workers as a whole benefited from the growth of the postwar economy, poverty persisted after 1960 as a serious social problem. The problem of rural poverty became the problem of urban poverty. As late as 1980, 29,300,000 people, or 13 per cent of the total population, lived in poverty. Most of these poor were, as we will also see, nonwhite. As America entered the last quarter of the twentieth century, the work force appeared divided between the "haves," who possessed technological skills, and the "have-nots" without them.

3. DIVERSITY IN THE AGE OF AFFLUENCE

Afro-Americans, 1945 – 1982

The postwar period was one of the most important eras in American history for blacks. During the 1950s and 1960s, blacks fought for and won the civil rights which had been denied them during the early twentieth century. They thus earned the right to vote, the right to equal housing, and the right to equal economic opportunity. Most important, the federal government established instrumentalities to guarantee that these rights would not be abridged in the future (see pp. 264–67, 288–89, and 297).

Less noted, but equally revolutionary, was the transformation of the social and economic status of Afro-Americans. Most important, blacks began to emigrate from the rural South en masse after the conclusion of the Second World War. Mass black migration to northern cities was a long-term development; during and after the First World War, and especially during the 1920s, thousands of blacks traveled north in search of work. The restriction of European immigration beginning in the 1920s resulted in a labor shortage and drew blacks to urban areas. Moreover, after 1945, when southern cotton farmers began to mechanize agriculture, an even more substantial number of rural blacks—most of them desperately poor—packed trains and buses bound for northern and southern cities throughout the rest of the 1940s, 1950s, and 1960s.

The mass migration of rural blacks to cities had several effects. The twin curses which had historically plagued the South—extreme poverty and racial conflict—now became national problems. As blacks moved into northern and midwestern cities, whites tended to move from city centers to the suburban fringe. In 1950, 43 per cent of American blacks lived in central metropolitan areas; by 1970, that figure had increased to 55 per cent.

The black migrants to urban areas lived in an environment which was more segregated than the rural South. Urban blacks remained poor and faced increasing problems of social disintegration and rising crime in the cities. Changes in the structure of the black family paralleled the transformation of all American families. In spite of an overall decline in the birthrate among blacks, it grew proportionately higher than the birthrate among whites. In 1960, for example, the black birthrate was 141 per cent higher than that among whites; ten years later, that figure had increased to 163 per cent. An equally important development was the rise in illegitimate births and in female-headed households among blacks. Illegitimate births, which, in 1969, composed a third of all live births among blacks, also tended to affect black women differently than they did white women. Most importantly, the tendency was for more black mothers to keep and raise their illegitimate offspring. In 1969, it was estimated that, while two thirds of white mothers put illegitimate babies up for adoption, the figure among black mothers was only 7 per cent.

Many sociologists pointed out that these developments tended to perpetuate a cycle of poverty among urban blacks. Undeniably, weak family structures also contributed to an extremely high crime rate among urban blacks in the postwar period. Even before 1945, blacks in the United States—partly because of racial oppression by whites—had a high crime rate. During the postwar period, this higher crime rate increased. While the arrest rate for blacks in 1950 was five times that for whites, twenty years later blacks were twenty times more likely to be arrested than were whites.

The story of the migration of blacks to urban areas has not been an altogether dreary one. Blacks, like all Americans, enjoyed a significant increase in income, measured both in absolute standards and as compared against income for whites. The number of black males who earned less than $2,000 (in 1969 dollars) decreased from 40 per cent in 1959 to 22 per cent in 1969. At the same time, black income increased proportionately. In 1947, black family income was only 54 per cent that of white families; in 1974, that figure stood at 62 per cent. If blacks found greater opportunity for economic advancement, they also found larger opportunities for educational advancement. In 1940, only about 2 per cent of blacks in the twenty-five- to twenty-nine-year-old age group had attended colleges; by 1970, that figure had increased to 10 per cent.

The most visible evidence of the advancement of Afro-Americans was the growing presence of a black middle class. College-educated and professionally trained, the new black middle class of the postwar era grew rapidly during the 1960s and 1970s; by 1980, about 25 to 30 per cent of blacks could be classified—to varying extents—as "middle class." The growth of a black middle class, in turn, stimulated class divisions among blacks, as increasing numbers of affluent Afro-Americans left the inner city for the safety of the suburbs.

The Coming of Age of Ethnic America

One of the most important socioeconomic developments of the postwar era was the increasing prominence of so-called ethnic Americans, the descendants of the millions of Europeans who had immigrated to the United States during the nineteenth and twentieth centuries. The descendants of Irish, Jewish, Italian, Polish, and other immigrants achieved a degree of socioeconomic upward mobility unparalleled in the history of the world. Moreover, by the early 1980s, they exerted a high degree of leadership in the economy, politics, and culture.

The most striking feature of the development of ethnic Americans was a very large increase in income within a few short generations. The best-known success story has been that of the Jews. Although most eastern European Jews arrived in the United States with little money, they came with the significant advantages of literacy and strong familial organizations. In New York City, Jews moved rapidly up the socioeconomic ladder within a generation. They first employed the skills which they brought with them—mainly in the clothing industry—and then used education as a means to achieve upward social mobility. In 1900, about 68 per cent of American Jews worked in manual professions; by 1953, 66 per cent of them worked in nonmanual occupations. By the 1960s, moreover, the average family income of Jews was higher than that of any other ethnic group in the United States—including the "older" ethnic groups of the English, Scotch-Irish, and Afro-Americans.
'   Other ethnic Americans who traced their ancestry to the "new" immigrants of the early twentieth century experienced similar upward social mobility. Unlike the Jews, the Italians arrived in the United States without any concrete economic or educational skills. The Italian immigrants and their children thus first moved into the ranks of skilled labor and became involved in such industries as construction and real estate. After 1945, Italians began to move into the professions—university teaching, engineering, the medical profession, and the law—and, like the Jews before them, they used the educational system as a vehicle for social mobility. A similar success story also occurred in the case of the Slavs—particularly the Poles—who enjoyed substantial economic gains during the postwar period.

The Changing Character of Immigration

During the postwar period, a shift in the character of immigration to the United States occurred which was just as important—and equally troubling to many Americans—as the "new" immigration of the early twentieth century had been. A growing proportion of these new Americans—like the "new" immigrants seventy-five years before—came in search of economic opportunity, but more of them came from Latin America, the Caribbean, and Asia. This shift was partly a consequence of the revision of the immigration law. As we have seen, the National Origins Act of 1924 successfully prevented the immigration of southern and eastern Europeans; it also blocked immigration from Asia. Congress put into effect an entirely new immigration policy in

1965. Although the Immigration Act of that year continued to limit the total number of immigrants, it abolished the proviso which barred "undesirable" immigrants. The law permitted 170,000 immigrants to enter annually, and no more than 20,000 of this total could come from any single country. The law liberalized policy toward Asians and other nonwhite groups, since they now possessed equal status with any other immigrant group.

The liberalization of immigration policy resulted in a transformation in the number and type of immigrants. Although only 700,000 immigrants arrived in the United States during the 1930s, more than 2,000,000 immigrants arrived during the 1960s. The numbers of legal immigrants during the 1960s and 1970s were augmented by a growing number of illegal immigrants, particularly from Asia and Latin America. Moreover, in four separate instances, the United States Government permitted the migration of refugees —from Hungary in 1956, from Cuba in the early 1960s, from Vietnam during 1975 and 1978–1979, and from Cuba again in 1980.

The most important tendency of the postwar immigration was the growth of the Hispanic community in the United States. The oldest and most numerous of the Hispanic groups were the Mexicans, who, at the time of the Mexican Cession of the southwestern United States in 1848, numbered about 75,000. The Mexican-American population continued to grow throughout the nineteenth and twentieth centuries, for immigration between Mexico and the United States was unrestricted (no border patrols were even established, for example, before 1924). Because of the intensive labor shortage caused by immigration restriction during the 1920s and 1930s, thousands of Mexicans moved into the United States. During the 1920s alone, about 1,000,000 Mexicans moved north of the Rio Grande; of these, about one half were legal immigrants.

During the Second World War, the federal government, on account of the severe labor shortage, began to permit the importation of *braceros,* or contract laborers, from Mexico; and, between 1942 and 1947, about 220,000 *braceros* worked in twenty-one states, about half of them in California. The *braceros* program was extended during the period of labor shortage from 1947 to 1964; in addition, farmers of the Southwest continued to hire a large number of "wetbacks," or illegal immigrants, throughout the postwar period. Many of these remained in the United States and lived in conditions of extreme poverty. During the 1970s, Mexican Americans composed about one third of the poor in Texas and New Mexico and about a quarter of the poor in Arizona and Colorado. In 1972, the median annual family income for Mexican-American families was $8,759—higher than that of blacks but substantially lower than that of "Anglos," or non-Mexican Caucasians.

At the same time, by the early 1980s it was clear that the Mexican Americans were making progress up the socioeconomic ladder. Having left extreme poverty, overpopulation, and a rigid caste and class system in Mexico, Mexican immigrants achieved an immediate increase in income when they first crossed the border. Moreover, the vast majority of Mexican Americans lived in cities, where they discovered many opportunities for economic advancement and the acquisition of wealth. In 1950, for example, about two thirds of persons of Mexican ancestry lived in urban areas; twenty years later, that figure stood at 85 per cent. Many Mexican Americans also moved into the ranks of skilled labor, particularly high-paying jobs in aeronautics and automobile manufacturing. Even during the 1950s, Mexican Americans composed about one fifth of all automobile workers in California.

Women in the Work Force

Another striking way in which American society was remade in the postwar period was the growing prominence of women in the work force. The transformation in the position of women—and the change in sexual roles which it implied—was very much a part of the wholesale expansion of the American economy after 1945, for, as in the case of blacks and ethnic groups, economic growth brought a variety of opportunities and possibilities.

The expansion of the role of women in the work force carried forward the same socioeconomic tendencies which had prevailed during the late nineteenth and early twentieth centuries. The intensive demand for labor on the home front during the Second World War resulted in the hiring of millions of American women. The massive entry of women into the work force continued during the postwar period, as women began to enter heretofore exclusively male occupations. Between 1940 and 1950, the number of women accountants increased by 300 per cent, compared to an increase of about 60 per cent for male accountants during the same period. During the 1960s and 1970s, moreover, women began to enter the professions, particularly engineering, the law, medicine, and higher education.

The most important fact about the involvement of women in the economy was the growing incidence of married women in the work force. In 1940, only about 15 per cent of all married women in the United States worked; thirty years later, more than 44 per cent worked. Women with children also joined the work force in increasing numbers. Whereas, in 1940, only about 10 per cent of women with children worked, by 1975, that figure had increased to about 37 per cent.

The large-scale influx of women into the economy after 1945 was not accompanied by full equality for the sexes in the workplace. Indeed, the overall inequities between men and women workers in many respects widened. In 1945, for example, white women on the average earned 63 per cent of the average income of the white male; almost thirty years later, that proportion had declined to 57 per cent. The postwar influx of women into the work force, in short, was an influx into low-paying jobs.

4. THE MATURATION OF AMERICAN CULTURE

Mass Media in the Age of Affluence

In many respects, the best example of the social transformation after 1945 is the almost complete remaking of the cultural landscape. Although the seeds of cultural change were planted in the early twentieth century, they came to full fruition in the postwar period. In general, postwar American culture evolved in two overlapping directions. The first was the *nationalization* of culture—the transmission of culture, that is, increasingly took place through national means, particularly through television. Second, culture—partly because of its national orientation—became more geared toward a mass, popular, and highly commercial market.

These trends were nowhere more evident than in the emergence of the mass media as the most important instrumentality of culture in the United States. The most important element in the mass media was television. Although the technology of television existed as early as the 1920s, full commercial production of television sets did not take place until the late 1940s. In 1948, the first full year of the television, the number of stations increased from seventeen to forty-one; by the end of that year, twenty-three cities had television service. The purchase of television sets continued apace. In 1948 alone, the number of people owning sets increased by 4,000 per cent; ten years later, there were as many sets as there were families in the United States.

From its inception, television was under the control of the major radio networks—NBC, CBS, and ABC. As a result, the television of the 1940s and 1950s was much like radio in the type of programs offered. Early television, like radio, used live performances; during this "golden age" of television, viewers enjoyed comedy and drama of exceptionally high quality. *Studio One*, a live drama series which ran from 1948 until the late 1950s, attracted a variety of playwrights. Moreover, the same persons who had dominated radio—Jack Benny, Bing Crosby, and Bob Hope—found an even more successful medium in television.

By the late 1950s, however, television had acquired a style and mode which was quite distinctive from radio of the 1920s and 1930s. The advent of the video recorder, which became available to television in 1956, revolutionized television by making possible a variety of prerecorded comedies and dramatic series. Television news reporting also had become extremely sophisticated by the late 1950s, so much so that the newsreels, which had been shown in theaters across the nation, were extinct by the mid-1960s. The evening news report, first produced by NBC's Chet Huntley and David Brinkley in 1956, became a common feature of American life. Other varieties of national network news, particularly documentaries and investigative reporting, were pioneered by the CBS reporters, Edward R. Murrow and Mike Wallace.

Television continued to develop as a medium in the 1960s and 1970s. Yet, despite the incredible amount of technological innovation in television between 1960 and 1980, many critics charged that the medium in general experienced a decline in quality. As the chairman of the Federal Communications Commission, Newton Minnow, put it in 1964, television was a "vast wasteland" of commercialization, violence, and boredom. Whether the expansion of television after the mid-1950s has resulted in a general decline in quality is, of course, subject to debate. What is indisputable is that the commercialization of television made it extraordinarily sensitive to a mass, national audience.

Moreover, the emergence of television to cultural prominence in the postwar era had a profound and wide-ranging effect on American society. It exposed Americans to a national mode of living and to a national popular culture. It undoubtedly had an important, and, at this date, indeterminable, effect in erasing the distinctions of regional culture and isolation which had existed for centuries. Television, and the mass media in general, also played a significant role in influencing and shaping popular opinion, including opinion

about politics and political leaders. For example, television played a deci
sive role in the fall of Senator Joseph McCarthy from popularity in 1954. In
that year, the broadcast of McCarthy's investigation into alleged Communist infiltration of the army, in combination with slashing exposés by
Murrow, galvanized public opinion against McCarthy. National news coverage of the civil-rights movement in the South had a similar effect in
coalescing national public opinion. The broadcast of the congressional
investigations of the Watergate scandal (see p. 326) also helped to cause the
downfall of Richard Nixon.

The Culture of Youth

Another prominent feature of postwar American culture was the emergence
of cultural modes designed specifically for youth. The growing prominence of
public education and the diminishing role of children and teenagers in the
labor force tended to segregate children and adolescents from adults. The
affluence of postwar society, moreover, meant that American youth had more
time for leisure than did their ancestors; they also had much more disposable
income, around which grew a market for products geared to youth. Most
important of all, the "baby boom" meant that young Americans after 1945
composed an increasingly large—and demanding—market for goods and
cultural forms.

The clearest example of the emergence of youth culture was the growth
and development of the music and entertainment industries. Most prominent
of all was the demand for rock music. By the 1970s, the record industry alone
recorded multibillion-dollar sales. Rock music as such did not exist before
1950; most popular music was either swing, jazz, blues, or white folk music.
The nationalization of the market for cultural goods in the 1950s—and the
intense commercialization of culture—encouraged the development of rock
music, a combination of black and rural white music which employed unique
innovations in content and in the use of electronic equipment. Unlike any
other musical form in American history, rock-and-roll was youth-oriented,
distinctly designed to appeal to the large adolescent market of the 1950s.
Rock musicians, such as Elvis Presley, Chuck Berry, and Jerry Lee Lewis,
wrote music about youth and the problems of adolescence; they also
embodied the youthful rebellion against moral and sexual strictures of adults,
not only in lyrics but also in their performances. Even more significant and
unique was the fact that rock music was also nonregional and national in
orientation.

The appeal of rock music to a national, young audience continued into the
1960s and 1970s. Particularly after 1964, rock represented "counter-
culture"—a rebellion of youth which was directed against sexual repression
and involved the use of drugs. The Beatles, probably the best product of the
age of rock-and-roll, dominated popular music after 1964; they were followed
by such groups as the Rolling Stones, the Jefferson Airplane, Jimi Hendrix,
and the Doors. During the late 1970s and early 1980s, rock music began to
lose its vitality and appeal, a development which was a product of the aging
of the "baby boom" generation. Nonetheless, the musical tradition and
cultural style of rock-and-roll survived. After 1978, the important new rock
music was "New Wave," a mode which embodied the rock traditions of

repetition and rhythm but also stressed—and even exaggerated to the point of absurdity—youth, violence, rebellion, and sexuality.

Professional Sports

Another important component of popular culture in the postwar United States was professional sports. Organized spectator sports were not new to the postwar era; the spectator sports of horse racing, boxing, and baseball were extremely popular as early as the 1870s. Yet, following the end of the Second World War, professional spectator sports began to play a growing role in American culture, one which, in turn, also displayed the twin characteristics of the commercialization and nationalization of American culture.

A veritable explosion of the sports industry occurred in the postwar era. The oldest of the professional team sports, baseball, grew even larger after the 1960s as the industry grew out of the old franchises in the Northeast and Middle West and found hospitable climates in the South and particularly in the West and Pacific Northwest. Between 1960 and 1980, the number of major league baseball franchises increased from sixteen to twenty-six; attendance, at the same time, substantially increased. Meanwhile, even more impressive growth took place in the newer sports, particularly basketball and football.

Closely linked to the professional sports franchise were college and university team sports, particularly football and basketball. College team sports served as something of a "farm system" for professional leagues; but, at the same time, they became extremely commercialized activities. Large colleges and universities found it profitable and advantageous to establish successful sports programs; the athletes themselves also became less students and, in general, more like professionals.

The emergence of spectator sports as an industry and as a leisure activity for a majority of Americans was closely related to the growth of television. Next to news reporting, sports telecasts—manned by armies of analysts and technicians—composed the most important aspect of network programming. In addition, the biggest source of revenue for college and professional sports came from television; the fortunes of both, in a very real way, were intimately connected.

Organized Religion in the Age of Affluence

The transformation of American culture after the Second World War affected the oldest cultural institution—American churches—in different ways. On the one hand, religion undeniably was a less influential force in postwar society. With the advent of radio and television, churches no longer held a cultural monopoly; secular forms of leisure activity grew increasingly more important. On the other hand, organized religion remained a powerful force in American life.

The main-line churches of the United States, above all, faced an enormous challenge to retain the membership and attention of the mass of Americans. On the whole, churches and synagogues held on to, and even expanded, their membership; even in the 1980s, affiliation with organized religion in the United States ranked as the highest in the western world. Immediately after the Second World War, indeed, the percentage of Americans who were members of churches increased from 43 per cent in 1940 to 61 per cent in 1955. Church membership declined in the 1960s and, after 1970, stabilized and began to increase.

The Protestant evangelical groups (particularly those which exploited the use of radio and television) constituted the fastest growing segment of organized religion. Almost without exception, these television evangelists were "fundamentalist" in orientation and, in general, politically conservative. The pioneer evangelist of this type, Billy Graham, established himself as the most prominent and important evangelist of the postwar era, primarily through the use of television. Television evangelists such as Rex Humbard, Oral Roberts, Pat Robertson, and Jim Baker enjoyed similar success during the 1970s and 1980s.

In the late 1970s, moreover, evangelical "fundamentalists" increasingly began to involve themselves in the cause of conservativism. Many of them believed that the stunning changes in the nature of the family and in sexual roles were the product of excessive permissiveness, which, they believed, was embodied in postwar "liberalism." Before the 1970s, most fundamentalists were apolitical; that is, they avoided tainting themselves with any involvement in the worldly pursuit of politics. By the 1970s, this had begun to change, most particularly with those evangelists closely associated with television. In 1978, Jerry Falwell, pastor of the Thomas Road Baptist Church of Lynchburg, Virginia, and a prominent television evangelist, organized the Moral Majority, a coalition of right-wing religious groups, but mainly Protestant fundamentalists. The Moral Majority subsequently played a prominent and well-publicized role in the victory of Ronald Reagan in the presidential election of 1980.

The Educational Revolution

After 1945, public education on all levels grew at an unprecedented rate. Americans by the 1960s could boast the most extensive and the best-financed educational system in the world. Although the basic pattern of educational expansion was clear by the 1920s, it was not until after the Second World War that the wholesale expansion of education, mainly public education, took place. The dreams of early twentieth-century reformers came to fruition. Elementary schools were consolidated and standardized, and the yellow and black school bus symbolized the vast extension of the authority of the state in the upbringing of American children. An even greater expansion took place in high schools in the nation as substantially more Americans had the opportunity to receive secondary education.

While the number of "baby boom" children filled public elementary and secondary schools, enrollments at state universities and private schools rose significantly. In this wholesale expansion, higher education grew in size and scale; huge bureaucracies emerged to administer universities and huge faculties to teach large numbers of students. Closely connected to institutional growth in higher education was the expansion of professional education —training in graduate education, medicine, engineering, and the law.

Just when the vast system of American education appeared to be most successful—in the late 1960s—stresses and strains began to appear in the entire system. The end of the "baby boom" by the latter part of that decade made clear the fact that higher education, and perhaps the entire educational system, had overexpanded. By the early 1980s, the declining population of schoolchildren had already affected enrollments in elementary and secondary education. Among universities and colleges, moreover, competition for students, as a result of declining population, became intense, and jobs for recent Ph.D.s increasingly rare.

The postwar expansion of American public education itself also came under criticism. In the United States, the proportion of adolescents and young adults who attended colleges and universities was the highest in the world, and yet many of them found the job market competitive and shrinking. During the early 1970s, there were growing indications that general educational standards and levels had begun to decline. Standardized test scores dropped throughout the early and mid-1970s, and the public elementary and secondary schools were blamed for providing inadequate instruction in basic skills of reading and writing.

Nonetheless, in spite of growing uncertainty about public education in general—and in spite of growing numbers attending private schools—public education had become an integral part of American culture. Especially during the postwar period, it became the primary instrument of the socialization of American youth and one of the most important extensions of the state into society. In spite of its problems, moreover, the American system of public education provided opportunities and avenues for advancement—especially after 1945—for untold numbers of the disadvantaged, minority groups, and the poor.

SUGGESTED READINGS

The standard reference for up-to-date social and economic data is the *American Almanac* (formerly *Statistical Abstracts of the United States*), which is published annually. See also summary volumes of the decennial census. Scholarly studies of demography and social changes include John L. Shover, *First Majority—Last Minority: The Transformation of Rural Life in America* (1976), and Jean Gottman, *Megalopolis: The Urbanized Northeastern Seaboard of the United States* (1961).

The scholarship on the family in modern America is voluminous. Several important studies are Christopher Lasch, *Haven in a Heartless World: The Family Besieged* (1977); Joseph F. Kett, *Rites of Passage: Adolescence in America, 1790 to the Present* (1977); Carl N. Degler, *At Odds: Women and the Family in America from the Revolution to the Present* (1980); and Andrew J. Cherlin, *Marriage, Divorce, Remarriage* (1981).

For a comprehensive treatment of the impact of the new media on American life, see David Halberstam, *The Powers That Be* (1979). On the growth of television, consult Erik Barnouw's definitive account, *A History of Broadcasting in the United States* (1966) as well as Alexander Kendrick,

Prime Time: The Life of Edward R. Murrow (1969).

General economic trends can be followed in W. Elliott Brownlee, *Dynamics of Ascent: A History of the American Economy* (1979). The structure of economic life is discussed in Alfred D. Chandler, Jr., *The Visible Hand*, already cited; John Kenneth Galbraith, *The New Industrial State*, 2nd ed. (1972); and Robert Sobel, *The Age of Giant Corporations: A Microeconomic History of American Business* (1972). The role of American-based multinational firms is discussed in Richard J. Barnet and Ronald E. Muller, *Global Reach: The Power of the Multinational Corporations* (1974); and C. Fred Bergsten, *Toward a New International Economic Order* (1975). The problem of poverty is discussed in James T. Patterson, *America's Struggle against Poverty, 1900–1980* (1981). Elting E. Morison, *From Know-How to Nowhere: The Development of American Technology* (1974), is useful, as is Michael Mandlebaum, *Nuclear Reactor Safety: On the History of the Regulatory Process* (1981).

Changing sex roles and the women's movement are discussed in Degler, *At Odds*, just cited; William H. Chafe, *The American Woman: Her Changing Social, Economic,*

and Political Roles, 1920–1970 (1972); and
Peter Filene, *Him/Her/Self: Sex Roles in Modern America* (1975).

Of the general treatments of Afro-American history, the best are John Hope Franklin, *From Slavery to Freedom,* and August Meier and Elliott Rudwick, *From Plantation to Ghetto,* both cited earlier, but see also the earlier and important Gunnar Myrdal, *An American Dilemma* (1944). Important studies of black leaders and black movements for liberation and equality include Martin Luther King, Jr., *Stride Toward Freedom* (1958); David L. Lewis, *King: A Critical Biography,* 2nd ed. (1978); Peter Goldman, *The Death and Life of Malcolm X* (1973); August Meier and Elliott Rudwick, *CORE: A Study in the Civil Rights Movement, 1942–1968* (1973); and William Chafe, *Civilities and Civil Rights: Greensboro, North Carolina, and the Black Struggle for Freedom* (1980).

White opposition to social change is described in Numan V. Bartley, *The Rise of Massive Resistance: Race and Politics in the South during the 1950s* (1969). For the Brown

decision, see Kluger, *Simple Justice,* cited in the next chapter. The urban upheavals of the 1960s are analyzed in Joe R. Feagin and Harlan Hahn, *Ghetto Riots: The Politics of Violence in American Cities* (1973).

The best general guide to immigration is Leonard Dinnerstein, *Ethnic Americans: A History of Immigration and Assimilation* (1975). The Hispanic experience in America is summarized in James S. Olsen, *The Ethnic Dimension in American History* (1979). The largest segment of the nation's Hispanic population is the subject of Matt S. Meier and Feliciano Rivera, *The Chicanos: A History of Mexican Americans* (1972). The economic struggles of Mexican-American laborers in the Southwest are discussed in Ronald B. Taylor, *Chavez and the Farm Workers* (1975).

The best general treatment of religion after the Second World War is found in Sidney E. Ahlstrom, *A Religious History of the American People* (1972). See also D. F. Wells and J. D. Woodridge, eds., *The Evangelicals* (1975); and Marshall Frady, *Billy Graham* (1979).

CHAPTER 14
THE EISENHOWER YEARS,
1952 – 1960

1. THE FIRST EISENHOWER
ADMINISTRATION

The Eisenhower Presidency

The election of Dwight David Eisenhower in 1952 gave new proof that the American people still loved military heroes. Eisenhower, born in Denison, Texas, on October 4, 1890, grew up in Abilene, Kansas. His appointment to West Point began a military career which culminated in leadership of the Anglo-American military forces which, along with their Russian allies, defeated Germany in 1945. No American was more popular than "Ike" in the days following the end of the Second World War. Eisenhower remained in the army as Chief of Staff until 1948, when he accepted the presidency of Columbia University. Three years later he was called back into public service as the first Supreme Commander of NATO forces in Europe. He resigned his command on June 1, 1952, to return home to campaign for the Republican presidential nomination. The American people respected Eisenhower for his qualities of leadership, but they elected him to their highest office because they admired him as a person who stood above ordinary political conflict and exuded personal integrity.

It seems safe to say that Eisenhower will not be ranked as a great domestic leader among the Presidents of the United States. His background and personal temperament appear to be most responsible for his shortcomings. Although the greatest opportunity existed for constructive leadership since the 1930s, he took any action which required vigorous presidential leadership only reluctantly. He refused to confront domestic problems in civil rights, air and water pollution (which he dismissed as a peculiarly local problem), or hard-core unemployment and poverty. In foreign policy, Eisenhower demurred from changing the parameters of the Cold War. Immensely popular, he had at his disposal a reservoir of good will and loyalty such as few Presidents in American history have ever possessed. He had behind him a resurgent party with many creative elements. His presidency coincided with a period of general prosperity. Finally, he came to national leadership at the end of a period of intense partisanship, when the great mass of people were yearning for domestic quietude. Yet, Eisenhower did not take advantage of his opportunity to give the dynamic leadership which can be exercised through the presidential office.

Part of Eisenhower's deficiencies stemmed from his view of the presidency and of leadership. He strongly emphasized the principle of the separation of legislative and executive functions because he was convinced that Roosevelt and Truman had concentrated too much power in the White House. Eisenhower therefore never exerted decisive leadership over Congress, nor even over his own party. Moreover, Eisenhower believed that he could lead a nation in the same way he had led the Allied and NATO commands. Such leadership consisted almost exclusively of conciliating differing points of view, not of planning and working for programs and causes.

Probably the most important reason for Eisenhower's failure as a leader was his fundamental lack of interest in and knowledge about American politics, largely because he had been a professional soldier for so long. Although a magnificent campaigner, he did not enjoy the quest for votes and tired easily of crowds and adulation. Mere politicians, with their quarrels over party policies and patronage, bored him, and he much preferred golf games with businessmen. He therefore failed to rebuild the Republican party, although many of his associates urged him to organize and lead the progressive and internationalist wing which had obtained his nomination in 1952. The Republican party actually was weaker at the end of his tenure than it had been in 1952, because it remained bitterly divided between conservatives and progressives and isolationists and internationalists.

Nevertheless, Eisenhower made some important contributions to American political traditions, if not to the presidency itself. In foreign policy, Eisenhower not only guided the government through a series of crises without resort to violence, but he also maintained firm continuity with the American diplomatic policies of the 1940s. He helped to heal deep wounds in the body politic by his own simple decency and fair play. It was a tribute to the reconciling effect of his leadership that Americans in the important presidential election of 1960 were once again able to demonstrate that they could disagree and even fight hard for control of the federal government without using destructive tactics. Finally, Eisenhower helped to consolidate and strengthen the New Deal's economic and social programs. Eisenhower won Republican support for the extension of Social Security, public housing, and aid to education, and thus made such welfare measures the common property of both parties. This was a significant accomplishment. As a domestic leader, it can be said that Eisenhower accomplished most of what he set out to do.

The Middle of the Road

Although some Democrats rather gloomily predicted that Republicans, once in power, would try to turn the clock of history back to the 1920s, Eisenhower tailored his domestic policies to the moderate majorities in both parties. He once characterized these policies as follows: "When it comes to dealing with the relationships between the human in this country and his government, the people of this administration believe in being what I think we would normally call liberal, and when we deal with the economic affairs of this country, we believe in being conservative." This approach, Eisenhower explained, was "dynamic conservatism"; it implied caution and conservatism in financial policies but the protection, and even extension, of social-welfare programs. In short, "dynamic conservatism" meant staying in the middle of the political road and avoiding the extremes or even the near extremes of both radicalism and reaction.

Rhetoric and Reality

As a candidate in 1952, Eisenhower had put himself at the head of a great crusade to clean up the "mess" in Washington, and he had called upon all good Americans to join him in the effort. Yet, he arrived in Washington only to discover that his predecessor had done a thorough job of cleaning up whatever "mess" formerly existed. The crusade was quickly adjourned, and Eisenhower did not mention it again. Eisenhower also talked much in 1952 about the evils of centralization in federal governmental functions at the expense of local and state power. Yet he did not initiate any measures toward diffusing federal power, and the federal system was, if anything, more centralized when he left office than when he entered the White House. The presidential candidate in 1952 discoursed on the utter necessity of what he called "fiscal integrity," of not spending more than one received in revenue. And yet the federal deficit in 1959 was the largest in American peacetime history to that time, and there were deficits in other years as well. Although Republicans pledged to purge the federal government of Communists, they soon found little or nothing to be done. Eisenhower did institute new standards of security, and their severe application resulted in the dismissal of 3,002 so-called security risks. But the costs, both to individuals and the nation, were high. Even distinguished individuals, whose loyalty was not questioned but who were deemed to be security risks because they had once had friends or acquaintances who were Communists, were excluded from federal employment.

Less Government in Business

One promise—to reverse the tide of direct governmental participation in business and manufacturing—Eisenhower carried out to a considerable degree. Almost at the outset of his term, the new President ended all price and wage controls imposed during the Korean War. He let the Reconstruction Finance Corporation, which had lent about $40 billion since its founding by Herbert Hoover in 1932, go out of business. In April 1953, Eisenhower obtained authority from Congress to sell to private industry government-owned and government-operated synthetic rubber manufacturing plants capable of producing some 800,000 tons per year. And in August 1954, Eisenhower obtained amendment of the Atomic Energy Act of 1946 to permit private industry to participate more widely in the development of atomic materials and facilities.

Significant though all these actions were, they passed without much notice or debate. What did stir sometimes violent controversy were Eisenhower's determined efforts to halt the trend toward governmental development of natural resources. These efforts led to three major conflicts:

1. *Offshore oil lands.* The discovery of evidently vast oil deposits off the coasts of California and the Gulf states raised the question of the ownership of these coastal areas. Twice, in 1946 and 1952, Congress had passed bills giving title to the claiming states. On both occasions, Truman blocked such action with ringing vetoes. Eisenhower denied such sweeping national claims and gladly signed a compromise measure on May 22, 1953. It transferred title to submerged coastal lands to the states, but only within their historical boundaries. The Supreme Court, in May 1960, set these at the usual three-mile limit, except for Texas and Florida. Their historical boundaries were said to extend ten and a half miles into the sea.

2. *The development of Hell's Canyon.* Between 1953 and 1955, a bitter battle took place between the privately owned Idaho Power Company and certain advocates of public-power development. The power company wanted to build three dams in the Hell's Canyon area of the Snake River. Advocates of public power fought back and pleaded for one large dam to be built and operated by the federal government. Eisenhower supported the power company, which won approval of its plans in 1955.

3. *The Tennessee Valley Authority.* Eisenhower revealed his opposition to further extension of public power most significantly in his attitude and policies toward the TVA. In 1953, he referred to the TVA as an example of "creeping socialism." Although he later retracted the remark, it revealed his fundamental opposition to governmental development when private utilities could do the same job. In 1954, he directed the Atomic Energy Commission to sign a contract with certain private power companies, the Dixon-Yates group, to supply 600,000 kilowatts of power to the TVA. This agreement was to replace an equal amount of power to be delivered by the TVA to the AEC's plants at Paducah, Kentucky. The opposition grew so strong and bitter, and evidence of irregular activity in the contract negotiations so pervasive, that Eisenhower finally admitted defeat, and the contract was later canceled.

Agricultural Policy

One of the most stubborn problems which faced the Eisenhower administration was the serious decline in farm income which occurred after 1952. Between that date and 1960, farm income fell 23 per cent, while the national income as a whole increased by 43 per cent. There were several reasons for agricultural distress, the most important of which was a tremendous increase in production which resulted from the use of machinery, hybrid corn seed, and fertilizers.

Everyone agreed that overproduction was the basic problem after 1952, but considerable disagreement existed over the best means to curtail production and to maintain something like fair prices. Spokesmen for the farmers pleaded for maintenance for high price supports, such as the 90 per cent of parity level provided by the Agricultural Act of 1949. They also suggested that the government should use surpluses to combat hunger throughout the world. In contrast, Eisenhower's Secretary of Agriculture, Ezra Taft Benson of Utah, urged Congress to adopt low and flexible price supports. The government, Benson insisted, could never solve the problem of mounting surpluses until it stopped paying farmers to overproduce.

The tug of war between the farm spokesmen and the administration continued throughout the Eisenhower era. The alignment did not always follow partisan lines. However, the Democrats tended increasingly to support what most farmers wanted, while the Benson program drove more and more farmers out of the Republican camp.

Neither side had had its way completely by the end of the Eisenhower administration. Benson could point to the progressive lowering of price supports—from a flexible scale of 82.5 to 90 per cent under the Agricultural Act of 1954, to a general scale of 65 per cent under the Agricultural Act of 1958. Congressional representatives of the farmers could point to the program initiated by the act of 1954 to use American agricultural surpluses abroad. Between 1954 and 1960, agricultural products with a total market value of nearly $4.5 billion were sold for foreign currencies.

Neither side, however, could claim credit for any solution. Farmers produced more every year, despite lower price supports—or perhaps because of them. Farm income continued to decline, in spite of an outpouring from Washington of about $4 billion in 1959 and of $2.6 billion in 1960 in subsidies of one kind or another. Surpluses so huge as to be almost unmanageable continued to burden the warehouses and granaries. By the end of 1960, the government still owned more than 1,000,000,000 bushels of wheat and nearly 1,500,000,000 bushels of corn, much of which was rotting in federally owned or rented warehouses.

Economic Growth

During the campaign of 1952, one commentator quipped that the best hope for the survival of the New Deal and Fair Deal was the election of a Republican President. He meant simply that a Republican administration would have no choice but to continue the Democratic programs for economic security and that talk of repealing these programs would end once both parties could claim credit for them.

This appraisal, as it turned out, was accurate. Eisenhower and his party leaders never contemplated turning back the clock of economic and social reform. Such an undertaking, they realized, entailed excessive political risks, since most Americans considered a limited welfare state—particularly the Social Security system—as necessary and desirable. Moreover, because conservatives lacked a working majority in the Republican-controlled Congress from 1953 to 1955—and because the Democrats controlled it thereafter—repeal of the New Deal-Fair Deal laws was probably not possible anyway.

In any event, a fundamental part of Eisenhower's middle-of-the-road policy was not only to preserve, but also to strengthen and extend, programs for social and economic security. In many instances, the only differences between Republicans and Democrats in Congress, or between Democrats in Congress and the President, involved the questions of cost and speed. The President and Congress thus agreed in 1954, and again in 1956, to increase Social Security benefits and to broaden the system to include an estimated 10,000,000 new workers. In 1955, Congress and Eisenhower compromised on a new minimum-wage law which increased the minimum from seventy-five cents to $1 an hour. Greater disagreement occurred between the two branches of government over providing low-cost public housing for poor people. Democrats endorsed generous measures and were disappointed when forced to accept administration bills. Even so, the Housing Act of 1959 provided most of what the Democrats demanded, and, despite Republican occupancy of the White House, federal expenditures for public housing continued. Between 1953 and 1961, the federal government spent some $1.3 billion for slum clearance and public housing.

In health and medical welfare, as much as in housing and slum clearance, Eisenhower carried forward the programs which Roosevelt and Truman had begun. On April 1, 1953, Eisenhower signed a bill (earlier proposed by Truman) which raised the Federal Security Agency to cabinet rank as the Department of Health, Education, and Welfare. Although Eisenhower opposed Truman's plan for broad national health insurance, he asked Congress in 1954 to provide federal support for the nonprofit health insurance plans which had been growing rapidly since the 1940s. A Republican Congress refused this request, but bills which provided federal funds for medical research and the construction of hospitals were adopted with little opposition throughout the 1950s. In 1960, the federal government spent $80 million on the construction of hospitals alone, and Congress passed the Kerr-Mills bill, which authorized the federal government to match state funds on a three-to-one basis to provide medical assistance for needy people over sixty-five years of age.

Eisenhower also appointed a commission to study the entire program of immigration and naturalization. This commission recommended complete revision of the McCarran-Walter Immigration and Nationality Act of 1952. Congress refused to alter the basic features of American immigration policy, but it did adopt the Refugee Act of 1953, which permitted an additional 214,000 immigrants to enter during the next three years. Thousands more were admitted under special provisions when Russia suppressed a revolt in Hungary in 1956.

Beginnings of the Civil Rights Movement

Truman, who failed to win civil-rights legislation, used every executive power at his command to launch a national war against Jim Crow laws and customs. Eisenhower carried this program forward from the White House with no great personal enthusiasm. But presidential action could provide only limited effectiveness in any event, for only Congress held the power to strengthen civil rights by legislation, and threats of a filibuster by southern senators prevented civil-rights bills even from coming to a vote before 1957, when the logjam was finally broken in a most unexpected way. Senator Lyndon B. Johnson of Texas, Democratic majority leader in the Senate, persuaded administration Republicans and northern and western Democrats to accept a limited bill which sought only to protect the right of black

Americans to vote in the southern states. In return, southern senators permitted the measure to pass without a filibuster.

The Civil Rights Act of 1957 created a bipartisan Commission on Civil Rights with power to subpoena witnesses and authority to investigate violations of the right to vote. It also provided for a new Assistant Attorney General to initiate suits in federal district courts when this right was denied. The Civil Rights Act of 1957 was a landmark—the first federal civil-rights legislation since 1875. In 1960, Congress adopted a second bill which extended additional protection for blacks who attempted to vote; it empowered federal courts to appoint referees to consider state voting qualifications whenever a petitioner had been deprived of the right to register or vote on account of race.

The Warren Court Takes Shape

Chief Justice Frederick M. Vinson died in September 1953. In the appointment of Earl Warren as Chief Justice—a decision which Eisenhower later described as the "biggest damnfool mistake I ever made"—the President opened a new chapter in the history of the Supreme Court.

In 1953, however, the choice seemed a satisfactory one to Republicans. A loyal partisan, Warren was the most popular governor in the history of California. He achieved political success on the basis of an energetic career, first as a crime-fighting district attorney in San Francisco, and then as Attorney General of California. His political career provided no augury for the future of his career as Chief Justice. In 1941, he supervised the internment of the Japanese Americans in California in a manner which grossly violated their constitutional rights. As governor, Warren opposed reapportionment plans which would have given cities such as Los Angeles, San Francisco, and Oakland representation in the state legislature consistent with their proportion of the state's population. Moreover, Warren had also accused the Truman administration of "coddling" Communists.

Yet, as Chief Justice, Warren manifested concern for civil liberties, a burning social conscience, and a desire to extend the role of the court in government. A skillful politician, Warren was a persuasive advocate, and he frequently won a majority of the court to his position. From 1953 until his retirement in 1969, Warren directed a judicial revolution which made the Supreme Court the most important instrumentality for political and social change in the United States during the 1950s and 1960s.

Desegregation and Public Education

This judicial revolution had been long gathering. After a series of rulings from 1944 to 1953, the legal basis of segregation was eroding. The court had ruled, first, that blacks could not be excluded from state primary elections on account of race; second, that persons could not be excluded from jury service on account of race; third, that so-called restrictive covenants (agreements by buyers of houses not to sell them to persons of certain races and religions) were unenforceable; and, fourth, that segregation was illegal in the District of Columbia, in interstate transportation, and in public recreational facilities.

The vanguard of the challenge to Jim Crow in the courts was the NAACP's

Legal Defense Fund. The organization consisted of black lawyers such as Thurgood Marshall, many of them trained during the 1930s at Howard University's School of Law. The NAACP pursued a long-term strategy. It first insisted on a strict interpretation of the Plessy decision; if public facilities were separate, they maintained, let them be truly equal. By the Second World War, however, the NAACP had begun to challenge the constitutionality of the Jim Crow system as it applied to elementary, secondary, and higher education. In 1950, the Vinson Court ruled in Sweatt v. Painter that a law school for blacks in Texas—which was quickly established to meet the requirements of Plessy—did not, and could not, constitute a legal education equal to the one offered by the Law School of the University of Texas at Austin. The court thus ordered the university to admit the claimant, Herman M. Sweatt, as a student in the white law school. But in this and other cases, the Supreme Court had refused to overturn Plessy.

The legal assault on the constitutionality of segregated schools culminated in 1954 in the Supreme Court's landmark ruling in Brown v. Topeka Board of Education. The case, which included the NAACP's challenges to segregation in public schools in Virginia, South Carolina, Delaware, as well as in Kansas, was argued before the court during 1953. Backed by a unanimous decision, Chief Justice Warren read the decision in the Brown case on May 17, 1954. It reversed the Plessy decision and decreed that enforced racial segregation in public schools violated the Fourteenth Amendment's equal-protection clause. Warren, to a large extent, accepted the arguments which the NAACP had presented, particularly the assertion by the black sociologist, Kenneth Clark, that segregation impaired learning by black children. Separate schools were therefore inherently unequal because they stamped black children as inferior and denied them equal protection under the law. It was one of the most important decisions in the history of the Supreme Court and the opening blast in the civil-rights revolution.

In 1955, the court established the guidelines for the implementation of the Brown decision. Warren deliberately left the enforcement of the decision vague by instructing federal district courts to require local authorities to show "good faith," to "make a prompt and reasonable start toward full compliance," and to move with "all deliberate speed" toward desegregation of all public schools.

School desegregation was fairly well accomplished in the District of Columbia and the Border States by 1957. By the same date, a beginning toward school desegregation had been made in North Carolina, Tennessee, Arkansas, and Texas, while more than half of the formerly all-white publicly supported colleges and universities in the South had opened their doors to blacks.

But in Virginia and the Deep South, the Brown decision met with a concerted and well-orchestrated program of "massive resistance." The legislatures in these states passed legislation which denounced the Supreme Court's ruling as unconstitutional and which mandated the closing of public schools if they were desegregated. The first and strongest defiance of the federal courts took place in Little Rock, Arkansas, where, in September 1957, violence erupted in response to the desegregation of Central High School and where Governor Orval E. Faubus dispatched the National Guard to prevent the matriculation of black pupils. Although Eisenhower privately deplored the Brown decision, he found such defiance of federal authority unacceptable. He ordered the National Guard of Arkansas into national service and also sent in federal paratroopers to reopen the school and to maintain the peace. Thus the power of the federal government, for the first time since Radical Reconstruction, was marshaled—through the courts, the presidency, and even the army—to guarantee basic civil rights for blacks.

Early in 1959, another antiintegrationist citadel surrendered. Virginia, led by Senator Harry F. Byrd and most other state politicians, had spearheaded the "massive resistance" in the South. Nonetheless, in 1959 the Old Dominion allowed local school boards to obey federal court orders if they wished to continue their public schools. Two years later, the Georgia legislature followed by permitting limited desegregation in Atlanta. By the inauguration of John F. Kennedy in 1961, only South Carolina, Alabama, and Mississippi still maintained all-out resistance.

In cases relating to internal security, the Warren Court moved to restore traditional constitutional protection to individuals. In Pennsylvania v. Nelson (1956), it barred enforcement of state sedition laws on the ground that Congress had preempted antisubversion legislation. However, in the following year the court struck boldly in defense of civil rights in Yates v. United States. In this decision, the court overturned the decision in the Dennis case. The Smith Act, Warren said in the Yates decision, had forbidden only conspiracies and overt *acts* to overthrow the government by force, not the *teaching or advocacy* of the overthrow of government as an abstract principle. Thus, without openly invalidating the Smith Act, Warren made it a dead statute.

Warren's judicial activism in the area of civil rights earned him widespread criticism and hatred. Calls for his impeachment appeared on billboards, fences, and car bumpers throughout the country, but especially in the South and the Southwest. The court was criticized for legislating rather than interpreting the law—an accurate assessment to some extent—although Warren responded by maintaining that only an activist Supreme Court could guarantee the higher law of the Constitution. Moreover, it is important to remember that the Warren Court operated in something of a power vacuum, especially in the area of civil rights. Eisenhower deliberately and scrupulously avoided making decisions—especially about an issue such as civil rights—and Congress remained unable to form a consensus on most important issues. As we will see (pg. 300), the Warren Court's revolution in constitutional interpretation had only just begun by the end of the Eisenhower administration.

2. THE EISENHOWER FOREIGN POLICY

The New Look

John Foster Dulles, long-time leading Republican spokesman on foreign policy, was, from 1953 until 1959, one of the most controversial Secretaries of State in American history. A nephew of Wilson's Secretary of State, Robert Lansing, Dulles had been an active participant in American foreign policy during the Paris Peace Conference and between the two world wars. Armed with supreme self-confidence which partly arose from experience and partly from his own peculiar personality, he thus became the director of American foreign policy in 1953. Above all, Dulles was a rigid absolutist, particularly about what he considered the threat from international communism. Shortly after the First World War, Dulles became convinced that a monolithic "world Communist movement"—"an unholy alliance of Marx's communism and Russia's imperialism"—imperiled the world. Events after 1945 only strengthened this belief. Dulles, it should be noted, was an adept politician; his most important role was to protect Eisenhower and the administration's foreign policy from McCarthy and the Republican right wing.

The controversy surrounding Dulles is in large part the product of his undeniable gift for coining catchy phrases and slogans. In the Republican platform of 1952, he inserted a promise that a Republican administration would repudiate all "secret understandings," such as the Yalta agreements, and find a substitute for the "negative, futile, and immoral" policy of containment. Dulles suggested that the United States could somehow win the Cold War against the Soviet Union. He hinted about the liberation of "captive peoples" under Soviet domination—an apparent reference to eastern Europe and the Baltic states—and about the use of "massive retaliation" against the Soviet Union or Communist China if they committed serious aggression. On still another occasion, he warned of the "unleashing" of Chiang Kai-shek on the Chinese mainland. Meanwhile, there would be "agonizing reappraisals" of American foreign policy; and in some cases Dulles talked about carrying the country to "the brink of war" (giving rise to the term "brinkmanship") in order to preserve the peace of the world. The implied meaning of "the brink," of course, was that the United States would go over it if that policy failed and use "massive retaliation" against its enemy.

It was unfortunate that the Secretary of State possessed such a talent for phrasemaking. His slogans frightened not only the allies of the United States, who took them seriously for a while, but also a good many Americans. Even more significantly, they obscured the reality of Eisenhower's foreign policy. First, Eisenhower, not Dulles, made almost all important decisions in the field of foreign affairs, and, on several important occasions, the President overruled his Secretary of State. Both held similar views about American foreign policy—firm commitment to a continuation of the Cold War, certainty of the moral superiority of the American position in this conflict, and the precedence of European affairs over problems which arose elsewhere. Second, Eisenhower and Dulles carried forward policies whose foundations had been firmly laid by Roosevelt and Truman. Third, Dulles, in spite of his bombast, was a cautious and resourceful diplomat, and his accomplishments were considerable.

Containment in the Far East

The first task in foreign policy which faced the Eisenhower administration was the conclusion of the war in Korea. The Chinese and North Koreans had opened armistice negotiations with General Ridgway in the summer of 1951. The discussions proceeded until October 1952, when North Korea broke them off.

One of Dulles' first important acts as Secretary of State was to send a message to the Chinese leaders that the United States would open a wholesale offensive, perhaps against China as well as North Korea, if the North Koreans did not bargain in good faith. Although neither Dulles nor Eisenhower would have risked an invasion of China, their bluff was effective. Negotiations were reopened, and the combatants finally signed an armistice at Panmunjom, Korea, on July 27, 1953. It provided for the return of prisoners on a voluntary basis and established a demilitarized buffer zone along the battle line not far from the thirty-eighth parallel.

In spite of criticism about the lack of a clear-cut victory, to many contemporaries the Korean War seemed a significant triumph for the United Nations. Invaders from North Korea, later fully supported by Communist China's finest armies, had attempted to conquer the UN-sponsored Republic of Korea. The aggressors had been defeated with terrible losses to themselves. American aid had made it possible for the infant world organization to win its first major test at arms. More than 1,500,000 American soldiers participated during the three years of fighting in Korea, and of this number 54,246 gave their lives.

However, no sooner had peace talks begun in Korea than a new crisis broke out to the south. In northern Indochina, the Viet Minh, led by the Communist and nationalist, Ho Chi Minh, had waged a successful guerrilla war against the French, who sought to maintain their colonies in Southeast Asia. The war went badly for the French, who were able to control cities but conceded the countryside to the Viet Minh. In 1954, the Vietnamese rebels, commanded by Nguyen Van Giap, captured a large French force at Dien Bien Phu, and the French soon afterward sued for peace. The considerations of the Cold War—particularly the determination to prevent the "fall" of another Asian nation—promptly deepened American involvement in what was a colonial war. As early as 1950, the United States subsidized French forces; by 1954, it paid for 80 per cent of their expenditures. When the hard-pressed French were near defeat, Dulles, supported by Vice-President Nixon among others, proposed to extend American involvement through the use of tactical nuclear weapons and American troops. With public opinion clearly lukewarm for American military participation, Eisenhower vetoed these plans and supported the calling of an international conference, which met in Geneva in April 1954. The Geneva Conference not only ended the war but also provided a Final Declaration, which—after a temporary truce—provided for the reunification of Vietnam (that is, the French-controlled South with the northern part of the country) through elections to be held in July 1956. Dulles, who was aware that Ho would overwhelmingly win these elections, immediately worked to undermine the Geneva accords. Dulles and the Americans first refused to sign the Geneva treaty. In June 1954, American-trained sabotage teams conducted operations, apparently unsuccessfully, all over Vietnam to destabilize the Viet Minh. Most important, the United States swung its full support behind Ngo Dinh Diem, a South Vietnamese Roman Catholic who had collaborated with the French colonial forces.

Out of a fear that all of Asia might soon fall under Communist control, Dulles promoted a new anti-Communist alliance. Soon after the Geneva Conference, delegates from Australia, Great Britain, France, New Zealand, Pakistan, the Philippines, Thailand, and the United States signed a pact on

September 8, 1954, which created the Southeast Asia Treaty Organization (SEATO). Like the North Atlantic Treaty, the Manila Pact pledged joint action in the event of aggression against any member nation, and it provided special protection for Cambodia, Laos, and the new Republic of Vietnam (South Vietnam). The new security system in the Pacific was completed in December 1954, when Dulles signed a mutual defense treaty with the Chinese Nationalist government on Taiwan. It provided protection against an attack by mainland China, as had a similar mutual security treaty which Dulles signed with South Korea in October 1953.

German Rearmament

Just as crises shook the Far East, so a controversy in the West threatened to split NATO. It involved the question of whether to rearm Germany and incorporate it into the western defense system. Truman had made such a suggestion as early as 1950. France, Italy, Belgium, the Netherlands, Luxembourg, and West Germany had signed a treaty on May 27, 1952, which provided machinery for the formation of a European Defense Community (EDC) as soon as the parliaments of each nation approved. The important feature of the EDC was its plan for a tightly integrated western European army with German contingents.

Trouble soon developed because no majority could be found in the French Chamber of Deputies for any plan to put rifles in the hands of German soldiers. Dulles entered the fray by warning that continued French refusal to ratify the EDC treaty would force the United States to make an "agonizing reappraisal" of its foreign policy—in other words, perhaps to abandon NATO. The threat, empty at best, only further angered the French, who replied by rejecting the EDC treaty again in August 1954.

A solution proposed by the British foreign secretary, Anthony Eden, resulted in the signing of the compromise Paris Pact on October 23, 1954. In this treaty, the western powers gave full sovereignty to the Federal Republic of Germany. The Brussels Treaty Organization was expanded to include West Germany and Italy. West Germany was admitted to NATO and permitted an army of 500,000 men to serve under NATO command. Finally, the United States and Great Britain promised to keep troops on the continent so long as the Brussels Treaty Organization wanted them to remain there.

The First Summit Conference

The Soviet dictator, Stalin, died in 1953, and a new government, headed, first, by Georgi Malenkov and, soon afterward, by Nikolai A. Bulganin, came to power in Moscow. For a time, at least, these new Soviet rulers seemed to want sincerely to reduce the tensions of the Cold War. Eisenhower met suggestions for a summit conference of the leaders of the great powers with some enthusiasm. Like Franklin D. Roosevelt, Eisenhower believed that he could accomplish much by personal diplomacy. The conference met at Geneva in July 1955, in an atmosphere of strained cordiality. Although the chiefs of state of the United States, Russia, Great Britain, and France adopted no concrete measures to end the Cold War, they did refer four major problems to their foreign ministers for further discussions. These were European security, disarmament, German unification, and increased communication across what was now called the "iron curtain" which separated the western and eastern blocs. The "spirit of Geneva" quickly evaporated when the foreign ministers returned to Geneva in October 1955. Since both sides were still determined to have their way on all issues, the conference broke up without a single agreement.

The St. Lawrence Seaway

The relations of the two North American neighbors, the United States and Canada, presented a different story. Their main problem at the beginning of the Eisenhower administration was cooperation in building a seaway from the St. Lawrence River to Lake Ontario. The seaway would open the Great Lakes to large freighters and passenger ships and make possible the development of vast new hydroelectric power.

Both Roosevelt and Truman had tried to win congressional approval for the project, and both had failed because of opposition from the eastern states and railroads. Finally, in May 1954, Congress yielded to pressure from the new President (and from Canada, which threatened to go ahead on its own); and digging for new locks and dams began almost at once. The seaway, completed in the spring of 1959, was formally opened by Elizabeth II and Eisenhower.

3. THE SECOND EISENHOWER ADMINISTRATION

The Election of 1956

Two events caused Democrats to look to the presidential election of 1956 with increasing confidence. The first was the somewhat surprising result of the mid-term election in 1954—the election of a Congress with small Democratic majorities in both houses. The second event shocked the country. On September 24, 1955, Eisenhower suffered a heart attack. He was soon out of danger, but for several months all observers took it for granted that he would not run again. But Eisenhower's recovery was almost complete by early 1956, and he announced on February 29 that he would be a candidate for reelection. Eisenhower and Vice-President Nixon were renominated by acclamation by the Republican national convention.

The Democrats had met in Chicago only a week earlier. Ex-President Truman tried to rally old-line liberals behind Governor W. Averell Harriman of New York, but Stevenson, who had conducted a spirited and successful fight in the presidential primaries, easily won the nomination on the first ballot. Senator Estes Kefauver of Tennessee, Stevenson's chief rival in the preconvention campaign, was named as Stevenson's running mate.

Both parties waged short campaigns which, for the first time, intensively employed television advertising. The Republicans had the advantage of Eisenhower's enormous popularity and of continuing prosperity. "Everything," Republicans exclaimed, "is booming but the guns!" Democratic hopes lay in better local organizations and in support from labor and blacks. In the final analysis, the campaign was a popularity contest between a candidate who did not seem able to rouse the voters and a President who remained a hero to many Americans. Indeed, the actual differences on issues between the two party platforms and the two candidates were narrow.

Eisenhower's victory was never in doubt, and the explosion of war in the Middle East in late October (see pp. 274–76) created a sharp crisis which turned many wavering voters to the President's side. He polled 35,590,000 popular votes and carried forty-one states. In contrast, Stevenson won only 26,023,000 popular votes and seven states. Once again, however, voters endorsed Eisenhower and not his party. The Democrats actually increased their majorities in Congress and elected governors in several hitherto Republican states. Not since 1848 had the party which won the presidency lost both houses of Congress in the same election.

Recession and Response

The most urgent problem confronting Eisenhower and the new Eighty-fifth Congress was a business recession which threatened to turn into a full-fledged depression. It began with a sharp decline on the stock market in the summer and autumn of 1957. The recession received further stimulation from a cutback in spending for new plants and machinery in the United States and by a decline in commodity prices and trade throughout the world. By January 1958, unemployment in the United States had reached a postwar high of nearly 4,500,000.

There never was any serious disagreement between the President and Congress as to whether the government should act to reverse the downward economic trend. Gone forever were the days when Americans would accept depressions as something which they could do nothing about. But sharp disagreement existed between the White House and Capitol Hill over the weapons to be used. Many Democrats urged drastic tax reductions and large federal spending in order to increase consumers' purchasing power. Eisenhower and his Council of Economic Advisers, in contrast, stood firmly behind a more limited program of increased credit, encouragement to home construction, a 7 per cent increase in Social Security benefits, extension of unemployment insurance payments, and some expansion of federal spending for highways, hospitals, housing, and schools. The administration had its way, mainly because a powerful group of Democratic senators who followed Majority Leader Lyndon B. Johnson also favored moderate policies.

The so-called built-in antidepression machinery worked perfectly during this recession. By May 1958, the economic downturn had ended, and the economy was growing at normal speed again by the beginning of 1959. Nonetheless, some Democrats pointed to a retarded growth rate in the 1950s, as compared with the rate of the 1940s, and to persistently high unemployment of about 6 per cent of the labor force, as proof that stronger countercyclical devices should have been used in the recession of 1957.

The Sputnik Scare

The development of missiles had been proceeding in Russia and the United States since the end of the Second World War, and Americans confidently believed that they were far ahead in the race for new weapons. Then, in October 1957, a new star appeared in the sky. It was Russia's *Sputnik I,* the first earth-launched satellite. Americans suddenly realized that, if the Russians had rockets powerful enough to launch satellites, they possessed rockets powerful enough to bombard the United States with nuclear weapons. The Russians had exploded an atomic bomb in 1949 and a hydrogen bomb in 1953, not long after the first American hydrogen bomb had been detonated. A second Russian Sputnik appeared in the sky a month after the first one. The successful launching of the first American satellite, *Explorer I,* in January 1958, did not quiet American fears that the Russians were considerably ahead in the rocket race. And Democrats and aerospace corporations encouraged widespread talk and fear of a "missile gap"—a period when the Soviet Union would command vastly more intercontinental missiles than the United States.

Congress therefore met in a state of high excitement, not to say alarm, when it assembled in January 1958. Eisenhower presented the largest peacetime budget in American history, which called for expenditures of nearly $74 billion. Congress increased this sum to more than $76 billion and provided an additional $4 billion for rocket and missile development and the conquest of outer space. (Appropriations for defense ran at the same level of about $40 billion during the next two years.) In addition, at Eisenhower's request, the lawmakers amended the Atomic Energy Act of 1946 to permit the sharing of atomic secrets with America's allies; created a National Aeronautics and Space Administration (NASA) to coordinate research and development; gave the Secretary of Defense much greater direct control over the three branches of the armed services; and adopted the National Defense Education Act, which granted funds to schools for special programs in science, mathematics, and foreign languages. Ironically, the Sputnik scare made possible a vast increase in federal aid to education.

Alaska and Hawaii were especially important to American defenses. Bases near Anchorage, Kodiak, and Fairbanks, and the Distant Early Warning (DEW) Line of radar outposts stood guard to signal possible attacks across the Arctic. The great naval base at Pearl Harbor in Hawaii controlled the vast Pacific to Formosa Strait. Alaska contained huge natural resources, including some of the world's most magnificent scenery. Hawaii, too, ranked among the earth's most beautiful regions. Nevertheless, Alaskan and Hawaiian pleas for statehood had repeatedly died in Congress; but the rocket and jet plane had annihilated the "too far from the mainland" argument. In June 1958, Congress paved the way for the admission of Alaska, and it entered the Union as the forty-ninth state on January 3, 1959. Nor was Hawaii's admission long delayed. After action by Congress in March 1959, it entered as the fiftieth state on August 21, 1959.

Democratic Resurgence

All signs seemed to point to a modest Democratic victory in the mid-term election in November 1958. Three developments turned what might have been a moderate Democratic gain into a landslide. First, a congressional committee discovered that Eisenhower's chief assistant, Sherman Adams, had been receiving gifts from a businessman in return for favors rendered. Eisenhower refused to discuss Adams and would not accept his resignation until September. Second, Republicans made open-shop, or "right-to-work," laws the main issue in many states and thus aroused the vigorous participation of organized labor on the Democratic side. Third, farmers blamed Republicans for the Agricultural Act of 1958, which cut price supports. A combination of these developments, together with some popular disillusionment about Eisenhower, resulted in a landslide victory which gave Democrats two-to-one majorities in both houses of the next Congress.

Democrats who expected to ride roughshod over the President in the Eighty-sixth Congress, which met in January 1959, underestimated Eisenhower's skill and popularity and the power of the presidential veto. With the resignation of Sherman Adams and the death of Secretary Dulles in May 1959, Eisenhower began to exercise a more direct leadership in domestic and foreign affairs. By the end of the first session of the new Congress, the President could claim as many victories as could his Democratic opponents.

The most important legislative accomplishment of the last two years of the Eisenhower era was a bipartisan one—the Labor-Management Reporting and Disclosure, or Landrum-Griffin, Act of 1959. It grew out of the recommendations of a special Senate committee headed by Senator John F. Kennedy of Massachusetts. For several years, the committee had been probing deeply into racketeering and corruption in some labor unions, especially the Teamsters' Union. An aroused public opinion demanded preventive legislation, and the Landrum-Griffin bill passed Congress by overwhelming majorities.

The new law required union officials to submit detailed financial reports to the Secretary of Labor. It also required employers to report on any payments to union officers and to labor-relations consultants. To protect union members who opposed their officers, a "bill of rights" guaranteed to members the right to vote in union elections and to speak up against union policies. Moreover, unions were required to hold regular elections. Finally, the act strengthened previous restrictions on secondary boycotts and blackmail picketing. These provisions hardly touched the powerful Teamsters' Union, which continued to contribute campaign funds liberally to key members of both parties.

4. INTERNATIONAL CHALLENGES, 1956–1960

The Suez Crisis

Except for the Korean armistice, the Eisenhower administration could claim no great diplomatic victories during its first years in power. Nevertheless, until mid-1956 it could say at least that the United States had suffered no major reversals and had more or less held its own in world affairs. Spokesmen of the administration could not make even these modest claims at the end of Eisenhower's tenure. The last four years, 1956–1960, were not only tumultuous but also full of reversals for the United States abroad. Even in Latin America, where the Good Neighbor policy had earlier won a host of friends, developments turned unfavorble after 1955. Vice-President Nixon's goodwill tour of Latin America in the spring of 1958 was marred by an outbreak of violence in Caracas, Venezuela. Moreover, in Cuba, the victory of Fidel Castro and his band of revolutionaries in early 1959 brought to power a regime soon bitterly hostile to the United States. Whether Castro was a dedicated Communist or was pushed toward dependence on the Soviets by the American administration's hasty opposition to the Cuban revolution remains a mystery. A repetition of the State Department's and CIA's coup, which helped to oust a pro-Communist government in Guatemala in 1954, could not be carried out immediately in the larger and more important Cuba, where it would have attracted worldwide scrutiny; but intensive planning for intervention began with Eisenhower's approval.

What seems to have been a chain of events in the Middle East began just before Eisenhower's smashing second electoral triumph. Israeli armed forces, goaded by Arab border raids and threats of destruction, attacked Egypt on

The Suez Crisis, 1956

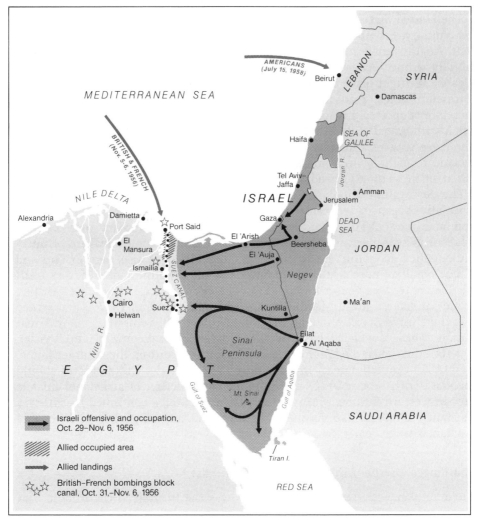

Israeli offensive and occupation, Oct. 29–Nov. 6, 1956

Allied occupied area

Allied landings

British–French bombings block canal, Oct. 31,–Nov. 6, 1956

October 29, 1956. Within four days, the Israelis had smashed the armies of President Gamal Abdel Nasser and had driven through the entire Sinai Peninsula. France and Great Britain had been angered by Nasser's aid to rebels against French rule in Algeria and by his recent seizure of the Suez Canal. Without the approval or knowledge of the United States Government, the British and French governments resolved to intervene to overthrow Nasser and regain control of the Suez lifeline. By a prearranged understanding with Israel, Great Britain and France demanded that Egypt and Israel stop fighting and withdraw from the area of the Suez Canal. When Nasser refused, the British destroyed what remained of the Egyptian air force and occupied the northern third of the canal.

The Soviet government was at this very moment suppressing an anti-Communist revolution in Budapest, Hungary. Soviet leaders sought to draw the spotlight of world opinion away from the Russian tanks, which were shooting down Hungarian workers, by condemning Great Britain, France, and Israel as aggressors in Egypt. The new Russian leader, Nikita S. Khrushchev, then threatened to send "volunteers" to help Egypt and to blast Great Britain and France with rockets carrying nuclear bombs.

The United States Government did not rush to the defense of its allies. On the contrary, Eisenhower and Dulles were personally angered by the independent Anglo-French military action. In addition, they thought that it was morally wrong because it smacked of old-fashioned imperialism, and unwise because it might drive the entire Arab world with its great, American-leased petroleum fields, into the arms of the Russians. Eisenhower and Dulles therefore supported a resolution in the UN which demanded a cease-fire and quick withdrawal of British, French, and Israeli forces from Egyptian territory. The three powers, threatened by Russia and opposed by their ally and friend, decided to comply. In contrast, the Soviets ignored a UN resolution which called upon them to withdraw their troops from Hungary.

The Suez affair shook the western alliance to its foundations. France, especially, began to reconsider its dependence on American military protection and the NATO alliance; it also began to develop its own nuclear weapons. The American government tried to restore some measure of unity and supplied economic aid to clear the Suez Canal. It also gave Britain and France credit to purchase huge quantities of oil from the United States until the Suez route was restored. Next, Eisenhower conferred with the new British Prime Minister, Harold Macmillan, in Bermuda in March 1957. They agreed that the United States should build intermediate-range missile sites in Great Britain. These advanced bases would provide some deterrence to Russian rockets. And, when disarmament talks with Russia during the summer failed, the NATO Council agreed, in December 1957, that the United States should negotiate with other NATO members for construction of additional missile sites in western Europe. Meanwhile, the United States continued its military assistance to NATO nations and others. By 1960, annual expenditures for this assistance were nearly $3.5 billion.

Challenges in the Middle East and Far East

The chief danger to world peace in 1957 was the turmoil in the Middle East which followed the Suez affair. American policymakers searched for a way that the United States could recover its influence in this oil-rich region. In an address to Congress on January 5, 1957, Eisenhower gave an answer in what was soon called the Eisenhower Doctrine. The United States, he announced, would help any middle eastern country to resist Communist military aggression and, in addition, would undertake aid programs for economic development.

Events soon revealed that the Eisenhower Doctrine contained fundamental weaknesses. It was based on the rather fatuous assumption that the dominant agent of change in the Middle East was worldwide communism and that American policy should therefore be geared toward maintaining the status quo. In practice, however, change in the Middle East was not a product of "Communist aggression." It was, rather, the result of a far-flung resurgence of Arab nationalism—at times directed against Israel, at times against the influence of the West—which was totally unrelated to Soviet-American competition. Moreover, the Eisenhower Doctrine could not be put into operation unless some government asked specifically for help. By sending some 14,000 marines into Lebanon at the request of the President of that country in July 1958, Eisenhower helped to prevent the overthrow of a government friendly to the United States. But the Eisenhower Doctrine provided no remedy when a much more serious crisis erupted in Iraq within the same week. There a group of army officers murdered the King and Prime Minister and knocked the props out from under the West's defensive system in the Middle East. America's only hope was that the new Iraqi government would at least remain neutral in the conflict between the great powers and not fall under the control of a pro-Soviet government. The same kind of threats which climaxed in Iraq existed in Syria, Iran, and virtually every other middle eastern nation.

No sooner had a kind of peace returned to the Middle East than the threat of war broke out on the other side of the globe. In August 1958, the Chinese Communists began to shell islands off the mainland held by the Nationalists. Eisenhower warned that the United States would join the fighting if the seizure of the offshore islands was part of a larger campaign against Taiwan. To back up his words, Eisenhower sent the powerful Seventh Fleet into Formosa Strait. This action was probably decisive; in any event, the threat of Communist invasion of the offshore islands had passed by November 1958.

The Berlin Crisis

A more severe test of diplomatic strength began on November 27, 1958, when the Soviet government submitted notes to Great Britain, France, and the United States which proposed that West Berlin be evacuated by Allied troops and be made a free city. Russia warned that it would sign a separate peace treaty with the East German regime unless the western Allies pulled out of Berlin within six months. If this happened, the western powers would have to make arrangements with East Germany for entry into Berlin; and if the East Germans forbade the Allies to enter the former German capital, the former would presumably have the military backing of their Soviet ally.

It was an obvious attempt either to split NATO or to force the western powers to abandon Berlin. The French, British, and American governments replied almost at once; they rejected Soviet demands and suggested a four-power meeting to consider the German problem. But how and when such a meeting could take place, no one seemed to know. Dulles, resolute in his opposition to a second summit meeting, proposed a conference of foreign ministers. Khrushchev, on the other hand, insisted upon a meeting of the heads of state to consider all the problems of the Cold War. The British Prime Minister, who visited Moscow and Washington in February and March 1959, tended to agree with Khrushchev.

The impasse was broken in a dramatic way not long afterward. Dulles died of cancer on May 24, 1959. He had been succeeded a month earlier by former Governor Christian A. Herter of Massachusetts. Eisenhower now took personal direction of foreign policy, and there were immediate results. In July, he sent Vice-President Nixon on a goodwill tour to Russia and Poland. In August, Eisenhower announced that he and Khrushchev would exchange visits. In the same month, Eisenhower flew to western Europe for conferences with leaders there; then, in mid-September, Eisenhower received Khrushchev. After he traveled to the West Coast and back, Khrushchev conferred again with Eisenhower in late September. The result was an agreement which seemed to promise an early end to the Berlin crisis: Khrushchev agreed to settle the Berlin question by negotiation and withdrew his six-month time limit, while Eisenhower made it plain that he would go to a summit meeting in the near future.

A Second Summit

During late 1959 and early 1960, all signs seemed to point to a solution of the Berlin crisis and a revival of American influence throughout the world. Eisenhower continued his efforts at personal diplomacy and made triumphal tours of eleven European and Asian nations in December 1959 and of four Latin American countries in February and March 1960. Secretary Herter and the Japanese Premier signed a new treaty of mutual security on January 19, 1960. It bound the United States and Japan in alliance and extended the American military presence in Japan. Leaders of the western powers met in a presummit conference in Paris on December 19, 1959, and invited Khrushchev to join them in a meeting during the coming spring. Negotiations with the Russians soon yielded agreement on May 16 as the date and Paris as the place of the conference.

At this point, bungling, bad luck, and bad temper spoiled all chances for an East-West understanding. On May 5, 1960, Khrushchev announced that, four days earlier, Soviet forces had shot down an American U-2 observation plane over the Soviet Union, but he gave no further information about the incident. Authorities in Washington immediately declared that the plane, on a routine meteorological mission, had strayed from its course. Two days after his original announcement, Khrushchev charged that the plane had been on an espionage mission over the Soviet Union. The pilot had been captured and had confessed. The Soviet evidence was so conclusive that Herter admitted the charge and implied that the espionage flights would continue. Eisenhower, in a television address, accepted personal responsibility for the aerial spying and, moreover, defended it. The atmosphere, consequently, was highly charged when the heads of state assembled in Paris in mid-May for the long-awaited summit meeting.

That conference actually never occurred. Khrushchev undoubtedly was genuinely upset by the U-2 incident. Perhaps he was determined already, as some American diplomats suspected, to wreck the Paris conference because he realized that he could not have his way on Berlin. Certainly, when Eisenhower presented him with an opportunity to vilify the American government, he was unwilling to pass it up. In any event, at the first meeting on May 16, Khrushchev made a violent personal attack on Eisenhower for continuing the spy-plane trips over the Soviet Union while he planned his meeting with Khrushchev; he also blamed the President for his attempt to justify their continuation rather than to apologize (as Khrushchev had requested) for the violation of Soviet air space and security. The Soviet leader also denounced the American lies about the U-2 plane when its crash was first announced, and he suggested that such untruthful announcements could have been made only with Eisenhower's consent. Khrushchev withdrew his earlier invitation to Eisenhower to visit Russia and announced that he would attend no more meetings until the President apologized for the U-2 incident. Eisenhower refused either to engage in personal recrimination or to apologize, and the conference broke up before it could begin.

Even though Khrushchev soon indicated that he was not prepared to force the Berlin issue, the unfortunate events at Paris were hard blows to hopes for the relaxation of tensions—and also to American prestige in the world. More bad news came in the months ahead. Eisenhower set out upon a visit of goodwill to Japan on June 12 and got as far as Manila. The Japanese government felt compelled to ask Eisenhower to cancel the tour after rioting mobs (which probably consisted mainly of Socialists and Communists) seemed to threaten his personal safety if he came to Tokyo. The Soviet delegation walked out of an East-West conference on the reduction of armaments at Geneva on June 27, 1960, when the American delegates refused to accept a Russian plan. A civil war rocked the newly proclaimed Republic of the Congo in July 1960, as mutinous Congolese troops went on a campaign of rapine and pillage. The dispatch of a UN task force prevented threatened Russian intervention and a serious international crisis, but brought no long-term solution to the new nation's basic problems.

5. THE ELECTION OF 1960

The Candidates

During all this turmoil abroad, the parties began to prepare for the presidential campaign of 1960. It soon became evident that the Republicans, forced by the Twenty-second Amendment to seek a new leader, would not be torn by violent struggles for the presidential nomination in 1960, as they had been eight years earlier. There were only two serious Republican contenders at the outset of the preconvention campaign—Nelson A. Rockefeller and Nixon. Rockefeller, elected Governor of New York in the face of the Democratic landslide of 1958, represented the progressive elements in the GOP. Convinced that he could not win the nomination without splitting his party, Rockefeller withdrew from the race on December 26, 1959. The road was cleared for the right wing's candidate, Nixon, and his triumph was assured when Eisenhower endorsed his candidacy on March 16, 1960.

Meanwhile, the Democrats had been hard at the game which they seemed to enjoy most—fighting among themselves for the leadership of their party. By the end of January 1960, four candidates openly contended for the nomination, while several others, including Stevenson, would not have refused a call. At first, the contest seemed to lie between Senator Hubert H. Humphrey of Minnesota, who hoped to rally New Dealers and Fair Dealers, and Senator John F. Kennedy of Massachusetts, a young leader of the eastern, urban wing and the first Roman Catholic to make a serious bid for the presidency since 1928.

The turning point of the Humphrey-Kennedy contest was the presidential primary in West Virginia on May 10. Kennedy polled 60 per cent of the votes in that predominantly Protestant state, and Humphrey withdrew from the race. From this point on, it was a question of whether Lyndon B. Johnson, who was sweeping the South and Southwest, and favorite-son candidates could prevent Kennedy's nomination on the first ballot. It also remained to be seen whether party leaders would risk running a Roman Catholic, despite the potential gain in votes from Catholics.

The questions were quickly answered at the Democratic national convention on July 11. With only token opposition from Southerners, the Democrats adopted the strongest civil-rights platform in their history. They proceeded with surprising speed to nominate Kennedy for the presidency on the first ballot. In a move which startled the convention as much as it did the country, Kennedy requested and obtained Johnson's nomination as his running mate.

Republicans gathered in Chicago ten days after the Democrats left Los Angeles. For a moment it seemed that conflict would break out over the platform, when Rockefeller threatened to take the fight to the floor and perhaps be a candidate himself if Nixon did not support his demands for a more progressive platform than had been drafted. Rockefeller had his way, and Nixon was named for the presidency almost unanimously on the first ballot. At Nixon's request, Henry Cabot Lodge, Jr., now Ambassador to the UN, was drafted for the second place on the Republican ticket.

The Debates

Dramatic events distracted American attention from the presidential candidates during the first weeks of the campaign. The Cuban government grew increasingly hostile to the United States and now turned openly for moral and material assistance to the Soviet Union. Then Khrushchev led a procession of heads of governments—including Castro—to the UN General Assembly which opened on September 20. For several weeks he both appalled and puzzled Americans by his antics, such as taking off his shoe and beating it on his desk in the General Assembly, as a means of protest against the proceedings.

Once it began, the presidential campaign became an exciting affair. Each candidate enjoyed certain advantages at the outset. Nixon benefited from Eisenhower's active support and had the advantage of having been much in the public eye for eight years. Nixon's supporters claimed that his great

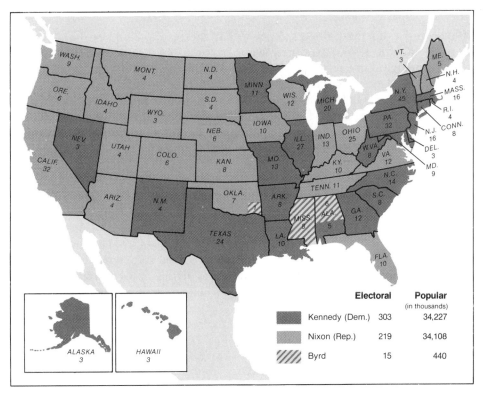

Electoral | Popular
(in thousands)

		Electoral	Popular (in thousands)
	Kennedy (Dem.)	303	34,227
	Nixon (Rep.)	219	34,108
	Byrd	15	440

The Election of 1960

experience made him the logical man to "stand up" to Khrushchev. Some Nixon supporters, although not the Nixon campaign organization itself, also circulated anti-Catholic literature, a tactic which apparently wored to Nixon's benefit. Kennedy enjoyed the advantage of greater party strength, better organization, personal attractiveness, and an electric personality. As might be expected, Catholics returned en masse to the Democratic fold. At the beginning of the campaign, the Democratic candidate tried, as he had done during the preconvention struggle, to eliminate the religious issue altogether by reaffirming loyalty to the historical American tradition of separation of church and state.

The turning point in the campaign came when the voters had an opportunity to judge the candidates in a series of four television debates between September 26 and October 24. It was the first time that presidential candidates had ever been brought face to face. The two men found it hard to grapple with issues, both for lack of time and because they agreed so much on fundamental principles. Consequently, they often discussed meaningless issues, such as American popularity abroad, or else questions which should never havebeen discussed in public, such as the defense of the Chinese offshore islands. Even so, Kennedy scored heavily by demolishing the Republican charge that he was inexperienced and badly informed. Moreover, Kennedy succeeded far better than his opponent in giving an impression of boldness, imagination, and poise.

Election Night

No one, not even the pollsters, knew what the result would be on election day, November 8, 1960, since there was a surge in Nixon's strength at the end of the campaign. First returns from the eastern states and big cities indicated a Kennedy landslide. Kennedy held his lead in the Northeast and most of the South Atlantic states, but, as election night passed into the morning of the next day, Nixon, who had carried most of the Middle West and West, whittled away at Kennedy's lead in the crucial states of Illinois, California, and Texas. Not since 1916 had a presidential election been so long in doubt. California finally went to Nixon after the absentee ballots were counted, while Illinois and Texas went to Kennedy by 9,801 and 45,264 votes, respectively. All told, of the nearly 68,500,000 popular votes cast, Kennedy won 34,227,000 and Nixon 34,108,000. Kennedy's popular plurality of two-tenths of 1 per cent was the smallest in the history of American presidential elections. The vote in the Electoral College was 303 to 219. The Democratic tide in the vote for congressmen and senators receded somewhat in 1960, but the next Congress would have Democratic majorities of sixty-four to thirty-six in the Senate and of 238 to 154 in the House of Representatives.

The election of 1960 had far-reaching meaning, to be sure, but the most significant result which could be read in the returns was the elimination of the religious issue—at least temporarily—as a decisive factor in American presidential politics. This is not to say that Kennedy's Roman Catholicism had not been a disturbing issue to many voters, but other issues probably were more important, and people who voted for and against the Democratic candidate because of his religion probably canceled each other out.

SUGGESTED READINGS

Most of the works cited in the Suggested Readings for Chapters 13 and 15 are relevant to the domestic issues of the Eisenhower administration. Herbert S. Parmet, *Eisenhower and The American Crusades* (1972); Charles C. Alexander, *Holding the Line: The Eisenhower Era, 1952–1961* (1975); Richard H. Rovere, *Affairs of State: The Eisenhower Years* (1956); and Robert J. Donovan, *Eisenhower, The Inside Story* (1956), are good surveys. The most complete accounts are by Eisenhower himself—*Mandate for Change* (1963) and *Waging Peace* (1965). Sherman Adams, *Firsthand Report* (1961); Lewis L. Strauss, *Man and Decisions* (1962); and Ezra T. Benson, *Cross Fire: The Eight Years with Eisenhower* (1962), are interesting personal accounts, while Emmet J. Hughes, *The Ordeal of Power* (1963), is a revealing discussion of the President and his administration as well. Richard Kluger, *Simple Justice: The History of Brown v. Board of Education and Black America's Struggle for Racial Equality* (1975), is an excellent book. On the period's legislation, the most valuable work is James L. Sundquist, *Politics and Policy: The Eisenhower, Kennedy, and Johnson Years* (1968).

Other important political figures in the Eisenhower administration can be studied in Patterson, *Mr. Republican*, already cited, and John W. Anderson, *Eisenhower, Brownell and the Congress* (1965), a study of the President and his Attorney General's relations with each other and with Congress concerning civil rights legislation.

The defense policy of the Eisenhower administration has been analyzed in numerous works. The best are Henry A. Kissinger, *Nuclear Weapons and Foreign Policy* (1956), Samuel P. Huntington, *Changing Patterns of Military Politics* (1962), and Robert A. Divine, *Eisenhower and the Cold War* (1981). Conflicting opinions on John Foster Dulles can be found in Emmet J. Hughes, *America the Vincible* (1959); John R. Beal, *John Foster Dulles: A Biography* (1957); Michael A. Hugin, *John Foster Dulles: A Statesman and His Times* (1972); and Townsend Hoopes, *The Devil and John Foster Dulles* (1973). Hugh Thomas, *The Suez Affair* (1967), is a good account of that crisis. For the problem of the underdeveloped nations, see Barbara Ward, *The Rich Nations and the Poor Nations* (1962).

CHAPTER 15
TURMOIL AT HOME
AND ABROAD,
1961 – 1968

1. THE KENNEDY ADMINISTRATION AND POLITICAL DEADLOCK

The New Frontier

It snowed heavily in Washington on January 19, 1961, and the following morning dawned clear and bitterly cold. But Democrats were rejoicing too warmly to mind the biting western wind. They had controlled both houses of Congress since 1955; on January 20, they would take possession of the White House as well. The world was about to witness democracy's most impressive drama—the peaceful transfer of control of the presidency of the United States from one person to another of a different party. Perhaps the country soon would see movement, too, toward the New Frontiers about which the successful candidate had talked so much during the campaign.

The inaugural procession moved slowly from the White House down a Pennsylvania Avenue which had been swept bare of snow. The presidential party, led by the tall, handsome forty-three-year-old President-elect and his beautiful, fashionably dressed, thirty-one-year-old wife, Jacqueline, walked briskly to the stands at the east front of the Capitol and faced the assembled throng. After the usual rituals, Chief Justice Warren administered the oath of office. The United States had a new and vigorous President; the western world, perhaps a new leader.

Tens of millions of Americans watched as John Fitzgerald Kennedy began his inaugural address. He began by reminding his fellow countrymen that they were heirs to the first successful constructive revolution in history. "Let the word go forth from this time and place, to friend and foe alike," he continued, "that the torch has been passed to a new generation of Americans." He called for a "grand and global alliance" against "the common enemies of man: tyranny, poverty, disease, and war itself"; he also pledged strong support to the United Nations and generous assistance to underdeveloped countries. He concluded:

> In your hands, my fellow citizens, more than mine, will rest the final success or failure of our course. . . . In the long history of the world, only a few generations have been granted the role of defending freedom in its hour of maximum danger. . . . The energy, the faith, the devotion which we bring to this endeavor will light our country and all who serve it—and the glow from that fire can truly light the world. And so, my fellow Americans: ask not what your country can do for you—ask what you can do for your country.

The New President

John F. Kennedy was born in Brookline, Massachusetts, on May 29, 1917, into a large Irish-American Roman Catholic family. His grandfathers on both sides had been prominent in Irish Democratic politics in Boston. Kennedy's maternal grandfather, John Francis ("Honey Fitz") Fitzgerald, was a legendary former mayor of Boston and a long-time "friendly" contender against James M. Curley for leadership of the Boston Democratic party. John F. Kennedy's father, Joseph P. Kennedy, had made a large fortune in business and finance and had served as ambassador to Great Britain from 1937 to 1940. Young John F. Kennedy was graduated with honors from Harvard in 1940. After distinguished war service, he entered politics and was elected to the House of Representatives in 1946 and to the Senate in 1952 and 1958. The greatest political influence on Kennedy, aside from his father, came from a group of Irish-American advisers and trusted aides. Kennedy ran unsuccessfully for the Democratic vice-presidential nomination in 1956. But no sooner had he failed in his bid than he began an unrelenting campaign for the presidential nomination in 1960.

Well before the campaign of 1960 was over, it was obvious that a new star had risen on the American political horizon. Kennedy was not only the youngest man ever elected to the presidency, but he was also one of the most fascinating. With reporters, he was relaxed, candid, and witty. To the people at large, he gave the impression of youthful vigor infused with intelligence.

To young Americans, especially, Kennedy seemed to promise a new quality of leadership. "Style" was the word most frequently used to describe the difference between Kennedy and the preceding generation of Presidents and presidential candidates. The new national leader possessed a sharp wit which effectively exposed the foibles of established institutions and politicians. He seemed imaginative and unconventional enough to be open to new ideas and to try new approaches. His presence in the White House gave hope to youthful citizens (who included some of the more rebellious ones) that they might still identify with their government and respect their country. This idealization of Kennedy was widespread enough for some to refer to it as a cult.

Kennedy also undeniably had weaknesses as well as strengths. Inexperience in the conduct of foreign affairs caused him to make costly blunders. His most striking weakness was his inability to establish his leadership of Congress in legislative policies. Circumstances over which he had no control were in part responsible. The acclaim which greeted his inaugural address gave the appearance of an overwhelming support for the new administration that did not exist. The Eighty-seventh Congress, which sat in 1961 and 1962, was at first glance solidly Democratic. Yet, because many southern Democrats broke ranks to vote with Republicans on crucial bills, Kennedy never enjoyed a reliable, working majority. Kennedy and his aides never admitted Vice-President Johnson into the inner circle of the White House; as a result, they did not exploit Johnson's remarkable skills at producing congressional support.

Kennedy also suffered the consequences both of his own political philosophy and of his own political past. Despite the somewhat misleading rhetoric of his inaugural address, he believed that the day of passionate commitment to causes was over. The United States, he thought, had reached a solid consensus on domestic policies. Therefore, his role was to use the resources of the political and intellectual communities to work out the details of legislation, not to lead a new reform movement. Moreover, as a representative and senator, Kennedy had never won the respect of his colleagues or been a member of the inner congressional circle because he was something of a dilettante and obviously ambitious for higher office. As President, he demonstrated a striking inability to use the techniques and power which a President must master in order to lead the men and women on Capitol Hill. He proposed legislation but allowed Congress to go its own way, without sufficient pressure from the White House or strong efforts on his part to rally public opinion. Kennedy was not a strong domestic leader, finally, because he was preoccupied with foreign affairs. With the exception of a few programs, he seemed to lack any serious interest in domestic policies.

It is important to remember, moreover, that Kennedy was a Cold Warrior. If anything, he was more aggressive and rigid in his anticommunism than Eisenhower. Kennedy was entranced, especially, by the possibilities of war conducted quietly by expertly trained special units, and he was an enthusiastic supporter of crack units, such as the Special Forces (Green Berets) and the 82nd Airborne Division of the army.

It is only fair to add that this evaluation is based upon Kennedy's brief tenure as President. He served only his apprenticeship in the White House. Kennedy was giving evidence of greater wisdom in foreign affairs and firmer mastery of domestic politics before his untimely death in 1963. We will never know whether he would have fulfilled the promise that he did begin to show.

Slow Progress

Kennedy outlined his domestic program in a State of the Union address on January 30, 1961, and in additional later messages and speeches. He spoke boldly and called for measures to "get the country moving again," but he soon discovered that unexpected circumstances have a way of defeating even the best-laid plans. Perhaps his most ironic defeat was the failure of his ambitious federal aid-to-education bill. Kennedy, on February 20, 1961, proposed to spend more than $5.6 billion to enrich and equalize educational opportunities. The states would receive about $2.3 billion over a three-year period for public-school construction and teachers' salaries. The rest of the money would go to colleges and universities for scholarships to needy undergraduates over a five-year period. The bill passed the Senate easily enough. Then Roman Catholic bishops and leaders insisted that the measure be amended to provide aid to parochial schools. Kennedy would not yield, because he thought that their proposal was unconstitutional; and enough Roman Catholic Democratic congressmen joined the bipartisan conservative opposition to defeat the administration's bill in the House of Representatives. The measure met a similar fate when Kennedy sent it back to Congress in 1962. Moreover, a new bill to aid higher education also ran aground on the shoals of religious controversy in 1962.

Opposition arose to other administration measures. An ambitious plan called Medicare—to provide medical care for the aged through the Social Security system—did not even receive serious consideration because of violent opposition from the American Medical Association. A new Food and Agriculture Act to regulate production of wheat was adopted in 1962 after much hard work on Capitol Hill. Then the measure was rejected by wheat farmers themselves in a referendum in 1963.

But the new President was not always disappointed during his first two years in office. The Housing Act of 1961 was a major administration victory. It authorized the expenditure of $4.9 billion over a four-year period for local urban renewal projects. It also included a provision for college dormitory construction and liberalized terms for home mortgages. Under Kennedy's prodding, the Democrats also honored their campaign promise to increase the minimum wage. A law which went into effect on September 3, 1961, raised the minimum from $1 to $1.25 an hour and extended protection of the Fair Labor Standards Act to an additional 3,624,000 workers. An Area Redevelopment Act, approved May 1, 1961, provided $300 million in loans and grants for new industries and the retraining of workers in some 675 "distressed areas" of high unemployment. This was supplemented in 1962 by a Manpower Development and Training Act to help workers threatened by automation. Amendments to the Drug Act, adopted in 1962, imposed new controls upon the manufacture and sale of drugs. However, the administration could probably have obtained a stronger bill pushed by Senator Kefauver if it had fought for it. The Twenty-fourth Amendment, which outlawed the poll tax as a requirement for voting for federal officials, was approved by Congress in 1962 and ratified in January 1964.

The Eighty-seventh Congress did not disagree with Kennedy about maintaining powerful defenses against possible aggression abroad. Congress appropriated nearly $47 billion in 1961 and more than $48 billion in 1962 for defense. It also authorized the President to call 250,000 reserves into active service for a year. All leaders in Washington continued to push the missile program because it seemed to offer the best hope of enabling the United States to deter war. Americans could feel reasonably secure by the end of 1961—and even more secure by 1965—for the first time since *Sputnik I* sailed across the sky. The missile gap with Russia had been closed—if, indeed, it had ever existed. The United States owned a fleet of nuclear submarines (twenty-nine of them by 1965) armed with Polaris nuclear missiles. The United States also had an arsenal of Atlas intercontinental missiles in position, and (by 1965) more than 500 new solid-fuel Minuteman missiles in underground "silos." Altogether, it constituted an awesome array of power.

Kennedy also met enthusiastic response from Congress when he recommended a vast expansion of the space program begun by the Eisenhower administration. Congress applauded and appropriated generously when Kennedy, on May 25, 1961, requested approval of a program aimed at putting a task force on the moon by 1970. Progress in space flight continued uninterrupted. In July 1969, television viewers around the world watched Neil Armstrong and Edwin Aldrin guide an Apollo spaceship on the moon. As the first humans to traverse the lunar surface, the astronauts planted an American flag and left a plaque that read: "We came in peace for all mankind."

On Dead Center

The country seemed to be on political dead center again by the summer of 1962. Congress was deadlocked on important domestic issues, much as it had been since the Truman administration. The administration faced its first test of public confidence in the mid-term election of 1962. Kennedy campaigned hard for Democratic candidates, and it seemed that the Democrats would hold their own or else suffer only minor losses, for most people enjoyed unprecedented prosperity—rising wages, salaries, and business profits with a low rate of price inflation. The Cuban missile crisis, which occurred in late October (see pp. 291–92), stimulated popular support for Kennedy and contributed to the Democrats' success in increasing, moderately, their majorities in both houses of Congress.

A Revolution in Civil Rights Begins

The Eighty-eighth Congress, which sat in 1963 and 1964, was politically top-heavy, with sixty-seven Democrats and thirty-three Republicans in the Senate and 258 Democrats and 176 Republicans in the House of Representatives. Nonetheless, Kennedy lacked a majority which supported his program.

It is clear in retrospect that Congress was fiddling while the country burned. Americans, or at least a majority of thoughtful people outside the South, were aroused by the brutal police suppression, in April and May 1963, of black civil-rights demonstrations led in Birmingham by the Rev. Martin Luther King, Jr., and, in September, by the bombing of churches and the murder of black children in that same city. Blacks and whites alike joined in sympathetic demonstrations across the country to protest against segregation in housing and public accommodations. Demonstrations sometimes went beyond the bounds of law and order, and police authorities resorted to fire hoses, tear gas, clubs, and dogs. Some 758 demonstrations occurred between early May and the midsummer of 1963, as blacks and their white supporters pressed to destroy the last vestiges of Jim Crow on this, the one hundredth anniversary of the Emancipation Proclamation. It seemed that a terrible showdown between whites and blacks in the South might be brewing.

Kennedy, heretofore, had shown no great zeal for bold new civil-rights legislation. He had used troops to suppress a bloody riot in Oxford, Mississippi, in September 1962, when a federal court had compelled the admission of a black student by the University of Mississippi. He dispatched troops again to force the admission of blacks by the University of Alabama. In addition, Kennedy sent a mild civil-rights bill to Congress in February 1963. But, despite increasing criticism from black leaders, he did not press the measure for fear of imperiling southern support in Congress for other New Frontier bills.

Kennedy was finally galvanized into action by the Birmingham disorders and the demonstrations which followed. Kennedy spoke to the nation by television on June 11, 1963. Eight days later he sent a strong new civil-rights bill to Congress with the warning that continued federal inaction would cause leadership on both sides to pass "to the purveyors of hate and violence." The response throughout the country was electric. Protestant, Catholic, and Jewish leaders joined hands with civil-rights groups and the AFL-CIO in a campaign to stimulate pressure at the grass roots on Congress. On August 28, more than 200,000 blacks and whites gathered before the Lincoln Memorial in Washington in a peaceful demonstration for the civil-rights bill. There was some floundering and partisan wrangling on Capitol Hill in the late summer and early autumn of 1963, but the President and his brother, Attorney General Robert F. Kennedy, hammered out a revised bill with leaders of both parties in the House of Representatives in October; the new measure was then put on its way.

2. THE KENNEDY COLD WAR

Foreign Policy Objectives

The style of American diplomacy changed somewhat after the succession in 1961. The new Secretary of State, Dean Rusk, gave the appearance of greater ability and assurance than his immediate predecessor, Christian A. Herter, and of greater caution than John Foster Dulles. Kennedy, too, seemed to be more vigorous and more of a natural diplomat than Eisenhower. However, events soon demonstrated that things are not always as they seem. Moreover, the substance of foreign policy did not change under the new administration; the foreign policies of the early 1960s were marked by an almost complete continuity with the policies of the 1950s. Actually, except for differences in age and Dulles' experience between the world wars, Dulles, Rusk, and Acheson were practically interchangeable in terms of ideas, values, affiliations other than political party, and the goals of their foreign policies.

One fact, surely, had not yet changed: the seemingly unending global struggle between Russia and the United States for the loyalty of the uncommitted majority of the world and for predominance along the perimeters of the two great powers. Kennedy soon decided that the Russian Premier, Khrushchev, did not intend to change course simply because a new President had come to power. Khrushchev, for his part, soon found that the relatively young American relished leading the non-Communist nations in their Cold War course as much or more than had any of his predecessors.

Trouble erupted in Laos during the early months of the new administration, but it turned out, for the time at least, not to be serious. The European area in greatest peril was still Germany, and, in Asia, Vietnam. Khrushchev's main target in Germany remained West Berlin, where the United States,

Great Britain, and France continued to maintain a precarious position. Kennedy, in order to explore any possibility that the Russian leader might be willing to moderate his continued threats against Berlin, flew to Vienna for a meeting with the Soviet Premier in June 1961. It was not a summit meeting; the two men were simply taking each other's measure. We can only guess what Khrushchev thought of the young American. We know, however, that Kennedy was shocked by Khrushchev's belligerence and threats against Allied rights in Berlin. Conferences with President Charles de Gaulle in Paris and Prime Minister Harold Macmillan in London strengthened Kennedy's determination to stand and fight for Berlin if necessary. Kennedy announced this decision to the world in a television address on June 28. A month later, he again went before the people to say that he was asking Congress for an additional $3.25 billion for immediate increases in the armed forces, especially to meet the Soviet challenge to Berlin.

There could be no doubt now what the United States would do, and Khrushchev announced that he was willing to negotiate to see if a settlement of the Berlin question was possible. Meanwhile, to prevent the escape of thousands of East Germans to the West, the East German government, in August 1961, walled off East Berlin. Conversations between the American and Russian governments proceeded while American and Russian troops faced each other across this barrier. These conversations failed, as earlier ones had, and West Berlin continued to be a powder keg. But after 1961 the Soviets did not again seriously endanger the western position, and the powder keg, at least for a time, was without a fuse.

The Cuban Revolution and the American Response

The hardest blow to American prestige and the gravest threat to world peace during the early 1960s occurred not in Europe, but in the Caribbean. Castro's defiance of treaty obligations, confiscation of American property, and alliance with the Soviet Union strained Cuban-American relations to the breaking point during the last two months of the Eisenhower administration.

In September 1960, Eisenhower approved a plan to dislodge Castro proposed by Allen W. Dulles, director of the CIA and brother of John Foster Dulles. The plan involved the supply of arms and money to equip and train a force of anti-Castro Cubans in Guatemala. They would invade Cuba, establish a stronghold there, rally the mass of supposedly disaffected Cubans to their banner, and then sweep through the country to Havana. American planes would protect the landing force.

Preparations progressed during late 1960 and early 1961. Kennedy, relying on the advice of his intelligence and military specialists, approved the invasion in early April 1961, but he would not agree that there should be a United States air cover for the invaders. Some 1,400 armed Cuban refugees left for their homeland on April 17. Castro's forces easily destroyed and captured the little army as it became bogged down in the marshes of the Bay of Pigs on the southern coast of Cuba.

For the United States, the ill-planned, ill-timed, and futile project was more than a fiasco. Khrushchev, on April 18, threatened to go to Cuba's assistance if the United States did not "call a halt to the aggression against the Republic of Cuba." Kennedy replied in a public address on April 20; he warned that the

United States did not intend to permit the Russians to establish a military foothold in Cuba or elsewhere in Latin America.

New Confidence and New Horizons

The Cuban fiasco had unnerved the young President and his administration, and a pall of gloom hung over Washington. Then confidence slowly returned. However, Kennedy's conference with Khrushchev in Vienna made it clear that there were no quick and easy solutions to conflicts between the United States and the Soviet Union, and that the struggle with Russia might be prolonged and dangerous.

Kennedy's main reply to the Soviet challenges consisted of a foreign-aid program to help peoples in underdeveloped countries, particularly in Latin America. Overpopulation, underdevelopment, and poverty were acute in the Latin American countries, which had been much neglected by Truman and Eisenhower. Congress followed Kennedy's lead by approving a five-year Development Loan Fund of $7.2 billion. Next, on August 16, 1961, the United States worked through an Inter-American Conference at Punta del Este, Uruguay, and launched the Alliance for Progress. This program looked forward to the extension of some $20 billion in United States economic aid of various kinds over a ten-year period. It was designed to improve the relations of the United States with Latin America and to prevent Cuban-style revolutions. As it turned out, in many cases the Alliance for Progress supported repressive and unpopular dictatorships, and in some cases, because of corruption, little American aid reached poor sectors of the population.

Meanwhile, other signs indicated that the United States was seizing the initiative in its foreign policy. Soviet prestige suffered when the Russians resumed atmospheric testing of large nuclear bombs in the summer of 1961, and many people worldwide worried about the consequent increase in atmospheric radioactivity. One of Kennedy's answers was the creation of the Peace Corps to train thousands of young Americans for voluntary educational, medical, and technical services to people in underdeveloped countries. The immediate, enthusiastic response of young people showed that idealism remained very much alive on American college and university campuses, and the Peace Corps had become well established by the mid-1960s.

The Cuban Missile Crisis

All during the summer and autumn of 1962, the United States Government became increasingly alarmed at the buildup of Soviet arms in Cuba. Congress, in a joint resolution signed by Kennedy on October 3, warned that the United States was "determined to prevent by whatever means may be necessary, including the use of arms, the Marxist-Leninist regime in Cuba from . . . creation or use of an externally supported military capability endangering the security of the United States."

This warning went unheeded in Moscow and Havana. Aerial reconnaissance revealed to Kennedy unmistakable proof that the Russians were installing sites in Cuba for missiles capable of hitting nations in the western hemisphere, even targets in the United States. The Russian ambassador, summoned to the White House, denied the existence of the missile sites.

Kennedy and his advisers then decided to force a showdown at the risk of war. Kennedy announced his decision to the world in a dramatic television address on October 22, 1962. He denounced "this secret, swift, and extraordinary buildup of Communist missiles" and said that he had already ordered the United States Navy to begin "a strict quarantine on all offensive military equipment under shipment to Cuba"—in other words, a blockade against Russian ships which carried such equipment. Kennedy also said that he was calling an immediate meeting of the Organization of American States to rally Americans to self-defense under the Treaty of Rio de Janeiro of 1947. He furthermore announced that he was requesting an emergency meeting of the UN Security Council to consider a resolution to demand prompt dismantling and removal, under UN supervision, of all offensive weapons in Cuba. "It shall be the policy of this nation," Kennedy went on, "to regard any nuclear missile launched from Cuba against any nation in the Western Hemisphere as an attack by the Soviet Union on the United States requiring a full retaliatory response upon the Soviet Union." What was more: "Any hostile move anywhere in the world against the safety or freedom of peoples to whom we are committed—including in particular the brave people of West Berlin—will be met by whatever action is needed."

American naval vessels then began the sensitive and potentially dangerous task of turning back Soviet ships approaching Cuba. Khrushchev, who undoubtedly realized that he had overreached himself, responded promptly in a conciliatory tone. This led to an exchange between the President and the Premier; Khrushchev promised to dismantle and remove the offensive missiles (which he did), and Kennedy promised to launch no attack against Cuba. Although the bargain salvaged some Russian prestige and the peace of the world, it also resulted in a long-term Soviet military buildup both in conventional and nuclear weaponry; the Soviets were determined to prevent any such humiliation in the future.

Strains in the Alliance

The Cuban missile crisis and subsequent increased expenditures for armaments revealed that the two superpowers soon would be tied in a nuclear deadlock. Neither would be able to inflict serious injury on the other without suffering nearly mortal damage in return. Each, therefore, had to refrain from threatening the other's sphere of vital interest. This condition seemed likely to prevail—and control diplomacy—for decades to come. The approaching nuclear standoff also had immediate consequences.

For one thing, the coming stalemate, along with rapid economic progress throughout Europe, gave much greater diplomatic confidence and freedom to the smaller powers within the two alliance systems than they had known since the end of the Second World War. Fear of Russian attack had drawn the western powers into close alliance in NATO in 1949. Fear of German resurgence had kept eastern Europe dependent upon Russia. The waning of these fears inevitably encouraged nations hitherto under the shadow of the superpowers to assert independent policies.

Few persons in Washington read these signs correctly in 1961 and 1962. On the contrary, the Kennedy administration was working at this very time on what was called a Grand Design to draw the western community into closer association, a plan which Kennedy revealed in his Annual Message of January 11, 1962. The United States, he declared, should join in economic partnership with the European Common Market by mutual slashing of tariffs.

The Common Market, established in 1957 by France, Germany, Italy, and the Benelux countries, had been working toward a customs union and had already stimulated the rapid economic growth of its members. Congress did its part at once by approving the Trade Expansion Act in October 1962. This measure permitted the President to reduce tariffs generally by 50 per cent, and to remove tariffs altogether on articles heavily traded by the United States and western Europe. The latter provision depended upon the entry of Great Britain into the Common Market.

But President De Gaulle interpreted the Grand Design as a plan to fasten Anglo-American control on western Europe. He vetoed Great Britain's application for membership in the Common Market in January 1963. De Gaulle hoped to create a new power bloc—a Third Force—under French leadership; thus, he built his own nuclear weapons and strike force, and he greatly reduced French participation in NATO. The result was considerable disarray in the western alliance in 1963. Kennedy, who sought to prevent any widening of the breach, offered to give Polaris missiles to France and proposed to create a NATO naval force with nuclear weapons. De Gaulle would not accept the Polaris missiles and rejected the plan for a NATO naval force because the United States retained final control over use of the nuclear weapons. Great Britain did not like the plan for a NATO naval force, either; it feared that it was the first step toward putting nuclear weapons in German hands.

At the same time that NATO seemed to be coming apart at the seams, a similar loosening of bonds proceeded apace within the Communist world. Eastern European nations, particularly Poland and Rumania, were no longer content to be hewers of wood and drawers of water for Russia. Following Yugoslavia's earlier example, they struck out on their own projects of internal development and began to show diplomatic independence. But the great rupture in the Communist world took place between the Soviet Union and China. The split had been long gathering. Both countries, sharing a long contiguous border, had a historic animus and competition over border areas. Soviet support of the Nationalists in the Chinese civil war left a legacy of suspicion between the two countries. Moreover, both China and the Soviet Union considered themselves the true exemplars of Marxist-Leninist dogma.

By the end of the 1950s, therefore, the Chinese had ended their dependence on Soviet arms, machinery, and replacement parts. A series of subsequent quarrels led to the abrupt withdrawal of all Russian advisers from China in 1960. During the next two years, the two powers glowered at each other along their long common border. Russia supported India when China attacked that country in 1962. The Chinese Communists accused Russia of being a "paper tiger" after Khrushchev's retreat in the missile crisis. Khrushchev, in return, accused the Chinese leaders of reckless insistence that the world could be communized by war. Beginning in the late 1960s, reports reached the West of sporadic fighting along the Chinese-Russian border. During 1969, China and the Soviet Union shifted large military forces to the frontier areas, and Chinese newspapers and posters warned of possible war with their former ally.

Soviet-American Détente

Tension between the United States and Russia lessened as their respective alliance systems were weakening. The leaders of both superpowers seemed to acquire a new respect for each other during the missile crisis. They now realized that coexistence was the only alternative to mutual annihilation.

The first sign of what diplomats call a détente, or relaxation of tension, came in 1963. Kennedy appealed to Khrushchev for a ban on all nuclear testing in the atmosphere and outer space and under water. After months of negotiation, such a treaty was signed; it was approved by the Senate on September 24, 1963, by a vote of eighty to nineteen. But neither France, which recently had exploded her own atomic bomb, nor China, which would detonate one in 1964, agreed to join the more than 100 nations which signed the treaty.

Growing Involvement in Vietnam

By the autumn of 1963, the success of the Communist-led revolution in South Vietnam, along with the pro-American government there, formed a dark cloud on the horizon. After 1954, the United States had supported the creation of a separate rump republic in South Vietnam. Most of the American commitment came in the form of military aid. About 90 per cent of all financial help to South Vietnam between 1954 and 1963, for example, went into military training and supplies; only a small portion remained for agricultural and industrial development.

Despite massive American aid, by 1963 the South Vietnamese regime had not established its ability to govern or even to survive. Sporadic attacks by a South Vietnamese nationalist and largely Communist force, the National Liberation Front (NLF)*, supported by Ho Chi Minh's Communist government in North Vietnam, began to burgeon into a full-scale civil war by 1961. The South Vietnamese dictator, Ngo Dinh Diem, had aroused considerable opposition from virtually all quarters. He used a law which permitted the arrest of any person deemed to be dangerous to the state, suspended habeas corpus, and established a nationwide system of prison camps.

Diem never created a stable political apparatus. Much of the local governmental machinery was the same as the French colonial regime; in 1959, indeed, over a third of Diem's civil servants had begun their service with the French. Diem's regime was also unpopular because it was rife with corruption and nepotism from Diem's family, the Ngo family. His wife's father and his youngest brother served as ambassadors to the United States and Great Britain, respectively; his other three brothers—Ngo Dinh Can, Ngo Dinh Nhu, and Ngo Dinh Thuc—were his most important officers in the South Vietnamese government. The Diem regime came to a bloody end in November 1963, when it crumbled before a Buddhist-led rebellion and, ultimately, a military coup. A succession of military rulers followed until June 1965, when Nguyen Cao Ky seized control of the government.

Meanwhile, the American military involvement in South Vietnam grew larger. By the autumn of 1963, some 16,000 American military "advisers," who were allegedly sent to train the South Vietnamese army, had arrived. In

*Called the Viet Cong by the South Vietnamese dictatorship and then by the Americans to imply that all NLF members were Communists.

practice, they served a much larger role. They flew airplanes for South Vietnamese forces, helped to supply troops in the field, and led some of these troops into action. But the domestic political situation in South Vietnam could best be described as chaotic, and the war against the National Liberation Front made little progress. Sooner or later, and probably sooner, Kennedy would be forced either to withdraw or else greatly to increase American commitments to the beleaguered Asian nation. His friends claimed later that he planned to withdraw American forces altogether from Vietnam after his reelection in 1964. These reports may or may not be true; in any event, while he lived, Kennedy continued to build up American forces in South Vietnam.

The Kennedy Assassination

Relaxation of international tensions during the summer and early autumn of 1963 freed Kennedy to repair some badly broken political fences at home. He needed to build popular support for items in his unfulfilled program, such as the civil-rights bill, a tax cut to stimulate the economy, Medicare, and federal aid to education. To do this, he embarked upon a speaking tour in mid-November, traveling first to Florida, then to Texas. The crowds were large and enthusiastic everywhere that he went. Nowhere were they more friendly than in Dallas, where he arrived just before noon on November 22, 1963.

The presidential entourage, which included Mrs. Kennedy, Vice-President and Mrs. Johnson, and Governor and Mrs. John B. Connally of Texas, passed through cheering throngs on its way to deliver a luncheon address. Just as the presidential car turned into an expressway, bullets from a high-powered rifle ripped through Kennedy's body and seriously wounded Connally. Kennedy died before his car reached a hospital. His death is recorded officially as having occurred at 1 P.M., November 22, 1963.

The killing of Kennedy has long been shrouded in controversy. A blue-ribbon commission, headed by Chief Justice Warren, conducted an intensive investigation into the assassination and concluded that Lee Harvey Oswald, a solitary miscreant, acted alone. Since the issuance of the Warren Commission's report, numerous conspiracy theories have been advanced, none of which has adequately explained the assassination. Perhaps the only person who could have provided all the answers was Oswald, who was murdered in front of a television camera on November 24 by Jack Ruby, a Dallas nightclub owner.

John F. Kennedy was the fourth American President to die at the hands of an assassin. No single tragedy in American history, except perhaps the death of Lincoln, had ever caused such national trauma. Most Americans seemed genuinely shocked that a person so young and vital should have been struck down, and the entire nation and much of the world shared the feeling of bereavement and loss.

3. JOHNSON AND THE GREAT SOCIETY

Johnson as President

Lyndon Baines Johnson, who took the presidential oath in Dallas soon after

Kennedy's death, was born near Stonewall, Texas, on August 27, 1908. Johnson entered public life as director of the WPA's National Youth Administration for Texas in 1935. Elected to Congress in 1937, he served in the House until 1949 and in the Senate from 1949 to 1960. So formidable were Johnson's political talents that he was elected minority leader of the Senate in 1953, while still a freshman senator, and majority leader in 1955. He made a strong bid for the Democratic presidential nomination in 1960, only to be engulfed by the Kennedy tidal wave. Kennedy asked Johnson to be his running mate in part because the Texan's support was essential to party harmony and victory in the South and Southwest. Johnson accepted because he wanted to be a national, not merely a sectional, leader. Certain labor and liberal spokesmen objected, but the offer had been made and accepted, and Johnson became the vice-presidential nominee.

Few men outside of Congress really knew what the new President was like when he took the oath of office on that sad autumn day in 1963, but he would reveal his driving personality and political philosophy under the stress of events in the years ahead. In politics, Johnson was a New Dealer: Franklin D. Roosevelt had been the idol and mentor of his young manhood. This heritage, in addition to his own experience of growing up a poor boy, imbued in Johnson a sympathy for the downtrodden and dispossessed. It gave him the strong conviction that governmental power should be used to improve the human condition.

Johnson also was a master manipulator of other politicians. No man ever came to the presidency with greater knowledge of Congress or deeper experience in managing it. In addition, he strongly believed that politics is the art of the possible. He usually had the uncanny ability to find and represent the consensus. He willingly accepted half a loaf if he could not obtain a whole one, and he seldom asked for more than he thought that he could get. His greatest deficiency, when he succeeded Kennedy, was lack of experience and knowledge in foreign affairs.

Johnson lacked Kennedy's suavity, wit, and flair; his personal coarseness, ruggedness, and his Texan manners and drawl reflected American rural, even frontier, traditions. His most striking personal characteristic—an almost superhuman energy which drove him, in spite of a severe heart attack in 1957, to herculean labors—might have made him a great President. However, his hypersensitivity to criticism deprived him of sound advice and advisers, and his mental rigidity, when events and facts failed to fit his preconceptions, prevented him from changing courses. This man of burning intensity, who was eager for approval and determined to earn a high place in the annals of the presidency, failed to earn that place. Johnson left the presidency under humiliating conditions; he was despised by the younger generation in his own party as a symbol of all that was wrong in American society. But he did not fail because he lacked lofty ambitions or the political skills and experience to carry them out—except in the crucial area of foreign policy, where he depended unduly upon the advice of others who supposedly knew more than he.

Reaching the New Frontiers

The succession was carried out smoothly even while the nation mourned, and Johnson appeared before a joint session of Congress on November 27, 1963. He urged rapid completion of what he called the most urgent unfinished legislative business—tax reduction and adoption of the pending civil-rights bill. Johnson did not hesitate to invoke the memory of the martyred Kennedy when he asked for passage by Congress of the administration measures, which had remained locked in committees while Kennedy lived.

Congress soon knew that it had a new rider—with sharp spurs. The large Democratic majorities in both houses also had their eyes on the coming election campaigns. Hence, in February 1964, they approved a bill which reduced taxes by some $11.5 billion over a two-year period. The reduction had more than proved its worth as a stimulant to economic activity by the end of 1966. Before the presidential election, Congress also provided funds for public housing. It continued the National Defense Education Act of 1958 for another three years and authorized more than $1 billion for a five-year program to improve college facilities. Furthermore, Congress established a food-stamp plan for families who received welfare assistance. After he brought all these Kennedy measures to fruition, Johnson submitted one of his own—the Economic Opportunity Act. This measure, approved August 20, 1964, authorized the expenditures of about $1 billion in the following year alone to inaugurate a massive, coordinated national war against the causes of poverty.

The most significant legislative event of 1964 was the adoption of the new Civil Rights Act. The House approved the bill on February 10. The Senate endured a filibuster by southern senators for eighty-three days and then adopted cloture (a rule ending debate, which requires a two-thirds majority) on June 10 and the bill itself on July 2. The Civil Rights Act of 1964 was one of the most ambitious and far-reaching pieces of legislation ever adopted by Congress. It forbade discrimination on account of race in most places of public accommodation; attempted to protect the right of blacks to vote; forbade (in Title VII) discrimination on account of race or sex by employers, employment agencies, and labor unions; created an Equal Employment Opportunity Commission, to begin its duties in 1965; forbade discrimination in any form in the use of federal funds by states and other local authorities; empowered the Attorney General to initiate cases to speed the desegregation of schools; and created a Community Relations Service to assist individuals and officials to deal with racial problems on the local level.

The Election of 1964

These mighty events on Capitol Hill served as a prelude to the battle for control of Congress and the presidency. The Democrats had not been as united behind a leader since 1944, in spite of the disaffection of many whites in the Deep South because of the Civil Rights Act. The Democratic national convention nominated Johnson by acclamation. It adopted a platform promising full-scale mobilization of national skills and resources to create what the President called "the Great Society." It thundered its applause when Johnson asked for a mandate to continue the war against poverty. The only question before the Democrats remained the choice of a vice-presidential nominee, and Johnson answered it while the convention reveled in Atlantic

City. The President had already rejected Robert F. Kennedy and named Hubert H. Humphrey of Minnesota, one of the most ardent progressives in the Senate.

The Republicans, meanwhile, had been torn by dissension. The GOP suffered most from lack of available leaders and spokesmen of national stature. Nixon suffered a stunning loss while running for governor of California in 1962. Therefore he appeared to be out of this presidential race. Most other Republicans of national stature knew that 1964 would be a Democratic year and refused to enter the contest for the presidential nomination. Only two serious candidates eagerly challenged the Texan in the White House. They were Governor Nelson A. Rockefeller of New York, a progressive, and Senator Barry M. Goldwater of Arizona, a conservative. Rockefeller ruined whatever chances he had by a divorce and a remarriage just before the campaign began. Goldwater, popular with most of the powerful state Republican organizations, and extremely conservative groups, won most delegations chosen in state conventions by Republican activists. When former President Eisenhower refused to rally the progressive and internationalist wing of the GOP against Goldwater, Governor William W. Scranton of Pennsylvania made a solitary and vain effort at the end of the preconvention campaign. Goldwater won the presidential nomination with ease on the first ballot at the Republican national convention. Conservative delegates heckled and booed progressive leaders when they tried to persuade the convention to denounce extremist groups. Goldwater widened the split by naming an obscure congressman from New York, William E. Miller, an extreme conservative, as his running mate. Goldwater also alarmed moderates by saying in his acceptance speech that "extremism in the defense of liberty is no vice."

A New Mandate

Not since 1936 had there been a presidential campaign in which the contenders were so unevenly matched. Johnson conducted a strenuous campaign. Concerning foreign affairs, he gave the impression of wisdom and restraint and warned that Goldwater's proposals about Vietnam might involve the nation in an Asian war—perhaps even in a third world war. On domestic issues, Johnson stood forthrightly behind the Civil Rights Act of 1964, the war against poverty, for Medicare, and for federal aid to education. The public response was overwhelming. Everywhere that the President went, he was engulfed by cheering throngs who wanted to shake his bruised, outstretched, and eager hand.

Goldwater, on the other hand, moved steadily downhill from the moment of his nomination. Most Republicans in Congress had supported the Civil Rights Act, and there had been strong Republican support for other Kennedy-Johnson measures. The majority of Republican voters differed little from the majority of Democrats. Most Americans clearly wanted the federal government to take the lead in meeting the changing problems of their day and differed only in details and on the speed of change. This consensus seemed to characterize American political attitudes more in 1964 than at any other time in American history, except, perhaps, in 1912.

However, Goldwater had promised the voters "a choice, not an echo." He had voted against the Civil Rights bill, the Test Ban Treaty, and most of the Kennedy-Johnson welfare measures. During the campaign, Goldwater continued to oppose the very things for which a majority of his own party stood. He intimated that he would like to repeal the Social Security Act, sell the TVA to private investors, and wipe out as much progressive legislation as possible. He also gave the impression of believing that violent conflict with the Soviet Union was inevitable (for example, he referred to the Soviet Union as the "enemy"). Finally, he refused to denounce the support of the right-wing John Birch Society and other extremely conservative organizations which said that Eisenhower and Dulles, as well as Democrats, had been traitors to the United States.

Goldwater hoped to carry the segregationist South and what he believed to be the conservative Middle West and Far West. His strategy failed. The voters did not like the choice which he offered, and he probably lost a million votes every time that he made a major address. The result was a Democratic landslide on November 3, 1964. Johnson and Humphrey amassed more than 43,000,000 popular and 486 electoral votes, to some 27,000,000 popular and fifty-two electoral votes for Goldwater and Miller. The Arizonan carried only five states in the Deep South and his home state. The Eighty-ninth Congress (1965 – 1966) would have sixty-eight Democrats and thirty-two Republicans in the Senate and 295 Democrats and 140 Republicans in the House of Representatives.

The Great Society

Johnson's inauguration on January 20, 1965, seemed more like a second inaugural than the beginning of a first regular term, so entrenched in leadership was the President. However, the situation on Capitol Hill now appeared radically different. For the first time since 1938, a President had a firm working majority in both houses of Congress. For the first time since 1938, a Democratic President could obtain legislation without the help of conservative southern Democrats.

No one understood the significance of this fact better than Lyndon B. Johnson. With furious energy, he pushed through a willing Congress the most comprehensive domestic program since the high tide of the New Deal.

The President finally broke the logjam which had damned up a comprehensive education bill. The Education Act of 1965, adopted and approved in mid-April, authorized $1.3 billion for direct federal assistance to public schools. It sidestepped the religious issue by providing aid to parochial school children in a number of "shared services." The Education Act, Johnson said when he signed the measure, was "truly the key which can unlock the door to the Great Society." In addition, a Higher Education Act of 1965 authorized $650 million in federal aid to colleges and universities for scholarships to needy students and to strengthen teaching and research.

An Appalachian Regional Development Act, approved in March 1965, provided $1.1 billion for highways, health centers, and development to the poverty-stricken mountainous region which stretched from Pennsylvania to Alabama and Georgia. A Medicare bill, enlarged to include low-cost insurance against doctors' bills as well as against hospital and nursing expenses for all persons over sixty-five, was overwhelmingly approved by

Congress and signed by the President on July 30, 1965. Medicare, administered by the Social Security Administration, effected the first fundamental change in the Social Security Act since its adoption in 1935. Congress approved the President's bill to cut excise taxes by $4.6 billion in several stages, which began in June 1965. The Housing and Urban Development Act of 1965 was the most important housing act since 1949. It provided assistance for the construction of approximately 240,000 units of low-rent public housing and authorized $2.9 billion in federal grants for urban renewal over a four-year period. A supplementary act of May 1966 provided funds to subsidize the rents of some low- and moderate-income families. In addition, Congress created a federal Department of Housing and Urban Development of cabinet rank. Robert C. Weaver, the first black ever named to the cabinet, became the head of the new department in January 1966.

Johnson and Congress also responded to growing popular demands that steps be taken to improve the ecological conditions in which Americans were forced to live. Legislation enacted in 1966 attempted to control both air and water pollution. Another measure gave the government authority to set safety standards for automobile manufacturers and on highways.

The Immigration Act of 1965 signified a fundamental change in American immigration policy. The National Origins Act of 1924 had provided for quotas which heavily favored immigration from northern Europe. The Immigration Act of 1965 put all nations on an equal footing by providing for the admission of some 170,000 "regular" immigrants annually with a limitation of 20,000 per year from any single country.

The Voting Rights Act of 1965

Johnson, meanwhile, had added another measure to his program in response to new convulsions on the civil-rights front. Various organizations had begun campaigns to encourage black registration and voting throughout the South in 1964, and both were heavy in many southern states. But white reaction across a chain of black-belt counties in Mississippi and Alabama had been violent. Whites and blacks were murdered. Black churches, usually the centers of local political activity, had been bombed or burned, and local registrars had succeeded in preventing most blacks from registering. Local police seemed more intent upon obstructing efforts at registration than upon apprehending the arsonists, bombers, and murderers.

National indignation was at fever pitch by early 1965. Public outrage greatly intensified in March, when Alabama state troopers used clubs and tear gas to break up a demonstration in Selma, led by Martin Luther King, Jr. Some 400 ministers, priests, and rabbis flew at once to Selma to join the demonstrators. Johnson went before Congress on national television and in one of the most moving presidential addresses since Roosevelt's acceptance speech of 1936, denounced the denial of basic constitutional rights. He demanded adoption of a bill for federal registrars in all counties where blacks did not vote in normal numbers. These registrars would enroll blacks under rules so rigid that no person could be denied the right to vote on account of race.

This measure, called the Voting Rights Act of 1965, was put on its way to passage even while thousands of Americans took airplanes, cars, and buses to

Alabama to join the marchers from Selma. Passage of the bill, probably already assured, was made inevitable by the murder of three civil-rights workers near Selma. The measure quickly passed the House. Then it went through the Senate with unusual dispatch, because the majority in that body tolerated only a brief southern filibuster. President Johnson signed the bill on August 6, 1965.

The Supreme Court and Judicial Revolution

The Supreme Court, now completely under the influence of Chief Justice Warren, in the 1960s completed the revolution in constitutional interpretation which it had begun in the 1950s. This, actually, is an understatement, for the court did nothing less than to effect a fundamental reinterpretation of laws which affected individual rights.

It is not surprising that the Supreme Court threw the weight of the entire American judiciary behind the civil-rights revolution, for the court had been one of the principal originators of the revolution (see pp. 265–67). In Heart of Atlanta Motel *v.* the United States (1964), the court upheld the Civil Rights Act of 1964 in sweeping language. In other cases, the court upheld the Voting Rights Act of 1965 and struck down local segregation statutes. It outlawed the poll tax as a requirement for voting in local and state elections and thus supplemented the ban against the poll tax in federal elections in the Twenty-fourth Amendment.

The Warren Court also struck death blows at another ancient political inequity—rural control of state legislatures in urban states, accomplished until then by the refusal of rural state lawmakers to reapportion voting districts to give equal representation to urban areas. Certain citizens of Tennessee brought suit in federal court to compel their legislature to grant to Tennessee's urban citizens representation equal to that enjoyed by the rural population. The Supreme Court, in Baker *v.* Carr (1962), in effect declared that the federal courts should intervene in such cases to guarantee equal representation to all citizens in all states. Subsequent rulings, such as Westberry *v.* Sanders (1964) and Reynolds *v.* Sims (1964), compelled state legislatures throughout the country to reapportion both of their houses and their congressional districts on the principle of "one man, one vote."

At the same time, the court more clearly defined the First Amendment's affirmation of the principle of separation of church and state in Engel *v.* Vitale (1962) and School District of Abington Township *v.* Schempp (1963). These decisions outlawed state or local laws which required the reading of the Bible and prayers in public schools on the ground that they constituted establishment of religion contrary to the First Amendment.

Finally, the court threw up a variety of new safeguards for individuals accused of crime. In Gideon *v.* Wainwright (1963), the court ruled that a defendant too poor to hire an attorney had to be furnished one at public expense. The court, in Escobedo *v.* Illinois (1964), Miranda *v.* Arizona (1966), and other cases extended the right of the accused to be informed of self-incrimination, the option of silence, and rights to counsel and to confront prosecution witnesses in most categories of offenses.

4. INTO THE QUAGMIRE OF VIETNAM

American Power Finds a Limit

Johnson disturbed many Americans and outraged even more Latin Americans when, in April 1965, he sent some 20,000 American troops to intercede in a civil war in the Dominican Republic out of fear—groundless, as it turned out—that Communists were about to take over the government of that Caribbean country. Johnson reinforced these doubts about his wisdom in foreign policy—and destroyed his political coalition—with his decision in favor of a massive land war in Indochina. During the presidential campaign of 1964, Johnson had accused Goldwater of reckless statements about Vietnam and had assured the voters: "We are not going to send American boys nine or ten thousand miles away from home to do what Asian boys ought to be doing for themselves."

Although the army of South Vietnam (ARVN) outnumbered its guerrilla enemies, the NLF, by six to one, and although thousands of American advisers and enormous amounts of American military equipment and financial aid backed them up, the South Vietnamese forces by early 1965 had been barely able to hold their own. Johnson, almost unanimously supported by his chief policy planners, was certain that the "free world"—which included dictatorships and right-wing military regimes—confronted a worldwide threat from international communism. Vietnam, accordingly, represented only one phase of a larger Soviet-inspired expansionistic thrust, and if Vietnam "fell"—according to this "domino theory"—then further expansion might ensue throughout Asia.

Few of Johnson's advisers disagreed. Many of them, including military theorists, confidently predicted that a calculated escalation of the scope and intensity of the Vietnamese War—largely involving American troops—would sooner or later force an enemy to sue for peace. Others were optimistic advocates of counterinsurgency techniques and strategic bombing. Faced with an imminent collapse of the South Vietnamese government and convinced that the war could be won, Johnson in February 1965 ordered the bombing of North Vietnam and sent units of American combat troops to South Vietnam. He acted on the basis of a joint resolution of Congress in August 1964 which had been adopted after North Vietnamese attacked American destroyers in the Gulf of Tonkin, off the coast of North Vietnam. Approved by overwhelming majorities, the Gulf of Tonkin resolution supported action by the United States in Vietnam "to promote the maintenance of international peace and security in Southeast Asia."

A steady buildup of forces followed. But, just as steadily, reinforcements streamed down from North Vietnam to fight the Americans. Previously, the North Vietnamese had given the southern rebels little but training and moral support. By the time that Johnson left office, 535,000 United States soldiers were stationed in Vietnam and were assisted by 800,000 South Vietnamese regular troops, 200,000 South Vietnamese militia, and 72,000 allied troops. They opposed about 320,000 North Vietnamese soldiers and the remnant of the NLF. The bombing of North Vietnam, in an effort to disrupt the flow of men and materials southward, mounted to the dropping of 100,000 tons of explosives monthly. The tonnage of bombs dropped on North and South Vietnam by American planes by 1970 had already exceeded by over 50 per cent the total dropped in all theaters during the Second World War. Attempts to starve and expose the guerrillas included chemical defoliation of almost 1,000,000 acres, which transformed South Vietnam from a major rice exporter as late as 1967 into a large-scale importer of rice in 1968, and into an impoverished area later.

Nevertheless, as United States casualties and expenditures in Vietnam increased, the Americans and South Vietnamese seemed no closer to victory, or even to a negotiated peace, than before the United States had intervened. A series of promises from American officials that triumph was near and American soldiers would soon be home accompanied each stage in the escalation of the war. Those who had doubted the wisdom of Johnson's policies from the beginning now pointed to the danger of continuing the costly battle. Even old friends of the President, such as Clark Clifford and Dean Acheson, found that Johnson refused to take advice to deescalate the war, and that he reacted with hypersensitivity to suggestions that he had made any kind of mistake. High officials who made such suggestions—such as Secretary of Defense Robert McNamara, who earlier had believed that intensive bombing would soon bring North Vietnam to its knees—were forced to resign.

Johnson learned somewhat tardily the limitations of his country's resources. Since the Vietnam War was costing over $20 billion annually, Johnson was obliged to resort to large deficits in order to maintain expenditures on the Great Society programs. Johnson's refusal to ask for new taxes to pay for the Vietnam War set off a cycle of increased deficits and inflation. Then, in January 1968, a series of incidents further exacerbated Johnson's problems. On January 31, the NLF launched a major offensive—called the Tet offensive after the Vietnamese New Year—and assaulted almost every important base, city, and town in South Vietnam as 84,000 men struck five of six cities, thirty-six of forty provincial capitals, and sixty-four district capitals. The NLF invaded the center of Saigon, and nineteen commandos held the United States embassy in that city under siege for six hours. In Hue, the ancient capital of Vietnam, the NLF captured the city and were driven out a month later only after American marines and bombs had destroyed the city. All told, after three weeks of fighting, 165,000 Vietnamese civilians were killed and 2,000,000 new refugees created.

The Tet offensive represented a turning point in the war. It marked the end of the NLF as an effective political and military force; henceforth, their ranks were now more than filled by North Vietnamese regulars. Although the Americans won a military victory, the political costs of Tet at home were extremely high. General William C. Westmoreland, commander of the American forces, requested another 206,000 troops to extend the war into Cambodia and Laos, and even to invade North Vietnam. Yet, the domestic reaction to the Tet offensive prevented such an escalation as public opinion of the war and of Johnson—whose approval rating dropped to a low of 35 per cent—galvanized against the war.

5. THE ELECTION OF 1968

The Democratic Challenge

In November 1967, Senator Eugene McCarthy of Minnesota announced his candidacy for the Democratic presidential nomination on a peace platform. At the time, McCarthy's action seemed a token gesture on behalf of the peace advocates, or "doves," within the Democratic party, and Lyndon Johnson's renomination appeared to be a foregone conclusion. McCarthy, a moderate liberal, was virtually unknown in most of the country. His campaign suffered further from his subdued, whimsical speaking style, and from his refusal either to dramatize his differences with the administration or to appeal directly to ethnic groups. His campaign workers frequently found him diffident, almost unwilling to take actions necessary to win—a tendency which may have reflected McCarthy's deep desire to avoid the overwhelming political and administrative problems which the next President would have to face.

Nevertheless, thousands of young Americans, almost all of them college students, grasped at the opportunity presented by McCarthy's candidacy to oppose actively Johnson's policies. Students on the East Coast spontaneously descended upon New Hampshire, site of the earliest presidential primary, and swamped the local McCarthy offices. Quickly, and with little help from professional politicians, the students systematically canvassed the whole state and spoke to almost every registered Democrat and many Republicans about the necessity for a change in Washington. Americans were startled in mid-March 1968, when McCarthy won 42 per cent of the Democratic vote to 48 per cent for Johnson, with enough write-in votes for McCarthy on Republican ballots to make the two candidates almost even.

Robert F. Kennedy, now senator from New York, opposed the continuation of the Vietnam War but had refused to enter the Democratic preconvention race. After Tet, however, Kennedy decided to speak out, and at the same time he moved to the edge of entering the campaign. During a major speech in Chicago, before the New Hampshire primary, Kennedy declared that the United States was not winning the Vietnam War and should no longer attempt to do so.

As evidence mounted that Johnson could not muster dependable support from anyone but established Democratic politicians, and that the nomination might go to a political unknown who could easily lose the general election, Kennedy announced his active candidacy. Not only did Kennedy thus provide Johnson with truly formidable opposition—Kennedy's popularity, especially among blacks and Hispanic voters, may even have exceeded that of his older brother—but Johnson also now faced the possibility of losing to a man who had treated him with humiliating condescension when he served as Vice-President.

McCarthy's young campaign workers had already moved to Wisconsin, where hordes of midwestern college students helped to organize a statewide canvass similar to the successful New Hampshire venture. Polls in Wisconsin indicated that the Minnesota senator, now a figure of national importance, would win an overwhelming victory over the President. Two days before the

Wisconsin primary election, on April 2, Johnson announced that, in the interest of national unity, he would not be a candidate for reelection. During the same speech, Johnson also announced an end to American bombing of a large portion of North Vietnam in the hope, he said, that this action would lead to early peace talks. An American mission headed by W. Averell Harriman met with North Vietnamese delegates in Paris in May for preliminary talks. Following Johnson's announcement of a total cessation of the bombing of North Vietnam on October 31, the negotiators in Paris began formal discussions in early 1969. However, peace remained elusive at the end of the Johnson administration.

Meanwhile, in the Democratic preconvention contest, Kennedy won every presidential primary which he entered, most by large margins, except for Oregon, which went to McCarthy. Just after the California primary, on June 5, a young Palestinian immigrant, Sirhan Sirhan, mentally deranged and infuriated by Kennedy's statements favorable to Israel, shot the senator at a victory celebration which followed Kennedy's triumph in the California primary election. Kennedy died the next day.

The Chicago Convention

Kennedy's supporters and delegates were reluctant to swing behind McCarthy. Most of them tended to drift into the camp of either Vice-President Hubert Humphrey or Senator George S. McGovern of South Dakota, neither of whom had directly participated in the primaries. At the Democratic national convention in Chicago, which opened on August 26, Humphrey won the presidential nomination on the first ballot; he chose Senator Edmund S. Muskie of Maine as his running mate.

The attention of most observers at the Democratic convention focused not on floor votes, but rather on the battles which raged outside the convention hall between representatives of the nation's radicalized youth and the Chicago police. The protesters had no clear unifying purpose, except perhaps to express anger at a political system which obviously would ignore their strong wishes as well as the results of the primary elections. Words were exchanged with police; objects were thrown by demonstrators. Then television viewers were given a demonstration of what "police brutality" meant. Police used night sticks and tear gas indiscriminately. Members of the press, television and radio crews, and onlookers were assaulted along with the demonstrators. Stimulated by the excitement outside, guards inside the convention hall treated delegates roughly and even arrested a few who failed to display proper identification. Most of these events were captured by the ubiquitous eyes of the television cameras. Somehow Humphrey managed to keep smiling and in his acceptance speech termed the theme of his campaign "The Politics of Joy."

The Nomination of Nixon

The struggle for the Republican nomination in 1968 did not even last until the New Hampshire primary. Republicans opposed to former Vice-President Nixon, who again made a strong bid for Republican leadership, backed Governor George Romney of Michigan. However, Romney withdrew before the first primary, and the other possible candidates—Governors Nelson Rockefeller of New York and Ronald Wilson Reagan of California—did not campaign actively until just before the Republican convention. However, they acted too late, and Nixon won on the first ballot when the Republicans opened their national convention in Miami Beach on August 7. Nixon chose Spiro T. Agnew, governor of Maryland, as his vice-presidential nominee.

Two minor parties also entered the contest. George Wallace, ex-governor of Alabama, founded the American Independent party, a southern-based conservative organization, which obligingly nominated him for the presidency. As his running mate, Wallace named Curtis LeMay, retired air force general. On the left, a coalition of pacifists and advocates of "black power" formed the Peace and Freedom party; they named the Black Panther leader, Eldridge Cleaver, to head their ticket. It soon became obvious that the American Independent party presented by far the greater threat to the two major parties.

The Election

The presidential campaign of 1968 opened with Humphrey trailing far behind Nixon in the polls. Wherever he went in September and early October, student hecklers hounded the Vice-President. To these young people, Humphrey represented the Vietnam War, the suppression of the Chicago demonstrators, and, in general, the continuation of Johnson's policies. On the major

The Election of 1968

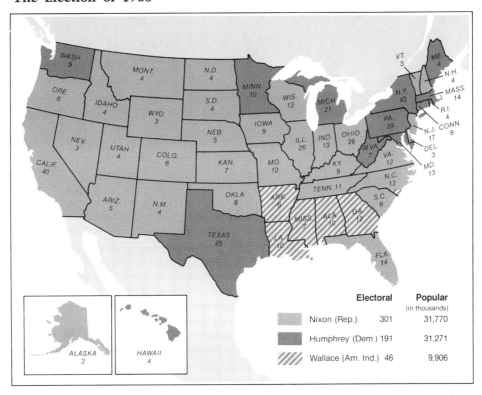

	Electoral	Popular (in thousands)
Nixon (Rep.)	301	31,770
Humphrey (Dem.)	191	31,271
Wallace (Am. Ind.)	46	9,906

issue of the campaign—Vietnam—Humphrey encountered almost insurmountable difficulties. He badly needed the antiwar vote to win, but he could not repudiate Johnson without alienating many Democrats. When asked what changes he would make in Johnson's policies, Humphrey could not reply. Not until late September, in a speech in Salt Lake City, did the Vice-President appear to move away from the administration's position by calling for an end to all bombing of North Vietnam in order to make possible meaningful peace talks. Johnson's announcement on October 31 that he had ended the bombing of North Vietnam infused new vigor into the Democratic campaign.

In contrast to their opponents, the Republicans began their campaign confidently. Nixon, and particularly his running mate, Agnew, talked of "law and order" and the need to stop crime in the streets. Nixon also declared that he had a "secret plan" for peace in Vietnam but refused to divulge any particulars of it. Nixon increasingly stressed the need for national "unity." He spoke to a nation torn by racial animosities and deep disagreements over the Vietnam War and promised to end the war, without saying how, and to bring the American people back together again. These were widely shared desires, but Nixon said very little during the campaign about how he intended to accomplish these goals. Meanwhile, Wallace attacked "pointy-head intellectuals" and "anarchists" and made law and order his major issue.

There was a strong upsurge of support for Humphrey at the very end of the campaign, and, for a moment, it seemed that Humphrey might actually accomplish the impossible. Americans spent election night, November 5, 1968, much as they had done eight years before. They watched the Northeast go Democratic and then waited for returns from the South, Middle West, and West. By the early morning of November 6, it was clear that Nixon had carried the crucial states of Ohio, Illinois, and California by small margins and had barely won the presidency. Nixon's popular vote of 31,770,237 was 43.4 per cent of the total; Humphrey's 31,270,533, 42.7 per cent. Wallace received 9,906,141 popular votes, or 13.5 per cent of the total, and carried Alabama, Arkansas, Georgia, Louisiana, and Mississippi. The final tally in the Electoral College was Nixon, 301; Humphrey, 191; and Wallace, forty-six.

SUGGESTED READINGS

Arthur M. Schlesinger, Jr., *A Thousand Days: John F. Kennedy in the White House* (1963), although distinctly partisan, remains the most comprehensive account. Theodore C. Sorenson, *Kennedy* (1965), is another good account, but it should be supplemented by Henry Fairlie, *The Kennedy Promise: The Politics of Expectation* (1973), perhaps the most thoughtful evaluation. James M. Burns, *Kennedy: A Political Profile* (1959), although to some extent a campaign biography, nevertheless holds up well as a perceptive study of Kennedy as a politician. More specialized works on Kennedy's short administration include Haynes B. Johnson, *The Bay of Pigs* (1964); John Kenneth Galbraith, *Ambassador's Journal: A Personal Account of the Kennedy Years* (1969); Robert

F. Kennedy, *Thirteen Days: The Cuban Missile Crisis* (1969); Elie Abel, *The Missile Crisis* (1966); Lewis J. Paper, *The Promise and the Performance: The Leadership of John F. Kennedy* (1975), a political scientist's evaluation; and Carl M. Brauer, *John F. Kennedy and the Second Reconstruction* (1977). B. Miroff, *Pragmatic Illusions: The Presidential Politics of John F. Kennedy* (1976), deals with what may well have been Kennedy's basic intellectual weaknesses. For an examination of Kennedy's policy toward the Soviet Union, see Glenn T. Seaborg and Benjamin S. Loer, *Kennedy, Khrushchev, and the Test Ban* (1982).

In addition to the supposedly objective studies by Schlesinger and Sorenson, other members of Kennedy's staff whose memoirs now are in print include Kenneth P. O'Donnell and David F. Powers, *"Johnny, We Hardly Knew Ye"* (1972), which includes a fine account of the start and early years of Kennedy's political career; and Pierre Salinger, *With Kennedy* (1966). The definitive account of domestic surveillance of the civil rights movement during the Kennedy and Johnson years is David J. Garrow, *The FBI and Martin Luther King* (1981). The official account of the Kennedy assassination is the Warren Commission, *Report* (1964). Among the many criticisms of this report, E.J. Epstein, *Inquest* (1966), remains the best. William R. Manchester, *The Death of a President* (1967), is a popular description.

The election of 1964 is the subject of Theodore H. White, *The Making of the President 1964* (1965). For an analysis of the problems of the Republican party, see Robert D. Novak, *The Agony of the G.O.P. 1964* (1965).

Conflicting opinions on Johnson are offered by Rowland Evans and Robert Novak, *Lyndon B. Johnson: The Exercise of Power* (1966); William S. White, *The Professional: Lyndon B. Johnson* (1964); Eric F. Goldman, *The Tragedy of Lyndon Johnson* (1969); and Robert Sherrill, *The Accidental President* (1967). Doris Kearns, *Lyndon Johnson and the American Dream* (1976), is a highly personal analysis; Johnson gives his own version in *The Vantage Point* (1971). Johnson staff members with recollections now in print include Harry McPherson, *A Political Education* (1972), and Jack Valenti, *A Very Human President* (1975). Sar A. Levitan and Robert Taggart analyze the effects of Johnson's Great Society programs in *The Promise of Greatness* (1976). They produce a vast array of evidence that these programs have been much more beneficial to American society than is generally realized. Eugene McCarthy has offered his own history of his presidential campaign in *Year of the People* (1969); also see Jeremy Larner, *Nobody Knows: Reflections on the McCarthy Campaign of 1968* (1970). Norman Mailer has written a fascinating piece of journalistic autobiography

about the confrontation of police and demonstrators at the Democratic national convention of 1968 in *Miami and the Siege of Chicago* (1968). Philip L. Geyelin, *Lyndon B. Johnson and the World* (1966), is a sympathetic study of that President's foreign policy. More critical is J. William Fulbright, *The Arrogance of Power* (1966).

A blueprint for the Nixon administration was presented by a young member of Attorney General John Mitchell's staff: Kevin P. Phillips, *The Emerging Republican Majority* (1969). A perceptive account of the election of 1968 can be found in Joseph McGinnis, *The Selling of the President* (1969). A more general account is Theodore H. White, *The Making of the President 1968* (1969), a rather naive description, especially of the "new Nixon."

The origins and early years of American intervention in Vietnam have received a great amount of attention. Among the better works are George C. Herring, Jr., *America's Longest War: The United States and Vietnam, 1950–1975* (1979); David Halberstam, *The Making of a Quagmire* (1965); Bernard B. Fall, *Viet-Nam Witness* (1966); and Townsend Hoopes, *The Limits of Intervention* (1969). The most comprehensive treatment can be found in Frances FitzGerald, *Fire in the Lake* (1972). Those who wish to know more about the staged deceptions of the Johnson administration, connected largely, but not solely, with Vietnam, should read Neil Sheehan et al., *The Pentagon Papers* (1971).

As with the Eisenhower administration, most of the works cited in the Suggested Readings for Chapter 13 are relevant to the domestic issues of this period. To this should be added Anthony Lewis, *Gideon's Trumpet* (1964), a good analysis of Gideon v. Wainwright, and Robert G. Dixon, Jr., *Democratic Representation: Reapportionment in Law and Politics* (1968). For general studies of the Warren Court, see Stanley Kutler, *The Supreme Court and the Constitution* (1969); Archibald Cox, *The Warren Court* (1968); and Anthony Lewis, *The Warren Court: A Critical Evaluation* (1969).

CHAPTER 16
RICHARD M. NIXON AND THE CRISIS OF CONSTITUTIONAL GOVERNMENT

1. DOMESTIC POLITICS DURING THE FIRST NIXON ADMINISTRATION

The Tragedy of Richard M. Nixon

To historians and contemporaries alike, Richard Milhous Nixon has remained an enigma. He was born on a farm in southern California on January 9, 1913, and grew up in nearby Whittier, where he helped his father run a small grocery store. The Nixons were Quakers, but, like many of that denomination who had settled in the West, they never were pacifists, and the church in which Nixon was reared was little different from any other Protestant church in the United States.

Nixon worked his way through both Whittier College and Duke University Law School, practiced law briefly in Whittier, and then moved to Washington in search of government employment. During the Second World War, he served as a naval supply officer, and, in 1946, returned to southern California, where, in a frenetic campaign in which he engaged in red-baiting, Nixon defeated the incumbent Democrat, Jerry Voorhis, a congressman from the state's twelfth district. Four years later, Nixon successfully employed the same tactics against the liberal congresswoman Helen Gahagan Douglas in a race for the Senate. A leading anti-Communist, Nixon in the Hiss case and on other issues quickly earned a reputation as a Cold Warrior and a champion of the right wing of the GOP. Because of this reputation, Eisenhower twice selected him as his running mate. In one of the closest elections in American history, he lost the presidency to John F. Kennedy in 1960, and, when the incumbent governor of California, Edmund G. Brown, decisively defeated him in the gubernatorial election of 1962, Nixon's political career appeared at an end. His subsequent comeback to win the presidency six years later was the result of his unflinching tenacity and political skill.

Nixon entered the White House aided by extraordinary good fortune for the future of his party. The Republicans, it appeared, would benefit during the next decade and beyond from the popular frustration with and reaction against racial violence, crime, and the new sexual revolution. In the South, Nixon hoped to forge a permanent Republican majority composed of a coalition of former conservative Democrats and suburban and urban middle-class whites. In foreign policy, Nixon had promised to end the Vietnam War, and an unparalleled opportunity beckoned for a thaw in the Cold War.

Yet, on almost every count, Nixon's presidency was a failure, largely because of deficiencies in his personality and character. Nixon was fundamentally shy; he therefore sought advice only from a small circle of family and friends. He was consumed by insecurity to the point of paranoia, an intense need for recognition (because of his modest origins), and a passion for power. Nixon was, above all, determined to succeed—to win reelection in 1972. One reason for his determination to stay in power was that he immensely enjoyed its trappings and display.

Although Nixon was driven by ruthlessness and insecurity and was a pure political opportunist, he also possessed a deep sense of patriotism. A conservative in ideology, Nixon was pragmatic and even progressive in his policies; for example, he was a fervent advocate of the extension and use of governmental power. Finally, Nixon genuinely believed that he could unify the country and heal the wounds of the Johnson presidency.

It is thus not only tragic but also ironic that, when Nixon left office in disgrace in August 1974, he imparted a legacy of popular mistrust of government. Like Theodore Roosevelt, Nixon practiced the plebiscitory style of presidential leadership. The people, he thought, had vested their sovereignty in him; he considered, therefore, that he was a sovereign with virtually unlimited power. In the process of governing, however, Nixon inflicted such damage on the relationship between the presidency and Congress that he impaired the strength of the presidency for almost a decade. Through the excessive use of power in foreign affairs—particularly military power in the Vietnam War—Nixon also damaged the relations of the United States with other countries. The paradox of the Nixon presidency—the vast gulf between ideals and personality and opportunities and achievements—was tragic not only for Nixon but also for the entire world.

The Nixon Cabinet

The Nixon cabinet reflected the direction of the new President, and most of the new appointees were moderate conservatives who had had considerable experience in government. William P. Rogers, a negotiator with experience in international law, was the new Secretary of State; Melvin R. Laird, a veteran Republican congressman from Wisconsin, was chosen as Secretary of Defense. Nixon's chief economic advisers were Secretary of Labor George P. Shultz, formerly dean of the University of Chicago Business School, Paul McCracken, chairman of the Council of Economic Advisers, and Maurice H.

Stans, Secretary of Commerce. The new Nixon cabinet also included several prominent moderates and progressives: Robert H. Finch, head of the burgeoning Department of Health, Education, and Welfare (HEW); Secretary of the Interior Walter J. Hickel, a former governor of Alaska; and Clifford M. Hardin, the Secretary of Agriculture.

Yet, the political views of the new cabinet members revealed very little about the future of the Nixon presidency. Progressives, particularly Finch and Hickel, quickly discovered that their policies represented only one side of Nixon's program; and they soon fell victim to political necessity. Most cabinet members also suffered from Nixon's isolation, and they soon lost access either to his support or to his ear. The new Secretary of State, William P. Rogers, found himself in an impossible situation because Nixon was determined to assume personal direction of diplomacy. Indeed, Nixon saw himself as a Wilsonian, not only in ideals, but also in practice; he would assume personal control of foreign relations and use American power as an incentive to reduce international tension. In the cabinet, only the Attorney General, John N. Mitchell, Nixon's former law partner, enjoyed Nixon's confidence and had direct access to the President.

Nixon thus turned to personal advisers—most of them not in the constitutional position of cabinet officers—for the direction of the government. For example, he systematically ignored and humiliated Rogers and turned to Henry A. Kissinger for advice in diplomacy. Kissinger, Special Assistant to the President for National Security Affairs and head of the National Security Council, had distinguished credentials. Author of several widely acclaimed books, Kissinger was a professor of government at Harvard and had served as a consultant for the Eisenhower, Kennedy, and Johnson administrations; he was also closely associated with Nelson A. Rockefeller. Nixon was partly attracted to Kissinger because their views on the international role of the United States coincided. Both believed that the reduction of international tensions was consistent with vigorous diplomatic as well as military competition between the two superpowers; both advocated ending the Cold War but extending the bipolarity of diplomacy even further into the world. Nixon and Kissinger also agreed about the ruthless use of American power to further national objectives, a strategy which they pursued, not only in Vietnam, but also in Greece, Chile, and Pakistan. Finally, both saw an opportunity to cultivate China and exploit the Sino-Soviet split as a means to alter the world configuration of power.

In the conduct of domestic affairs, Nixon also turned to noncabinet officials. H. R. ("Bob") Haldeman, White House chief of staff, and John Ehrlichman, special adviser on domestic affairs—known collectively as the "German shepherds" because they so zealously guarded access to the Oval Office—soon became Nixon's most influential advisers. Neither had had any experience in running the federal government, but both had unswerving loyalty to Nixon and an ardent desire for his reelection.

The new cabinet thus reflected vividly the ambiguity of the Nixon administration. While Nixon appointed such progressives as Finch and Hickel to take charge of the important issues of school busing, desegregation, and the environment, he unleashed a vicious attack on civil liberties through Mitchell, the FBI, the CIA, the army, and other intelligence organizations. While he appointed competent and experienced men to the cabinet, he bypassed them and instead lodged virtually complete power in the hands of a few close advisers.

The First Nixon Administration

In retrospect, it is clear that a significant expansion of the federal government took place during the Nixon administration. Federal outlays stood at about $180 billion in 1969; when Nixon left office almost six years later, they had reached almost $270 billion. Nixon did not challenge the heritage of the welfare state left by Democratic Presidents; indeed, it grew during his administration. Social Security coverage was expanded in 1969, 1971, and 1972; prompted by Nixon, Congress passed a tax reform bill in 1969 which, although it fell short in several respects, provided for a more equitable distribution of the tax burden. Nixon also supervised the expansion of benefits both for elementary and secondary schools and for higher education.

Nonetheless, Nixon's domestic program suffered from several handicaps. To begin with, Nixon lacked a working majority in Congress. In the election of 1968, the Republicans gained a total of nine seats in Congress, but were outnumbered fifty-eight to forty-two in the Senate and 243 to 192 in the House. During the congressional elections of 1970, despite strenuous campaigning by both Nixon and Agnew, Democrats still retained control of both houses. Nixon's problems with Congress were exacerbated by his confrontational style and the vulgar attacks by his Vice-President. Most important, Nixon had no consistent domestic policies, largely because he had little interest in domestic affairs other than in securing his reelection. His consuming passion was the practice of diplomacy.

Nixon's lack of any firm principles on domestic issues was best demonstrated in the fates of Finch and Hickel. Before 1970, Nixon gave his old friend Finch considerable freedom in running HEW. Finch announced early in 1969 that he would press for desegregation in public schools by withholding federal funds from those districts which had not made adequate efforts at integration. Like many other strong civil-rights advocates, Finch supported the massive busing of white and black students to achieve racial balance, a policy which aroused strenuous opposition from parents wherever it was imposed. In the face of a storm of protest, Nixon promptly called a halt to busing in Mississippi and gave that state more time in which to integrate its public schools. When the Supreme Court ordered the immediate desegregation of schools in Mississippi, Finch began to implement the decision by cutting off federal funds to segregated school districts. But Nixon instructed HEW to permit delays in school desegregation, and Finch and his followers in HEW resigned. Nixon had thus reversed his earlier position on civil rights and undermined the policy of a key subordinate in order to forestall opposition —and indeed to galvanize support in the South—for his reelection. Ironically, the final desegregation of southern public schools took place during the Nixon administration; mainly on account of the efforts of the judiciary and officials such as Finch, the proportion of blacks in segregated schools in the South declined from 80 per cent in 1968 to 20 per cent in 1972.

Ambivalence and opportunism also characterized Nixon's relationship with Hickel. Hickel promulgated regulations which protected the public domain and the environment. He halted construction of the Trans-Alaska oil pipeline until the consortium which was to build it had devised a route which did not damage the fragile tundra. After a well blowout in the Santa Barbara Channel in 1969—an unparalleled environmental disaster—Hickel halted all offshore drilling. Hickel also prohibited the erection of billboards on federal lands. Before 1970, Nixon strongly supported Hickel's efforts to protect the environment. Yet, when substantial opposition from the business community developed, Nixon began to undermine Hickel's authority, and, in late 1970, the Alaskan resigned in frustration.

The progressive phase of the Nixon administration came to a climax in two of his most important legislative proposals, the Family Assistance Plan (FAP) and "revenue sharing." Introduced in Congress in 1969, the FAP had been devised by Nixon's adviser on urban affairs, Daniel P. Moynihan, a sociologist who had worked for both the Kennedy and Johnson administrations. An advocate of the transfer of responsibilities for welfare to the states, Moynihan had captured Nixon's attention in 1967 in a speech in which he cited the "limited capacities of government to bring about social change." Under the FAP, the federal government would abandon the traditional welfare system altogether and would, instead, guarantee to a family of four an income of $1,600 a year and food stamps worth $800; all families earning less than $3,920 annually would be eligible. The FAP soon encountered opposition in Congress. Conservatives objected to what they called governmental "hand-outs"; progressives believed that the plan would maintain poor Americans only at a level of subsistence. The House passed a version of the bill in 1970 and 1971, but the Senate rejected it on each occasion. Two years later, Congress again rejected the bill. By 1972, however, Nixon had lost his enthusiasm for the FAP, and he abandoned any program to reform the welfare system.

The second cornerstone of Nixon's domestic program, his "revenue-sharing" plan, was also introduced in 1969. Yet, it, too, fell considerably short of expectations, largely because of problems with Congress and because of ineffectual support from Nixon. In October 1972, Congress passed the State and Local Assistance Act, which provided for the "sharing" of $30.2 billion in federal revenues over a five-year period, beginning with an allocation of $5.3 billion in 1972. Some of the beneficiaries of "revenue sharing," mainly governors and mayors in urban states, complained that fewer federal funds were available than before; they also objected when specific projects, such as the Job Corps program, were ended.

Economic Pragmatism

As President, Nixon exhibited an extraordinary amount of flexibility in his economic policies. Although elected as a conservative, he presided over an unprecedented involvement of the federal government in national and international economies and was the first President in the history of the United States to impose wage and price controls during peacetime. Moreover, budget deficits rose to the spectacular levels—or so it appeared to contemporaries—of $23 billion in 1971 and 1972 and $25 billion in 1973.

One of Nixon's most pressing problems in 1969 was inflation. Largely because of Johnson's decision to finance the Vietnam War through the expansion of the money supply and budget deficits, prices had risen at an accelerating rate at the end of the 1960s, and during 1970 and 1971 they rose by 4 to 5 per cent. At first, Nixon adopted conventional means—reduced spending, tighter credit, and higher interest rates—but prices continued upward. In the Economic Stabilization Act of 1970, Nixon then asked for and received authority from Congress to impose wage and price controls. Nonetheless, he promised never to impose controls, no matter how "politically expedient that may seem."

Yet, on August 15, 1971, in the midst of an apparent crisis, Nixon reversed himself and imposed a freeze on wages and prices for six months. Three months later, in Phase Two, he established a cost-of-living council which limited increases in wages to 5.5 per cent and increases in prices to 2.5 per cent. By the time that Nixon lifted controls and shifted to a voluntary program of restraint in January 1973, the results of his antiinflation program were mixed. Controls of any kind inevitably cause disruptions in allocation and supply, even in wartime; and these disruptions probably contributed even further to the growth of inflation.

Even as he fought inflation, Nixon faced a continuing and nagging problem of unemployment, which rose from 3.5 per cent in late 1969 to 6.2 per cent in 1970. Largely because of the restrictive monetary policy pursued by the Federal Reserve Board, the economy stagnated during 1970 and 1971 even while inflation, fueled by large outlays for the Vietnam War, continued to grow. Facing reelection in 1972, Nixon and his advisers—Secretary of the Treasury John B. Connally and the new chairman of the Council of Economic Advisers, Herbert S. Stein—aggressively pursued an expansionary fiscal policy. Nixon persuaded Congress to lower taxes and put heavy pressure on the Federal Reserve Board to lower interest rates. At the same time, he and his subordinates urged agencies to step up their spending. Nixon's policies resulted in a surge in the economy which began during the summer of 1972; at the same time, these policies soon caused more inflation.

By 1971, Nixon also faced an international monetary crisis. The United States had enjoyed a trade surplus every year since 1893; after the collapse of the British pound as a medium of international exchange during the Second World War, the American dollar supplanted it under the Bretton Woods agreement in 1944. After that year, international trade was based on the dollar, which was convertible at the fixed rate of $35 per ounce of gold. But this system rested on the unquestioned dominance of American trade; and, when the economies of the western European countries and Japan began to grow, and when the United States began to experience trade deficits for the first time in early 1971, gold supplies in the United States declined precipitately, from a postwar peak of $25 billion to a nadir of $10.5 billion in 1971.

When Nixon froze wages and prices in August 1971, he also took action to reshape the international monetary system. He proclaimed that the dollar was no longer convertible into gold and, at the same time, slapped a 10 per cent surcharge on all imported goods. During the following December, representatives of the leading commercial nations met and formulated a new system which abolished gold as the medium of international exchange and devalued the dollar by 8 per cent. Thereafter, all currencies would "float" in relative value.

The Assault on Civil Liberties

The Nixon administration mounted the gravest assault on civil liberties during peacetime since the ratification of the Constitution. Much of this campaign was implemented by Attorney General Mitchell, to whom Nixon gave a free hand. Mitchell was zealous; he was also the most determined enemy of civil liberties in American history. Much of his effort was directed against the opponents of the continuing Vietnam War. Along with J. Edgar Hoover, the director of the FBI, he expanded surveillance and ordered illegal break-ins; he also attempted to obtain the right from the Supreme Court to wiretap without a court order. Mitchell initiated wide-ranging indictments of the leaders of the demonstrators at the Democratic national convention in 1968. He also advocated preventive detention (if insufficient evidence existed for holding suspects) and asked Congress to give police in the District of Columbia authority to conduct "no-knock" searches of houses.

The peak of Nixon's and Mitchell's onslaught against dissent came after the publication of the so-called Pentagon Papers, a forty-seven volume compilation of the evidence of American involvement in Vietnam. The study had been conducted on the order of Secretary of Defense McNamara after he had decided that American intervention was a mistake. Daniel Ellsberg, one of the leading authors of the "Pentagon Papers," secretly duplicated them and gave a copy to the *New York Times*, which began to publish excerpts in June 1971. Mitchell and Nixon responded in two ways. They first appealed to the courts to suppress the publication, but the Supreme Court, in a quick decision, ruled that the danger to national security caused by the publication of the "Pentagon Papers" was not sufficient to warrant their suppression. At the same time, the White House ordered a campaign to discredit Ellsberg and even went to the length of ordering the burglary of the office of Ellsberg's psychiatrist in an attempt to find damning evidence.

Nixon and the Supreme Court

During the campaign of 1968, Nixon promised that he would, if elected, work to change the character of the Supreme Court. He contended that the Warren Court had made, not interpreted, the law, and he promised to appoint strict constructionists and advocates of judicial restraint. As it turned out, Nixon was presented with an unusual opportunity to shape the character of the court, for between 1969 and 1972, four justices of the Warren Court retired. Nixon also saw an opportunity to win support in the South and to strengthen his position among conservatives in general.

Warren resigned in 1969 as Chief Justice, and Nixon replaced him with Warren E. Burger, an undistinguished jurist from Minnesota who had served for thirteen years on the United States Court of Appeals in the District of Columbia. Soon thereafter, Abe Fortas resigned from the court because he had been paid an annual retainer of $20,000 by a foundation whose chief backer was under investigation by federal authorities. Nixon was determined to replace Fortas with a Southerner, but he encountered unprecedented difficulty in overcoming opposition to his nominees. Nixon first nominated Clement Haynsworth, a federal judge in South Carolina, who not only was conservative on civil-rights and labor issues, but also had conducted dubious financial dealings while on the bench. In spite of a massive lobbying effort by the administration, Haynsworth's confirmation in November 1969 fell short of the necessary two-thirds majority by twelve votes. Stung by this rejection, Nixon then nominated another Southerner, G. Harrold Carswell of Florida. But in their hurry to obtain a southern justice, Nixon and Mitchell had found in Carswell an even more unqualified candidate. In April 1970, Nixon was again dealt another blow when the Senate rejected Carswell; this time, his nominee lacked sixteen votes. Nixon then nominated Harry A. Blackmun of Minnesota, and the Senate quickly confirmed him. In December 1971, Nixon nominated, and the Senate approved, two other justices of conservative reputation—Lewis F. Powell, Jr., a Virginian and a former president of the American Bar Association, and William H. Rehnquist, an assistant attorney general from Arizona with unimpeachable conservative credentials.

What was soon called the Burger Court did not depart in a dramatic way from the rulings of the Warren Court, although in several key areas it tempered the latter's judicial revolution. In civil rights, it extended the rulings which were the outgrowth of the Brown decision. In Alexander v. Holmes County Board of Education, it ordered that all forms of school segregation should end immediately and directly rebuked the Nixon administration's attempts to slow integration in Louisiana, Oklahoma, and Mississippi. In an even more important case—Swann v. Charlotte-Mecklenburg Board of Education—the court extended its ruling by justifying busing as a legal way to end school segregation.

The Burger Court also addressed the issue of women's rights. In 1971, for example, it ruled against various forms of discrimination against women in employment. In general, however, the Burger Court fell short of pressing for absolute sexual equality. In January 1973, it said that women officers in the armed forces were entitled to dependency benefits for their spouses, but it refused to issue a general decision about the constitutionality of sexual discrimination. In 1981, the court similarly refused to rule that the drafting of only men for combat was unconstitutional. In another important decision, Roe v. Wade (1973), the court decreed that a state could prevent abortions only during the last six months of pregnancy.

The change from the Warren Court to the Burger Court was most evident in the field of criminal law. The Burger Court ruled in Williams v. Florida (1970) that a jury of six people was constitutional; two years later, the court, in Milton v. Wainwright, said that an illegal confession did not sufficiently violate a defendant's constitutional rights to force an acquittal. In general, the court limited the rights of criminal defendants; however, it stopped short of destroying the structure of constitutional safeguards erected in the Miranda decision and in Gideon v. Wainwright a decade earlier. Moreover, the Burger Court, in 1972, struck down the death penalty (when it was applied without mandatory provisions) as an unconstitutional violation of the Eighth Amendment's prohibition against cruel and unusual punishment. At the same time, the court held that an equitable application of the death penalty was constitutional, and many states moved quickly during the mid-1970s to rewrite their laws.

By its moderation, the Burger Court fell far short of Nixon's expectations. Nixon's disappointment could not have been more complete when, in 1974, the court, in a unanimous decision written by Burger himself, decreed that the President could not ignore a court subpoena by appealing to executive privilege or by invoking national security. Moreover, both Powell and Blackmun proved to be moderate in their decisions; and, in frequent decisions, Blackmun in particular swung to the liberal majority. The appointment of John Paul Stevens in 1976 (by Gerald R. Ford) to succeed William O. Douglas—even though Ford thought that he had appointed a conservative—resulted in the strengthening of the moderate-liberal coalition.

2. NIXON AND THE SEARCH FOR WORLD ORDER

The Cold War Thaws

By the end of the 1960s, there were signs that the long era of confrontation and conflict between the United States and the Soviet Union was coming to an end. Both Kennedy and Johnson had begun to relax the atmosphere of tension which had prevailed between the two countries, but it was Nixon and Kissinger who actually began the era of détente. Détente largely centered around the reduction and control of nuclear weapons. In 1969, Nixon supported the ratification of the Nuclear Nonproliferation Treaty, which banned the spread of nuclear weapons beyond those countries—the United States, the Soviet Union, Great Britain, France, and China—which already possessed nuclear armaments. For the most part, nonproliferation has been successful, although India's explosion of a nuclear device in 1974, along with the nearly certain possession of such weapons by Israel and South Africa and aggressive development programs by Argentina and Pakistan, have clouded the horizon for the rest of this century. Soviet-American relations were also improved by extensive arms-control negotiations held between the two countries at Vienna and Helsinki between 1970 and 1972. In 1972, the two countries signed the first of the SALT (Strategic Arms Limitation Talks) agreements, which limited the development of antiballistic missiles and set ceilings on the numbers of offensive warheads which each nation could deploy.

The control of nuclear weapons made possible a series of agreements which eased tensions in eastern Europe. In 1971, the foreign ministers of the western nations and the USSR agreed to refrain from the use of force in Berlin, to provide easier movement between the two Germanys, and to define and make permanent the status of eastern and western Europe. In 1972, the two Germanys signed a treaty which recognized existing borders and normalized relations. Nixon's transformation of relations with Russia culminated in his visit to that country in 1972, where he signed the SALT treaty and began negotiations on an extensive trade agreement which lowered tariff rates and paved the way for large purchases of American wheat by the Soviets.

At the same time that Nixon effected a thaw in relations with the Soviet Union, he engaged in active global competition with it. Although Nixon began arms-control negotiations, he oversaw a large buildup in nuclear weapons to undreamed of and almost suicidal proportions. At the same time, to finance increases in strategic power and to maintain the war in Vietnam, Nixon reduced conventional strength and permitted the Russians to attain superiority in such weapons as submarines and naval vessels, to say nothing of land armaments. This shift of military priorities—away from conventional toward strategic strength—was supported by senators who maintained that the defense establishment should be reduced.

Nixon firmly believed that the United States could be most effective in its dealings with the Soviet Union by negotiating and competing from a position of relative strength. Along with the buildup of strategic forces, he bolstered the network of pro-American allies to defend American interests on the borders of the Soviet Union. Thus Nixon gave full support and encouragement to the military government of Greece as a buttress against the Soviets in the Mediterranean, even though the former had overthrown a duly elected and constitutional government in 1967 and had earned the enmity of most Greeks. Similarly, in Iran, Nixon gave full support to the Shah and, particularly after 1974, permitted him to purchase sophisticated weapons in almost unlimited quantities.

Beginnings of Rapprochement with China

Probably one of Nixon's greatest accomplishments as a diplomatist was the breakthrough in Chinese-American relations which he accomplished during the early 1970s. As Nixon realized, the United States possessed a unique opportunity. The Sino-Soviet split of the early 1960s had made China receptive to any opponents of the Russians in international relations, and the Chinese now recognized the USSR, and not the United States, as the chief threat to their security. At the same time, Nixon and Kissinger realized the benefits which would flow from opening diplomatic exchanges with the Chinese, particularly in negotiations with the Soviet Union. Moreover, because Nixon's reputation as an anti-Communist was well established, he had the political strength to carry his conservative supporters with him.

Nixon startled the entire nation in July 1971 when he announced that he planned to visit the People's Republic of China. His visit occurred in spectacular fashion in February 1972, and he signed a joint communiqué with the Chinese leaders, Mao Tse-Tung and Chou En-lai, which looked toward the establishment of normal diplomatic relations between the two countries. They avoided dealing directly with the thorny issue of Taiwan, however, and agreed to defer settlement of the issue to the future, and not until Jimmy Carter broke relations with Taiwan in 1979 did the United States and China formally establish diplomatic relations. Nonetheless, even today Richard Nixon is revered in China as one of the greatest American leaders and friends of China.

3. NIXON AND THE INDOCHINESE WAR

"Winding Down the War"

During the presidential campaign of 1968, Nixon stated that he had a "secret" plan to end the Vietnam War. In fact, Nixon intended, not to end the war, but to reduce the numbers of Americans in combat by putting heavier military responsibilities on South Vietnam. Soon after he took office, Nixon announced this program of "Vietnamization," and the ARVN was supplied with huge amounts of military equipment and training. At the same time, Nixon was under considerable pressure at home to withdraw American troops. In 1969, a Senate resolution banned the use of American troops without congressional approval. In 1971, Congress repealed the Gulf of Tonkin resolution and ordered an end to all American military involvement as of August 15, 1973. In response, Nixon began a phased withdrawal of American combat troops, from a level of 541,000 in March 1969 to 27,000 in December 1972.

In practice, "Vietnamization" failed miserably. American equipment made ARVN troops only more effective at destroying their own villages and alienating what remained of popular support for the Thieu government. At the same time, because of the almost complete collapse of support for the South Vietnamese government and because of the ineptitude or unwillingness of the ARVN troops to fight, Nixon increasingly came to rely on widening the war to maintain the American position in Vietnam. He therefore increased aerial bombing, particularly after 1972, when it had become clear that the war was beginning to turn in the North's favor. Bombing, along with the use of napalm and the creation of "free-fire" zones, also drove millions of Vietnamese from their homes and to the shattered cities.

Another corollary to "Vietnamization" was the extension of the war to other areas of Indochina. In March 1969, in what Nixon described in his memoirs as the "turning point" in his policy toward Vietnam, the President ordered the secret bombing by B-52s of NLF and North Vietnamese sanctuaries in Cambodia. To prevent knowledge of the bombing of Cambodia—and the first significant expansion of the war outside Vietnam—Nixon, Kissinger, and the staff of the National Security Council created an elaborate cover-up. Records of the B-52 missions were falsified or destroyed; numerous superiors, including the Secretary of the Air Force, were not told of the bombings. Moreover, when the *New York Times* reported on May 9, 1969, that the Americans were bombing Cambodia, Nixon and Kissinger ordered the wiretapping of five journalists and three members of the National Security Council, Morton H. Halperin, Daniel I. Davidson, and Helmut Sonnenfeldt.

Widening the War

Nixon's expansion of the war soon took a dramatic new turn. On April 20, 1970, Nixon announced to the nation that 150,000 combat troops would soon come home. Yet, ten days later, he again went on television, this time to tell a startled nation that United States ground forces had launched a massive invasion of Cambodia to destroy the alleged headquarters of North Vietnamese operations. Striking a firm pose, Nixon promised to accept the consequences of his action: "I would rather be a one-term President," he declared, "and do what I believe was right than to be a two-term President at the cost of seeing America become a second-rate power and to see this nation accept the first defeat in its proud hundred-and-ninety year history."

The Cambodian invasion, despite Nixon's optimism, did nothing more than widen the war and hasten the destruction of what had been a peaceful and neutral nation. American troops did not discover the enemy headquarters, although they were able to destroy bunkers and caches of arms and materiel. Since the neutralist Prince Sihanouk had been deposed by General

Lon Nol in early 1970, the Americans found a pro-American government in power in Cambodia. Yet, the invasion, and the massive bombing by B-52s which followed it, greatly undermined popular support for Lon Nol, drove the North Vietnamese and NLF further inside Cambodian territory, and ravaged the economy of Cambodia. This unparalleled destruction of a defenseless nation, in fact, aided the triumph of the Khmer Rouge, a rebel group who called themselves Communists, which by 1972 numbered 30,000 and controlled about two thirds of the country.

Nixon expanded the war even further in February 1971, when he ordered the invasion of Laos, an operation which this time was conducted by about 16,000 ARVN troops and was supported by massive American air power to strike at the heart of North Vietnamese supply lines. Because the Defense Appropriations Act of 1970 banned the use of American troops in Laos, this operation was a rugged test of "Vietnamization." The South Vietnamese troops failed miserably and were forced to beat a hasty retreat. Nixon had hoped, if the Laotian invasion was successful, to launch an invasion of North Vietnam, in the name of protecting the phased American withdrawal but actually as a way to force concessions at the peace table. With the defeat of the ARVN forces in the Laotian campaign, however, Nixon realized that "Vietnamization" was a bankrupt alternative to direct American involvement. Increasingly, in Laos, Cambodia, and Vietnam, he was forced to rely on the B-52s to enable the South Vietnamese government to survive.

Opposition at Home Continues

The antiwar movement gathered considerable steam after Nixon's inauguration. In fact, largely because of the successful campaigns of Kennedy and McCarthy during the spring of 1968, the movement picked up support from journalists, authors, and politicians of all stripes. By the autumn of 1969, indeed, a majority of Americans (57 per cent) favored, at the very least, a phased withdrawal of American troops from Vietnam by a specific date.

A series of antiwar demonstrations during the autumn of 1969 thus attracted considerable popular support. Suddenly, news of antiwar marches filled the newspapers. On October 15, 1969, massive demonstrations took place in Washington, New York, and Boston. A month later, on November 15, antiwar activists, who had recently organized a nationwide "moratorium" against the war demonstrated, 250,000-strong, in Washington.

The White House now launched a major counteroffensive to discredit the antiwar movement. The White House's hatchet man was Vice-President Agnew. In a series of speeches, Agnew denounced the antiwar protesters variously as an "effete corps of impudent snobs"; as "hard-core dissidents and professional anarchists"; and as "anarchists and Communists" who were aided by "ideological eunuchs." In a speech televised on November 3, Nixon appealed to the "great silent majority" to support the American position in Vietnam; at the same time, he denounced the "minority" of Americans who were taking their cause to the streets.

Despite Nixon's counteroffensive, the antiwar movement gathered new momentum in the storm of the popular reaction which followed the invasion of Cambodia in April 1970. The outbreak of popular outrage was unequaled during the twentieth century. On hundreds of college campuses, students and faculty combined to stage "strikes" which closed down their campuses. In some universities, violence erupted. On May 4, 1970, National Guardsmen at Kent State Univerity in Ohio—inexplicably armed with loaded guns—shot and killed four student protesters and wounded eleven others; at Jackson State University, a predominantly black institution in Mississippi, police fired at a dormitory after student protests and killed two students. All told, 400 colleges and universities were disrupted, and another 200 were closed down entirely.

The reaction of the White House to antiwar sentiment was, predictably, defensive. After the shootings at Kent State, Nixon issued a statement which said that they should "remind us all once again that when dissent turns to violence it invites tragedy." Agnew called the deaths of the students "predictable and avoidable," but went on to denounce "psychotic and criminal elements in our society," "elitists," and "traitors and thieves and perverts."

"Peace Is at Hand"

American, South Vietnamese, NLF, and North Vietnamese representatives, had been conducting intensive, if futile, negotiations to end the war and achieve a political settlement. Yet, in Nixon's overall strategy to bring the Vietnam War to a close, the peace talks, which had begun during the spring of 1968, were to play an integral part, for his strategy called for an impressive array of American military power—through bombing and through "Vietnamization"—sufficient to convince the North Vietnamese that they could not win on the battlefield.

Particularly after 1970, therefore, Nixon and Kissinger increasingly relied on the B-52s to extract concessions from the North Vietnamese. In 1972, Nixon pursued an even more aggressive strategy in order to win an acceptable peace. In May of that year, he ordered the mining of Haiphong and six other North Vietnamese ports to interdict military supplies from China and the Soviet Union. At the same time, Nixon resumed bombing sorties against targets in North Vietnam. By October, a breakthrough at Paris appeared imminent when Kissinger, after intensive secret negotiations, was prepared to conclude an agreement with Le Duc Tho, the North Vietnamese foreign minister. "Peace," Kissinger announced, "is at hand." But objections from the South Vietnamese aborted the agreement, and Nixon again resorted to the B-52s to persuade the enemy. On December 17, Nixon initiated the most destructive bombing—the notorious "Christmas bombing"—in history. The bombing was aimed at military targets, but it was so intense that few civilians were spared. On December 30, Nixon halted the bombing and announced that the North Vietnamese had promised to reopen negotiations.

Finally, on January 27, 1973, all the belligerents signed a peace treaty in Paris. It was, in fact, essentially the same agreement which Kissinger (now Secretary of State) had hammered out in the preceding October. It gave the NLF and North Vietnamese forces control of large portions of the South; it also stipulated that all United States troops would be withdrawn within sixty days and that an exchange of prisoners of war would take place. In order to persuade Thieu to sign the treaty, Nixon promised him large amounts of military aid, and the fighting continued throughout 1973 and 1974 and even grew in intensity. However, the treaty ended American involvement in the war, and, with the adoption of the War Powers Act of 1973, Congress formally ended American intervention in Vietnam. This act stipulated that future Presidents should not commit American combat forces without prior and explicit congressional approval. Congress also specifically limited the use of American aircraft to the support of American allies in either Laos, Vietnam, or Cambodia.

The Legacy of Vietnam

The American intervention in Indochina—a tragic chapter in the history of

---

The Collapse of South Vietnam, 1975

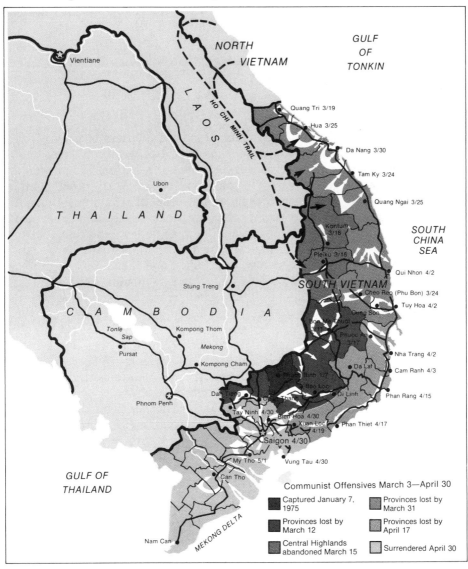

the United States—came to a close in 1975, when Communist forces achieved complete victory throughout Vietnam, Cambodia, and Laos. In 1975, the North Vietnamese routed the bulk of the ARVN. Despite urgent requests by Secretary Kissinger and President Ford, Congress refused to give military aid to the collapsing Thieu government. The collapse of South Vietnam was accompanied by Communist victories in Cambodia, where a cruel regime headed by Pol Pot took charge, and in Laos, where the Pathet Lao peacefully assumed control of the government. The ravages of the Vietnam War were extensive. About 56,000 Americans lost their lives and about 300,000 were wounded; thousands more were addicted to heroin when they returned. Moreover, we do not know even today how extensive were the effects of the main defoliant, Agent Orange, on the thousands of Americans who came into contact with this highly toxic substance. The losses for Vietnam were, of course, even heavier. Over 1,000,000 Vietnamese were killed, and five times as many were wounded; even more were crowded into refugee camps in the nation's cities.

4. THE WATERGATE IMBROGLIO

The Election of 1972

Soon after his inauguration in 1969, Nixon and his advisers began to look ahead to the campaign of 1972. Republican strategists were convinced that they could forge a new majority coalition across the nation which would combine traditionally conservative Republican voters with other white Americans concerned and indeed deeply troubled about what they thought was the disintegration of their society. Nixon, backed by Mitchell, worked hard to present the image of an advocate of "law and order" and to associate race riots, high taxes, school busing, campus unrest, and a rising crime rate with Democrats and an orderly society with Nixon and the GOP. Nixon also had a "southern strategy," which was aimed at establishing his control of that region. He thus made his well-publicized effort to appoint southern justices to the Supreme Court; he also publicly opposed busing and the extension of affirmative action programs.

Nixon's general strategy not only worked in 1972, but he was also helped by several critical events. One was the shooting of George Wallace in May 1972, which left him crippled and permanently out of presidential politics. After a long Democratic primary battle, George S. McGovern, senator from South Dakota and a long-time progressive antiwar leader, won the nomination, despite a last-minute campaign by Hubert H. Humphrey. At the Democratic national convention, which opened in Miami Beach on July 10, the nation watched as blacks, women, and minorities took control. The convention also antagonized key elements of the Democratic party, because it denied organized labor and Richard Daley's Chicago organization their dominant positions. Both George Meany, president of the AFL-CIO, and Daley (who was denied a seat at the convention) withheld their support from McGovern.

If the Democratic convention played into Nixon's hands, McGovern also suffered from bad luck. Because of the wrangling and speech making at the convention, he was not able to deliver his acceptance speech until the early morning, long after most Americans had gone to sleep. The same strategy which had captured a sizable bloc of the Democratic party in the preconvention campaign—advocacy of an immediate withdrawal from Vietnam and the introduction of a guaranteed annual income for all Americans—now alienated many Democrats. McGovern also did not display qualities of presidential leadership after his running mate, Senator Thomas F. Eagleton of Missouri, admitted in July that he had been hospitalized on two occasions for psychological problems. McGovern impulsively said that he was behind Eagleton "1,000 per cent," but, when that position appeared unpopular, he requested Eagleton's resignation. Sargent Shriver, the popular former head of the Peace Corps and a brother-in-law of John F. Kennedy, replaced Eagleton on the ticket, but the McGovern candidacy was already doomed.

The Republicans, who also met in Miami Beach, renominated Nixon and Agnew on August 21. In spite of the fact that the Twenty-sixth Amendment, ratified earlier in the year, had enfranchised some 14,000,000 young people between the ages of eighteen and twenty-one (McGovern appealed especially to young people), the outcome of the election was never in doubt. On November 7, 1972, Nixon won one of the most stunning presidential victories in American history. He and Agnew received more than 47,000,000 votes, or 61 per cent of the total vote cast, as against 29,200,000 votes for McGovern and Shriver. Even more striking was Nixon's electoral sweep; the President carried forty-nine states and 521 electoral votes, compared with seventeen electoral votes from Massachusetts and the District of Columbia for his opponent. Nonetheless, the election was probably more a repudiation of McGovern than it was an unqualified mandate for Nixon, for the Democrats retained control of Congress and even added two seats to their majority in the Senate. Democratic candidates also won eleven of eighteen gubernatorial races.

The Watergate Break-in

Just as the Democrats were falling into disarray and the Republicans were uniting behind Nixon, the seeds for the destruction of the Nixon presidency were sown. In 1971, Nixon and his campaign managers created the Committee to Reelect the President (CREEP) as an organization independent of the Republican National Committee and which was led by Mitchell, who resigned as Attorney General. CREEP, which by 1972 had collected nearly $60 million in campaign contributions, not only worked for Nixon's reelection but engaged, often in alliance with the White House staff members, in actively subverting the Democratic preconvention campaign. But the most serious of the dirty tricks by CREEP was the series of break-ins at the headquarters of the Democratic National Committee offices in the Watergate complex in Washington. There, burglars implanted the offices with microphones and copied files. On June 17, 1972, a security guard alerted policemen, who caught five burglars, led by the CREEP officials, James McCord, G. Gordon Liddy, and E. Howard Hunt.

Nixon's spokesmen, for a time, were able to suppress the ill effects of the Watergate burglaries. Mitchell immediately disavowed any connection, official or otherwise, with them; Ronald Ziegler, Nixon's press secretary, denounced the last episode as a "third rate burglary." As late as August, Nixon publicly denied any knowledge of the break-ins and announced that a White House investigation (which actually had not occurred) had turned up nothing in "this very bizarre incident."

The Cover-up

Despite a placid public posture, the White House staff was in a state of near panic about the implications of the Watergate affair during the summer and autumn of 1972. Two days after the last break-in occurred, John Dean, Nixon's personal counsel, revealed most of the details of the burglary to Haldeman. On the following day, June 20, Haldeman discussed the affair with Nixon and revealed the implications of the burglary, but also, more seriously, the methods which should be used to prevent any further legal repercussions. The Watergate cover-up had begun. From late June onward, the White House's preeminent concern was Watergate and its impact on the election. On June 23, Haldeman told Nixon that he had ordered L. Patrick Gray, Hoover's successor as director of the FBI, not to go "any further into this case, period." Along with CREEP officials, Gray destroyed records which documented the long trail of campaign illegalities, the full extent of which historians will probably never know. Meanwhile, through his subordinates, Nixon worked to keep the Watergate burglars quiet. He promised large amounts of "hush money" and presidential pardons in exchange for their silence; in fact, more than $400,000 in CREEP funds went to legal fees, family support, and various forms of bribery. The cover-up was completely successful during the presidential campaign. Although McGovern tried hard to make an issue of the Watergate burglaries, few Americans believed that members of the Nixon administration and of CREEP had been implicated.

Beginnings of the Crisis

Soon after Nixon's second inauguration, which occurred with great pomp and ceremony, the Watergate cover-up began to collapse. The trial of the Watergate defendants began in January 1973. John J. Sirica, judge of the district court of the District of Columbia, an Eisenhower appointee and a stern jurist, presided. The trial proceeded quickly—the defendants pleaded guilty—but Sirica declared that he was "not satisfied" with its results. In late March, he announced that he was imposing harsh sentences—thirty-five years for Hunt and forty years for four others—unless they cooperated "completely and entirely" with the Watergate investigation. At the same time, Sirica revealed that the other defendant, McCord, had sent him a letter which alleged that pressure had been applied to keep the burglars silent.

Meanwhile, in early February, the Senate, by a vote of seventy-seven to nothing, had voted to establish a select committee, which Samuel J. Ervin, Jr., of North Carolina, headed, to hold hearings to determine the full truth of the Watergate affair. The dam of the cover-up soon broke, and an array of Nixon aides—John Dean, Jeb Stuart Magruder, Haldeman, Ehrlichman, and Attorney General Richard Kleindienst—divulged increasingly lurid details, not only about Watergate, but also about the wider dimensions of the criminal activities of Nixon's aides. After he confessed that he had destroyed evidence concerning Watergate, Gray resigned on April 27; three days later, Nixon's chief aides, Haldeman, Ehrlichman, and Dean, along with Kleindienst, all resigned.

By the summer of 1973, Nixon's position was further imperiled. Dean revealed that Nixon had been aware of the cover-up at an early stage and had even discussed the distribution of "hush money." Yet, it remained a case of Dean's word against Nixon's. The Watergate affair assumed a new dimension on July 16, 1973, however, when Alexander Butterfield, a former Secret Service agent, testified that Nixon had installed a taping device to record all telephone and other conversations held in the Oval Office and elsewhere in the White House. Archibald Cox, a professor at the Harvard Law School, whom Nixon had appointed as Special Prosecutor, subpoenaed the tapes on July 23. On August 29, Cox won a court order from Sirica to receive portions of the tapes. Nixon then appealed Sirica's order to the court of appeals, which on October 12 upheld Sirica and set a one-week deadline for compliance. Nixon then tried to compromise and, when Cox rejected the compromise, Nixon ordered his dismissal.

The firing of Cox was a costly mistake, for Nixon's Attorney General, Elliot Richardson, and his immediate subordinate, William Ruckelshaus, both resigned rather than carry out Nixon's order. The Solicitor General, Robert Bork, finally carried out the order, but not before extensive political damage had been inflicted by what was called the "Saturday Night Massacre." Nixon, in an attempt to preserve his credibility, appointed another Special Prosecutor, Leon Jaworski, but he had to promise to give Jaworski unlimited powers of investigation. Moreover, a movement began in the House of Representatives to initiate proceedings for Nixon's impeachment, and there were demands across the nation for his trial and removal from office.

Crises in the Vice-Presidency and the Middle East

Nixon was rocked by two other crises at the very time that his popular support was plummeting. The United States attorney in Baltimore had uncovered substantial evidence that Vice-President Agnew had received kickbacks from local contractors while he was county executive of Baltimore County, governor of Maryland, and Vice-President of the United States. In early August 1973, reports leaked to the press that a substantial case had been prepared against Agnew. After a brief counterattack, Agnew bowed to heavy pressure from the White House and resigned on October 10, 1973. Attorney General Richardson negotiated a plea-bargained settlement in which Agnew pleaded "no-contest" to the charge of income-tax evasion in exchange for a guarantee that he would not be imprisoned. Thus, one of the most tireless advocates of law and order became the only Vice-President in American history to resign his office because he had repeatedly broken the law. Soon afterward, under Section Two of the Twenty-fifth Amendment, Nixon recommended, and Congress approved, the appointment of Gerald R. Ford, the House minority leader, as Vice-President of the United States.

Meanwhile, during the weekend of Yom Kippur, in October 1973, the combined forces of Egypt and Syria launched a full-scale attack against Israel. Egyptian forces crossed the Suez Canal and drove Israeli defenders into the Sinai; the Syrians meanwhile waged a fierce, if less successful, assault on

Israeli positions in the Golan Heights. The Israelis soon launched a massive counterattack, and, in a brilliant maneuver, outflanked the Egyptians and threatened to decimate them. Since they faced total defeat, the Egyptians and Syrians quickly agreed to a cease-fire.

Meanwhile, the United States, on October 12, had begun to supply Israel with military equipment on a massive scale. In retaliation, the Arab states, led by Saudi Arabia, imposed an embargo on the export of oil to the United States and those European countries, such as the Netherlands, which supported the Israelis. The oil embargo had a devastating effect upon the United States, western Europe, and Japan. It emboldened the Organization of Petroleum Exporting Countries (OPEC) to quadruple oil prices within six months, and it fueled inflation in the West and intensified the problem of balance of payments for many nations. The oil crisis also rudely awakened the American people—for the time being, at least—to the fact that there were shortages of all kinds of energy.

The Fall of Nixon

Nixon soon discovered that Jaworski was to be no less implacable than Cox in his demand for the crucial evidence—the White House tapes. From late 1973 to the summer of 1974, therefore, the drama largely centered around the control of the tapes. The battle against Nixon was waged on two fronts—by the Special Prosecutor and by the House Judiciary Committee, which, during the winter of 1974, was considering whether sufficient evidence existed to begin impeachment proceedings against Nixon.

Throughout 1974, meanwhile, Nixon conducted a vigorous campaign designed to fend off the attacks from Jaworski and the Judiciary Committee. Nixon hired James St. Clair, a prominent attorney of Boston, to press his argument that "executive privilege" justified withholding the tapes from the committee and Jaworski. At the same time, by the summer of 1974, Nixon had listened to the taped conversations and realized the extent of his implication in the crime of obstruction of justice. When Jaworski requested access to sixty-four tapes, Nixon therefore refused. He had more difficulty sidestepping a subpoena from the Judiciary Committee in late April, and he attempted instead to deflect the combined assault by publicly releasing 1,200 pages of edited transcripts of conversations which he had held between September 1972 and April 1973. Even though the transcripts contained questionable gaps in them—about 1,800 in all—they were extremely damaging to Nixon's political and moral standing.

The most telling blow, however, came from the Supreme Court. On July 24, 1974, it ruled that the principle of executive privilege, although valid in some instances, did not protect the President or his advisers in criminal cases; the principle of executive privilege, wrote Burger in *United States of America v. Richard Nixon*, did not "prevail over the fundamental demands of due process of law in the fair administration of criminal justice." About a week later, on July 30, the House Judiciary Committee approved three articles of impeachment against Nixon. Article I charged obstruction of justice in the Watergate cover-up; Article II accused Nixon of abuse of power; Article III condemned him for his refusal to obey the committee's subpoenas.

Nixon turned over to Jaworski the last of the tapes, some of which he had concealed from St. Clair, on August 5. It was now clear that both his impeachment by the House of Representatives and conviction by the Senate were imminent, and his closest friends in Congress and the chief of the White House staff, General Alexander M. Haig, urged him to resign. This Nixon did in a dramatic speech on August 8, 1974; he thus became the first President to resign from office. The chief reason for his resignation, which took effect on August 9, Nixon said, was not his guilt but the fact that he had lost his "political base in Congress." Although he had never been "a quitter," he was giving up the presidency in the interests of the nation. Ford was inaugurated at noon on August 9.

The Legacy of the Vietnam War and Watergate

The Vietnam War and the Watergate affair created two of the gravest constitutional crises in the history of the United States. Nixon and his subordinates, in almost all their actions, set out either deliberately or inadvertently to subvert the traditional limits of presidential power, either by flouting congressional authority and the authority of the courts, or by exceeding the constitutional limits of the Chief Executive in foreign policy. Moreover, the Nixon administration mounted a concerted effort to subvert the freedom of the press and the right of dissent in peacetime guaranteed by the First Amendment.

In a certain sense, Nixon merely extended and exaggerated tendencies which had existed in both the presidency and the federal government since about 1901. Nixon, like Theodore Roosevelt, was a plebiscitory President who acknowledged no limits to his authority, no law that bound him; indeed, he perceived himself and his office as the true embodiment of the sovereign will of the nation. But Nixon was simply the President with the greatest imperial pretensions and the worst offender insofar as flouting the law was concerned. For example, illegal wiretapping was begun during the administration of Theodore Roosevelt and continued at least until 1974 and probably beyond. Johnson favored intense surveillance of domestic antiwar protesters because he suspected that they had ties with some worldwide Communist movement.

The degree of continuity between Nixon and his predecessors began to become even clearer after his resignation. Investigation after investigation revealed a systematic violation of the constitutional rights of the American people and of sovereign peoples abroad, at least since the Eisenhower administration. Partly as a result of the disclosures of the illegal activities of such agencies as the CIA and the FBI, such severe restrictions were placed on their ability to act without clear and explicit authority that they soon complained of inability to gather intelligence vital to national security.

The Vietnam War and Watergate left an unprecedented legacy of popular apathy and mistrust of political leadership in general. For the rest of the decade, the same powers which had been instrumental in the fall of Richard M. Nixon—the press and Congress in particular—worked actively and perhaps even instinctively to prevent any effective exercise of presidential leadership.

SUGGESTED READINGS

An objective and comprehensive analysis of the Nixon presidency remains to be written. Many interesting, informative, and often provocative biographies of Nixon have appeared, and some biographies, autobiographies, and what can best be described as defensive memoirs now are available, including some by Nixon himself. See Nixon, *Six Crises* (1962), for self-revelations about the man, some of which are unintentional. Nixon's presently definitive autobiography is *RN: The Memoirs of Richard Nixon* (1978). Garry Wills, *Nixon Agonistes* (1970), is perceptive, but lacks the perspective which knowledge of the rest of Nixon's presidency would have brought. The same might be said for Jules Witcover, *The Resurrection of Richard Nixon* (1970), and Rowland Evans and Robert Novak, *Nixon in the White House* (1971). Bruce Mazlish, *In Search of Nixon* (1972), and Fawn M. Brodie, *Richard M. Nixon: The Shaping of His Character* (1981), are two psychobiographies.

On Agnew, see Jules Witcover, *White Knight: The Rise of Spiro Agnew* (1972), unfortunately written before the "white knight's" fall. Witcover and R. M. Cohen remedy this deficiency in *Heartbeat Away* (1974). Kevin Phillips' *The Emerging Republican Majority* (1969) has already been cited. On the rise to power of Haldeman and Ehrlichman, see Dan Rather and Gary P. Gates, *The Palace Guard* (1974). Moynihan gives an account of his intentions and his view of the probable effects of his guaranteed income plan, as well as an account of how he persuaded Nixon to adopt it, in *The Politics of a Guaranteed Income* (1972). Also see his *Coping* (1973). Other volumes on politics during the first Nixon administration include Arthur M. Schlesinger, Jr., *The Imperial Presidency*, cited earlier; Frank Mankiewicz, *Perfectly Clear: Nixon from Whittier to Watergate* (1973), and Samuel Lubell, *The Hidden Crisis in American Politics* (1970). Theodore H. White, *The Making of the President, 1972* (1973), is the least competent of White's series of books on presidential elections. Robert S. Anson, *McGovern* (1972), another campaign biography, almost does justice to its subject. Arthur M. Schlesinger, Jr., *Robert Kennedy and His Times* (1978), covers a wide period. Nixon's domestic policies are chronicled, again not quite satisfactorily, in R. L. Miller, *The New Economics of Richard Nixon* (1972). Richard Harris, *Decision* (1971), is a good treatment of Nixon's nomination of G. Harrold Carswell. The best general study of the entire Nixon presidency is Jonathan Schell, *The Time of Illusion* (1976).

Members of the Nixon administration have written about it in almost unprecedented numbers. Among the more informative is Henry Kissinger, *White House Years* (1979), and *Years of Upheaval* (1982), which should be read as the work of a man still ambitious for high office and a leading role in the making of foreign policy. Moynihan's volumes are mentioned above. Walter J. Hickel, *Who Owns America?* (1971); William Safire, *Before the Fall* (1975); and Clark Mollenhoff, *Game Plan for Disaster* (1976), are useful. The most valuable among the works by participants in the Watergate affair are John W. Dean, *Blind Ambition* (1976); Leon Jaworski, *The Right and the Power: The Prosecution of Watergate* (1976); Jeb S. Magruder, *American Life: One Man's Road to Watergate* (1974); and, particularly, John J. Sirica, *To Set the Record Straight* (1979).

In addition to the memoirs mentioned above, the Watergate scandals have given rise to numerous books. Among the best is Theodore H. White, *Breach of Faith: The Fall of a President* (1975). Carl Bernstein and Bob Woodward, *All the President's Men* (1974), will remain a classic journalistic account of the uncovering of the Watergate scandal—in part—by the two *Washington Post* reporters who played major roles in that process. Bernstein and Woodward's *The Final Days* (1976) completes their particular story. Raoul Berger, *Impeachment: The Constitutional Problems* (1974), is a sound analysis.

In addition to Kissinger's memoirs, mentioned above, other informative volumes on Nixon's foreign policy include Marvin and Bernard Kalb, *Kissinger* (1974); Robert Osgood et al., *Retreat from Empire?* (1973); Henry Brandon, *The Retreat of American Power* (1973); Lloyd Gardner, ed., *The Great Nixon Turnaround* (1973); Adam Yarmolinsky, *The Military Establishment: Its Impact on American Society* (1971); and Morton Halperin, *Defense Strategies for the Seventies* (1971). More likely to be of lasting value are John G. Stoessinger, *Henry Kissinger: The Anguish of Power* (1976); Schell, *The Time of Illusion*, already cited, which presents probably the finest analysis of Nixon's foreign policy as part of his overall presidential objectives; and John Newhouse, *Cold Dawn* (1973), on the shift in the relations between the United States and the USSR, especially concerning the SALT agreement. Ted Szulc, *The Illusion of Peace* (1977), provides another comprehensive account of Nixon's foreign policies. Frances FitzGerald, *Fire in the Lake*, already cited, contains an excellent chapter on "Nixon's War." It should be supplemented by William Shawcross, *Sideshow: Kissinger, Nixon, and the Destruction of Cambodia* (1979), and Frank Snepp, *Decent Interval: An Insider's Account of Saigon's Indecent End* (1977). A comprehensive account of the Indochinese war is available in Michael Maclear, *The Ten Thousand Day War: Vietnam: 1945-1975* (1981). Personal narratives, mainly written by soldiers and journalists, are also valuable. The best of these are Ron Kovic, *Born on the Fourth of July* (1976); Philip Caputo, *A Rumor of War* (1977); and Michael Herr, *Dispatches* (1977).

CHAPTER 17
FORD, CARTER, AND THE REAGAN REVOLUTION

1. THE FORD INTERREGNUM

"A Ford, Not a Lincoln"

On August 9, 1974, Gerald R. Ford was inaugurated as the thirty-eighth President of the United States, the first Chief Executive to achieve that office without election. At his inauguration, Ford announced the end of the constitutional crisis. "Our long national nightmare is over," he reassured the American people.

Gerald Rudolph Ford, Jr., was born in Omaha, Nebraska, on July 14, 1913. While an infant, Ford's parents were divorced, and his mother moved to Grand Rapids, Michigan, and married Gerald R. Ford, Sr., who adopted her child and gave him his name. Young Gerald attended the University of Michigan, where he played football and participated in the national championship teams of 1932 and 1933. In 1941, he was graduated from the Yale Law School, and, after serving in the navy from 1942 to 1946, he returned and practiced law in Grand Rapids. In 1948, Ford was elected to the House of Representatives, where he soon established a reputation for hard work, simplicity, and integrity. Because of these qualities and because Ford was also a loyal partisan, Nixon nominated him in November 1973 as the fortieth Vice-President following Agnew's resignation.

Ford was a competent and honest politician, but certainly not exceptional either as a congressman or as President. As Ford himself put it when he was inaugurated as Vice-President on December 6, 1973, he was "a Ford, not a Lincoln." But even had Ford possessed extraordinary political skills, he still would have faced almost insuperable problems as President. Because he was appointed by Nixon—and was his vigorous defender to the last—Ford was tainted, as was the Republican party, with the Watergate scandal. Most important, Nixon's struggle for political survival had so debilitated the presidency that Ford's effectiveness was hindered; Congress and the national news media, two institutions which were strengthened by the demise of Nixon, continued to oppose an extension of executive power throughout the 1970s.

Watergate Continues

The new President's association with the Nixon presidency was brought home when, in September 1974, Ford granted Nixon a "full, free, and absolute" pardon for any crimes which he had committed as President. Rumors and charges soon abounded that Ford had issued the pardon as part of an agreement for Nixon's resignation, but the most probable explanation was that Ford wanted to end Watergate as a political issue. Nonetheless, the pardon unleashed a fire storm of criticism of Ford, and it ended the month-long "honeymoon" period of good feeling toward the new President.

At the same time, other revelations were made public in 1974 and 1975 about systematic violations of the civil liberties of American citizens and of the sovereignty of foreign nations by the CIA and the FBI. Among other things, the Senate Select Committee on Intelligence discovered that the CIA had attempted to assassinate Fidel Castro by enlisting the help of organized crime and by concocting fantastic schemes, such as planting a cigar laced with poison. In an expressly illegal action, which violated the provisions of its charter, the CIA also conducted surveillance operations on about 10,000 American citizens. It was also revealed that the FBI had systematically violated the civil rights of American citizens. The FBI had freely engaged in "black bag" operations—illegal burglaries—and, during the 1960s and 1970s, the agency had attempted to infiltrate and to destroy certain political groups. In the South, the FBI in the 1960s successfully infiltrated the Ku Klux Klan; by 1970, as a result, that group was almost completely moribund. Most of the efforts of the FBI and its director, J. Edgar Hoover, were aimed at left-wing dissent. The agency also conducted a program of wiretapping and intimidation against Martin Luther King, Jr.; it conducted a vigorous and occasionally even violent campaign against the Black Panthers; and it sent countless agents against radical and antiwar groups. All told, Hoover and the FBI carried out some 2,370 covert operations against alleged subversives.

Economic Problems and Conflicts with Congress

Ford's political problems were compounded by the results of the congressional elections of 1974, in which voters elected overwhelmingly Democratic majorities in both houses of Congress. In the Senate, Democrats outnumbered Republicans by sixty-one to thirty-seven; in the House, they had a majority of 291 to 144. The results of the mid-term elections were a clear mandate against Nixon which was directed at the Republican party in general and against Ford's pardon of Nixon in particular.

The subsequent intractability of the Ninety-fourth Congress made effective cooperation in dealing with the growing economic problems almost impossible. Most of these problems were a result of the end of the age of cheap energy. During the Yom Kippur War in the Middle East, Arab oil-producing nations, led by Saudi Arabia, prohibited the export of all oil to the United States from October 1973 to March 1974. In the ensuing shortage, American oil companies scrambled to buy oil from non-Arab oil producers; this intense demand for oil permitted the OPEC producers to quadruple prices in early 1974. This "shock" of reduced supply and increased prices had a traumatic effect on the American economy. During late 1973 and early 1974, lines appeared in many American cities at gasoline stations, while more expensive oil accelerated the rate of inflation.

Ford and the Democratic Congress were soon in almost complete disagreement about economic policy. In November 1973, Nixon had proposed "Project Independence," which promised self-sufficiency in energy by 1980, but neither Ford nor Congress formulated any national energy policy. Meanwhile, Ford pursued a restrictive monetary policy of high interest rates. This move, along with the shock of the increases in the price of oil, set off in 1975 the worst recession since the Great Depression. During 1975, more than 1,000,000 workers lost their jobs; by the end of the year, unemployment was over 9 per cent.

Both Ford and Congress were reluctant to advocate a strong energy policy because of the lack of public support. By late 1975, lines at gasoline stations had disappeared, and, during the next four years, Americans renewed their long love affair with large, gas-guzzling automobiles. Congress did pass the Energy Policy and Conservation Act in December 1975, but it posed little threat to the enormous (and growing) consumption of petroleum products in the United States. Congress was more aggressive in proposing alternatives to Ford's economic policies. Democrats in Congress, for example, proposed and passed the Humphrey-Hawkins bill (which Ford vetoed) to create extensive federal public works programs to hire unemployed workers.

The result of this conflict between the executive and legislative branches was that Ford's administration was one of the most ineffective in American history. In spite of mounting economic problems, neither the President nor Congress possessed sufficient power to formulate and put into effect a coherent program. Ford's most effective instrument was the presidential veto, a power which he exercised fifty times during the short two and one-half years in which he held office. Indeed, by the end of the Ford administration, the federal government was locked in a virtual stalemate.

The Ford Foreign Policy

In contrast to his position at home, Ford, in the conduct of foreign affairs, possessed wide discretionary powers which he could exert without the approval of Congress. Although Ford largely continued Nixon's foreign policies, by the time that he left office in 1976, those policies had begun to unravel in the various "trouble spots" around the globe.

The largest element of continuity between the Nixon-Ford foreign policies was the dominant presence of Secretary of State Henry A. Kissinger. Like Nixon, Kissinger was a fervent advocate of intense competition with the Soviet Union and, at the same time, a reduction of tensions through détente.

Trained as a political scientist, Kissinger also saw diplomacy in terms of balance of power and larger "geopolitical" forces; he also believed in the firm assertion of the worldwide interests of the United States through the use of military power. Although an advocate of détente, Kissinger saw world diplomacy almost exclusively in terms of Soviet-American competition. He therefore often equated socioeconomic change—and the political instability which accompanied it—in terms of an ever-present Soviet threat.

As a sort of foreign-policy "czar" under Ford, Kissinger enjoyed a widespread reputation as an effective diplomatist. In a series of negotiations, conducted through "shuttle diplomacy," Kissinger helped to ease tensions between Israel and the Arab world after 1973. Yet, Kissinger's most spectacular successes—in easing tension with the Soviet Union and, in particular, opening relations with China—had faded somewhat by 1975. Particularly after that year, substantial opposition in the United States to détente with the Soviet Union developed, especially after Marxist forces in Angola, financed in part by the USSR, took power. The unraveling of the Kissinger system was, however, largely the result of the erosion of worldwide American military supremacy after the debacle in Vietnam, as well as of the increase, relatively speaking, of Soviet military strength during the 1970s. Kissinger also confronted a Congress which was reluctant to engage American ground forces in military conflicts abroad. Indeed, the War Powers Act, as well as the Clark Amendment (which specifically ended all American involvement in Angola in early 1976) were expressions of growing congressional restrictions on the war-making powers of the President.

In all, the United States entered an increasingly precarious position in the world during the late 1970s. To many Americans, détente with the Soviet Union seemed to be working decidedly in the Soviets' favor. In the summer of 1975, at Helsinki, Finland, the United States, the USSR, and thirty-one other nations signed a European Security Treaty, which established as permanent the postwar boundaries of the Soviet empire. In exchange for this recognition, the Soviets formally agreed to respect the human rights of persons within its empire. No sooner had the Soviets signed the Helsinki agreements than it became clear that they had no intention of abiding by their human-rights provisions.

The Election of 1976

Despite his problems at home and abroad, and despite an earlier intention to serve only as a "caretaker" President, Gerald Ford had, by early 1975, decided to campaign to stay in the White House. Yet, Ford did not have the Republican nomination for the asking, for he faced a serious challenge from the party's right wing, whose hopes rested with Ronald W. Reagan, former governor of California. In the earliest stages of the primary battles, Ford had the upper hand, but in the late spring, Reagan won crucial victories, first in North Carolina, and then in Texas and California. By the time that the Republican national convention met in Kansas City in August, neither candidate could claim a majority of the delegates. Despite a last-minute move in which Reagan announced that, should he win the nomination, he would support liberal Senator Richard Schweiker of Pennsylvania as his running mate, Ford won the nomination by a majority of sixty votes out of more than 2,000 cast.

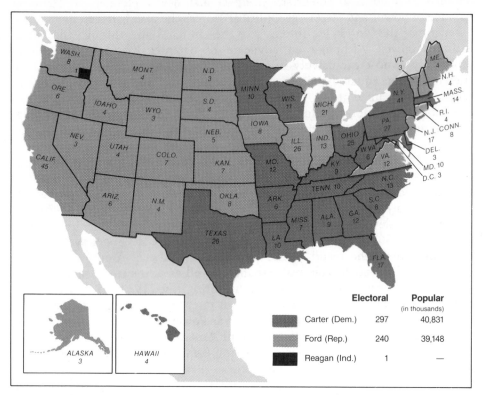

	Electoral	Popular (in thousands)
Carter (Dem.)	297	40,831
Ford (Rep.)	240	39,148
Reagan (Ind.)	1	—

The Election of 1976

Meanwhile, Ford's obvious political weakness attracted a plethora of candidates for the Democratic nomination. Vigorous campaigns were waged by congressional Democrats such as Henry M. Jackson, Humphrey, and Morris Udall, congressman from Arizona. But it was a dark-horse candidate, Jimmy Carter of Georgia, who had emerged as the clear victor in the primaries by the early spring of 1976. Carter entered the campaign with an effective strategy. He began to campaign, first informally, then with increasing vigor in 1972, and cultivated opinion makers throughout the country during the next four years. Carter and his advisers, Hamilton Jordan, Jody Powell, and an Atlanta lawyer, Charles Kirbo, were adept at influencing the media by emphasizing such "symbolic" issues as integrity, competency, and honesty. Carter and his strategists also deliberately avoided specific issues and campaigned on a vague, "populist" platform strongly tinged with anti-Washington overtones. In his most important political strategem, Carter staged an all-out battle in early caucuses in Iowa and in the first presidential primary in New Hampshire. When he won both with only a plurality of the votes cast, he soon established himself as the front runner in the campaign, and, despite a last-minute challenge from Udall, the Democratic convention, which met in New York for the first time since 1924, nominated Carter for President and Walter F. Mondale, a liberal senator from Minnesota, for Vice-President.

Carter held a huge lead in the presidential race at the outset of the campaign, but the gap between him and Ford began to close in September. The highlight of the campaign was the series of three televised debates held between the two candidates on September 22, October 6, and October 18, 1976. In the first debate, which was watched by approximately 100,000,000 Americans, Carter appeared uneasy and Ford reassured and "presidential"; post-debate polls gave the contest to Ford. But in the subsequent two debates, while Carter held his own, Ford inflicted serious damage on his own campaign by stating that eastern Europe, and Poland in particular, was not under Soviet domination.

By early November, Ford and Carter were running neck to neck. The Georgian polled 40,827,000 popular votes, or 50.1 per cent of the vote and won 297 electoral votes; Ford, 39,146,000 popular votes, or 48 per cent and 241 electoral votes. Carter carried key states in the East and swept the South—and thereby won the election—by small margins. But Carter won the presidency, in the final analysis, because the New Deal Democratic coalition came together again. Carter's strongest base of support was in the South, where he polled the largest percentage of voters by any Democratic presidential candidate since Harry S Truman. Unlike Truman, however, Carter's support in the South came mainly from those blacks reenfranchised by the Voting Rights Act of 1965. Although Carter received as much as 94 per cent of the black vote, he attracted only a minority of white votes in the South. Next to blacks, Carter's strongest supporters outside the South were labor-union members, about three quarters of whom voted for him. In all, however, the election was a verdict against Richard Nixon, the recession, and the mounting economic problems of the mid-1970s.

2. JIMMY CARTER AND POST-WATERGATE POLITICS

"Why Not the Best?"

James Earl Carter, Jr., was born in Plains, Georgia, on October 1, 1924. "Jimmy" grew up in surroundings which were rural but, by the standards of southern Georgia during the 1920s and 1930s, surroundings which were also prosperous. His father, Earl Carter, was a hardworking and successful businessman who made money, even during the Great Depression, in farming and in real estate. From his father, Jimmy acquired a determination to work and an obsession to succeed. In 1946, he was graduated from the United States Naval Academy at Annapolis, where he received training in engineering, and during the next seven years he served in the navy. In December 1948, Carter received an assignment on U.S.S. *Pomfret,* a conventionally powered submarine; in 1952, Carter was accepted into the new nuclear-powered submarine fleet which was being developed by then Captain (later Admiral) Hyman Rickover. Carter came to regard Rickover as a model; in his autobiography, *Why Not the Best?,* Carter later recalled that Rickover had had a "profound effect on my life—perhaps more than anyone except my own parents." Above all, Carter emulated Rickover's work habits and his systematic approach to problems.

In the autumn of 1953, Carter left the navy and returned to Plains to run the various businesses of his father, who had recently died. In 1962, Carter was elected to the Georgia State Senate, and, after an unsuccessful gubernatorial bid in 1966, he won election to the governorship four years later. As governor of Georgia, Carter began to receive national attention as a new breed of southern politician—liberal on race relations and conservative on fiscal matters and foreign affairs. As governor, his administration left behind no substantial accomplishments, and, when he left office in 1974, he left behind a large number of opponents in Georgia.

When Carter broke tradition by walking with his family a mile and a half to his inauguration as President on January 20, 1977, he also became one of the most enigmatic Chief Executives in American history. He was, on the one hand, a man of high principles and integrity who was deeply committed to peace and to avoiding bloodshed overseas or American military involvement. At the same time, Carter was insecure and extremely self-conscious; he was, above all, afraid of failure. Carter won the presidency by exploiting his "populist" image and by manipulating the media. Yet, by 1980 he was a deeply isolated man, unable to communicate to the American public his own high aspirations or the achievements of his presidency.

Carter and the Democratic Congress

Elected with the new President in the election of 1976 was an overwhelmingly Democratic Congress. In the Senate, sixty-one Democrats held seats; in the House of Representatives, the party commanded a majority of 292 to 144. Not since Lyndon Johnson did a President seem to hold such power over the other branches of government. Yet, four years later, the most common criticism of Jimmy Carter's presidency was his ineffectiveness in dealing with Congress. In fact, the contention that Carter was "ineffective" is not true, for, in terms of legislative accomplishments, he ranks among the most effective Presidents in American history. But Carter confronted enormous obstacles in Congress. When he took office, Carter faced the same Congress which had so effectively prevented the assertion of presidential power under Nixon and Ford. Equally important, Carter was elected in 1976 as an "outsider." He was largely elected on an anti-Washington platform in which he appealed to popular mistrust of government and of "bigness" in general. Because he exploited the reformed system of presidential primaries, Carter won the nomination without the support of party leaders in Congress. Carter's relationship with the members of his own party in Congress was therefore contentious, stormy, and, in many ways, "ineffective."

One of Carter's earliest actions as President which evoked conflict with Congress involved multibillion-dollar federal programs in the western states for irrigation and water-management systems. There was substantial evidence that these systems inflicted heavy damage on the ecosystem; they were also enormously expensive. In early 1977, for these reasons, Carter vetoed a number of water projects. Since water projects were also a prime form of patronage, Carter alienated a major portion of his own party on Capitol Hill.

More important, Carter's efforts at a domestic program in energy, tax reform, and welfare were stymied in Congress. In the spring of 1977, Carter delivered a nationally televised address in which he told his fellow citizens that the United States faced a major challenge in energy, and that the answer lay in equating the energy problem as the "moral equivalent of war." Carter then sent a comprehensive energy program to Congress which emphasized conservation through higher energy prices. For various reasons, little of Carter's energy program survived its journey through the Congress. The main feature of his plan to raise gasoline prices and thus encourage conservation—a "wellhead" tax on crude oil—met strenuous opposition in the Senate and died thereafter. Carter was more successful in his program for natural gas. Congress passed an act in October 1978 which provided for a phased deregulation of natural-gas prices.

Superpower Diplomacy and the Human-Rights Crusade

In many respects, Carter followed the major foreign policies of the Nixon-Ford administrations. Soon after he took office, Carter dispatched his Secretary of State, Cyrus R. Vance, to Moscow to press for drastic and immediate reductions in levels of nuclear armaments. The Soviets indignantly rebuffed Carter's initiative, which they interpreted as a move to negate their supremacy in certain areas of nuclear weaponry. In fact, the Soviets had become more accustomed to the procedures of SALT, and it was only after Carter had abandoned his original approach that he succeeded in coming to an agreement. Negotiations for a SALT II treaty progressed throughout 1978, and Carter and Brezhnev signed it in Vienna in June 1979.

But by the autumn of 1979, if not earlier, détente was in trouble. Throughout the 1970s, the Soviets engaged in a massive buildup in conventional and strategic weapons which began to alarm foes and friends of détente alike. Having achieved parity with the United States in military power by the end of the decade, the Soviet Union pursued an aggressive foreign policy, especially in southern Africa and central Asia. In 1975–1976, the USSR sent massive aid and approximately 20,000 Cuban soldiers to support one of the rebel groups in Angola. Two years later, the Soviets airlifted more Cubans and about $1 billion worth of equipment to Ethiopia, which was simultaneously fighting a rebellion by Eritreans in the North and an invasion by Somalia in the South.

Although Carter had campaigned in 1976 on a platform of cooperation with the Soviet Union, by 1979 he had found himself assuming an increasingly rigid anti-Soviet position. Early in his administration, Carter made the protection of human rights a centerpiece of his foreign policy. He thus gave active encouragement to dissident intellectuals inside the Soviet Union, and, during the summer of 1978, when the Soviets began a strenuous crackdown against the dissidents, Carter responded by imposing sanctions on Soviet-American trade. Two subsequent events during late 1979 reinforced the position of hard-liners within the Carter administration, such as Zbigniew Brzezinski, head of the National Security Council and adviser on foreign policy to the President. The first was the controversy which raged in September 1979 over the alleged presence of Soviet combat troops in Cuba. This "revelation," which had been known by American Intelligence since the 1960s, was disclosed by Senator Frank Church, a liberal Democrat from Idaho who was facing a challenge, ultimately successful, from a right-wing Republican. The administration completely mishandled the controversy, first by discounting the report, then by demanding the withdrawal of the troops, and, finally, by accepting the presence of Soviet troops as something over which it had no control.

A much more serious and ominous development was the Soviet Union's invasion of Afghanistan in December 1979. Earlier, in May 1978, the Soviets had supported a coup by Afghan Communists who seized power from a neutralist government. A struggle among several factions inside the Afghan Communist party followed, even while it attempted to begin the collectivization of the economy and a modicum of land reform. The Communists soon confronted growing opposition from Afghans, particularly from rural Moslems. Facing the disintegration of an ally on its borders, the Russians, in December 1979, sent about 80,000 troops into Afghanistan, murdered the President, and installed a puppet in his place.

The reaction against the Soviet invasion of Afghanistan was overwhelming, and it galvanized congressional and popular support in the United States for an anti-Soviet foreign policy. In January 1980, Carter outlined several steps in a nationally televised address. He ordered a halt to any grain shipments above the 8,000,000 tons already under contract for sale to the USSR and ordered the Soviets to close several trade missions in the United States. In the same address, Carter announced his support for a boycott of the Olympic Games, which were to be held in Moscow in July 1980. The United States Olympic Committee voted in March to boycott the Games, and, by July, a number of other nations, including Japan and West Germany, had followed suit. In January 1980, Carter announced a more elaborate program to contain Soviet expansionism. The President declared, in what was called the "Carter Doctrine," that the United States considered the oil-rich Persian Gulf region an area of vital national interest to the United States and that, accordingly, he would meet any threat to that region with military force. Carter also announced increases in the budget for military expenditures and for the creation of a new Rapid Deployment Force (RDF), a highly mobile, interservice group capable of quickly reaching the area of the Persian Gulf. Finally, opposition to the SALT II treaty was so great that Carter did not attempt to obtain the Senate's consent to its ratification.

Although Carter found circumstances pressing him into an increasingly anti-Soviet position, he achieved more success in other areas. His greatest successes occurred in China and in the Middle East. Chinese-American relations had been stalemated over the issue of Taiwan. The United States had adhered to the approach of Nixon in 1971, when he announced a "two-China" policy, which normalized relations with the Peoples' Republic but maintained a diplomatic and military presence in Taiwan. While American diplomats pressed for full diplomatic relations, particularly after 1974, the Chinese demanded that the United States break diplomatic relations with Taiwan and recognize the government in Peking as the sole representative of China. In January 1979, American negotiators gave the Chinese everything they asked for, and the two countries established full embassies in the spring of 1979.

Carter also charted a new course for foreign policy in the so-called "third world" nations in Africa, Asia, and Latin America. Early in his administration, Carter made clear that his human-rights crusade applied to nations other than the Soviet Union. Even steadfast friends of the United States,

Carter maintained, would be expected to make efforts to improve the climate for political freedom. The human-rights emphasis in Carter's foreign policy, especially before the Soviet invasion of Afghanistan, also meant that, particularly in the "third world," considerations other than simple Soviet-American competition were important.

Carter also confronted, head-on, a nagging problem with Panama over the Panama Canal. American control over the canal, which dated back to the administration of Theodore Roosevelt (see pp. 45–46), was a visible sign to many Latin American nations of American domination over the entire western hemisphere. Three American Presidents—Johnson, Nixon, and Ford —recognized the necessity of yielding sovereignty over the canal to Panama, yet all three had avoided the issue because of substantial popular opposition in the United States to any "giveaway" of the waterway. The treaties which Carter and the Panamanian strong man, Omar Torrijos, signed in September 1977 represented an act of considerable political courage, for Carter gained almost nothing in the ensuing fight for their approval by the Senate. Despite well-organized, and largely partisan, opposition, the Senate gave its consent to the ratification of the Panama Canal treaties on March 16 and April 18, 1978. Actually, despite the rhetoric of their opponents, the treaties were generous to the interests of the United States. The first gave the United States control of the canal until the year 2000; the second guaranteed the neutrality of the canal, and Torrijos consented to an "understanding" under which the United States might intervene militarily to protect that neutrality.

The most important initiative and achievement of the Carter administration in foreign policy involved the Middle East. In September 1977, the President of Egypt, Anwar el-Sadat, decided to chart a course independent of the Arab world by negotiating directly with Israel. Sadat visited Jerusalem in October 1977 and addressed the Knesset, Israel's parliament. Intense negotiations between the two countries followed but, by the summer of 1978, they were stalled over the issue of autonomy for the West Bank territories taken by Israel in the Six Day War of 1967. In September, Carter invited Sadat and the Israeli Prime Minister, Menachem Begin, to the presidential retreat at Camp David, and, in a rare act of presidential and personal diplomacy, he hammered out an agreement between the two sides.

Although thorny problems remained during late 1978 and early 1979, Carter supervised the signing of the first Arab-Israeli peace treaty on March 26, 1979. It stipulated that Israel would withdraw from the occupied Sinai peninsula by the spring of 1982; it also provided for the establishment of normal trade and diplomatic relations between the two countries. Israel thus secured its southern flank by concluding what was, in essence, a separate peace with Egypt. Moreover, the treaty gave Israel more freedom to move against its Palestinian enemies in Lebanon and in Syria. The treaty also gave Egypt a virtual alliance with the United States and billions of dollars worth of American economic and military aid. Although Sadat earned the enmity of the Arab world, he also won substantial popular support in Egypt.

Energy and Economic Problems

More than any other single event, the Iranian Revolution of January 1979 determined the fate of the Carter presidency. Since early 1978, the absolute ruler of Iran, Mohammad Reza Pahlavi, otherwise known as the Shah, had experienced increasing domestic opposition. After the quadrupling of oil prices in 1974, the Shah embarked on an ambitious campaign of modernization for his country. But problems in his plans soon became apparent. The Shah had a particular taste for expensive military equipment, and he spent billions on costly and sophisticated armaments from the United States. Extensive corruption also accompanied the Shah's huge outlays of oil wealth, corruption which largely involved the Pahlavi family. Thus when the Shah—partly in response to Carter's human-rights campaign—relaxed his repression of his domestic opponents in 1977, a series of anti-Shah demonstrations occurred, most of which were led and orchestrated by fundamentalist Moslem clerics, or mullahs. By the autumn of 1978, these demonstrations had become pitched battles in the streets of Teheran, Iran's capital. Unwilling, or perhaps unable, to conduct and lead a civil war, the Shah, who had held the Peacock Throne of Iran for thirty-seven years, took a permanent "vacation" from his native country and fled to Mexico.

The departure of the Shah from Iran was soon followed by the coming to power of a new, revolutionary regime. On February 1, 1979, the Ayatollah Ruhollah Khomeini, a religious opponent of the Pahlavi regime who had been in exile in Paris, returned in triumph to Teheran. Despite the return of Khomeini, the government of Iran remained in turmoil. Oil production fell off dramatically, from close to 6,000,000 barrels a day to under 2,000,000 barrels. This in turn caused a worldwide shortage and a rapid increase in the price charged by the oil-producing nations from about $15 per barrel in 1978 to more than $30 per barrel by 1980.

Long lines at the gasoline stations in the United States undermined public confidence in the Carter administration, while price increases stimulated a significant jump in the rate of inflation. Carter's response to the crisis caused public support to erode even more. In a well-publicized sojourn at Camp David, Carter consulted with advisers and experts from all over the nation. Then, in mid-July 1979 he delivered one of the most candid speeches in the history of the American presidency. He described a "malaise" which he said was gripping the nation and virtually declared that he had failed as leader of the American people. Shortly thereafter, Carter announced a major reshuffling of his cabinet and White House staff. Carter promised a more vigorous fight against inflation and appointed Paul Volcker—an advocate of tight money and high interest rates—to replace William G. Miller as head of the Federal Reserve Board. Moreover, Carter announced an ambitious energy program which included a phased decontrol of all price controls on oil in order to encourage the further exploration for energy sources and—by raising prices—to discourage the consumption of oil. At the same time, Carter proposed a "windfall profits" tax on the decontrolled oil, the revenues from which would finance a range of alternative energy programs.

Although Congress passed most of Carter's energy program in the spring of 1980, neither it nor his antiinflation program did much to boost his declining standing with the American people. As the shocks of the increases in oil prices hit the American economy, inflation became an ever-present problem. Volcker also pursued a rigorous policy by imposing credit controls in early 1980 and by stimulating an increase in the prime rate to 20 per cent by the early spring.

The Hostage Crisis

The Iranian Revolution affected the future of the Carter administration in yet another way. Under pressure from a number of the Shah's friends in the United States, Carter, on October 22, 1979, made the fateful decision to admit the deposed monarch into the United States. The Shah's advocates claimed that, stricken with cancer of the lymph nodes, which would eventually kill him in July 1980, the Shah desperately needed medical attention available only in New York City. In fact, unknown to Carter and his advisers, the Shah did not need to come to the United States; the proper medical facilities existed in Mexico.

For whatever reason, the decision by Carter to admit the Shah had momentous consequences. Soon thereafter, Iranian religious fundamentalists engaged in a series of street demonstrations outside the American embassy to protest against the Shah's visit to the United States. On November 4, about 400 Islamic students rushed the gates of the American embassy, and they soon had captured the compound and about eighty American hostages. These students had originally intended simply to stage a "sit-in" in the American embassy and then to leave after four or five days. However, their action immediately electrified Iran and set off a wave of enthusiasm for the occupation, and anger against the United States.

It was soon clear that the occupation was to be of long duration. The crisis, to begin with, swept away what had remained of the moderate, secular leadership in Iran and strengthened the hand of the Islamic fundamentalists, largely because they themselves had engineered the occupation. Even after Iran approved a new constitution which abolished the Peacock Throne and established an Islamic republic, nothing resembling a coherent government emerged with which the United States could negotiate. On several occasions in late 1979 and early 1980 Carter came close to solving the hostage crisis only to discover that Iranian negotiators—most particularly President Abdul Bani-Sadr and his foreign minister, Sadegh Ghotbzadeh—did not command the support of the student militants or of Khomeini.

In mid-April 1980, the hostage crisis took a new turn. Facing a presidential campaign at home, Carter was experiencing increasing pressure for some kind of military response such as, for example, the mining of the Persian Gulf. Instead, Carter chose another alternative—a rescue mission to free the American hostages. On the morning of April 24, six C-130 transports left from Egypt and surreptitiously flew to a secret airstrip inside Iran which was nicknamed "Desert One." There they rendezvoused with eight RH-53D helicopter gunships which had taken off from the aircraft carrier *Nimitz*, then in the Arabian Sea. On the way, however, the helicopters encountered a dust storm, which disabled two of their number; another helicopter, meanwhile, had suffered equipment failure. Left with only five helicopters, Carter issued the order to abort the mission; but, as one helicopter took off, it collided with a C-130 transport and killed eight persons. Carter went on national television early in the morning of April 25 and announced the failure of the mission.

The failure of the mission ended any hopes which Carter may have had of freeing the hostages before the autumn. Vance, who had opposed the rescue attempt, resigned and was replaced by Senator Edmund S. Muskie. Moreover, the catastrophe ended the political advantage which Carter had enjoyed as a result of the crisis; by the summer of 1980, the hostage crisis had begun to undermine public confidence in his administration. Movement on the hostages did not resume, indeed, until September, when the Iranian Parliament was elected that summer and announced conditions for the release of the hostages. In October, it appeared that a breakthrough was imminent; but negotiations stalled on the critical issue of the return of close to $9 billion in Iranian assets which were frozen in American banks. Not until the last day of Carter's presidency did Iran and the United States agree to terms for the hostages' release; on January 20, 1981, as Ronald Reagan took the inaugural oath on the steps of the Capitol, the American hostages were released after 444 days of captivity.

3. THE REAGAN REVOLUTION

The Election of 1980

The combination of economic problems and the Iranian crisis spelled the doom of the Carter administration. Even before the hostage crisis, during the summer and autumn of 1979, it appeared that Carter would not only certainly lose the presidency but that he would also drag the Democratic party down to defeat in the process. Scores of Democrats—ranging from the liberal George McGovern to the conservative Henry M. Jackson—implored the still popular Senator Edward M. Kennedy to challenge Carter for the nomination, since it appeared that the nomination was his at the asking. As late as November 1, 1979, an opinion poll indicated that Democratic voters preferred Kennedy over Carter by 54 per cent to 20 per cent. Despite public doubts about Kennedy's involvement in the Chappaquiddick episode, most Americans, according to public-opinion polls, distrusted Carter more than Kennedy. Indeed, by the autumn of 1979, Carter's approval rating was lower than Nixon's when he left office in disgrace.

Nonetheless, Kennedy's popularity in opinion polls did not translate automatically into victory. Kennedy entered the race in early November 1979, but his campaign was something less than spectacular. In thirty-four primary contests, he won only ten; in twenty-five caucuses, he defeated Carter only five times. Kennedy was, in a certain sense, a victim of bad fortune. His announcement of his candidacy was overshadowed by the surge of popular support for Carter which accompanied the seizure of the American hostages in Teheran. Kennedy could also not dispel the growing public doubts about his character and his ability to lead the nation. In a nationally televised interview on November 4, 1979, Kennedy appeared tentative, bumbling, and inarticulate.

The low point in Kennedy's standing coincided with the onset of the grueling preconvention primary season, and the resurgent Carter beat him decisively in state after state. In the first contest, the Iowa caucus, held on January 21, 1980, Carter received 59 per cent of the vote as compared to 31 per cent for Kennedy. Carter then went on to win other early primary victories in the Middle West, East, and South. By late April, despite a last-minute surge by Kennedy, Carter had enough delegates to guarantee his renomination. But the bitter Carter-Kennedy struggle left deep divisions in the Democratic party. Carter had waged his primary campaign mainly by remaining in the White House, portraying himself as "presidential," and portraying his opponent as unfit to be President. A deep personal animosity between the two men persisted even into the Democratic convention in New York in August, when Kennedy, in a well-publicized address and incident, gave only lukewarm support to the leader of his party.

The ultimate beneficiaries of Democratic infighting were the Republicans. By the spring of 1980, Reagan had emerged as the clear choice of the Republican party for President. The Republican national convention, which met in Detroit in July 1980, was thus a festive occasion in which all elements of the party—moderates and conservatives alike—united behind Reagan. The convention not only nominated Reagan, the hero of the party's right wing, but also endorsed a platform which was a manifesto of Republican conservatism. It opposed the ratification of the ERA, thus reversing a forty-year-old Republican policy. It also included planks opposing abortion, endorsing school prayer, and supporting sweeping reductions in taxes and a wholesale reduction of the role of the federal government in the economy.

The presidential campaign also included what, at the time at least, appeared to be the strong candidacy of John B. Anderson. The Illinois congressman, who was a staunch, right-of-center conservative Republican of twenty years' standing, had by the summer of 1980 mounted a successful campaign to lure the support of disaffected voters. He conducted a campaign which was geared to a maximum degree of media exposure; he also emphasized, without committing himself to specific policies, his general adherence to liberal principles in order to attract dissatisfied supporters of Kennedy.

When Reagan accepted the Republican nomination in July, public opinion polls showed that he held a commanding lead over the incumbent President. Nonetheless, during August and September, Reagan's lead eroded, and, by the beginning of October, Carter had drawn within striking distance. Reagan, as the front-runner, conducted a cautious campaign—especially after a bad start in early September, in which he committed a number of well-publicized "gaffes." Carter, on the other hand, followed the same strategy which he had used against Kennedy—that is, to denigrate the abilities of his opponent, while, at the same time, to appear "presidential." Carter thus reminded voters that Reagan had once been a vociferous opponent of the Medicare program and Social Security; the President also intimated that Reagan would be willing to involve the United States in military adventures abroad.

Throughout October, it appeared that the election would be extremely close. Most polls had the candidates dead even or "too close to call." Reagan, however, appeared to lead in most tallies of the electoral votes. Yet, the public-opinion polls revealed an unprecedented degree of voter volatility. The outcome of the election, it appeared, would hinge on the results of the presidential debate. The League of Women Voters had issued invitations to Reagan, Carter, and Anderson to debate each other in September. The debate took place, but, because Carter insisted on a "one-on-one" debate with Reagan, the chief result of the Anderson-Reagan debate was a steady decline in Anderson's standing in the polls. By mid-October, he commanded under 10 per cent of the voters. Reagan strategists took advantage of Carter's refusal to participate in a three-way debate during September and early October; but, by the end of October, when it appeared that Carter's onslaught against Reagan was succeeding, they shifted tack and approved a "one-on-one" debate.

The debate, which took place a week before election day, was crucial in deciding the contest. Reagan, in fact, "won" the debate by all accounts because he presented himself as affable, responsible, and articulate; Carter, on the other hand, appeared nervous and stiff. Moreover, Reagan skillfully used the format of the debate to hammer home to Democratic voters the theme that the economic problems—recession and inflation—were the responsibility of the Carter administration. During the week following the debate, Carter's momentum was not only stalled, but a tremendous shift occurred in favor of Reagan, even in as short a period as the two days before the election.

On November 4, 1980, therefore, Reagan was overwhelmingly elected President. In fact, the size and extent of Reagan's victory surprised even his most loyal supporters. Reagan won 43,500,000 popular votes (or 51 per cent) and 489 electoral votes as against 34,900,000 popular votes (or 41 per cent) and forty-nine electoral votes for Carter. Anderson received about 5,600,000 popular and no electoral votes. Reagan's victory was so decisive that the major television networks projected his victory as early as 8 P.M.; by 9:30, Carter had delivered a concession speech. On the West Coast, where the polls remained open three hours after the networks had proclaimed Reagan the winner, millions of Democrats stayed home, and, as a result, Republicans won at least four additional congressional seats in the West. According to one estimate, the early projection of the Reagan victory caused as many as one fourth of the potential voters to stay home.

The most important feature of the Reagan landslide was the resurgence of the Republican party in Congress. For the first time since 1952, the Republicans captured the Senate; at the same time, they made inroads in the House, where, because of the large bloc of conservative Democrats from the South and Southwest, they appeared to have good prospects.

Many observers described Reagan's victory as a "landslide," but it probably represented more a decisive anti-Carter and anti-Democratic vote than a vote of confidence in Reagan. Inflation, which had been a persistent problem since 1979, raged at an annual rate of 13.5 per cent in 1980; unemployment, at the same time, rose above 8 per cent of the work force during the summer of 1980. Worse still, the ravages of inflation had by 1980 virtually wiped out all the economic gains obtained by higher wages during the 1970s. Median family income, adjusted for inflation, rose only from $20,939 in 1970 to $21,023 a decade later. It was the smallest decennial increase since the worst years of the Great Depression. The American hostages in Iran, above all, were a heavy liability for Carter on election day, the first anniversary of the storming of the American embassy in Teheran. In fact, Reagan's victory was made possible by the defection of about one fifth of Democratic voters to the Republican ticket. This defection took place at all levels of the Democratic coalition—labor, Jews, and Southerners. Indeed, the only traditional Democratic voters who remained faithful to Carter in 1980 were blacks.

Reagan and the Republican Renaissance

Ronald Wilson Reagan was inaugurated as the fortieth President of the United States on January 20, 1981. The news of the release of the American

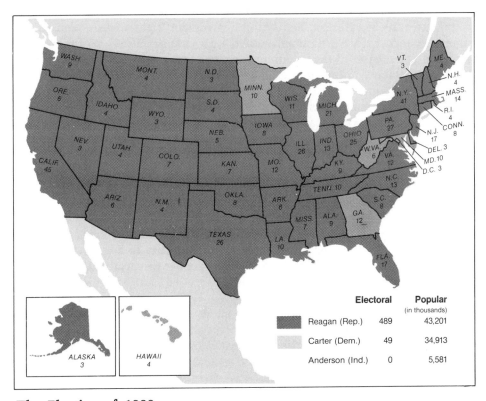

	Electoral	Popular (in thousands)
Reagan (Rep.)	489	43,201
Carter (Dem.)	49	34,913
Anderson (Ind.)	0	5,581

The Election of 1980

hostages, which came at about the same time that Reagan was inaugurated, added an even more festive tone to the gala series of inaugural balls organized by Reagan supporters in Washington and throughout the country. Two weeks shy of seventy, Reagan was the oldest man ever to be inaugurated President.

The election of Reagan to the presidency in 1980 was the culmination of a long quest for that office, at least since 1966, when he was first elected governor of California. Reagan was born in Tampico, Illinois, on February 6, 1911, the younger of two sons. His father, John E. ("Jack") Reagan, was a shoe salesman, an Irish Catholic, and an active Democrat; his mother, Nellie Reagan, was a Protestant of English and Scottish background who was interested in drama and the fine arts. In 1932, young Ronald was graduated from Eureka College in Illinois, where he majored in economics and sociology and was an active dramatist and athlete. After graduation, "Dutch" Reagan soon emerged as a well-known sports announcer based in Des Moines and Chicago. In 1937, Reagan became a film actor, and, during the next twenty years, he starred in successful films such as *Brother Rat* (1938), *Knute Rockne—All American* (1940), and *Kings Row* (1941).

In spite of his acting career, Reagan had always been interested in politics, and he gained his first experience in politics as president of the Screen Actors' Guild from 1947 to 1952. While president of the union, however, Reagan underwent a political conversion; and, by the mid-1950s, he had switched from an advocacy of the New Deal to right-wing conservatism. Although he had supported Truman in 1948, he supported Eisenhower in 1952 and 1956. By the early 1960s, Reagan had become a fervent right-winger; and, in a dramatic speech before a national audience in October 1964, he announced his formal conversion to the Republican party and his support for Goldwater. Reagan was elected, by a large margin, governor of California in 1966 and served in that office until 1974. Thereafter, he pursued the presidency relentlessly, and despite his loss to Ford in 1976, he was the resounding choice of his party four years later.

A man of deep integrity and honesty, Reagan was committed to his long-held principles of conservatism. He believed with genuine enthusiasm that the nation needed less governmental intrusion in the economy; at the same time, he believed that the nation required a massive military buildup and a more aggressive stance toward the Soviet Union. Although committed to a well defined, and relatively simple, set of political values, Reagan was also a superb politician. As he would soon prove, he possessed not only a superior political instinct and timing, but also an unusual ability to communicate his programs to politicians and to the American people, especially through the use of television.

"A New Beginning?"

Reagan wasted little time in acting on what he perceived to be a mandate for change. His cabinet appointments, which were announced in December 1980, revealed that the new President's most important advisers would be conservatives. Among them was a new Director of the Office of Management and Budget, David Stockman, a young, aggressive, and ambitious conservative Republican congressman from Michigan. Reagan chose as Secretary of the Treasury Donald T. Regan, then chairman of the board of the investment firm, Merrill-Lynch. Reagan's chief advisers on foreign policy were similarly conservative: for National Security Adviser, he chose Richard V. Allen, his long-time associate and an advocate of an anti-Soviet posture; for Secretary of State, Reagan chose Alexander M. Haig, White House chief of staff under Nixon and commander of NATO forces from 1974 to 1978.

From the outset Reagan and his advisers kept the attention of the American public on their new economic program, what they called a "new beginning." Its basic premise was simple: if the federal government's role in society could be decreased, then economic growth and renewed prosperity would result. These economists and politicians believed that economic policies since the New Deal have favored demand rather than supply. By unleashing the "supply-side" of the economy—mainly by reducing federal income taxes —they held that the tremendous productive capacity of the American economy would undergo a new era of growth and that a renaissance in economic creativity would ensue.

In February 1981, Reagan proposed a reduction of expenditures by the federal government amounting to about $43.5 billion; at the same time, he called for a massive cut in federal income taxes of about 30 per cent over three years. In a series of dramatic meetings with Democrats in the House of Representatives, Reagan was able to shepherd his budget and tax proposals intact through Congress. With a few exceptions, Congress, in June 1981, passed almost all of the budget cuts proposed by Stockman and Reagan; about a month later, the President scored another victory when he pushed through a 25 per cent, three-year reduction in federal income taxes. In both instances, defections were high among Democrats, especially among the conservative "Boll Weevils" from the South and Southwest.

Recession and the Budget Crisis

Following his victory in Congress, Reagan began to face a series of problems on the domestic front. Inflation, which had been above 10 per cent during the last two years of the Carter administration, had abated to just over 7 per cent by the summer of 1981, largely as a result of sharp declines in the price of crude oil, food, and housing. The reduction in the rate of inflation was, however, also the result of growing economic problems, particularly a stifling level of interest rates. By January 1981, when Reagan took office, the prime rate of interest (that charged by banks to their most preferred customers) was above 20 per cent, and it remained above 14 per cent through the late summer of 1982. High interest rates, in turn, pushed the American economy into severe recession during 1981 and 1982. Particularly hard hit were agriculture and basic industries such as steel, mining, and textiles. Other industries, especially automobiles and housing construction—each of which depended on cheap credit—went into a tailspin. By the fall of 1982, 11.1 per cent of the American work force was unemployed, the highest rate since the Great Depression. All told, between 1980 and 1982 the American people suffered a decline of 3.5 per cent in real income.

Along with recession, the "new beginning" faced other problems. Supply-side economics soon began to lose its attractiveness among some of its political supporters. In the fall of 1981, a furor erupted when Budget Director Stockman characterized the tax cut of 1981 as a "Trojan horse" which disguised within it "trickle-down economics." Even more serious was a crisis in the federal budget which occupied Congress and the President throughout 1982. The tax cuts, which came into force in the fall of 1981, had little immediate effect in stimulating economic growth and prosperity. In fact, the reduction of income taxes, combined with tremendous increases in military spending, produced budget deficits which, by the summer of 1982, approached $140 billion.

Reagan responded vigorously to the crisis and to the erosion of his political support. In August 1982, he pushed further cuts in social programs through Congress. Over a three-year period, $30 billion would be cut from Medicaid, Medicare, food stamps, federal pensions, and government-guaranteed home mortgages. Reagan was forced, at the same time, to compromise one of his most important principles—the reduction of federal taxes. On August 19, after hard lobbying by the White House for a tax increase, Congress passed a measure that would increase taxes by $98.3 billion. Over three years, the tax increase would result from new excise taxes on cigarettes and telephone service; a withholding tax for income earned from interest and dividends; and reduced deductions for medical expenses on income taxes. A significant consequence of the tax increase—which was passed in an election year—was that conservative Republicans in the House broke ranks with Reagan and voted against the bill.

James Watt and the Environment

Reagan also proposed to reduce the role of the federal government in society through a relaxation of environmental regulation. He thus appointed as his Secretary of the Interior James Watt, a lobbyist from Colorado, whose chief qualification was his rigid opposition to environmentalism. Watt soon demonstrated his commitment to the philosophy of the New Right and his willingness to pursue its objectives vigorously. He appointed as head of the Environmental Protection Agency Anne Gorsuch and as chairman of the Council on Environmental Quality A. Alan Hill, both antienvironmentalists. Watt proposed a general relaxation of antipollution standards. Moreover, he made the public domain accessible to private enterprise in a way unprecedented in American history. To promote the exploration and development of domestic oil, Watt opened up almost all of the coastal waters to oil producers. Federal lands were similarly made available for mineral exploration, and he proposed that 80 million acres of wilderness be opened by the year 2000. In his most publicized action, Watt planned to offer 35 million acres of federal land for sale to the public.

It soon became clear that environmental deregulation not only was unpopular but was a distinct liability to the administration. Public-opinion polls revealed that an overwhelming majority of the American people supported federal protection of the environment. By 1982, every major environmental group in the country not only opposed Watt but also demanded his resignation. In addition, the Secretary of the Interior experienced significant opposition in Congress—forty members of the House by 1982 had joined in the demand for his resignation. In that year, the House voted overwhelmingly to ban mineral exploration in national wilderness preserves, while the Senate refused to revise antipollution legislation.

Foreign Policy Initiatives

Although the Reagan administration was at first preoccupied with domestic affairs, urgent problems in foreign affairs soon emerged. From the beginning of his presidency, Reagan adopted a strident anti-Soviet tone in his comments and addresses. Indeed, he and his chief advisers were determined to reinstate Soviet-American competition as the primary, if not the only, foreign-policy concern of the United States.

One of the earliest tests came in Central America. In Nicaragua, a landed oligarchy dominated political and economic affairs through electoral fraud and repression, and in July 1979 a Marxist-led group, known as the *Sandinistas,* overthrew the ruling dictator, Anastasio Somoza Debayle, with considerable aid and support from Cuba. Similar problems of maldistribution of land, a rapid rate of population growth, and a repressive military government were also present in nearby El Salvador. In 1979, a moderate junta in El Salvador deposed a right-wing government and began, with American advice and cooperation, an extensive land-reform program. But the junta was not able to stop the insurgency; instead, political and social reform seemed to initiate a new era of violence in El Salvador as right-wing "death squads" and left-wing guerrillas grew stronger during 1980. During three years of civil war between 1979 and 1982, about 34,000 Salvadorans—the overwhelming proportion of them civilians—were killed by government forces and guerrillas. In this context, Reagan, who was convinced that Central American political turbulence was an extension of Soviet foreign policy, made El Salvador a center of international attention.

Reagan had been forced to respond quickly to events in El Salvador, for, as he took office in January 1981, the insurgents announced the beginning of a "final offensive" to depose the government. The first blasts were largely rhetorical. In February 1981, Secretary of State Haig issued a State Department "White Paper" which detailed—but also exaggerated—extensive Cuban support for the Salvadoran guerrillas. Haig, meanwhile, claimed that El Salvador was on the Soviet "hit list." Through 1981 and 1982, the Reagan administration increased the American presence in the Central American country in two directions. The government in Washington first continued to support land reform in El Salvador, but the election of a right-wing regime in 1982, which was led by Robert D'Aubisson, effectively ended such economic reform. Reagan also placed a greater emphasis on military aid, and, during the first two years of his administration, sent American materiel and advisers to bolster the regime.

The most important test of the new anti-Soviet foreign policy occurred in Europe. There, the American military buildup provoked, during the summer and fall of 1981, widespread feeling against Reagan and stimulated a popular antinuclear movement which was particularly strong in Holland, Italy, and West Germany. Under pressure from its European allies, the administration began negotiations with the Soviets in the fall of 1981 on the mutual reduction of nuclear weapons in Europe. Then, in the spring of 1982, Strategic Arms Reduction Talks (START) began with the Soviets in Geneva.

Other tests of the administration's anti-Soviet policy in Europe occurred throughout 1981 and 1982. The most serious was in Poland, where, since August 1980, the Solidarity movement—organized and led by workers—had pushed through a series of political and economic reforms. Led by Lech Walesa, Solidarity was able to obtain the recognition of independent industrial and agricultural unions. By the summer of 1981, the Solidarity movement was carried by the momentum of reform, and under pressure from the union militants, in the fall it began to demand a more extensive reform of the Communist party and of the entire political system. By December 1981, however, the Polish military led by General Wojciech Jaruzelski, intervened with a coup. The Reagan administration denounced the crackdown, claimed that the Soviets were strongly implicated in it, and put into force a number of economic sanctions. The most important of these involved a multibillion dollar trans-Siberian pipeline, which was to be constructed during the mid-1980s to transport Soviet natural gas to western Europe. Although the Europeans desperately wanted the pipeline, the United States imposed an embargo on the use of any American technology or equipment. By the summer of 1982, when Reagan extended the embargo to include American firms in Europe, the issue remained a major source of tension within the western alliance.

Reagan also attempted to make anti-Sovietism his guiding principle in the Middle East, where his advisers tried to form a "strategic consensus" which would unite moderate Arab states such as Jordan, Saudi Arabia, and Egypt with Israel against the Soviet threat. In 1981, the United States thus expanded its military relationship with the Saudis by selling to them sophisticated military equipment such as the Airborne Warning and Command Systems (AWACS). Almost as soon as it was announced, the "strategic consensus" encountered significant obstacles, the most important of which was the fact that the main issue remained the animosity between Israelis and Arabs. In June 1981, the Israelis launched a successful attack on a nuclear-power plant in Baghdad, Iraq, which they suspected of producing nuclear weapons. The attack convinced the Arab world that their most serious threat came from Israel rather than from the Soviet Union.

An even more poignant reminder of the ancient enmity between Israelis and Arabs occurred in Lebanon. During the Lebanese civil war in 1975 and 1976, the Palestine Liberation Organization (PLO) and the Syrian army had become entrenched forces in Beirut and in the southern and eastern portions of the country. The Israelis, exposed on their northern flank, were determined to destroy their enemies by any means possible, and, in 1978, they launched a full-scale invasion of southern Lebanon. Although they soon withdrew, the Israelis continued to bomb Palestinian targets in Lebanon from 1978 to 1981. Then, in the summer of 1982, the crisis took a grave turn. In early June, the Israeli ambassador to Great Britain survived an assassination attempt, but Israel retaliated with an all-out attack on the Palestinians and Syrians in Lebanon. The outcome of the war was never in doubt, and within a week the Israelis had destroyed most Syrian air power, captured thousands of PLO fighters, and, in the process, devastated Lebanon. By mid-June, the Israeli army had encircled the military and political leadership of the PLO in West Beirut, and only through vigorous American mediation, conducted by the presidential envoy, Philip Habib, was an agreement reached in late August to evacuate the PLO.

4. THE ELECTIONS OF 1982

In the early days of the Reagan presidency, the White House hoped that the Pesident's popularity might bring the GOP further control of Congress in the elections of 1982. To both parties, these elections were crucial. Only once during the twentieth century (in 1934) had the party which occupied the White House *not* declined in strength during the "off-year" elections held two years after presidential contests. These elections in 1982, which would determine whether Reagan maintained control over the Senate and a working coalition in the House, hinged on several issues. Unemployment struck hardest in industrial areas—the Northeast, Middle West, and even the South—and there Reagan's support among blue-collar workers (a group which had voted Republican in significant numbers in 1980) had eroded. Organized labor, lukewarm in its support of Jimmy Carter in 1980, now campaigned hard against Republican candidates.

Republicans defended the record of the Reagan presidency. They claimed that the full impact of the tax cuts would come later, and they encouraged voters to "stay the course." Republican candidates also reminded Americans that inflation and interest rates had both declined during the Reagan administration. The Republicans expected that they would be able, at the least, to cut Republican losses to a few seats. Their hopes were based on both Reagan's popularity and a large party campaign chest. On the average, Republican congressional candidates in 1982 spent about $93,000 more than did their Democratic opponents in close races.

The Democrats, on the other hand, grew hopeful about their prospects as election day approached, predicting gains in the House as high as forty seats. Party leaders, such as Thomas P. "Tip" O'Neill of Massachusetts, Speaker of the House, and Charles T. Manatt, chairman of the Democratic National Committee, fashioned a strategy designed to attract moderate voters away from the GOP. Other Democrats, such as New Jersey Senator Bill Bradley and Colorado Senator Gary Hart, presented an image of moderation by suggesting a new version of liberalism. These "neo-liberals" proposed to modify New Deal liberalism so that government would intervene, not through regulation or social welfare, but through fiscal incentives to raise American productivity and make industry competitive in the international economy. But the main Democratic message was a rejection of the policies of Ronald Reagan, especially regarding economic issues. Democrats thus blamed Republican policies for double-digit unemployment, claimed that the tax cut was both inequitable and responsible for unmanageable budget deficits, and suggested that the Republicans were imperiling the Social Security system. To black voters, Democrats also stressed that they, and not the Republicans, were the most consistent defenders of civil rights, and Democrats claimed credit for the renewal of the Voting Rights Act in 1982.

Single-interest political action committees (PACs) injected other issues into the campaign. In groups such as the National Congressional Club, a PAC which was first organized by North Carolina Senator Jesse Helms in 1972, and the National Conservative Political Action Committee (NCPAC), right-wing Republicans successfully used direct-mail fund-raising and television and radio advertising. These conservative groups advanced an agenda of new "social" issues. They opposed, as a threat to the family, any further equalization of the status of women; they thus were instrumental in the failure of the Equal Rights Amendment, which fell short of ratification by the states in the summer of 1982. On the other hand, two of their cherished objectives—a federal ban on abortion and the introduction of voluntary prayer in public schools—languished in the Senate during 1982 because of tepid support and filibusters by Senate liberals.

The organizational innovations of the conservative Republicans spawned similar approaches by liberal Democrats. Thus, feminists also began to raise funds and to use them to promote their cause. But the most important liberal group consisted of antinuclear activists, who advocated a nuclear "freeze" which would stop the construction of new atomic weapons by both superpowers. The "freeze" movement culminated in June 1982, when a meeting in New York City attracted 1,000,000 people. Antinuclear organizers then pressed government at all levels to accept the freeze. By the autumn of 1982, 275 city governments and twelve state legislatures had passed pro-freeze resolutions, and in the House of Representatives such a resolution failed by only two votes. In the fall elections, the freeze issue took on a partisan quality as Democratic candidates tended to support it, while

Republicans tended to oppose it. Antinuclear PACs "targeted" congressmen who had opposed the freeze or had supported nuclear weaponry. These groups were able to get antinuclear referenda on the ballot in nine states.

The election results appeared to bring a Democratic victory. Actually, to a remarkable extent, the elections were tied to presidential policies; about 70 per cent of the voters viewed them as a referendum either for or against Ronald Reagan. Voters in 1982 reaffirmed their partisan allegiances; groups such as blacks, Jews, and the elderly voted with the Democratic party in overwhelming proportions. But particularly important in congressional races was the swing in the independent vote away from the GOP. Although the Republicans maintained control of the Senate, the Democrats gained twenty-six seats in the House of Representatives, and their majorities were highest in the crucial areas of the Middle West and the South. Republican losses were acute among Reagan's most loyal supporters, as twenty-four conservative Republicans in the House lost their seats. Even more significant was the dismal performance of right-wing PACs; NCPAC, for example, lost in thirty-five out of thirty-six congressional races in which it was involved. Perhaps more significant yet were the results of the gubernatorial races: the Democrats were swept to power in twenty-seven out of thirty-six states.

The results of the elections of 1982 were, however, less than decisive. Reagan now confronted a more moderate House, but he still held the legislative initiative. Although about $300 million was spent, campaign funding appeared to be less decisive than bread-and-butter economic issues —in particular, concern about the Social Security system, high interest rates, and unemployment. But election-day opinion polls suggested that voters believed that the Democrats offered little alternative to Reaganomics. Indeed, by a five-to-four margin, voters blamed the Democrats more than Republicans for their current economic woes.

American voters might also have confirmed a sense that life in 1982 was in many ways better than it was in 1900, but the dramatic changes of the twentieth century obviously brought not only new opportunities but also grave problems. Although America was clearly a nation of abundance, poverty persisted in the United States and in most of the world. Although American society in 1982 was one in which ethnic and racial interests were by law protected, color and group identity were still crucial. And, although the United States was still a world power, the American people and their leaders rarely felt less secure. Thus the direction of federal policy remained in doubt at the end of 1982. Voters obviously demanded a return to the center and more vigorous action to end the recession, and the forces of moderation were in control of both houses of the new congress in January 1983. However, the question remained unanswered whether President Reagan would "stay the course" through the heavy hand of vetoes or would shift course to adapt to new political and international realities.

SUGGESTED READINGS

The history of the Ford, Carter, and Reagan years is just beginning to be written. Much of the material for this chapter came from contemporary journalistic sources, including *Congressional Quarterly*, the *National Journal*, and major newspapers such as the *New York Times* and the *Washington Post*. Several general studies of recent United

States history include material on national politics and government in the late 1970s. The best brief account of energy and economic policies under Ford and Carter is found in Arthur S. Link and William B. Catton, *American Epoch, 1938–1980,* 5th edn. (1980). Richard S. Kirkendall, *A Global Power: America since the Age of Roosevelt,* 2nd edn. (1980), is also useful for the Carter years.

Gerald R. Ford describes his own brief presidency in *A Time to Heal: An Autobiography* (1979). The role of Henry Kissinger in shaping American foreign policy under Nixon and Ford will be a matter of scholarly debate for years to come. For a detailed but naturally self-serving account, see Kissinger, *Years of Upheaval* (1982).

The election of 1976 and the lengthy campaign which preceded it have already received book-length treatment from several political scientists and journalists. The most comprehensive journalistic account of the campaign is Jules Witcover, *Marathon: The Pursuit of the Presidency, 1972–1976* (1977). James T. Wooten, *Dasher: The Roots and the Rising of Jimmy Carter* (1978), is unsympathetic.

A growing number of books now exists about Jimmy Carter's personality and background. William Lee Miller, *Yankee from Georgia: The Emergence of Jimmy Carter* (1978), offers valuable information about Carter's personality, as does his autobiography, *Why Not the Best?* (1975). Gary M. Fink, *Prelude to the Presidency: The Political Character and Legislative Style of Governor Jimmy Carter* (1980), deals with his gubernatorial career. Book-length treatments of the Carter presidency are only now beginning to appear. Joseph E. Califano, *Governing America: An Insider's Report from the White House and the Cabinet* (1981), is the first memoir of an official in the Carter administration; others, including Carter's memoirs, will soon appear. For other views, see Clark R. Mollenhoff, *The President Who Failed: Carter Out of Control* (1980) and Betty Glad, *Jimmy Carter: In Search of the Great White House* (1980).

For good introductions to the Iranian Revolution and the Hostage crisis, consult Michael M. Fischer, *Iran: From Religious Dispute to Revolution* (1980); Michael Ledeen and William Lewis, *Debacle: The American Failure in Iran* (1981); Barry Rubin, *Paved with Good Intentions: The American Experience and Iran* (1981); and, Richard Queen and Patricia Hass, *Inside and Out: Hostage to Iran, Hostage to Myself* (1981).

For the fullest account of the election of 1980, see Jack W. Germond and Jules Witcover, *Blue Smoke and Mirrors: How Reagan Won and Carter Lost the Election of 1980* (1981) and Thomas Ferguson and Joel Rogers, eds., *The Hidden Election: Politics and Economics in the 1980 Presidential Campaign* (1981). The dimensions of the Reagan Revolution are explored sympathetically in Rowland Evans and Robert Novak, *The Reagan Revolution: A Blueprint for the Next Four Years* (1981).

INDEX

Classes, social
Social Democratic party, 33, 125
Social Gospel, 18; provides moral zeal for progressivism, 22; affected by socialism, 34; in 1920s, 115
Socialism, 33–34; and labor, 33–34
Socialist Labor party, 33
Socialist party, 33–34, 49, 53, 89, 90, 125, 150, 166–67; and Wilson, 83; *see also* Elections
Social Science Research Council, 114
Social Security Act (1935), 165–66, 299
Social Security Administration, 299
Social work, 31
Soil Conservation Act (1936), 170
Somalia, 337
Somoza: *see* Debayle, Anastasio Somoza
Somoza family (Nicaragua), 136, 348
Sonnenfeldt, Helmut, 318
Souls of Black Folk, The, 15–16
South Africa, 316
South Korea: *see* Korea; Korean War
Southeast Asia Treaty Organization, 269–70
Southern Education Board, 30
Soviet Union: *see* Union of Soviet Socialist Republics
Space exploration, 244–45, 287
Spain: and Cuba, 43; and Treaty of Paris, 43; *see also* Spanish-American War; Spanish Civil War
Spanish-American War, 43
Spanish Civil War, 178, 179
Sparkman, John J., 235
Spirit of St. Louis, The, 107
Spooner Act (1902), 45
Spooner Amendment, 44
Sports: growth of organized, 16; professional, 255
Sputnik I, 272–73
Stalin, Josef, 185, 205, 206, 207, 209, 219, 270
Stalingrad, 197, 198
Standard Oil Company, 4, 39

Standard Oil Trust, 23
Stans, Maurice H., 309–310
Stanton, Elizabeth Cady, 31
Stark, Harold Raynsford, 189
Stassen, Harold Edward, 223
State and Local Assistance Act (1972), 312
States' Rights Democratic party: *see* Dixiecrats
Steamboats, 2
Steel industry, 35, 39, 98, 169, 243, 346
Steffens, Lincoln, 23
Stein, Gertrude, 113
Stein, Herbert S., 313
Stettinius, Edward Reilley, Jr., 209, 218
Stevens, John Paul, 316
Stevens, Raymond Bartlett, 66
Stevens, Wallace, 115
Stevenson, Adlai Ewing, 235, 271–72, 280
Stimson, Henry Lewis, 136, 176, 185
Stockman, David, 346–47
Stock market: crash of, 143–44; regulation of, 158; decline of in 195, 272
Stone, Harlan Fiske, 123–24, 211
Strasser, Adolph, 35
Strategic Arms Limitation Talks: *see* SALT
Strategic Arms Reduction Talks (START), 349
Studio One, 253
Suburbs: growth of, 8, 104, 240
Sudetenland, 178
Suez crisis (1956), 274–76, *map* 275
Sullivan, Louis, 8
Supreme Court: and segregation, 15; and labor legislation, 28; and antitrust legislation, 39; and espionage and sedition acts, 90; and progressivism, 118–19; nullifies New Deal measures, 164, 167–68; and F. D. Roosevelt, 167–69; and Warren, 265, 300; and civil rights,

266–67, 300, 315; under Burger, 314–16; and Watergate, 326
Supreme Kingdom, 111
Suribachi, Mount, 200
Sussex crisis, 81
Swann *v.* Charlotte-Mecklenburg Board of Education, 315
Swanson, Claude A., 30
Sweatt, Herman M., 266
Sweatt *v.* Painter, 266
Swift, Edwin, 4
Swift, Gustavus, 4
Syria: and Arab-Israeli War (1973), 325–26; and Lebanon, 350

Tacoma Building (Chicago), 8
Taft, Robert Alphonso, 187, 214, 223, 226, 232, 234
Taft, William Howard, 44; and literacy tests, 11; and conservation, 42, 54, 55; and election of 1908, 53; administration of, 53–57; and reform, 54; and Ballinger affair, 55; and Republican insurgents, 55; and diplomacy, 56; and T. Roosevelt, 56–57; and election of 1912, 58–59, 60
Taft-Hartley Act (1947), 216, 226
Taft-Katsura Agreement, 52
Taiwan, 227, 277, 317, 338
Tammany Hall, 25, 60, 149, 152–53
Tarawa, 200
Tarbell, Ida M., 23
Tariff reform: T. Roosevelt and, 50; Taft and, 54–55; Wilson and, 63–64; in the 1920s, 126, 127; Hoover and, 141–42; and F. D. Roosevelt, 181; and Kennedy, 292
Taxation: and T. Roosevelt, 50; and Taft, 55; and Wilson, 73, 89; in 1920s, 126; in 1930s, 165; during World War II, 197; under Johnson, 296; and Nixon, 311; and Reagan, 347
Taylor, Frederick Winslow, 105